THE PHILOSOPHY
OF FREEDOM

CALEB NELSON

KENNETH JEPPESEN

"Therefore my people are gone into captivity, because they have no knowledge."
Isaiah 5:13

Contents

Authors' Note

Chapter 1: Principles of Existence 1
Chapter 2: Morality and Self-Interest 19
Chapter 3: Rights 35
Chapter 4: The Confusion of Rights 51
Chapter 5: The Proper Role of Government 59
Chapter 6: America's Government 71
Chapter 7: The Proper Environment for Mankind 97
Chapter 8: Capitalism 101
Chapter 9: Principles of Economics 107
Chapter 10: Collectivism and Statism 133
Chapter 11: The Philosophy of Evil 128
Chapter 12: The Politics of Evil 177
Chapter 13: Prosperity Principles 203
Chapter 14: The Attack on Capitalism 227
Chapter 15: Knowing the Enemy 267
Chapter 16: The Best Defense 287
Chapter 17: Immigration 303
Chapter 18: Education 311
Chapter 19: Welfare and Charity 321
Chapter 20: Health Care 329
Chapter 21: Principles of War 337
Chapter 22: Environmentalism 347
Chapter 23: Social Issues 357
Chapter 24: Voluntary Funding 365
Afterword: What Now? 375

Appendix A: List of Principles 380
Appendix B: Recommended Reading 382
Photo Credits 384
About the Authors 386

AUTHORS' NOTE

This book is designed to be read the first time from front to back, like a novel. The concepts and facts we discuss are built up from a foundation carefully laid in the beginning chapters. This foundation is essential to understand before reaching the higher-level applications found later in the book.

For ease in writing, the words "man" and "he" are often used throughout the book, and are intended to represent individuals of any gender.

To our international readers: While much of this book is centered in the context of American life and history, its principles are still universally applicable to all nations of the world. Freedom and prosperity can be enjoyed anywhere.

Freedom is never voluntarily granted by governments; it must be claimed by the citizens. Knowledge is the first step in claiming the liberty and prosperity possible to the human race. This book was written to assist in that first step and as such is primarily concerned with principles, not issues. Since principles are common to all mankind, this book is also completely unconcerned with the arbitrary divisiveness of political parties.

Our aim is to present, in one comprehensive introductory volume, an explanation of the origins and applications of the philosophy of mankind's freedom.

The American Founders knew they had laid the foundation for the most spectacular experiment in freedom in the known history of the world. This book is to assist us all in honoring that inheritance and completing it.

About the Second Edition: The core content of this book remains unchanged from the First Edition. Spelling and grammar errors have been corrected, and some small portions have been rewritten for better understanding. Some stories, pictures, and illustrations have been added to better personalize and visualize the ideas presented.

About the Third Edition: Endnotes have been changed to footnotes. A large chapter was divided into three chapters for better flow. Some editing and rewriting for better understanding.

CHAPTER 1

PRINCIPLES OF EXISTENCE

"There are certain primary truths or first principles upon which all subsequent reasonings must depend."[1] - Alexander Hamilton

"Mom!" my daughter whined. "It just isn't fair!"

"What isn't fair, sweetie?"

We were waiting in line to enter our school's Fall Carnival where already throngs of families were enjoying the possible festivities. Bobbing for apples, searching for prizes in the hay, having their faces painted, and shooting foam darts at scarecrows were just a few of the games that had children screaming with glee.

"Liam has a lot of money and I don't," she replied, her eyes focused on the cotton candy machine just inside the fence.

It was true that my oldest child, a boy of eight, who was currently dressed as a ninja, had more money than my daughter, age five, a princess in a golden gown.

---

[1] Hamilton, Alexander. Madison, James. and John Jay. *The Federalist Papers* (New York: Bantam, 2003), 176.

"What about that isn't fair?" I asked. Though it may seem like quite the question for a five-year old, both my kids were pretty clever. Not to mention, you take life lesson teaching moments wherever you can in this day and age, and by the look of things we were going to be in this line for a while anyway.

As with most children, her answer was entirely reactionary, "He'll get to do all the fun things and buy stuff and I won't!"

I believe in encouraging her when she recognizes fact and so answered, "Yep, he will."

"But I want money!"

I knelt down to chat on her level, "River," I began, "Remember earlier today when I had a lot of jobs around the house and asked who wanted to earn money?"

She avoided my gaze but answered, "Yeah."

"And what did you say?"

"But Liam is bigger than me!"

I tickled her, "That's not what you said, silly girl!" She laughed. "What did you say?"

She was now sitting on one of my knees, "I didn't want to do it."

"That's right." She had chosen to watch a Barbie movie and dance around in her Halloween costume, complete with tiara and cape. "But what did Liam say?"

My son piped up, "I said, 'I DO, I DO!'"

"And he did, didn't he?" My son had cleaned the kids' bathroom, washed the windows of the kitchen door, and even picked up his sister's toys and put them away to earn a total of $5 over the course of the day.

River moved the hair out of her eyes before going on, "I didn't want to do the jobs you wanted me to do. I want you to pay me for doing what I want to do."

"That would be awesome," I answered with enthusiasm. "What did you want to do?"

"Not jobs."

"Ah." Of course. It would be nice if we could be paid to dance about in pretty dresses and watch movies. "Well, River, at least you still have the $2 left over from your birthday. So you have some money for fun things."

This did not placate her, "Not as much as Liam."

"But, honey, you didn't work as hard as Liam."

"But I want it!"

By now we had reached the head of the line, showed them our pre-purchased admission wristbands and were allowed into the carnival. But River was still a basket case over her desire for Liam's money, and Liam was concerned about her happiness, as he often was. So we made our way over to a picnic table and I sat my daughter on my lap.

"Let me ask you something, kids. Let's say that you each earned $10 and came to the carnival. But another kid didn't have any money and went to your teacher and demanded that she take half of your money from you and give it to them. Would that be right?"

Again reactionary, my daughter emphatically answered, "NO!"

"Why not? If you had half and the teacher gave the other kid half, then it would be fair, wouldn't it?"

"No. It was my money! It's not fair to take it from me."

"That kid could have done jobs, too, and earned money like me," my son added.

This scenario seemed to upset them both as they began eyeing the grownups around them, seeing a money-stealing-tyrant in every one. So I steered it another direction.

"But what if you had the $10 and saw a kid—a friend maybe—who didn't have any money. You know he would need money to do fun things, and because you want to do things together, you give him a few dollars. Would that be okay?"

"Yeah," they both answer.

"Why is that okay, but the other way isn't?" I asked.

"Because no one made us!"

"Because then maybe they get to say 'Thank you.'"

"Because then we get to have fun together."

"Because I got to say what I do with my money."

As all these answers were right, I hoped the lesson was learned. But to be sure, I asked my daughter another question, "So should I force Liam to give you some of his money, even though he worked hard to earn it while you played around?"

It seemed to pain her to say it, but only a little, "No. I'll be okay with my $2."

Then Liam's eyes lit up and he dug his hand into his pocket, pulling out another $2 and handing it to his little sister, "Here, River. Now we can both find prizes in the hay!"

River needed no prompting from me to say an exuberant, "THANK YOU, LIAM!" and wrap him in her grateful arms, squeezing the air out of him with her love.

I watched my children go off to play and had a chance to realize that the battle isn't between the Have's and the Have-Not's. It's between the Do's and the Do-Not's. When a person has worked for their life, wage, and place, they may chafe under the idea that what they've earned must be taken from them and given to someone else who has NOT worked.

Many arguments between children—or in fact between any members of a family—can be traced back to principles of property and liberty.

"That's mine!"

"Don't touch me!"

"You aren't the boss of me!"

"Get out of my room!"

"As long as you live under my roof, you'll obey my rules!"

Even my children saw that when we Have, that means we have something to share, and when we Do, we Have.[2]

This story illustrates the soul and purpose of this book. Such is the importance of a foundation of principles to a happy and fulfilling life. Even the young have little trouble recognizing these ideas. But they often get confused as they get older, especially if they have never learned to identify the truths they know in specific words. If we are going to understand how to prosper in the world around us, we first need to understand how that world works.

But when we look at our understanding of how the world works, we should ask some basic and vital questions, such as, "Is my view of reality accurate?" and "How do I know it?" and "Can I prove it?"

THE SEEN AND THE UNSEEN

Have you ever thought about the way you process information, what you choose to focus on, and what you ignore? The information you bring in can be broken down into two basic categories: sensing and perceiving.

Those who prefer sensing like concrete, tangible data.

---

[2] As told by Chelsea Nelson to the authors.

Those who prefer perceiving like information that is abstract or theoretical and can be linked to other information in patterns.

More simply, we could say Sensors focus on concrete facts and Intuitives focus on abstract concepts. "Intuition" sees the forest, "sense" sees the trees. Sensors tend to focus on the details and implementation, while Intuitives focus on the big picture and overall direction.

You could think of these two functions as a rally driving team. The Sensor does the work of driving the car, but the Intuitive is the one with the map that tells the driver where to go. The driver and the navigator are a team who can't win the race without each other. Neither function is better than the other—they each serve an important purpose. When it comes to understanding the world, we have to be able to see details as well as how those details fit into the big picture.

Another way to think of it is that sensing is a bottom-up approach; perception, or intuition, is a top-down approach. Two mechanics could perform a repair job equally well from each perspective. The Sensor would likely look at the parts, how they are shaped, and how they fit together. The Intuitive would think about the larger function of the system, considering how the parts conceptually work together and go from there. Each function has its strengths and weaknesses, but both are vital.

Chances are, you're a Sensor rather than an Intuitive (for more information, see the Myers Briggs personality test.). While everyone has some ability to use both functions, many people have a preference for one over the other. Roughly 75% of the population prefers sensing to intuition.[3] Furthermore, studies have shown that roughly 75% of the population never learn to fully think abstractly.[4] Perhaps this reflects the sensor vs. intuitive preference of the population. Regardless, Sensors tend to have a hard time seeing how abstract concepts apply to their lives or what value they have. This book focuses on abstract concepts, so it will be a challenge to those who haven't strengthened their intuition muscles.

---

[3] MBTI Manual, 1985. As cited by Ickes, William, John. ed. *Empathic Accuracy* (New York: The Guilford Press, 1997), 45.

[4] *College Teaching and the Development of Reasoning*. Edited by Robert G. Fuller, Thomas C. Campbell, Dewey I. Dykstra, Jr. (IAP, 2009), 228. Online. books.google.com/books?id=7B65NOZYdrQC&pg=PA228&lpg=PA228&dq=25 %25+of+population++Formal+Operations&source=bl&ots=hdsCVTMwy1&sig =INbUEUKGGS35BvQEvDX9WGJfSv8&hl=en&sa=X&ei=hCiKU7r1Ns2aqAaG k4KADw&ved=0CHcQ6AEwBw#v=onepage&q=25%25%20of%20population% 20%20Formal%20Operations&f=false. Accessed 2 June 2014.

But every principle we share is discussed precisely because it does apply to concrete reality, but is usually ignored.

Even if you find abstract thinking distasteful, it is still absolutely necessary to understand. Consider the less tangible ideas like justice, mercy, love, health, and freedom. Do these things matter to you? You can't hold them in your hand, you can't observe them under a microscope, yet they exist as concepts, and without them life is meaningless.

Intuition makes connections between things, seeing how they relate to one another. Concentrating solely on isolated facts leads to range-of-the-moment decisions, while ignoring long-term consequences. This is illustrated in Nancy and Eric Gurney's book, *The King, the Mice and the Cheese*. The king wants to keep his cheese, but has a problem with mice. Perplexed, he goes to his advisors for a solution. They recommend using cats to chase the mice out. The plan works splendidly, except for the subsequent cat infestation. So the advisors bring in dogs to chase out the cats. To get rid of the dogs they bring in lions. To get rid of the lions they bring in elephants. And finally to get rid of the elephants, they bring the mice back in.

This is a humorous children's story, but it is more than that. There is a moral to the story, and that moral is an abstract principle—specifically, short-sighted fixes can cause long-term problems. The moral of the story is a general guideline to inform our decisions in any given situation, not just ones involving cheese hoards and animal control.

If we know a principle in the abstract, we can apply it to whatever circumstances we find ourselves in. Without the abstract principle to guide our self-taught actions, we have to spend valuable time treating every problem in life as novel and unique. In effect, we are forced to reinvent the wheel every time we need to go somewhere.

America's government has demonstrated the same sad comedy of errors as the king in the story because we too have failed to understand important conceptual connections between cause and effect. The political and economic problems we face as a country and as a world are largely because humans do not grasp the connections between freedom, government, prosperity, and peace. Many don't even know that they are connected at all. Hence laws are passed to fix things that can't be fixed by law. Those laws violate principles and cause a cascade of other problems. Then, to fix the new problems ten more laws are made, more principles are broken, and the problems multiply exponentially.

Intuition is needed to understand the broader, unseen connections between things. In America, when we have heart problems we go to a cardiologist. When we have nerve problems we go to a neurologist. Specialization has the benefit of detailed knowledge, but a weakness of our healthcare system is that in treating these systems as separate, we sometimes forget they are part of the same body. We forget that systems, like those in the body, do not function in isolation, but affect each other.

Because Sensors are not used to thinking intuitively, they can easily dismiss or miss connections between systems.

Sometimes there are connections between systems that we would have never considered before. Many times, the connection between things has more than one step, making it almost impossible to see how they are intertwined. Such subtle or distant connections that we've never considered can seem downright crazy. What would you think if you were told that wolves can change the course of rivers and streams? Sounds insane, doesn't it? There doesn't seem to be any logical connection between those two things, yet it is true.

George Monbiot described how, in 1995, wolves were reintroduced into Yellowstone National Park. For the seventy years before that, there had been no dominant predator to thin the deer population. Without

predation, the deer herds grew, and since more animals means more food is needed, the vegetation in the park was heavily grazed on. When the wolves got there, aside from eating some deer, they changed the behavior of the deer. The deer would now avoid areas where they could be easily trapped like valleys

COLLARED WOLF FROM THE DRUID PACK, YELLOWSTONE NATIONAL PARK

and gorges. Without deer there to graze, the vegetation sprang back with vigor. Impressively, the trees in some areas quintupled in height in only six years! More trees attracted more birds and beavers.

"And beavers, like wolves, are ecosystem engineers. They create niches for other species. And the dams they built in the rivers provided habitats for otters and muskrats and ducks and fish and reptiles and amphibians. The wolves killed coyotes, and as a result of that, the number of rabbits and mice began to rise, which meant more hawks, more weasels, more foxes, more badgers. Ravens and bald eagles came down to feed on the carrion that the wolves had left. Bears fed on it too, and their population began to rise as well, partly also because there were more berries growing on the regenerating shrubs, and the bears reinforced the impact of the wolves by killing some of the calves of the deer.

"But here's where it gets really interesting. The wolves changed the behavior of the rivers. They began to meander less. There was less erosion. The channels narrowed. More pools formed, more riffle sections, all of which were great for wildlife habitats. The rivers changed in response to the wolves, and the reason was that the regenerating forests stabilized the banks so that they collapsed less often, so that the rivers became more fixed in their course. Similarly, by driving the deer out of some places and the vegetation recovering on the valley sides, there was less soil erosion, because the vegetation stabilized that as well. So the wolves, small in number, transformed not just the ecosystem of the Yellowstone National Park, this huge area of land, but also its physical geography."[5]

Mr. Monbiot goes on to explain how whales and their excrement are connected to phytoplankton and how phytoplankton trap and reduce the amount of CO_2 in the atmosphere. Thus, indirectly, whaling can have an impact on the amount of greenhouse gas in the atmosphere. These connections are surprising and not in the least bit obvious. There is no "common sense" that would have ever told us about these systemic connections. We couldn't have dreamed of these connections, yet they exist.

What else don't we know? What else exists that we haven't considered? We should keep open and curious minds since, as fallible mortals, we are grossly ignorant of most things.

As we've seen, even small changes to a system can have massive effects on the whole, for good or ill. America has governmental and cultural and societal systems made up of thousands of smaller interlocking systems. If our solutions are not systemic, our problems will persist.

THE TREE OF FREEDOM

The information in this book addresses the larger philosophic system that supports all the rest. Think of it as a tree. Everything you enjoy in life is like the fruit of a great tree. Your free time, modern conveniences, safety, etc. are all caused by the tree. The trunk of that tree can be viewed as our form of government, our institutions and policies that work to create the fruit. But most important is the seed it started with. That seed is philosophy. A specific view of the purpose of a government and the nature of mankind. It is the seed that causes the tree that produces the sweet fruit. America's blessings came from a clear, unambiguous,

---

rational philosophy, and its modern problems are the result of forgetting or ignoring that.[6]

Whether you've ever thought about it or not, you already have a philosophy! It is operating in all areas of your life, and you base your decisions, thoughts, and worldview on it. Despite philosophy being the foundation of our lives and minds, most people are never fully aware of it!

Just as humans can digest food without having any idea how stomachs and intestines work, so the mind performs its operations without our awareness. We can have an unconscious, contradictory, implicit philosophy; or we can work to achieve a conscious, cohesive, explicit philosophy.

You cannot escape philosophy because it provides the meaning and the reason for all you think and do. Why do bad things happen to good people? What is the purpose of my life? How can I be happy? How should I treat others? What kind of person am I attracted to? Who should I vote for? These are all very practical questions, and the answer to every one of them is philosophical. "As a human being, you have no choice about the fact that you need a philosophy," Ayn Rand explained,

"Your only choice is whether you define your philosophy by a conscious, rational, disciplined process of thought and scrupulously logical deliberation—or let your subconscious accumulate a junk heap of unwarranted conclusions, false generalizations, undefined contradictions, undigested slogans, unidentified wishes, doubts and fears, thrown together by chance, but integrated by your subconscious into a kind of mongrel philosophy and fused into a single, solid weight: self-doubt, like a ball and chain in the place where your mind's wings should have grown."[7]

It was philosophy that led America to fight its war of independence.

It was philosophy that led Stalin to murder millions of people.

It was philosophy that started slavery thousands of years ago, and it was philosophy that ended it.

Philosophy is the hidden engine that turns the wheels of history. And philosophy is also one of the first things to be ignored and swept under the rug.

Philosophy is the ultimate foundation of human action, and as such, it is absolutely crucial to make sure our philosophy is rational, and based on facts.

---

[6] Analogy borrowed from David Barton.

[7] Rand, Ayn. *Philosophy: Who Needs It?* (New York: Signet, 1984), 5.

Whether you like it or not, philosophy is at the core of your life and character. It is therefore practical, and useful. Philosophy holds an indispensable place in your life, and it's important to understand its role.

The happiness, prosperity, and freedom of your life are dependent on the extent to which you understand and apply true principles to your life. Is anything more practical than that? Before we get into the nitty-gritty nuts and bolts of freedom and prosperity, we need to spend a little time talking about the nature of reality and what we should base our knowledge on.

REALITY IS REAL

The most basic axiom of life to understand is that existence exists. If we don't understand that reality is real, it becomes a problem. We might choose to believe that hemlock isn't poison, that prosperity can be obtained through deception, or that violent discipline produces happy and loving children, but these beliefs do not correspond to reality, and believing them will not change their consequences.

Metaphysics is the science of the nature of reality. Reality is there, concrete, static, external to our minds, existing independently from our consciousness. It is not an illusion, not a dream, and will not change how it works in a moment's notice. Closing your eyes doesn't make the world cease to exist; it only limits your perception of it.

How do you know existence exists, that reality is real? First and foremost, because you exist, you are conscious and aware of yourself. It is an axiom that is proof of its own truth. (You cannot argue against this fact without first accepting it, because things that don't exist can't form arguments.) We know that we exist, and we know that other things exist because we perceive them through our senses.

Isn't perception faulty and unreliable? In many little ways, yes. In the "Monkey Business Illusion" by Daniel Simons, observers are shown six girls, all are wearing dark jeans, and half have white shirts while the other half have black shirts. Participants are asked to count how many times the players wearing white pass the ball. The players begin to move around in a small area, frequently shifting places and crossing in front of one another. Midway through this exercise a person in a gorilla suit walks from one side of the screen to the middle, pounds fists on their chest, then continues off camera. The gorilla is very prominent and visible, yet many people do not see it at all, nor do they notice that the curtain in the background slowly shifts from red to orange.[8]

Upon reflection it isn't that surprising. We have been asked to track multiple players and count their passes. Because we have been given the specific task to watch the ball moving only from the players in white our minds naturally screen out the players wearing black, and in all that movement, it is little wonder that we miss another moving black element in our field of vision and unimportant color changes in the background. The mind can be fooled, and the eye tricked; emotion can influence what we remember; focus is selective; and memory can be altered.

On these small scales we show our human frailty, but in the larger scheme we function just fine and our mental failings do not significantly hinder our lives. Reality still exists even if we do not process it flawlessly. We may not see a person in a gorilla suit during an experiment, but that doesn't mean we are unfit to observe reality. Nor does it change fact that we must use our minds to obtain the necessities of life. Not being able to perform multiple tasks at once doesn't change the principles of growing food, for instance. A farmer can still understand and use the principles of raising crops even if he misses seeing a curtain changing colors. Our minds are far from perfect, but they are perfectly suited to discern the requirements for survival and happiness and then act on those requirements.

"Facts are stubborn things, and whatever may be our wishes, our inclinations, or the dictums of our passions, they cannot alter the state of facts and evidence."[9] – John Adams, at the Boston Massacre trial

The universe is run by natural laws. Reality is real and natural laws govern all of it. These laws govern nature, physics, economics, and politics—and to a more personal degree, your career, your home, and your life.

The knowledge that there are laws of nature and that man can discover them is part of what brought mankind from millennia of dark ages into an explosion of advancements in the last few centuries. Descartes, Locke, Newton, and others united in telling the world that the universe is intelligible and that man can know it and discover the unknown if he us-

---

[8] Simons, Daniel. "The Monkey Business Illusion." Available online. illusioncontest.neuralcorrelate.com/2010/the-monkey-business-illusion/. Accessed 2 Aug 2012.

[9] Quoted in McCullough, David. *John Adams* (New York: Simon & Schuster Paperbacks, 2001), 68.

es his faculty of reason. This was known as the Enlightenment era. It only spanned a few brief decades, but it left a nation as its lasting monument: The United States of America. During this time man discovered that life was governed, not by the arbitrary whims of some unpredictable and mystical god or gods, but by predictable, knowable laws.

The two basic laws of nature that man discovered were the laws of identity and causality.

The Law of Identity

- The self-evident truth that everything is what it is, everything has properties that make it what it is.
- A is A.

The Law of Causality

- The Law of Identity applied to action: a thing can only act in accordance with its nature.

The law of identity tells us apples are food, arsenic is poisonous, and grizzly bears can be dangerous. The law of causality tells us that if we make a grizzly angry we might become an entrée, or if we come in contact with sufficient levels of arsenic we will die. It tells us if we get vaccinated we won't get polio. These laws are why we refrigerate certain foods, why we don't drink drain cleaner, why we put wings on airplanes, and why we wear warm clothing in the winter.[10]

FREEDOM AND REASON MAKE US MEN

Reason is the process of logic.

Man uses logic, the art of non-contradictory identification, to compare his ideas against facts. This means being able to identify concrete things, like chairs and hummingbirds, as well as abstract things, like justice and theft, without contradiction.

A toaster is a toaster; it is not a puppy. Freedom is freedom; it is not slavery, etc. The use of non-contradictory identification is the only way that man can gain accurate knowledge of the world. Not by emo-

---

[10] Biddle, Craig. Loving Life: *The Morality of Self-Interest and the Facts That Support It* (Richmond, Virginia: Glen Allen Press, 2002), 14 -15.

tions, wishes, or feelings. Knowledge can only be gained through reason (though the emotions do play a role as a feedback mechanism).

Reason is the use of logic in thinking and decision making. This is the first rule of a proper epistemology—the science of how we know things.

Metaphysics

• The first branch of philosophy studies the nature of reality.

Epistemology

• The second branch of philosophy studies how we gain knowledge.

Amazingly, we can arrive at certain political and ethical truths when we start with correct foundational truths about reality and the nature of mankind.

The basic rule of logic is the law of non-contradiction—that a thing cannot be what it is and what it is not at the same time and in the same respects. A contradiction cannot exist in nature, therefore if a contradiction exists in our thinking we can know for certain that we must be mistaken and need correction.

This does not mean nature is simple. The fact that light has properties of particles and of waves does not mean it is a contradiction—it is merely complex.

The law of non-contradiction tells us that the identifications we make do not change. Rat poison will not become nutritious if we label it "oatmeal"—it remains rat poison.

Over time, mankind continues to learn and more fully understand the laws that govern physical health, positive personal relations, financial prosperity, and spiritual peace. We don't know everything, but we have the capacity to keep learning and discovering and progressing. Understanding and utilizing the governing principles of existence leads to a life of joy and prosperity. The misunderstanding, ignorance, and violation of natural laws leads to death, misery, and poverty.

As your parents may have told you, "You can choose to do anything you want, but you can't choose the consequences." This means that we can live by principles or not, and there are consequences, or results, from either decision. Thomas Jefferson admonished, "Only lay down true principles, and adhere to them inflexibly."[11]

Some things are true whether we want to believe them or not.

Other things are true whether we understand them or not.

And still other things are true whether or not we even know they exist.

We often hear that "the truth will set you free." The truth allows us the knowledge to be able to act while also offering a reasonable promise of the outcome of those actions.

Denying the existence of governing principles makes us captive to seemingly irrational or unpredictable consequences. Imagine how confusing and painful life would be to a pedestrian who was unaware of the frictional properties of ice and banana peels! Knowing the principles of life allows us to achieve the greatest happiness and accomplishments possible.

The alternative to knowing principles is to try and live in a world of shifting whims and partial truths, which are unstable because they are decided arbitrarily or by opinion. It is trying to operate on the belief that whatever people wish to be true is true, and whatever people wish to exist does exist—as long as most people agree on it.

OPINION OR FACT?

Reality and truth are not subjective, but opinions and preferences are.

Reality is an absolute. A speck of dust is an absolute, as is a human life. Whether you live or die is an absolute.[12]

What you prefer to eat for lunch is subjective. Whether you have bread in your belly or whether that bread is given to another is an absolute.

What sports team you like is subjective—it is a preference. Whether they win or lose is an absolute. As the old Latin maxim says, *de gustibus non est disputandum*; in matters of taste, there can be no dispute.

Let anyone who claims that existence is subjective try to create a microchip, or launch a satellite under the assumption that nature has no

---

[11] Peterson, Merrill, ed. *The Political Writings of Thomas Jefferson* (Annapolis Junction, Maryland: Thomas Jefferson Memorial Foundation, 1993), 191.
[12] Rand, Ayn. *For the New Intellectual* (New York: Signet, 1963), 173.

laws and could change at any moment. Try to manufacture fireworks without rigid principles.

A businessman related a story about a time when he was involved in a motorcycle accident. "I learned a principle from that frightening experience: gravity works," he said. "One can't disagree with gravity. Imagine how silly it would have been if, while flying through the air looking at the pavement, I quickly shouted, 'Gravity, stop working!' But we do exactly that in our economic lives all the time. We say, 'I'm not really sure what to do; I just hope the stock market does well.'"[13]

As he goes on to point out, many of us act in the same manner today with similar, painful consequences. When a politician passes a law or a bureaucrat issues an order contrary to the laws of economics or human nature, he is wishing reality to be other than it is, to conform to his whims. Such thinking always leads to unintended consequences.

PRINCIPLES GOVERN

"Men do not make laws. They do but discover them. Laws must be justified by something more than the will of the majority."[14] - Calvin Coolidge

> **Principle**: a fundamental, primary, or general truth, which describes an aspect of reality, and upon which other truths depend.

Principles often describe a specific application of the law of causality. In this way, "principle" can be synonymous with "law."

For example, one of the principles of physical motion is: If an object is traveling at a certain speed, then it will continue to do so unless acted upon by another force.

Notice that principles can be expressed as an if-then statement as above, or as a simple observation of truth: Inertia is a property of matter; people respond to incentives; etc.

If you get nothing else out of this entire book, we hope you take away this most important truth: principles govern.

---

[13] Koerber, Rick. "Individual Prosperity: Putting It All Together." *The FreeCapitalist Project Primer* (Provo, Utah: The FreeCapitalist Project, 2007), 77.

[14] Safire, William, ed. *Lend Me Your Ears: Great Speeches in History* (New York: W. W. Norton & Company, 1992), 55.

This primary truth—that life doesn't happen by chance, that every effect has a cause or causes, that every action has consequences, that a thing is itself—will set you free.

Watch any "National Geographic" television special and be witness to the laws governing the survival of life. Plants, insects, and animals all have fundamental natures that require them to engage in certain activities or find certain environmental conditions in order to live. Each animal has unique requirements for life. These requirements can't be changed according to the animal's whim or changed through a vote by its fellow animals. As is evidenced in both the death of individual animals and in the extinction of entire species, failure to meet the requirements of nature means death. Humans, on the other hand, do not live by major survival instincts—they have the ability to reason.

We are not exempt from the requirements of existence merely because we are the only creatures on earth which must rely alone on rational thought. We can't ignore these requirements for long before the natural consequences of illness, starvation, misery, and death set in.

It is this very attribute of man—his mind—that becomes his basic tool of survival. While animals can get by on their instincts, man cannot. Man can't live like an animal. There aren't many animals man can chase down for food—he has no claws with which to make the kill, he has no fur to prevent him from freezing in the cold. Man's only tool of survival is his rational mind which allows him to plant food, create clothing, find shelter, design and create weapons to hunt and tools to farm with, and interact with and learn from his fellow men. Man's survival must be by conscious choice, not instinct. A man's failure to think results in death, unless others think for him, in which case he is not living as a man, but as a parasite or a vegetable.

Man must live by conscious choice. Animals adjust themselves to their environment; man adjusts his environment to himself. Ayn Rand contrasted this idea, "If a drought strikes them, animals perish—man builds irrigation canals; if a flood strikes, animals perish—man builds dams; if a carnivorous pack attacks them, animals perish—man writes the Constitution of the United States. But one does not obtain food, safety, or freedom by instinct."[15]

All of existence is governed by principles, whether we know and understand them or not. The more we can align our life with true principles the more prosperous and happy we become.

---

[15] Rand, Ayn. *For the New Intellectual* (New York: Signet, 1963), 15.

REVIEW

Q1: What is the primary truth about reality upon which all other principles rest?

Q2: What are the laws of identity, causality, and non-contradiction?

Q3: How can you discover principles?

Q4: How can you know what is true?

Q5: What is man's means of survival?

Q6: Can you name some principles that have helped you in life? Is there something you used to believe was true that you have come to discover was in error?

CHAPTER 2

MORALITY AND SELF-INTEREST

"Man's mind is his basic tool of survival. Life is given to him, his sustenance is not. His mind is given to him, its content is not. To remain alive he must act, and before he can act he must know the nature and purpose of his action. To remain alive he must think."[1] - Ayn Rand

THE PURPOSE OF LIFE

You are a completely unique entity, different and independent from all the rest. And while your existence may not matter to the majority of people on earth, it matters to at least one person—you. Whether you live or die, whether you are happy or miserable, makes a difference to you. This is why you are here. Your life is an end to itself, and your enjoyment of it—your happiness—is the only moral purpose of it. You exist to be happy; and it is up to you to create the kind of life you want and have as much happiness as you choose.

There's good news and bad news that goes along with that, and it's actually the same news: happiness doesn't come by chance; it comes by obeying certain rules, or laws.

---

[1] Rand, Ayn. *Atlas Shrugged* (New York: Signet, 1957), 938.

That's the good news because you can discover those rules, and by following them, be happy.

That's also the bad news because joy and fulfillment in life won't come by wishing, hoping, and waiting for some big roll of universal dice for things to finally go your way. If you want to have the feelings of happiness, you must do what it takes to be happy. The same is true if you want to be wealthy, or respected, or have a loving, committed relationship, or a free and prosperous country. You must perform the cause to get the effect.

These rules, or principles, were not invented—they simply are. No one invented the principle of inertia; it is an inescapable fact of physical matter. No one decided that trees need sun, soil, and CO_2 to live.

Just as discovering principles of physics and chemistry and biology

IMMANUEL KANT

helped mankind cure diseases and manufacture cars, so principles of prosperity and economics and personal happiness can provide predictable results when they are followed.

As for your happiness, there have been those throughout history that have told individuals that happiness is not your purpose. They have done this for a variety of motivations, and they instead taught that the design of your existence was to be used for someone else's happiness. To do this effectively, they often had to downplay the role of rational thought.

Philosopher Immanuel Kant claimed this. He claimed that our reason and choice were ineffective tools to be given to us by nature if man's purpose was to be happy. He said that "by instinct . . . [we would have been happier] much more certainly than . . . by reason," and that "our existence has a different and far nobler end, for which, and not for happiness, reason is properly intended."[2] Happiness was not a noble goal in Kant's view. He had other things in mind for the human race. More on that later.

---

[2] Kant, Immanuel. *The Critique of Pure Reason, The Critique of Practical Reason and Other Ethical Treatises, The Critique of Judgment* (Chicago: Encyclopedia Britannica, 1978), 257.

While happiness is the purpose of your life, it is not provided by default of the fact that you're alive. It does not come by doing whatever you want or whatever you feel like doing. It cannot be had by acting on every capricious impulse that floats through your mind.

Our whims are rarely in our self-interest, and blindly following them is not the way to be happy. You might really enjoy eating an entire box of Oreos at once, easily mistaking the temporary rush of dopamine as happiness, but you would soon find it overshadowed by the later consequences. Your life isn't better, it's actually worse because your stomach hurts, you're nurturing an addiction, your health is damaged, and soon your pants will not fit. In this example, you are basing your happiness on an external chemical substance, rather than on something internal and ongoing. It is artificial, temporary, and damaging, rather than natural, sustained, and healthy. It is not rational.

How then do we find happiness? What natural and internal source will give us steady happiness and satisfaction?

One of the best ways to describe this is that happiness lies in achieving life-serving values. Such values you can achieve will not come to you by instinct, but must be deliberately chosen. Lasting joy comes in the achievement of your rational values. This can be called doing what is in your best self-interest. Those values have to be life-serving, because if you're dead, you can't do anything else.

THE VALUE OF VIRTUE

To achieve the values that make us happy, we must cultivate virtues in ourselves.

For example, reason is a value; its corresponding virtue is rational thinking.

A career is a value; productive work is a virtue.

Self-esteem is a value; doing what it takes to gain and keep it is a virtue.[3]

Knowledge and wisdom are values; pursuing education is a virtue. Without virtues, you have no way to achieve values.

Job training programs can be viewed as "virtue training programs" in this sense. It is a program designed to help people learn the virtues of showing up regularly to work, of consistent responsibility, of good social

---

[3] Biddle, Craig. *Loving Life: The Morality of Self-Interest and the Facts That Support It* (Richmond, Virginia: Glen Allen Press, 2002), 4.

interaction. Such virtues are necessary to achieve higher values than would be possible without them.

Principles, in this context, are the laws in which virtues are the cause and values are the effect.

For example, if you decide that a healthy and trusting relationship with family and friends is a value you desire to have, then you must discover the principles that describe how to achieve the desired results, and then take the virtuous actions that will get those results. To obtain the value of a trust-filled relationship, you must follow, among others, the principle of integrity, which will require you to exercise the virtue of honesty.

The same formula can be applied to weight loss. A healthy body is the value you desire, principles of good diet and physical activity dictate to you the virtues you must cultivate, such as the discipline and knowledge for proper exercise and nutrition.

Virtuous actions conform to principles and lead to the achievement of values. This makes us happy. This concept can be expressed visually in a simple manner:

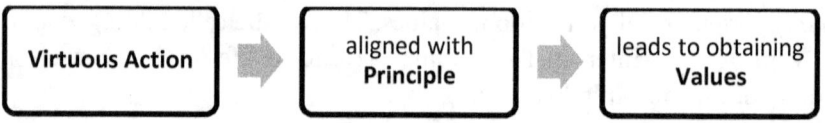

How do we determine if values are good or bad? Are all values the same? Is there a way to judge which values should be held in higher esteem? Are there some deceptive "values" which are actually evil and lead to misery and destruction? Shouldn't we just go with whatever society says is good or whatever feels good?

Good and evil can be defined clearly and objectively[4]:

> **Good:** That which is suitable to the life of a rational being.
> **Evil:** All that which destroys the life of a rational being.[4]

Please notice that the standard used to judge good and evil is life—our ultimate value. Notice also that this standard is objective—existing independently of feelings and opinions. Life and its requirements are empirical; they are observable and discernible to any person with natural senses. Since life is universal to all people, such a standard of good and evil is also universal to every person.

---

[4] Rand, Ayn. *The Virtue of Selfishness* (New York: Signet, 1964), 23.

"Good" is that which is proper, or necessary by nature, to the life and joy of man—be it physical, mental, social, or spiritual values to support and sustain man's life. It is focused on what is—in reality and not by whim—good or best for each individual (always in context, accounting for who he is and what is possible to him). "Evil" is that which destroys life or man's ability to sustain his own life, or enjoy it, i.e. his ability to act according to his judgment in pursuit of his self-interest.

Our (Caleb's) family recently acquired two pet rabbits. As I learned about what rabbits need, not only to survive, but to thrive as a pet, I realized that they needed a rabbit run area by their shelter to get exercise and have room to explore and play. They needed toys to avoid cage boredom. They do better with another rabbit to socialize and communicate with and share grooming. As I worked to provide these things, my wife mentioned she thought it was cute I was "spoiling" them. She had seen a neighbor's pet rabbit that was cranky and lonely because of a lack of these things in its life. I observed that providing what rabbits need to thrive wasn't "spoiling" them, but merely complying with their nature.

In the case of humans, acting morally requires having virtues and pursuing values—living according to principles.

It is important to identify whose life is the standard of value: yours. You cannot be given happiness from someone else nor give it to them. (You may derive happiness from your association with another person, but they do not force you, it is still a choice.)

You cannot tell someone what to value, nor have values forced upon you. It takes a conscious, rational, mental recognition to discover what kind of life is proper to man's happiness, and to live that life.

Even when you have found the values necessary to a proper life, you cannot require that others be forced to embrace them. While your knowledge allows you to live a principled life of happiness, it does not provide you with any authority to hold others to your standards and coerce them to choose your same values.

IDEAS HAVE CONSEQUENCES

Cancer happens when a cell reproduces itself with an abnormality. The abnormal cell continues to go through the same motions of life its predecessors did, reproducing and growing. But as it takes nourishment from the body it is supposed to be supporting, it unwittingly sabotages its own existence.

A POOR FOUNDATION CAUSED THE FAMOUS "LEANING" OF THE TOWER OF PISA.

Such is the case with a false premise, which supports a false belief, which in turn leads to actions of destruction. Ideas have consequences.

A false premise has terrible ramifications because of this progression from belief to action. It is compounded when the error is laid early in the foundation of cognition. An error laid at the bedrock of a person's cognition has a devastating cascade effect because every subsequent thought is warped by passing through its filter. As if that weren't bad enough, it destroys a person's very ability to detect false premises!

Many people who destroy life today do so inadvertently by attacking that which is necessary to support and sustain life—man's mind and the product of man's labors. Attacks on the mind are pernicious because they will often call into question the validity of our senses. They engender doubt that we possess the necessary faculties to make wise decisions and choose what is in our best interest.

The process of discovering and defining what actions we should take is the purpose of the philosophy of ethics.

> **Ethics**: the third branch of philosophy seeks to answer the questions: "What should I do with my life?" and "What code of values should guide my decisions?"

Ethics is a term that most people often interchange with morality, but it will be used in this book in its philosophical meaning as the process of seeking and defining morality—a code of values.

WHAT IS MORALITY? WHY DO I NEED IT?

"Matters of truth and morality are not determined by consensus."[5]
- Craig Biddle

Moral choices determine the purpose and the course of a person's life. It is by a code of morality that we judge what is right or wrong, good or evil.

> **Morality:** a code of values to guide man's choices and actions.

Much of society today operates under a moral code which claims that man has no right to live for himself, that service to others is his primary reason to live, and that self-sacrifice is his highest goal.

You may hear that if you oppose the majority you must be antisocial or have some other varying degree of mental disorder.

You may hear that the needs of the many are more important than the rights of a few, and that a little sacrifice is simply the price of living in a society, or the only way possible for civilization to exist. Such moral codes are not true because they are contrary to man's nature and the requirements for his life. When most of mankind acts on a morality that is directly in opposition to the nature of their life and survival, the result is misery and destruction.

Others today may say that there is no way to know for sure what to do logically or objectively, that "my truth is different from your truth," but that people just need to go by what they feel. They say that morality is relative or subjective and changes with each individual and culture—and that one morality is just as good as any other.

They may say that there is no way to know what is good or evil, or that defining ideas or actions as good or evil is narrow-minded and arrogant. Who are you to decide what is right or wrong?

The world is plagued with moral subjectivism. Two common forms of this are personal subjectivism and social subjectivism. These have been accepted over the centuries with many twists and variations.

---

[5] Biddle, Craig. "Capitalism and the Moral High Ground." *The Objective Standard*. Winter 2008-09. Online. theobjectivestandard.com/issues/2008-winter/capitalism-moral-high-ground.asp. Accessed 9 Aug 2011.

Personal Subjectivism

- The idea that truth and morality are creations of the mind of the individual.
- Truth is a matter of personal opinion.

Social Subjectivism

- The notion that truth and morality are creations of the mind of a collective (a group of people).
- Morality is a matter of social convention. [6]

A subjective morality can be used to justify any action, even murder, rape, or genocide. This is the problem with subjective standards—they aren't firmly fixed to anything. When they can be whatever we want them to be, how can we even say they are a standard? (The history of the word "standard" has been proposed to be related to "stand hard", to stand fast or firm—in other words, an unchangeable thing to count on.) It is a symbol of how subjective we have become politically when these days we talk about someone's *stance* on such-and-such an issue, rather than their *stand*.

Subjective morality is a line in the sand that can be drawn anywhere by anyone at any time. It doesn't matter whether the subjectivity is based on feelings, whims, opinions, political expediency, or religious beliefs; none of those things have a firm footing in observable reality.

The good news is that there is a code of morality that can be proven to be true by the facts of reality, but a tool is required. That tool is reason.

Humans need moral guidance, without which we wouldn't know the right way to spend our time. Do we work for a living or steal from others? Do we lie or tell the truth? Should we befriend someone, marry them, vote for them, or trust them with our children? In order to achieve happiness, we need to know how to evaluate our choices. We need a principle to guide our decisions.

But it's not as easy as it sounds. We can't just pick a goal and take actions to achieve it. We must first ask, "What is a proper goal?" What is the standard by which we should measure the rightness of our goals? The issue of morality is not an issue of effective means. It is an issue of proper, appropriate, or necessary ends.

What is a proper end? There are many ends for which people take action. We study to learn. We get a job to get a paycheck. We get a

---

[6] Biddle, *Loving Life*, 7.

paycheck to buy other things for other purposes and so on. But where does it all end? Philosopher Craig Biddle asked it this way, "We need to discover a final end—one toward which all of our other goals and values are properly aimed. Such an end is . . . the standard against which we can objectively assess the value of all our choices and actions. So then the question becomes: What is our ultimate goal?"[7]

The answer: Life and joy.

A moral life is one that both protects that life and provides it with the conditions of happiness.

It is important to keep in mind the meaning of "moral" and how to know such a morality.

Morality does not mean "whatever God commands," although in most religions, many of the precepts are indeed moral.

Morality does not mean "whatever is legal," although in most countries, many of the laws are indeed moral.

Morality does not mean "whatever the majority decides," although a large group can sometimes vote for what is moral.

Morality does not mean, "whatever appears expedient or necessary at the moment." Whims and range-of-the-moment decisions are not made with rational moral judgment.

The correct morality, or the good, is all that which is suitable to the life and joy of a rational being. *Morality is self-evident in the nature of man.* Morality stems from the fact that existence is what it is and that man is what he is. And it does not matter how many people believe differently. Popular sentiments and ideas aren't necessarily true.

COLLECTIVE ACTION HAS NO UNIQUE MORAL AUTHORITY

Here we discover a principle to guide us. Businessman Garrett Gunderson described it this way, "It is also important for us to realize that collective action has no unique moral authority. In other words, fifty million people saying a dumb thing doesn't make it any less dumb. True principles exist regardless of whether or not we are aware of them or believe in them."[8]

---

[7] Biddle, *Loving Life*, 36.

[8] Gunderson, Garrett. and Stephen Palmer. *Killing Sacred Cows* (Provo, Utah: Decade Media, 2007), 17.

"Moral Authority": The principle states that a group of people, no matter how large, has no unique moral authority. In many cases the majority does, indeed, carry unique authority as seen in many democratic institutions or tribal actions. The authority of the majority to carry out its will can be enforced by brute strength of numbers or through the action of peaceful democratic processes such as voting. (If the majority votes for slavery, it's still wrong.) However, the idea here is that the collective has no unique moral authority. This means the collective has no authority over the establishment and defining of right and wrong, truth and falsehood, good and evil. "Mainstream" thought, if such a thing can exist, is not an ultimate source of truth. In other words, contrary to the old song, fifty million Frenchmen can be wrong. Reality is what it is regardless of what any number of people wish it to be.

"Unique": A large number of people can recognize the truth and advocate it. But, in that case, the truth is still simply the truth which happens to be recognized by a number of individuals. The truth they advocate gives them moral authority, but increasing the number of individuals by any amount does not add to or detract from the moral authority that would already be had by a single individual who is advocating true principles.

Some things are true whether you believe them or not. It doesn't matter if you, your President, your church, or your neighbors think the sun revolves around the earth—belief doesn't change reality. The number of people who believe an idea does not affect whether that idea is true or false, merely its popularity.

RATIONAL SELF-INTEREST

We've identified our ultimate goal as the furtherance of lives filled with joy. Such a goal requires us to recognize whose life it is that we seek to protect and enhance—our own. Thus, if we choose to keep living, we must recognize the morality of rational self-interest.

Man's primary motivating force begins with self-interest.

This principle stems from the fact that for those who choose to live, each individual's own life is logically his own ultimate value. Every other decision is based on that foundation.

Scottish economist Adam Smith helped lay some groundwork for this principle in 1776, with his description of "self-love." The principle of "self-love," he explains, is not displayed in force or deception, but in persuasion and exchange:

"But man has almost constant occasion for the help of his brethren, and it is in vain for him to expect it from their benevolence only. He will be more likely to prevail if he can interest their self-love in his favour, and show them that it is for their own advantage to do for him what he requires of them. Whoever offers to another a bargain of any kind, proposes to do this. Give me that which I want, and you shall have this which you want, is the meaning of every such offer . . . . It is not from the benevolence of the butcher, the brewer, or the baker, that we expect our dinner, but from their regard to their own interest. We address ourselves, not to their humanity but to their self-love, and never talk to them of our own necessities but of their advantages."[9]

In other words, a man's self-interest is one of the primary and most powerful motivators to inspire men to action. The baker and the butcher do not bake bread and prepare meats to be charitable. They do so to exchange with others and create wealth.

Rational self-interest does not hold pleasurable feelings as the standard of value, but man's life. This means that whims do not amount to self-interest. There is never a conflict of interest between rational men because rational men do not expect the unearned. And since one's rational self-interest is employed in improving and enjoying one's life, then self-interest must be counted as a moral virtue.

ADAM SMITH

The Founders recognized that man's pursuit of his own life (i.e. his own happiness) was a natural and moral phenomenon. Jefferson wrote that, "If we are made in some degree for others, yet in a greater are we made for ourselves. It were contrary to feeling & indeed ridiculous to suppose that a man had less right in himself than one of his neighbors or indeed all of them put together."[10] He recognized that not only does man

---

[9] Smith, Adam. *The Wealth of Nations* (New York: Bantam, 2003), 23-24.
[10] Peterson, Merrill, ed. *The Political Writings of Thomas Jefferson* (Annapolis Junction, Maryland: Thomas Jefferson Memorial Foundation, 1993), 48.

exist for his own life, but that the claims of others, no matter how many, do not outweigh a man's claim on himself.

When rational self-interest is examined as a code of ethics, it can be described as **egoism**. Biddle explained that every individual ought to act in their own best interest and ought to benefit from their own moral actions. Since humans have free will, they can choose to live or not. If they choose to live, then life is their ultimate value, and the actions required to sustain that life must be considered moral.[11]

It's okay to work towards your own happiness.

It's more than okay, it's a moral imperative.

ISN'T THAT SELFISH?

Let's make sure we distinguish between what most people think of as selfishness, and egoism, or rational self-interest.

Egoism can be thought of as the view that you should derive benefit from what you do every day.

Selfishness, or hedonism, holds desires and pleasures as the standard of value, and feelings as the source of truth. However, many actions that might make you feel good for a while are not life-promoting (i.e. not in your self-interest).

It might feel good for a while to get high on drugs, but that action is not going to promote and enhance your life. You can cheat on your spouse and get some pleasure, but if it destroys your integrity and self-esteem (as it surely will) it is not good for you. A ballerina might get pleasure from binging on ice cream and Twinkies all day, but if that action causes her to gain weight, lose energy, and ruin her career it is not in her self-interest. Murderers, robbers, swindlers, and embezzlers are not acting in their self-interest—and none of them are happy, even before they get caught.

Then how do we know what is in our best self-interest? It can be hard work. We have to turn to the facts of reality to discover which values to pursue. Biddle gives us an outline of how to proceed, explaining that we need "both long-range and wide-range guidance: long-range guidance to account for the span of our lifetime, and wide-range guidance to account for the broad spectrum of our needs." To know if an action is good or bad we have to "project both the physical and the psychological consequences, and not only with regard to the present, but also with regard to the more distant future."[12]

---

[11] Biddle, *Loving Life*, 50.
[12] Biddle, *Loving Life*, 52.

It is unfortunate that the word "selfish" has a negative denotation, because to be interested in one's own welfare is good and proper, and the bedrock of moral action. The behaviors commonly associated with selfish behavior are in opposition to concern for one's well-being. In fact, such behaviors typically show disregard for one's rational self-interest; they are actions of self-destruction rather than self-preservation, actions that lead to misery rather than joy, self-*less* rather than self-*ish*.

They are also typically characterized by a lack of appreciation for the value of others—a violation of the principles we will discuss later that People Are Assets and that Exchange Creates Wealth.

FORCE DESTROYS FREEDOM AND PROSPERITY[13]

In order to live as human beings and pursue our rational self-interest in the furtherance of our life, we have to be free to act on our own judgment. The only thing that can stop us from doing so (wild animals and freak accidents aside) is other people. The only way they can do so is by using physical force. This involves the branch of philosophy known as politics.

> **Politics:** The fourth branch of philosophy seeks to answer the question, "How should I interact with my fellow men?"

The answer is, "Through any means except force."

Even a small child recognizes force easily. Watch a toddler react when a person takes an action that interferes with their choice and thwarts their desire. A sibling takes a toy; a parent turns off a movie; a child may even get angry when thinking that an inanimate object (e.g. a doorknob or a seatbelt) is uncooperative.

It's easy to recognize force in tyrannical governments. Ethnic cleansings, unjust imprisonments, and mass executions are fairly easy to spot. In other ways, force can be a bit more difficult to identify.

Physical force is the use or threat of physical harm to influence an individual to an action he would not have otherwise chosen.

Suppose you were walking to the store for the purpose of using your money to buy some groceries when you are suddenly held up by a

---

[13] Koerber, Rick. "The FreeCapitalist Project." *The FreeCapitalist Project Primer* (Provo, Utah: The FreeCapitalist Project, 2007).

mugger. He points a gun at your head saying, "Give me your wallet or you die."

Now you are unable, if you want to live, to continue to act according to your plan. To avoid getting shot, you must hand over your wallet. You are no longer going grocery shopping in either case. By placing a gun between you and your goal, the thief is forcing you to act contrary to your judgment—your means of survival. Yes, you still have agency. You can still choose what to think and do, but your choices have been artificially curtailed because now you must choose between alternatives that would not exist were it not for the threat of force.

If the thief leaves you alive, you're are free to continue to act on your own judgment, *but not with respect to the stolen money*. This won't thwart your life totally, but it will impede you partially. If you had your money, you could either spend or save it. Without it, you can do neither, and to that degree your life is now restricted. Thus it is that force destroys freedom and prosperity.

Biddle stated the principle this way: "To whatever degree physical force (or the credible threat thereof) is used against a person, it stops him from acting on his judgment; the greater the force, the less human a life he can live."[14]

As bad as physical force is, there is a worse form of force. Without this second form, physical force is harder to sustain. The second form is mental force, or deception. Proof of this can be seen in that no dictatorship was ever able to be maintained for any significant period without establishing censorship.[15]

Why is deception so evil? Because it destroys man's ability to act on his own judgment—his agency; it doesn't merely restrict his agency as the mugger did, but it destroys his agency.

Deception can also be viewed as indirect physical force. Suppose you buy a used car and the salesman lies to you about the condition of the engine. The car you drive away in is not the same as the car you thought you purchased. Thus, you have been forced against your knowledge and will to do something that you would otherwise not have chosen.

Whereas physical force violates agency by restricting the choices an individual can make, that individual can still make a choice based on the facts of reality. If I'm pointing a gun at your head, you can still choose your actions, though if your desire is to continue living, those choices will

---

[14] Biddle, *Loving Life*, 106.
[15] Rand, Ayn. *The Voice of Reason* (New York: Signet, 1990), 21.

be severely limited. Mental force is evil because it doesn't just violate agency, it destroys it. It doesn't limit our decisions based on reality; it takes away any possible ability to choose anything based on reality. If I hold out the good in my right hand and the evil in my left, but I tell you the opposite—that evil is in my right and good is in my left—what have I done? I have removed both your ability and opportunity to make a decision based on the truth. Or what if I hold out my hands and tell you that they are both holding good or holding evil? How can you choose? You can't! This is the only way to destroy the ability of someone to make decisions on what's best for them.

And it doesn't matter who's doing the deceiving. If I'm deceiving you, or your mayor's deceiving you, or your mother's deceiving you, or even if you are even self-deceived—it doesn't matter! The end result is the same. It's scary because you never know when you are deceived. That's the definition of "deceived;" you don't know what you don't know.

On the Jefferson memorial is carved an astounding sentiment in powerful language of the type that is rarely heard today: "I have sworn upon the altar of God, eternal hostility against every form of tyranny over the mind of man."[16] He wrote that in a letter in the year 1800 referring to his fight against certain religionists who wanted to establish a particular form of Christianity throughout the country. This is the conviction of a man who understands the power, the purpose, and the necessity of liberty of conscience—of a free mind, not just a free body.

We see now that man must be free to act on his judgment to live his life and achieve his values and happiness. Thus, in a social context, man needs a moral principle—a life-promoting and life-protecting law—to protect him from those who would seek to initiate or threaten the use of force against him. That principle becomes the concept of rights.

---

[16] Letter to Dr. Benjamin Rush. 23 Sep 1800. Text available online. lachlan.bluehaze.com.au/lit/jeff04.htm. Accessed 26 Apr 2011.

REVIEW

Q1: What is the difference between a value and a virtue? What are some examples?

_____

Q2: Why are values necessary for life? What other values do you personally pursue?

_____

Q3: What is the standard by which a value must be judged? Give an example of an irrational value.

_____

Q4: What is the problem with having a subjective morality?

_____

Q5: What is the difference between hedonism and rational self-interest?

_____

Q6: Why does force destroy freedom and prosperity?

_____

Q7: Why is deception a form of force?

_____

CHAPTER 3

RIGHTS

The concept of individual rights is relatively new to humankind. It is another key part of the foundation of all the spectacular advances in human civilization in the last three hundred years—and when this concept has been ignored, evaded, or twisted, the results have been the greatest horrors in human history. It is imperative in the cause of freedom to fully understand the origin, meaning, and application of the concept of rights.[1]

> A **right** is "a moral principle defining and sanctioning man's freedom of action in a social context."

(*Principle* in this sense means "A fundamental truth or proposition that serves as the foundation for a system of belief or behavior or for a chain of reasoning.")

Rights do not come from God or government, nor are they inherent or "natural" to mankind. They do not physically exist so they can't "come from" anywhere. They are concepts. Where they "come from" is from a rational mind that recognizes what man requires in order to live.

---

[1] Rand, Ayn. *Capitalism: The Unknown Ideal* (New York: Signet, 1967), 321.

They are moral principles based on the objective requirements of man's nature within a social context. They describe the requirements for our existence in relationship to other people.

The foundation of knowledge required for understanding rights is:

1. You exist.
2. Principles govern your pursuit of life and happiness.
3. To follow those principles of happiness, you must be free to act on your rational judgment.
4. The only thing that can stop you from doing so is the physical interference of others; therefore, rights describe how you should be left free from others' force.
5. Rights provide the link between ethics and politics, between personal principles of action and social principles of interaction.

The concept of individual rights was the core political philosophy of America's founding. It was recognized that rights are not created by human laws. As William Blackstone wrote in his *Commentaries of the Laws of England*, rights do not need human laws "to be more effectually invested in every man than they are; neither do they receive any additional strength when declared by the municipal laws to be inviolable."[2]

A major cause of America's problems today, however, was a failure by the Founders to explicitly define what these rights are and what constitutes a violation of them. Thanks to the hindsight of history and the work of many people before us, that oversight can now be corrected.

THE BASICS

The three basic individual rights were expressed by George Washington in 1786 prior to the Constitutional Convention, "Let us have [a government] by which our lives, liberties, and properties will be secured."[3]

1. **Life**—You are here, and so you have license to continue to be here. No one should try to take your life from you, and you

---

[2] Quoted in Skousen, W. Cleon. *The 5000 Year Leap: A Miracle That Changed the World* (Washington, D.C.: National Center for Constitutional Studies, 2006), 124.

[3] Allison, A., Parry, J., and W. Cleon Skousen. *The Real George Washington* (Washington D.C.: National Center for Constitutional Studies, 1991), 462.

shouldn't try to take anyone else's. How long do you have this right? As long as are alive and don't murder anyone else. You may have the right to exist, but it is your job, and your job alone, to maintain your existence by providing for your necessities. (Unless you are an infant or child, in which case it is the responsibility of your caregivers until you grow up.) This is the only basic right; all other rights stem from this one.

2. **Liberty**—Maintaining your life takes work, so you need to be free from other people beating you up and stuffing you in lockers and the like so that you can go about the business that will keep your heart pumping. Remember that your tool for maintaining your life is your mind, thus "survival requires that those who think be free from the interference of those who don't."[4] Your right to liberty includes liberty of conscience, and of religion, and the right to pursue safety and happiness. Basically, it is the right to do whatever you want to do unless that action would infringe on the rights of others.

3. **Property**—If you want to stay alive, which is a process of self-sustaining and self-generating action, you'll need food, shelter, clothes, water, and all the rest—that means you have a right to own, or control, things. Using your brain and your freedom, you can go about getting these things by working, creating, and exchanging with others for what you want. If you plant raspberries on your property, then if you want you can harvest and eat them until your stomach explodes. Your time is also yours; you are free to trade it to an employer for whatever pay you both decide is fair. Anything you earn is yours. If you trade your time and work for anything, that "anything" is yours to keep. You can share if you want, or consume it all yourself; it belongs to you, it is a product of your labor, and that means you have a right to control it. John Adams put it this way, "All men are born free and independent, and have certain natural, essential, and unalienable rights, among which may be reckoned the right of enjoying and defending their lives and liberties; that of acquiring, possessing, and protecting property; in fine, that of seeking and obtaining their safety and happiness."[5]

---

[4] Rand, *Capitalism*, 8.
[5] Allison, A., Parry, J., and W. Cleon Skousen. *The Real George Washington* (Washington D.C.: National Center for Constitutional Studies: 1991), 497.

Despite Adams' clarity, there is still much confusion in defining rights. But let's not take his word for it. It is best to make a fresh start, and rebuild our entire conception of rights from the ground up using only observable and self-evident facts of reality. That way, we can be sure we are on firm ground.

How do you prove that these concepts of natural human rights are true? Think of it this way: the fact that you are alive implies that nature declared you "existable" and you have the right to continue to be so. You have a mind and body independent of all others. You and you alone have direct control over your mind and body—no one else has that. Therefore, your life is yours to do with as you please.

JOHN ADAMS

You have the right to continue living on your merry way, free from anyone interfering with your existence. By this we mean people physically acting against you. Fall in a volcano, drown in a flood, get struck by lightning, have a heart attack, or be trampled by an elephant, that's "natural"—sad, but natural. The natural laws of causality have unfortunately revoked your life card. Getting shot, raped, or punched in the face—that is "artificial." It is not a natural condition or result of existing, it is a willful interference against your life which you did not choose, made by a person who lacks the prerogative to do so.

Since life is a process of self-sustaining and self-generating action, the right to life means the right to engage in self-sustaining and self-generating action. You have the right to take all the rational actions required by nature to support your life, to further your life, and to enjoy your life.

A right only means you have freedom to act. It means freedom from compulsion, or force, by other men. A right gives moral sanction to your voluntary actions and imposes no obligations on others except to abstain from violating your rights.

For instance, while the right to life means the right to keep yourself alive, it does not place the burden of your own survival on anyone around you. It does not mean that other people must give a man food when he is hungry, medicine when he is sick, or a job when he is unemployed. It does not mean that others must provide him with a community swimming pool, high-speed internet, or a recreational trail network.

Samuel Adams, often called the Father of the American Revolution, observed that man's rights "are evident branches of, rather than deductions from, the duty of self-preservation, commonly called the first law of nature."[6]

This means that your right to life is the one fundamental right to which all other rights are corollary. The first corollary of your right to life is your right to liberty. Your right to life is meaningless unless you also have the liberty to take the actions necessary to preserve that life. Your right to liberty means your right to dispose of your life as you see fit and pursue the activities you desire with only the restriction that your activities and pursuits do not physically harm, deceive, or coerce another human being. You have the right to life and the liberty to use that life, but not the liberty to infringe on the lives and liberty of others.

The most controversial right, the right to property, is the only means you have to implement all other rights. Without property rights, no other rights are possible! Your nature requires you to be free to think and perform those activities that will preserve your life. You must be free to work and to keep the product of your labor. This is the third basic right of man—the right of property. To deny it is, in effect, to deny that man has a right to life.

Everyone on earth begins life with a particular form of private property—their body. Man has the freedom to do with his body what he pleases, so long as it does not infringe on the rights of others—which means so long as he does not initiate physical force against others. Since man must sustain his own life by his own effort using his own body, the man who has no right to the product of his effort has no means to sustain his life. The man who produces while others take his product is a slave. The man who acts on the belief that others should, against their will, provide for his needs and wants is a tyrant.

The right to property does not mean the right to be given property by the government, but to produce and thereby earn it.[7]

Simply put, if you have no right to keep the product of your work, you have no right to liberty. If you have no right to liberty, you have no right to your life, because what you choose do with your liberty and property is what your life consists of. Those who argue that property is

---

[6] Quoted in Peikoff, Leonard. *The Ominous Parallels* (New York: Penguin, 1982), 110).

[7] Peikoff, *Objectivism*, 355.

not a right have said that having only some of your property taken from you does not impact your right to life—you are, after all, still alive. Technically you could be locked in a cage and fed just enough to keep you from starvation, but your right isn't just to be alive, it is to live!

Those who believe property is not a right would argue that even if some of your money is taken away, you still have your freedom to dispose of the rest of your property, but the range of possibilities open to you have been reduced. By the unwanted and arbitrary actions of others, your possible options have been reduced and your liberty has been restricted. The highwayman's ultimatum, "your money or your life" does not leave your freedom intact merely because you still have the choice to be robbed or murdered.

When the actions of others limit your choices, you lose the ability to do what you might have done. Paths that you may have chosen are now closed to you. Your ability to buy that special anniversary present, to save more for retirement, to pay off your home early, to go on that trip, to start a business, to give more to your charity, or anything else you might have done if you had the money cannot be done now. Your judgment has been overruled by another. You may eventually be able to do those things you wanted to do, but you have lost time, and time is the very currency of your life. Your life's potential and accomplishments have been quashed, and your pursuit of happiness shackled. Hence, your life is inexorably tied to your right of property. To the extent your property is taken away, your choices are limited, your liberty is restricted, and thus the right to your life is curtailed.

We have discussed the three fundamental human rights—life, liberty, and property. There are numerous ways to uphold, exercise, and enjoy your rights, but only one way to have them violated—physical force. Each of these rights is related to the right to act on our own judgment. But if someone holding a gun orders us to do anything, then we cannot act on our own judgment. In order to live we must act on the gunman's judgment—this is not freedom.

This is true with any form of force, even if it is as apparently small a matter as being required to pay taxes for a new city park with our alternative being a fine or even imprisonment. Our liberty has been restricted, and infringed upon by others.

Thomas Jefferson named these "unalienable" rights, meaning they cannot be changed; they are not granted or revoked by government, but are essential requirements of man's nature.

NOTE: In the Declaration of Independence, the traditional right of "property," is substituted by "the pursuit of happiness" as a broader, more sweeping term. However, most people at the time recognized that "property" was the right being referred to. As early as 1690, the philosopher John Locke claimed that "no one ought to harm another in his life, health, liberty, or possessions." Only two years before Jefferson's Declaration, the first Continental Congress's Declaration of Rights and Grievances made reference to "life, liberty, and property . . . secured by . . . the unchanging laws of nature."[8] In the same month that Jefferson was penning the Declaration, Virginia passed its own Declaration of Rights saying, "All men are by nature equally free and independent, and have certain inherent rights; . . . namely, the enjoyment of life and liberty, with the means of acquiring and possessing property, and pursuing and obtaining happiness and safety." (It has been suggested that Jefferson altered the traditional wording so as not to imply that slaves, which were considered property under the law, should be considered a right.[9] This helped pave the way to the abolition of slavery due to the inherent and fatal contradiction between slavery and individual rights.)

The Founders thought it was self-evident that property was a necessary requirement for any man's pursuit of happiness. The protection of these rights against infringement by others, Jefferson says, is the reason "governments are instituted among men." "To secure these rights" is the only proper purpose of government.

Respect for human rights is more than a political idea; it is a philosophy of peace. Every other philosophy might claim brotherly love as its ethic, but still reserves the use of coercion and theft against those supposedly beloved brothers.

Consider for a moment what a wonderful place it would be to live where everyone respected the rights of their neighbors, where "Do no harm" was the underlying theme of all action, and the only commandment was "Thou shalt not initiate force against another." Where the inevitable, but rare, infractions of law have simple legal recourse, and where government was never the aggressor wielding deception, theft, and coercion as tools of state, but only an impartial arbitrator and protector of all.

There are some additional principles to keep in mind regarding the right of property:

---

[8] Schweikart, Larry. and Michael Allen. *A Patriot's History of the United States: From Columbus' Great Discovery to the War on Terror* (New York: Penguin, 2004), 70.

[9] Peterson, Merrill, ed. *The Political Writings of Thomas Jefferson* (Annapolis Junction, Maryland: Thomas Jefferson Memorial Foundation, 1993), 15.

THE ORIGIN OF LAND PROPERTY RIGHTS

- The origin of real (land) property lies in its use and control;
- Private property includes intellectual property;
- Freedom requires private property.

Where does the right to own land come from?

John Locke identified labor—whether of the mind or body—as the source of land rights when that labor was exercised upon what had previously been unclaimed, or "common," to all mankind: "Thus labour, in the beginning, gave a right of property wherever anyone was pleased to employ it upon what was common."[10]

The primary basis for the concept of land ownership comes from control. It is this principle that operates among the animal kingdom. Whatever animal can stake out its own area and control it, gets it.

When there is no advanced government to record and protect the ownership of various tracts of land, a primitive people would have only one basis for such ownership—control. If an individual, family, or tribe could maintain control over a portion of land then it was theirs, whether a government was there to give them a "deed" or not. If the land was too large to protect effectively, portions of it might then be lost to neighboring peoples. Land might be acquired morally (received in fair trade) or immorally (stolen in conquest and invasion, or acquired through deception). Or it might simply be acquired and kept because no one else wanted it.

Eventually, when a new or advanced government rose up over the area, the owners/controllers experienced one of two scenarios. They were either given title and legal right to use the land protected by objective government arbitration, or else (if the government was more despotic) had it appropriated from them and subsequently issued "legally" to another party. (Recall that "legal" is not synonymous with "moral.")

Why is this important today?

It doesn't matter by what method a stretch of land was originally acquired in the recesses of history. It was either taken from nature or taken from others. If it was taken from others it was either voluntarily or through force. It doesn't matter today because the principle of control

---

[10] Locke, John. "Second Treatise of Civil Government." Online. constitution.org/jl/2ndtr05.htm. Accessed 9 Aug 2011.

operated until it could be replaced with objective government recognition and protection of ownership.

Whether land was ceded through war or traded for trinkets, it does not matter who owned the land hundreds or thousands of years ago or how they lost control of it. The principle to concern ourselves with today is the protection of property rights in a modern society which, finally in the history of mankind, uses objective means of determining, protecting, and maintaining such control.

Still, there are people today who, for some reason, are concerned with wresting control of land from its current owners and somehow "giving it back" to descendants of some native tribe. Generally, those who operate with this goal in mind aren't even consistent enough with themselves to ask how that ancient tribe acquired the land themselves (what if they stole it from someone else?!). These people do not care for, and understand even less, the aims of freedom and the consequences of the violation of rights. They fail to see the consequences of such impossible actions. Should the island of Manhattan be stolen away from the current owners to be given to a group of the descendants of those who traded it hundreds of years ago? You can see the absurd impracticality of such an idea when the original owners are long dead and since their time a government has been created which protects property. Two wrongs would make a quagmire, and certainly not make a right; thus the only principle to worry about now is current ownership.

INTELLECTUAL PROPERTY

Intellectual property is a relatively new concept as well, with its first recorded use less than one hundred fifty years ago. It refers to the recognition of certain mental creations which need to be protected by law. Included are musical, literary and artistic works, discoveries, inventions, phrases, symbols, designs, and trade secrets. We must note that intellectual property cannot be protected by law unless it exists in some physical form. A song, book, or piece of art cannot be intellectual property for recognition by objective law until it leaves the brain of its creator and exists in the physical world.

This type of property must be protected in a moral society. It is property because it is the creation of someone's mind—the product of their mental work. It is the fruit of their labors. No one who enjoys using cell phones, cars, or computers can argue that mental effort is not work or is somehow inferior to physical labor.

An inventor's right to life and his responsibility to provide for that life are the moral principles behind the existence, recognition, and protection of intellectual property.

PROPERTY AS AN ELEMENT OF PERSONAL FREEDOM

"[Man] has a right that is founded upon the constitution of the universe to have property that is his own. Ultimately, property rights and personal rights are the same thing."[11] - Calvin Coolidge

Personal Freedom Requires Private Property[12]

The phrase "personal freedom" is slightly redundant but is used to clarify and help us remember the important truth that liberty doesn't exist unless it is attached to a person. Only individuals can be described accurately as being free or not free.

The addition of the word "collective" would nullify the principle—"collective freedom" cannot exist unless referring to the freedom held by a group of specific individuals generally. The Declaration of Independence states that all men (individually) are endowed with certain rights. Life is not a collective right. Life cannot be had by a group. (The concept "group" is merely a collection of individual entities; you cannot have a group of something until you first have the somethings. A group does not exist in reality; it is a mental construct to help in sorting by attributes.) The pursuit of happiness is an individual activity—it is not a group right. A group could not achieve happiness, but only maintain a feeling of unified happiness, and this is only as long as each individual member does so.

The root of all liberty of action and private property is your own body.

The answer to the question, "Who does your body belong to?" is always, "You." That's one reason why slavery is a huge violation of principle. It violates all rights, beginning with the right to a person's sovereignty over their body.

---

[11] Safire, William, ed. *Lend Me Your Ears: Great Speeches in History* (New York: W. W. Norton & Company, 1992), 55.
[12] Koerber, Rick. "The FreeCapitalist Project." *The FreeCapitalist Project Primer* (Provo, Utah: The FreeCapitalist Project, 2007).

Barry Goldwater noted the necessary relationship between property and liberty, "We see in the sanctity of private property the only durable foundation for constitutional government in a free society."[13]

If someone is deprived by a person, group, or government the freedom to control the fruits of their labors and is dependent on others for their sustenance, they are essentially a slave to that entity, being subject to their control. The right and control of property is essential to pursue a career, exercise freedom of religion, freedom of the press, and to pursue an education by supporting yourself and paying those who educate you.

We cherish liberty because it makes our ultimate value possible—the value of our own happy life. But liberty, in turn, is only possible if we respect and protect the right to own and control property. Jefferson knew that "a right to property is founded in our natural wants, in the means with which we are endowed to satisfy these wants, and the right to what we acquire by those means without violating the similar rights of other[s]."[14]

The primary obstacle that prevents many people from living by and advocating principles is the failure to understand and accept that they are responsible for themselves and that this *agency implies stewardship*.[15]

Agency is a concept referring to an individual's power to:
1. Make decisions;
2. Act on those decisions.

Every person on earth, once they progress to a mental state able to evaluate choices and consequences, is, by nature, an agent for themselves. Small children and those with certain mental disabilities lack this agency, and their care necessarily falls to others who act as their agents. The United States attempts to recognize this principle politically in setting the voting age at eighteen. Until then, the parents or guardians legally speak for their children.

Agency is man's freedom to think, to choose, and to act. Agency means that each man is responsible for himself, his decisions, his actions, and his happiness. This freedom to choose and act necessarily implies stewardship, or responsibility, over his actions and property.

As a term, "stewardship" was historically a reference to the portion of a monarch's realm or household that was put into the care of a "stew-

---

[13] Safire, *Speeches*, 825.

[14] Peterson, *Writings*, 187.

[15] Koerber, Rick. "The FreeCapitalist Project." *The FreeCapitalist Project Primer* (Provo, Utah: The FreeCapitalist Project, 2007).

ard." Stewardship is also a common Biblical theme (e.g. Joseph of Egypt, and the Parables of Jesus).

Individually, a stewardship refers to everything you are responsible for in life. We sometimes use it in place of the word "ownership" to denote concepts beyond physical assets. It includes private, physical property, but also much more. What are you in charge of in life? Your body, first; your thoughts and actions; your responsibilities in a chosen career; your family and children; your home and vehicle; your relationships. All of these things fall within an individual's stewardship. You don't own your spouse, or your children, or your friends, but you are responsible for your actions concerning them (as well as your physical assets)—and your actions should result in improvement based upon an objective standard of values. It is with this view in mind that the Bible refers to good stewards as those who improve and increase what is under their care, and bad stewards as those who hide, hoard, misuse, abuse, and don't put to good use what is entrusted to them.

If you consider that everything around you is a stewardship, or responsibility, that you are meant to improve upon, does that change your attitude and actions?

Ask yourself, do things in your care get better or worse?

Is your car, no matter how expensive, well-kept and cared for?

Is your home or rental unit, no matter how modest or expansive, improved every day? (There are mansions treated like trash heaps and there are humble homes cared for like cathedrals.)

Are people around you uplifted for knowing you?

Is your body cared for?

Are your children's needs for development physically, mentally, and spiritually being met?

This is what it means to use your agency to improve the stewardship that comes within your power. Let's take these principles a step deeper and demonstrate how they don't merely apply politically, but personally as well.

PRIVATE PROPERTY AT HOME

There are ways to raise children to understand and respect private property.

In fact, one study reported by sciencenews.org shows that the majority of children have a better intuitive understanding of private property and personal body ownership than do adults.

In one part of the experiment, "Participants saw an image of a cartoon boy holding a crayon who appeared above the word "user" and a cartoon girl who appeared above the word "owner." After hearing from an experimenter that the girl wanted her crayon back, volunteers were asked to rule on which cartoon child should get the prized object.

"About 75 percent of 4- and 5-year-olds decided in favor of the owner, versus about 20 percent of adults."[16]

One way to consider giving material things is with strings attached (e.g. "This bike will remain in your control, son, under the following conditions: you take care of it, obey these specific rules of our household, use proper protective equipment, etc.").

Maybe you want to retain ownership of the bike as a parent and only release it for use (a stewardship) at certain times and under certain conditions.

Maybe you will truly respect the ownership you said you gave him and find a different, principled way to enforce household rules (e.g. rescinding of another privilege which you, as the parent, control).

To live by this principle at home it must be known to be taboo to take an item that is the property of another family member. Are we forcing our children to share what is theirs against their will, thereby showing that the person with the power gets to decide who receives what and for how long—showing that "might is right?" Violating this principle teaches that crying about a "need" gets more attention than respect for the possessions of others. If a child wants something, we can demonstrate that Exchange Creates Wealth (a principle we will cover later). If everything in a home has a specific owner, then everyone will know that each item has someone responsible for its upkeep and use.

Consider the difference between "Your brother is crying, give him your toy or we'll spank you!" and "No, that belongs to your sister. We can't force her to give it to you, but you're welcome to find out what it would take to persuade her to lend it to you." Not only does this teach clear principles for life (e.g. responsibility, ownership, communication free of emotional manipulation), it gives the positive benefits of living a principle-based life.

A child will have the self-esteem and self-confidence that comes from the certainty that life is abundant, not scarce.

A child will recognize, as we saw in the story at the beginning of this book, that when the things that are theirs are protected and respect-

---

[16] Bower, Bruce. "Kids Own Up to Ownership." *Science News.* Online. sciencenews.org/view/generic/id/74983/title/Kids_own_up_to_ownership. Accessed 18 Jun 2011.

ed, that all their needs are met, and that it is okay to be generous because being generous doesn't mean you get less.

A child will learn that since an item is theirs, if they want to continue to have good enjoyment of it, they will have to care for it properly.

A child will learn that communication is their tool, and emotion is not their thug.

A child will learn that by sharing, they often gain greater values, opening up avenues of exchange and friendship without hard feelings.

When possible, a child might be given their own room. If this room is protected, it would serve as a "safe place." The children from the opening story have been overheard to say things like: "You can't talk to me like that in my room," or "Yes, you can play in my room for a while if you pick up after yourself," or "May I come in your room?" An environment under the child's stewardship serves as a reassurance, a controllable place, a place where everything is as they want and as good as they can keep it up. Don't we all want that for ourselves? Children should be taught that it is possible, by word and example.

These are merely some ideas to get the wheels turning in your head. With any conflict at home, examine the issue carefully, identify the principles at work, and decide accordingly. Throughout this book, as you learn more about principles, we won't always pause to explain family and personal applications, but you can still pause in your reading and think how you can apply them to family and personal life, as well as professional and political life.

REVIEW

Q1: What is the definition of a right?

Q2: What are your individual rights?

Q3: What is the source of your rights?

Q4: Why are no other rights possible without property rights?

Q5: How is ownership of land determined when there is no objective government? How does this change when there is an objective government?

Q6: What form must intellectual property be in to be protected? Why must intellectual property be protected?

Q7: What does agency mean?

Q8: How are agency and stewardship connected?

Q9: Can you see any ways to better apply some of these principles we've discussed so far in your personal life? Discuss how.

CHAPTER 4

THE CONFUSION OF RIGHTS

"Ideas end where a gun begins."[1] - Ayn Rand

THE RIGHT TEST

In the previous chapter, it was shown that life, liberty, and property are the three rights which belong to every human being, and that to be moral, we must not only respect the rights of others, but act in accordance with our own rational self-interest. It was also shown that the only way to violate these rights is through the use of force, which includes deception. As simple as these concepts are, there is much confusion in the world about what rights are and how they are violated.

Other rights exist beyond life, liberty, and property, but not everything that is called a "right" today really is one. There's a test we can administer to tell if something might be a true "right."

Simply ask if anyone, or anything, must provide us with it.

If so, then it's not an actual right.

---

[1] Rand, Ayn. and Peter Schwartz, ed. *Return of the Primitive: The Anti-Industrial Revolution* (New York: Penguin, 1999), 177.

A right to life doesn't mean that nature will feed us if we lie down with our mouths open, nor does it mean the responsibility to feed us falls on anyone other than ourselves. Recall that rights are injunctions of non-interference. They do not require others to do anything, only to not do something—to not use force. They are merely what our nature requires in order for us to continue to live.

When someone says that two rights contradict each other, we can know immediately that one or both of the supposed rights aren't rights at all. Remember this: a right that infringes on another person is not a right. If someone claims that you have to provide their right to something (education, nutrition, health care, housing, etc.), then that thing, whatever it is, is not a right because it requires that property be taken from someone else.

What About Civil Rights?

One major factor contributing to today's confusion involving rights is that the term has broader common usage than its essential meaning. "Individual" rights and "natural" rights should be a redundancy since by definition rights only apply to individuals because of the "nature" of their existence. However, there has also come about a category of rights called legal rights. These are based on a society's customs, laws, statutes, and legislative actions. These can also be called civil rights or statutory rights—referring to the fact that these are granted via citizenship or statute (e.g. the "right" to vote, marry, or drive a car).

It is an unfortunate reality that these are often called "rights" rather than a more accurate term such as "privilege" or "license." Such a practice distorts both concepts—legal rights and individual rights. Legal rights are mistakenly given a sanctified view as being inalienable, and individual rights are lowered to the status of legal rights which *can* be alienated whenever the government or majority that granted them deems it necessary.

A person might recognize that rights can only exist in a social context, but then leap to the wrong conclusion, that it is the society which grants rights—that rights only exist where there is someone willing to grant or recognize them.

A person might even assume that our rights are codified in our Constitution and be exactly wrong.

Why is that wrong?

1. By viewing the Constitution, or the government, as the source of our rights, we implicitly give permission for those rights to be withdrawn, or alienated, any time the law changes.
2. The Constitution is not a codified list of natural rights. It is the framework for a republican form of government. Even the Bill of Rights is a misnomer. As some historians put it, "In retrospect, they more accurately should be known as the Bill of Limitations on government to avoid the perception that the rights were granted by government in the first place."[2]
3. The confusion largely stems from an unawareness or unwillingness to differentiate between natural rights, which exist whether or not a Constitution says they do, and legal rights (or privileges).

GOD-GIVEN RIGHTS?

The same fallacy of attributing the source of our natural rights to government applies to God as well. If God were the grantor of rights, then anyone claiming to speak for God could seek to take away those rights in His behalf. (Think Spanish Inquisition, the crusades, jihad, witch trials, etc.)

There is another reason why attributing the source of rights to God is problematic—there is no empirical proof of the existence of God. We are not going to make arguments here for or against the existence of God. We are simply making the point that God's existence cannot be proved empirically.

In other words, God cannot be readily perceived by everyone through their five senses—those senses which humans use to perceive the world around them. Those who believe in the existence of God usually base their belief on things other than the basic five senses. Because those experiences are subjective and internal, they are not verifiable. Anything that is not external and verifiable to the common senses of everyone has no bearing on political principles, and no place in the making of a proper earthly government.

The problems that follow basing rights on an unverifiable source are obvious. Any conflict about the substance of rights is because one group claims their god said one thing, and the other claims their god said differently.

---

[2] Schweikart, Larry. and Michael Allen. *A Patriot's History of the United States: From Columbus' Great Discovery to the War on Terror* (New York: Penguin, 2004),126.

Claiming that Lord Voldemort granted you authority to kill all unbelievers would have just as much validity and evidence (none) as any other religious claim in the field of political philosophy.

When a source is unverifiable by others, groups have no common ground upon which to settle their differences. With no way to verify which, if either, party is correct, there is an irresolvable stalemate, which history has shown leads very often to bloodshed and tyranny.

Any secular tyrant can justifiably claim that rights bestowed by an invisible, improvable entity are null and void; if we try to claim the existence of rights from an unverifiable source, it paves the way for their destruction. Rights must be grounded in observable reality where they can be defended with reason and power.

Remember, the source of our rights is not Government, and not God, but they are principles that we recognize as true by reason of our existence and of our nature as rational beings who exercise agency. Even if God gave you the gift of life, the *right* to preserve that life from other humans is a concept, not a gift.

FALSE RIGHTS

It is here we can apply the principle discussed earlier: Collective action has no unique moral authority. Just because it is the will of majority doesn't make it right. As Margaret Thatcher expressed it, "Right and wrong are not measured by a headcount of those to whom that wrong has been done. That would not be principle but expediency."[3]

The majority may vote that Jews be forced to wear a yellow star on their clothes, or that homosexuals wear a pink triangle on theirs. They may vote that everyone must tolerate all the actions of others, or else!

Majority does not equal morality.

Majority does not alter reality.

Jefferson observed that, "The will of the majority . . . to be rightful must be reasonable."[4] In other words, a thing is right (or wrong) no matter how many or how few people vote for it. Right or wrong must be gauged by a principled standard, not by a raise of hands.

An important distinction is that although you have the right to life, you do not have the right to be provided the means of existence. You

---

[3] Safire, William, ed. *Lend Me Your Ears: Great Speeches in History* (New York: W. W. Norton & Company, 1992), 146.

[4] Peterson, Merrill, ed. *The Political Writings of Thomas Jefferson* (Annapolis Junction, Maryland: Thomas Jefferson Memorial Foundation, 1993), 139.

have the right to morally obtain and keep personal property; you do not have the right to be provided with property.

"We believe that quality and affordable health care is a basic right" (Democratic Party Platform, 2009).

Additional "rights" listed in this platform include the right to a good job and good pay, the right to education, the right to a retirement check, etc. As you begin to look at things like this with a critical eye, some questions should start jumping out at you, such as: How do you define terms like "good," "affordable," and "quality?" Who gets to define those words? Who must provide that "right?" How is it paid for? Is this moral?

A much-touted false right today is sometimes couched in the term "economic rights." This is the claim that man has a right, by virtue of existing, to man-made services or goods, such as clothing, food, housing, education, employment, medical care, retirement, or even daycare and high-speed internet.[5]

There can be no such thing as a right to be given goods and services. It is a contradiction, for if someone has a right to be given something, then someone else has to be forced to produce and give it to him.

A right to money? Someone must earn it for him.

A right to a job? Someone is forced to hire him.

A right to a home? Someone is forced to build it for him.

A right to health care? Someone is forced to provide it for him.

A right to education? Someone is forced to teach him or pay to teach him.[6]

The Republican Party Platform of the previous year was almost as offensive through its contradictions and apologetic compromises. While it never explicitly calls these things "rights," it advocates the same ideas with language such as "Education is a . . . state and local responsibility, and a national strategic interest" (GOP Platform, 2008).

Remember the simple question to ask in order to determine if some idea, thing, or program is indeed a "right." Even the most unfamiliar and uninterested in politics can easily ask it and discover the answer.

> The question to ask of a proposed right is:
> ***At the expense of whom?***

---

[5] Peikoff, Leonard. *Objectivism: The Philosophy of Ayn Rand* (New York: Penguin: 1993), 356.

[6] Biddle, Craig. Loving Life: *The Morality of Self-Interest and the Facts That Support It* (Richmond, Virginia: Glen Allen Press, 2002), 97.

After answering this, you can know with utmost moral certainty the rightness of your position. If the answer to that question is anyone or anything at all, it is not a true right. The natural rights of life, liberty, and personal property are yours through the nature of your existence and are provided by no one.

There is no such thing as a right which must be provided by someone else. This is the only possible non-contradictory explanation of rights.

COLLECTIVE RIGHTS?

There is no such thing as collective rights. It is a contradiction. A collective, or group—be it a nation, a religion, a union, a family, a school, an economic class—is only a collection of individual human beings. The only possible way for a collective right to exist is if every single member of the group has that right individually to begin with. Jefferson explained, "What is true of every member of society individually is true of them collectively, since the rights of the whole can be no more than the sum of the rights of the individuals."[7]

A *collective* does not exist in concrete reality—it is an abstract concept. It is not an entity, not an "it," and therefore can have no attributes attached to it that are not represented in its constituent parts. The group must be boiled down to its most basic, irreducible unit before we can determine what the properties of its various parts would be.

A collective cannot provide us with rights we do not already have. How could a group of people have anything more than what each individual brings to the table? Where would it come from? Do two people together have more rights than two people separately? If so, how did that happen? 1+1 does not equal 3 or more. There's no visit from the Rights Fairy; no magical distilling of rights out of thin air. They are always attached to a person; the only source is the individual.

SUMMARY OF FOUNDATIONAL PRINCIPLES

We have shown that principles govern all of existence and that man must live by his own judgment and reason.

Man's life must be recognized as the proper standard of value. Morality consists of the principles defining the actions necessary to a prosperous and happy life.

---

[7] Peterson, *Writings*, 96.

Since that life is sustained through thought and action, we conclude that man must have the right to think and act and keep the products of thinking and acting—his individual rights.

Force is evil because it paralyzes man's mind and his freedom to use it.

We have therefore laid the foundation for the assertion that liberty is a fundamental social good. But what sort of association or society supports this idea? Which sort of government or social system is best designed to protect liberty and leave man's mind free? Those questions will be answered, but only after we understand the concepts of government and social systems, as well as become familiar with the foundational principles of American political philosophy.

REVIEW

Q1: What is the only thing that can keep us from acting on our own judgment?

_____

Q2: What is the test to determine if a "right" is actually a right?

_____

Q3: Can rights ever contradict one another? Why?

_____

Q4: What is the difference between a civil or legal right and a natural right?

_____

Q5: Why is the existence of collective rights impossible?

_____

CHAPTER 5

THE PROPER ROLE OF GOVERNMENT

"Life, liberty, and property do not exist because men have made laws. On the contrary, it was the fact that life, liberty, and property existed beforehand that caused men to make laws in the first place."[1]
- Frederic Bastiat

The philosophy of politics isn't essentially a discussion of issues, but of principles. Attention to principles is what is lacking in the modern popular discourse. Besides the subject of individual rights, the idea most avoided in popular dialogue is the principled question of the proper role of government.

"Security from domestic violence, no less than from foreign aggression, is the most elementary and fundamental purpose of any government."[2]
- Barry Goldwater

---

[1] Bastiat, Frederic. *The Law.* Online. constitution.org/law/bastiat.htm. Accessed 27 Apr 2011.
[2] Safire, William, ed. *Lend Me Your Ears: Great Speeches in History* (New York: W. W. Norton & Company, 1992), 821.

SHINYVILLE

Imagine we are part of a new settlement of pioneers in an uncharted territory. We settle happily, call it Shinyville, and go about our daily business. If there is no established government among us yet, then what powers properly belong to each and every person?

In this wild and primitive state, there is no doubt that each man would be justified in using force, if necessary, to defend himself against physical harm, against enslavement by another, and against theft of his property. He is also justified to punish an offender of any of these rights. For example, if you see a fellow pioneer break into someone's home, it would be proper for you to stop him if you could and punish him appropriately. If he was trying to kill someone, or had killed someone, it would be justifiable to banish or execute him. As the character Malcolm Reynolds of the TV show Firefly said, "[If] someone ever tries to kill you, you try to kill 'em right back!"[3]

As depicted in many Wild West films and novels, early pioneers did have to spend some time and energy doing exactly that—defending themselves, their property, and their liberty. However, in order to prosper, a man can't be spending all his time guarding his fields and his family from attack and theft. So what does he do? He gets with his neighbors and everyone decides to hire a sheriff.

Ta-da! Government is born!

The individual citizens delegate to the sheriff their natural and obvious right to protect themselves. Now it is the sheriff's job to do for them only what they had a right to do for themselves in the first place—and nothing more.

Remember the "Divine Right of Kings" you may have learned about in history class in high school (or possibly from *Monty Python and the Holy Grail*)? That was a useful concept for the ruling class to perpetuate because:

1. It made them accountable to no one on earth;
2. If the commoner didn't like what the King was doing—too bad! Because his power didn't come from the people, but ostensibly from God.

---

[3] *Firefly*. "Our Mrs. Reynolds." Episode No. 6, first broadcast 4 October 2002 by FOX. Written by Joss Whedon and directed by Vondie Curtis-Hall.

Keep in mind that Shinyville's governmental power and authority is from the people who created it. America was the first country in modern times to recognize this principle.

This is made clear in the Preamble to the Constitution of the United States, which reads: "WE THE PEOPLE . . . do ordain and establish this Constitution for the United States of America." The Declaration of Independence also states this principle when it says governments "derive their just powers from the consent of the governed."

Former Secretary of Agriculture, Ezra Taft Benson (Eisenhower Administration) gives the rest of the story in his speech on "The Proper Role of Government":

"The important thing to keep in mind is that the people who have created their government can give to that government only such powers as they, themselves, have in the first place. Obviously, they cannot give that which they do not possess. But now we come to the moment of truth. Suppose pioneer 'A' wants another horse for his wagon. He doesn't have the money to buy one, but since pioneer 'B' has an extra horse, he decides that he is entitled to share in his neighbor's good fortune. Is he entitled to take his neighbor's horse? Obviously not! If his neighbor wishes to give it or lend it, that is another question. But so long as pioneer 'B' wishes to keep his property, pioneer 'A' has no just claim to it.

"If 'A' has no proper power to take 'B's' property, can he delegate any such power to the sheriff? No. Even if everyone in the community desires that 'B' give his extra horse to 'A', they have no right individually or collectively to force him to do it. They cannot delegate a power they themselves do not have."[4]

A nineteenth century French economist named Frederic Bastiat wrote a brilliant little pamphlet called *The Law*. We urge our readers to study this remarkable work in its entirety. It is available for free online.

Bastiat defined "the law" (i.e. government) as: "the collective organization of the individual right to lawful defense."

In other words, since a man has the right to defend his life, liberty, and property, he logically has the right to gather a group of men and "support a common force to protect these rights constantly." This is the origin and meaning of free government, or "the law." This "law" has no

---

[4] Benson, Ezra T. "The Proper Role of Government." 1968. Available online. zionsbest.com/proper_role.html. Accessed 27 Apr 2011.

right to do anything else but what its individual members already have the right to do.

LEGAL PLUNDER

One of Bastiat's most powerful ideas was called *legal plunder*. Man, he observed, can pursue a living through either of two ways: production or plunder, he can work or he can steal. The only thing that makes people stop plundering each other is when it becomes more painful and dangerous than working honestly for a living.

Bastiat described how, instead of being a check against injustice, *the law* often becomes the "invincible weapon of injustice." When plunder is organized by law for the profit of those who make the law, then everyone tries to somehow enter into the making of laws.

"According to their degree of enlightenment," Bastiat said, "these plundered classes may propose one of two entirely different purposes when they attempt to attain political power: Either they may wish to stop lawful plunder, or they may wish to share in it."[5]

Thus we see today the war of lobbyists and pressure groups that are the symptom of a mixed economy and a corrupt government which has the power to legally plunder some citizens for the benefit of others.

FREDERIC BASTIAT

How are we to identify legal plunder today? Quite simply, Bastiat said, "See if the law takes from some persons what belongs to them, and gives it to other persons to whom it does not belong. See if the law benefits one citizen at the expense of another by doing what the citizen himself cannot do without committing a crime." Legal plunder can be committed in a number of ways: "tariffs, . . . benefits, subsidies, encouragements, progressive taxation, public schools, guaranteed jobs, guaran-

---

[5] Bastiat, *The Law*, Online.

teed profits, minimum wages, a right to relief, a right to the tools of labor, free credit, and so on."[6]

Let's take some time to examine our own ideas at this point. Do we agree that taking from one to give to another is wrong? Do we think minimum wage or government schools are a good idea?

If we answered yes to both those questions, we have contradictory ideas. There is no such thing as a contradiction in nature, only in the flawed thoughts of men. A contradiction cannot be true under any circumstances. As Aristotle's Law of Identity teaches, *A is A*. A thing is what it is. Either it is or it isn't. If one person does not have the right to do something, then they certainly cannot delegate it to a government.

Some may claim that taxation isn't theft—that it's some sort of voluntary "price" for living in a society. Being born doesn't force you into a "social contract" you didn't sign that demands you comply no matter your objections. That would constitute slavery. The only "price" for living in a society is a commitment to the principle of non-initiation of force.

Theft, or plunder, is the taking of another person's property without that person's freely-given consent. If you don't say I can have it, and I take it, then it is theft. The definition of theft does not change based upon who is doing the thieving, whether it be an individual or a government. The meaning does not change based on what happens with the stolen property afterwards. Robin Hood gave plunder to the poor; it was still theft (though in some versions he was merely returning plunder to its rightful owners that had been confiscated by government). Governments use the plunder to defend you against foreign aggressors; it is still theft, even if used for a good purpose.

Even if the person who steals from you uses the money to buy you something useful, they have still taken property which belongs to you, against your will—the definition of theft. A woman in Georgia, USA, reported that a thief had broken into her home, stolen her headphones, mopped her floor, cleaned a litter box, and taken out the trash. Despite his good intentions, he was still a thief.[7]

We are sometimes told that it's okay that the government takes our property because we get nice things in return. Even more often we are told that it's not our property to begin with, that it belongs to the gov-

---

[6] Bastiat, *The Law*, Online.

[7] Bankowski, Jennifer. "Police: Athens Burglar Breaks In, Cleans Up." Myfoxchicago.com. myfoxchicago.com/story/25996902/police-athens-burglar-breaks-in-cleans-up. Accessed 21 Jul 2014.

ernment and it's only the government's benevolence that lets us keep any part of what we produce.

To tax is to impose a financial charge or other levy upon an individual or legal entity by a State, such that failure to pay is punishable by law—by force. Whether or not we say the government can have it, it's taken under the threat of punishment.

The essential meaning of theft is taking something without the consent of the owner. Taxation is the State taking what we have, with or without consent, under threat of force. The essence of the concept of theft is present in the definition of taxation. The two are nearly identical. The only way they differ is in extraneous details. Whether by a thug in an alley, the IRS and federal prison, or a swashbuckling pirate, the agent and their methods do not change the fact that your property is being taken by force.

James Madison, who is often called the Father of the Constitution, described legal plunder this way, "Government is instituted to protect property of every sort . . . That is not a just government, nor is property secure under it, where the property which a man has in his personal safety and personal liberty is violated by arbitrary seizures of one class of citizens for the service of the rest."[8]

Simply put, with respect to the concept of a government, there are two principles to remember:

1. The proper role of government is the protection of individual rights, meaning the protection of individuals from the initiation of physical force.

2. The government is only morally authorized to act in those spheres in which you, the individual, also have the right to act.

---

[8] Saul K. Padover, ed., *The Complete Madison*, Harper & Bros., New York, 1953, p. 267. Quoted online. ar-chive.newsmax.com/archives/articles/2006/5/23/203004.shtml. Accessed 9 Aug 2011.

THE MONOPOLY ON FORCE

"It is to secure our rights that we resort to government at all."[9]
- Thomas Jefferson

A government is often defined as an institution that holds the exclusive power to enforce certain rules of social conduct in a given geographical area.

In order to live in a free society, all members partially give up, or delegate, one right and only one right—the right to forcefully protect and defend themselves. They have delegated that job to their government. You could say that government is the agent of man's self-defense. Government literally has (and must have in order for its citizens to live in a civilized nation) the legal monopoly on the use of retaliatory force. The only time you are authorized to use force under a proper government is if your life is under a threat so immediate that government has no power to respond in time to protect you. Examples include self-defense from mugging, rape, murder, or home invasion. Otherwise, you agree to delegate to the government your right to the retaliatory use of force.

If you lose your wallet, you are not allowed to search your neighbors' homes because you think one of them may have stolen it. If someone eggs your car, you are not allowed to go to their house and assault them and take their car as payment. If you break a contract with someone and don't pay them as agreed, they are not allowed to come and collect payment at gunpoint to enforce the contract (in mafia style). We have all given up the right of retaliatory force to a government that is meant to arbitrate and enforce objective law based on objective evidence. This is the only right that can be morally delegated to the government.

Just as government is only properly allowed to do that which you can delegate to it, so government is not properly allowed to do anything that you can't delegate to it. If you could not rightfully do it yourself, you cannot delegate that action to anyone else. If you aren't allowed to steal for a good cause, neither is the government. If you can defend your life, so can the government. If you aren't allowed to assault someone, neither is the government. If you aren't allowed to force someone to pay you a certain wage for your time, neither can the government. If you can't rob Peter to pay Paul, neither can the government. The created cannot rightly

---

[9] Peterson, Merrill, ed. *The Political Writings of Thomas Jefferson* (Annapolis Junction, Maryland: Thomas Jefferson Memorial Foundation, 1993), 120.

exceed the creator. Government prerogative cannot exceed the prerogative of the individual governed.

Force is ultimately the only power the government actually has with which to uphold the law. Let's give an example that, even if the specifics are simplified, demonstrates the only way government has to enforce its laws. Suppose that I break a minor law such as a moving violation, and receive a ticket for speeding. What happens? First, if my violation of the law was not too drastic, I may only be mandated to pay a fine. What if I refuse to pay the fine? Then a warrant is issued for my arrest. What if I resist arrest when the time comes? It could go two ways: either I am physically subdued and taken into custody, or if I resist in a certain manner that may endanger others, I may get myself killed. The end of a gun is all there is to enforce any law after you get past fines, liens, and other attempts at financial discipline. At the bottom of every bureaucratic stack of papers lies a gun.[10]

What does that mean to you? You have probably said or heard the phrase, "There ought to be a law . . ." This sentiment can sometimes be heard from customers at a place of business who are confused by the credit card reading machine. They might say, "There should be a law that all of these things have to be built the same way. Some swipe at the top, others on the side. Some machines ask you all kinds of questions; others don't. Some have you sign on the screen, others on paper, and others not at all."

Have you ever stopped to think what the person who utters that phrase is actually saying? "There ought to be a law" means that "the government ought to use its monopoly on physical force to execute such-and-such a policy or idea or ordinance." Which means: "If someone breaks such-and-such a law, I advocate the use of coercive action to get them to comply. And if that doesn't work, and they still resist, I advocate the steps to deprive them of their property, liberty, or life."

It sounds a little different when it's stated in its essential meaning, doesn't it? On an even more personal level, it means I, as a citizen, or as a public official, should only advocate laws that I would be personally willing to enforce and punish the violators. (If I'm not willing to, how can I expect others to?) Murder? I'm personally willing to enforce the law against it and punish the violators. Theft? Absolutely. Contract violation? Yes. Having a lawn that is too high or too dry? Uhhh, no. Requiring gas stations in Oregon to pump my gasoline for me? No way. Putting a roof

---

[10] Greenspan, Alan. "The Assault on Integrity." Edited by Ayn Rand. *Capitalism: The Unknown Ideal* (New York: Signet, 1967) 118-121.

on a community pool? Nope, sorry. Taxing my neighbor to send foreign aid to nations that are hostile toward the cause of freedom? Absolutely not.

A Minnesota man was arrested and jailed for two days after city leaders determined he had not finished installing siding on his house. The man had simply run out of money to finish the house in the failing economy. Are we willing to personally handcuff and jail our neighbors for not finishing construction on their house? "I was shackled, my wrists were handcuffed to my waist—for siding," the man said.[11]

So, the next time you say, "There ought to be a law," ask yourself if you are really willing to deprive someone else of their life, liberty, or property to enforce your law. And if you're okay taking their property, are you okay jailing or even killing them if they resist?

Thomas Jefferson defined proper government very well in his first inaugural address: "A wise and frugal government, which shall restrain men from injuring one another, which shall leave them otherwise free to regulate their own pursuits of industry and improvement, shall not take from the mouth of labor the bread it has earned . . . this is the sum of good government."[12]

ETHICS: REVISITED

Now that we've covered the proper scope of government and the role of human rights in the affairs of mankind, it's important to go back and add a vital distinction to ethics. Remember, when we refer to ethics, we mean the science of defining the code of morality by which one's life is governed. It seeks to answer the question, "What should I do with my life." The next step—politics—applies ethics to interactions with other people, answering the question, "What standard should I use to guide my conduct morally with others?" That standard is the principle of individual rights.

We have seen that ethical conduct in the political realm consists of respecting and protecting man's natural rights by not taking away his life or property, or infringing on his liberty. It is only after man has used his

---

[11] Starnes, Todd. "Man Jailed Over Unfinished Siding Project." Fox News Online. 21 Mar 2012. radio.foxnews.com/toddstarnes/top-stories/man-jailed-over-unfinished-siding-project.html. Accessed 17 Jun 2012.

[12] Allison, A., Maxfield, M., and W. Cleon Skousen. *The Real Thomas Jefferson* (Washington D.C.: National Center for Constitutional Studies, 1991), 461.

agency to infringe upon the rights of another that government should step in to punish the infraction.

Ethical conduct with regard to how individuals should treat each other is no different. Respecting the rights of others is the most basic standard of human conduct, and is termed **mandatory ethics**. Simply put, it means "Do no harm," and is the rule that should regulate the affairs of men. It is called "mandatory" because it is the very most we can rightfully demand of others.

This is not a perfect world and so unfortunately we can't expect others to use their turn signals, not cut in lines, donate to charity, or to be nice to us. Nor can we demand that they do so. As great as a world full of philanthropic, respectful, courteous boy scouts would be, those values are something to aspire to, but are not mandatory. We must make this conceptual distinction very clear between what is required, and what is desired. We can't force or use governmental force to coerce anyone to conform to these higher desired ideals.

Anything over and above the mandatory standard is **termed aspirational ethics**. These may include such things as personal charity, service to others, forgiveness, and courtesy.

The concepts of mandatory and aspirational ethics are predicated on one principle: Your life belongs completely to you and is made up of your choices.

The corollary is: You are free to make whatever choices you want as long as they do not prevent others from living according to their choices. Aspirational ethics relates to the first principle, mandatory ethics to the corollary. You are free to choose any code of values or none at all, but you may not impose it on others lest it violate the first principle.

Mandatory Ethics

• Do no harm.

Aspirational Ethics

• Be nice and do good.

It would be a pretty lonely, though peaceful, world in which no one did more than the mandatory standard. It is to the betterment of individuals and societies when people choose to rise above and achieve higher personal values. While we can't force others to be better, we can try to persuade them by word and by example. In fact, part of living by the higher ethic means that we help others to see that aspirational ethics function in their own self-interest and are part of the best path for their lasting happiness and enrichment. The only moral tools at our disposal are persuasion, patience, gentleness, kindness, sincerity, our ability to share knowledge, and showing the benefits of living by principles through the lives we lead.

CONCLUSION

It is important to understand how each part that we've covered so far fits together with the whole, because later ideas cannot be understood without the truths that come before them. These concepts can be viewed in a pyramid-shaped hierarchy, with the upper levels dependent on, and existing because of, the foundation of the first principles. Here's how everything is linked together so far:

LEVEL 1: Basic truth number one: you exist, and the purpose of your existence is to be happy. Your life and happiness are the standards by which to judge your decisions, your goals and values, and your interactions with others as good or bad. Your life and happiness are the ultimate "Why?"

LEVEL 2: In order to seek your rational self-interest, you must use your agency to choose life-serving values and work at the virtues that will lead to their attainment. Because you are alive it means you have a mind. Unless prevented by some major disability you also have the agency to control that mind. You have the responsibility to engage it in the use of productive, life-and-happiness-serving values. What you create with your mind and body in this endeavor is also considered your property—yours to do with as you see fit.

LEVEL 3: Because your life and happiness require it, you must be left free to act on your own judgment. Life is the standard by which all decisions should be judged; and happiness is not achieved by whim or chance, but by the achievement of rational values and obedience to the high-energy laws that govern joy. Thus any force initiated against you is evil since it prevents you from using your agency to pursue your fullest joy in the ways you decide.

LEVEL 4: Because force destroys your freedom and agency, your life, to be lived fully, requires that you recognize certain moral principles to guide your actions among other men. Such principles are called individual rights. Force isn't evil because it violates rights; rights exist because force is evil.

LEVEL 5: Because you must use moral principles in order to rationally guide your actions and protect your life and agency, you may join with other people to delegate the defense of those rights to a government.

Here we have demonstrated the proof that the only proper role of a government is the objective and equal protection of individual rights.

5. **Rights** need government **protection**.

4. **Freedom** necessitates **rights**.

3. **Action** entails **freedom**.

2. **Happiness** requires life-serving **action**.

1. The **purpose** of life is to be **happy**.

REVIEW

Q1: When are you justified in defending your rights, rather than letting the government do it?

Q2: Where does a sheriff get the authority to defend your rights?

Q3: What is theft?

Q4: What is legal plunder?

Q5: What is the difference between mandatory and aspirational ethics?

Q6: Why is force evil?

CHAPTER 6

AMERICA'S GOVERNMENT

"A new phenomenon in the political and moral world,
and an astonishing victory gained by enlightened reason over brute force."[1]
- George Washington, on the Constitution

At the peak of the Enlightenment, the Age of Reason, there was a nation founded differently than any other, almost without exception. Most countries are formed through warfare, language, custom, or geographical convenience. This new nation was founded on ideas. It was the first country in history to stand for something, to have an "avowed philosophical meaning."[2] That was the United States of America.

The source of the uniquely American character, and the cause of the country's spectacular achievements lies in the fact that the ideas of the Enlightenment became the actual foundation of its political institutions.

"Fix reason firmly in her seat," wrote Jefferson to his nephew, "and call to her tribunal every fact, every opinion. Question with boldness even

---

[1] Allison, A., Parry, J., and W. Cleon Skousen. *The Real George Washington* (Washington D.C.: National Center for Constitutional Studies, 1991), 505.
[2] Peikoff, Leonard. *The Ominous Parallels* (New York: Penguin, 1982), 103.

the existence of a God; because, if there is one, he must more approve of the homage of reason, than that of blindfolded fear."[3]

TYPES OF GOVERNMENT

"Government is a plain, simple, intelligent thing, founded in nature and reason, quite comprehensible by common sense . . ."[4] - John Adams

The primary meaning of the word *government* is "control, direction, restraint."[5] Before arriving at community government comes the first two kinds of government, without which the third is useless: self-government, and family government. The principle of liberty requires that individuals take direct, conscious control of themselves and their families. Koerber put it well, "When individual and family governments are failing, it is futile and destructive to glibly focus on trying to solve the myriad of individual, family, and social ills by the deceptive and false lure of compensating through city, county, state, and federal governments."[6]

Some basic types of community government worth understanding:

DEMOCRACY: Government decisions are made directly by the vote of the citizens.

Essential feature: The unlimited rule of the majority.

Primary fault: No recognition of individual rights.

Manifestation of fault: All at the mercy of the majority vote. Loss of freedom for the minority. "Two wolves and a sheep voting on what to have for dinner."

MONARCHY: All political power is carried by a single individual through family lines.

Essential feature: The rule of one.

Primary fault: No recognition of individual rights.

Manifestation of fault: No objective law, no recourse for citizens, no guarantee of individual freedom.

---

[3] Quoted in *ibid*, 106.
[4] Quoted in McCullough, David. *John Adams* (New York: Simon & Schuster Paperbacks, 2001), 60.
[5] "Government." Online Etymology Dictionary.
http://www.etymonline.com/index.php?term=government
[6] Koerber, C. Rick. "Free Capitalist Ideas & The 13 Principles of Prosperity."
www.freecapitalist.com/13-principles-of-prosperity/. Accessed 16 Oct 2016.

HEGEMONY/OLIGARCHY: Government is carried out by a small group of individuals.

Essential feature: The rule of a few.

Primary fault: No recognition of individual rights.

Manifestation of fault: Similar to monarchy, but with more than one tyrant, so it's less efficient—like an HOA.

ANARCHY: Absence of government; lawlessness; no governing by any individual or group.

Essential feature: The rule of none. No government at all.

Primary fault: No protection of individual rights.

Manifestation of fault: Immediately devolves into a dictatorship of the strongest gang. Mob rule.

REPUBLIC: Citizens have a voice in governmental decisions through elected representatives.

Essential feature: The rule of elected officials.

Primary fault: No inherent recognition of individual rights.

Manifestation of fault: Inherent possibility for tyranny is kept from growing only through an educated populace, constitutional restrictions, and honest officials.

EMPIRE: An aggregate of kingdoms ruled by a monarch called an emperor.

Essential feature: Monarchy over multiple kingdoms.

Primary fault: No recognition of individual rights.

Manifestation of fault: Inconsistent laws between kingdoms, fractious and unstable vassal states.

DICTATORSHIP: Strict rule by one or a few top leaders. Leadership is often aligned with the military.

Essential features: One-party rule, executions without trial for political offenses, expropriation or nationalization of private property, and censorship.

Primary fault: No protection of individual rights.

Manifestation of fault: Widespread governmental violence both to seize power and suppress dissent. Decisions made by the whims of one leader.

THEOCRACY: Government by religious leader(s).

Essential features: Officials are regarded as divinely guided. Laws based on religious texts and "revelation" from leader.

Primary fault: No recognition of individual rights.

Manifestation of fault: Ethical and moral foundation of laws is subjectively religious. No rational foundation or explanation of laws: "Why must you do that? Because I say that God said to." Historically, this has quickly led to oppression (e.g. Salem Witch Trials and Muslim Sharia Law).

There are, of course, many other different and intricate types of governments, but none are widespread or historically significant. There are also many variations and combinations of these governmental methods.

Democracy is not the essential feature of America's form of government. The most important feature, the one that is a primary source of this country's success, is a Constitution based on objective law and a balance of power. We elect representatives as a republic, and they vote on laws and policies democratically. However, those laws, to remain valid, must not contradict a written, objective code of principles—a constitution.

The most accurate description of American government as it was originally founded is a "constitutional republic"—which means: a state where officials are elected as representatives of the people, and must govern according to existing constitutional law that limits the government's power. Abraham Lincoln said, "A majority held in restraint by constitutional checks and limitations . . . is the only true sovereign of a free people"[7]

As Clinton Rossiter famously wrote, "[There is] no happiness without liberty, no liberty without self-government, no self-government without constitutionalism, no constitutionalism without morality."[8] This sentence would serve as a brief outline of this book thus far.

Happiness is the aim of existence.

To pursue it we must have liberty.

To protect liberty, we must have proper government.

---

[7] First Inaugural Address. Safire, William, ed. *Lend Me Your Ears: Great Speeches in History* (New York: W. W. Norton & Company, 1992), 744.

[8] Rossiter, Clinton. "Introduction." *The Federalist Papers*. Quoted online at notable-quotes.com/r/rossiter_clinton.html. Accessed 29 May 2014.

A proper government is founded on true, moral principles such as the protection of rights.

THE POLITICAL SPECTRUM OF LEFT VS. RIGHT

The problem with traditional approaches to defining politics as Left vs. Right is that these approaches usually define their terms by non-essentials. Every word we use is symbolic of a concept, and in order to make one concept distinct from another we have to make sure we include the essential qualities of the concept or else it loses its meaning.

For example, we could define "love" as "a warm feeling you get inside." It may be true that love gives you a warm feeling, but that is not the core—the essential—of what love is. Heartburn also gives you a warm feeling inside, and so does anger. To set love apart from other concepts requires defining love by its unique and essential characteristics.

"Dog" might be defined as "a faithful, four-legged companion." But that definition could include cats or any other animal possessing four legs and an attachment to you (and exclude any dog that is missing limbs). To make "dog" distinct from other concepts, it must have its core elements unique only to dogs, that is, any member of *canis lupus familiaris*.

In the case of the typical Left vs. Right dichotomy, we often see communism, socialism, and modern liberalism on the "Left," with fascism, conservatism, and capitalism on the "Right":

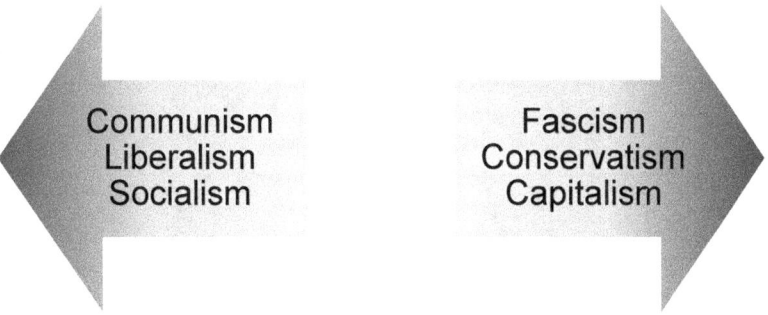

Grouping fascism, which shares many core attributes, together with capitalism is an absurd association. Conservatism also makes various calls for government to violate rights, and it makes no sense to lump it together with a social system of property rights, individual rights, and personal liberty. (We will discuss all of these "-isms" later in the book. For now, the subject is the nature of government.)

Another poor approach is a spectrum based on the size of government. This spectrum puts 0% government and anarchy on one side, and 100% government and totalitarianism on the other side:

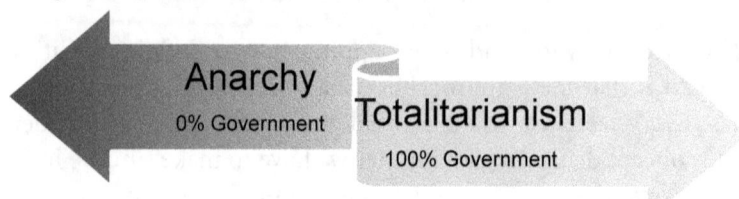

This is accompanied with the idea that somewhere in the middle is the right amount. But the size of government is not the essential issue in politics. A large military may be needed to defend against foreign aggressors. A large court system may be needed to deal with the countless contracts and disputes in a free market.

We can still use the Left/Right spectrum, but it must be redefined in terms of essentials. The essential issue in politics is not the size but the function of government—whether it protects rights or violates them. In this way, we can achieve a much clearer and more useful spectrum.

On the far left would be the ideologies and systems which use or allow extreme force in the violation of rights (communism, anarchy, fascism, etc.).

In the middle would be systems and ideologies that support various degrees of rights-violating force (modern liberalism, conservatism, progressivism, constitutionalism, etc.).

On the right would be all ideologies and systems which prohibit the initiation of force and protect individual rights (classical liberalism, capitalism):

Extreme Force	Some Force	Prohibited Force
•Communism •Fascism •Anarchy	•Liberalism •Conservatism •Progressivism	•Capitalism •Classical Liberalism

The essential issue of politics is one of absolutes—either man is free or not free; his rights are protected or violated. Such a shift in portraying the political spectrum would accurately reflect this essential knowledge.[9]

THE 3-PART AMERICAN REVOLUTION

The Revolution of America was more than just the struggle to win autonomy from Britain. It can be looked at as three important parts:

POLITICAL FREEDOM

This was the first significant transformation in America, and the easiest revolution to recognize in the history books. It was this revolution which involved armies and battles. The most obvious leaders for political freedom were George Washington and John Adams. Washington was General of the Continental Army, Chairman of the Constitutional Convention, and first President of the United States. Adams rallied the Congress to declare Independence and helped broker the Treaty of Paris to end the war. The Founders held sacred the idea that the rights and privileges of life belonged to no group, no collective, and no lone tyrant. Instead, they laid a political foundation upon the idea that each individual has sovereign rights. Among these rights is that of a people to establish their own rights-respecting government.

RELIGIOUS FREEDOM

The second transformation in America occurred in the religious world. Religious freedom was a long-running theme in America even before 1776. However, the goal of most religious groups coming to America was not freedom of religion, per se, merely freedom for them to practice their religion.

The Founders ensured that preserving liberty of conscience and its corresponding personal liberties was an essential role of all government.

In 1779, Thomas Jefferson wrote the Virginia Statute of Religious Freedom defending the right of any man to be free of compulsory religious involvement and financial support. Part of that Statute reads, "No man shall be compelled to frequent or support any religious worship . . .

---

[9] Some of the ideas in this section are borrowed from Biddle, Craig. "Political 'Left' and 'Right' Properly defined." The Objective Standard Blog. 26 Jun 2012. Online. theobjectivestandard.com/blog/index.php/2012/06/political-left-and-right-properly-defined/. Accessed 19 Sep 2012.

nor shall be enforced . . . or burdened in his body or goods, nor shall otherwise suffer on account of his religious opinions or belief, but that all men shall be free to profess, and by argument to maintain, their opinions in matters of Religion."

John Adams liked to remark in his later years that, ""The Revolution was effected before the War commenced. The Revolution was in the minds and hearts of the people; a change in their religious sentiments of their duties and obligations. This radical change in the principles, opinions, sentiments, and affections of the people, was the real American Revolution."[10]

ECONOMIC FREEDOM

The third transformation, and least understood, was a shift in economic thinking. The Founders knew that power over a man's sustenance amounted to power over his life in general. Economic freedom is essential to the protection and preservation of all other freedoms. Economic freedom is called capitalism or free enterprise today. This transformation revealed personal agency and self-interest as the source of all peace and prosperity for all people under all conditions.[11]

The primary Founding Father of this economic revolution was not even American, he was a Scotsman named Adam Smith. In his book, *An Inquiry into the Nature and Causes of the Wealth of Nations*, published the same year as the Declaration of Independence and widely read by the Founders, Smith did what no philosopher had done accurately before: identify the cause of wealth—or the root of money—not merely its effects. He identified self-interest as the most powerful motivation for all men and the relationship between freedom and wealth creation. This volume had a profound effect on early American thought.

---

[10] Quoted online. http://www.independentamericanparty.org/2015/04/the-real-american-revolution-a-quote-by-john-adams/. Accessed 27 Oct 2016.
[11] Koerber, Rick. "The FreeCapitalist Project." *The FreeCapitalist Project Primer* (Provo, Utah: The FreeCapitalist Project, 2007), 9. (The idea for dividing the American Revolution into these three parts comes from Koerber.)

THE DECLARATION OF INDEPENDENCE

Near the end of his life, Thomas Jefferson penned in a letter to Henry Lee, a description of the purpose, source, and design of his "Declaration":

> "The object of the Declaration of Independence [was] not to find out new principles or new arguments never thought of before . . . but to place before all mankind the common sense of the subject . . . Neither aiming at originality of principle or sentiment, nor yet copied from any particular and previous writing, it was intended to be an expression of the American mind, and to give to that expression the proper tone and spirit called for by the occasion. All its authority rests, then, on the harmonizing sentiments of the day, whether expressed in conversation, in letters, printed essays, or in elementary books of public right, as Aristotle, Cicero, Locke, Sidney, etc."[12]

Jefferson drafted the Declaration in a relatively short time, only a few weeks, with no references or assistance. How was he able to do this? Through his magnificent preparation of education. Like many of the Founding Fathers, Jefferson first learned Latin and Greek so he could read classical works in their original languages. He studied the law, physics, agriculture, mathematics, philosophy, chemistry, anatomy, zoology, botany, religion, politics, history, literature, and rhetoric. By adulthood he could read Latin, Greek, Spanish, Italian, and French.

So he could better study the laws of the ancient Anglo-Saxon freemen (early 5th century people in Britain), and learn about their "ancient principles," he taught himself to read the Anglo-Saxon, or Old English, language as well.

(How would the world be different today if Jefferson's attitude instead had been, "Well, they don't teach Anglo-Saxon at my school, so I guess I'm just out of luck"?)

---

[12] Allison, A., Maxfield, M., and W. Cleon Skousen. *The Real Thomas Jefferson* (Washington D.C.: National Center for Constitutional Studies, 1991), 71.

HENGIST AND HORSA

In fact, Jefferson was so impressed with the Freemen of early Britain that when he was appointed to be on the first committee to design a Seal for the United States, one of his suggestions included Hengist and Horsa, "the Saxon chiefs from whom we claim the honor of being descended, and whose political principles and form of government we have assumed."[13]

Jefferson's Declaration of Independence laid the foundational principles of America, and is the necessary document required to properly interpret the Constitution. Let us see how.

> *"When in the Course of human events it becomes necessary for one people to dissolve the political bands which have connected them with another and to assume among the powers of the earth, the separate and equal station to which the Laws of Nature and of Nature's God entitle them, a decent respect to the opinions of mankind requires that they should declare the causes which impel them to the separation."*

Notice the reference here to the "Laws of Nature." Basically, Jefferson was saying that he believed this Declaration to be based on, and made with the authority of the Natural Rights of Man; rights that man must have because of the nature of his existence. The rights stand on their own because they are objective. The reference to God could be removed, and the meaning and existence of rights would not change.

> *"We hold these truths to be self-evident, that all men are created equal, that they are endowed by their Creator with certain unalienable Rights, that among these are Life, Liberty and the pursuit of Happiness.—That to secure these rights, Governments are instituted among Men, deriving their just powers from the consent of the*

---

[13] As told by John Adams to Abigail Adams. Quoted in "Seal of the United States." monticello.org/site/research-and-collections/seal-united-states. Monticello.org. Accessed 5 May 2014.

governed,—That whenever any Form of Government becomes de-
structive of these ends, it is the Right of the People to alter or to
abolish it, and to institute new Government, laying its foundation
on such principles and organizing its powers in such form, as to
them shall seem most likely to effect their Safety and Happiness."

The phrase "all men are created equal" is not intended to imply that everyone is born with equal abilities or opportunities, but to state the correct political principle that all men ought to be protected equally, and treated as equal before the law, independent of circumstance or ability.

The pursuit of happiness means man's right to set his own goals, choose his own values, and achieve them. It was a purely individualistic idea.

The Founders discarded the traditional notion that the State was sovereign over the individual, who must submit to it. The Founders started with a new premise that the individual had primacy and sovereignty. Whether or not any social organization existed, each person had certain individual rights, which, as an early New Hampshire document stated, included "the enjoying and defending of life and liberty; acquiring, possessing, and protecting property; and in a word, of seeking and obtaining happiness."[14]

John Dickenson, a delegate to the Constitutional Convention, affirmed that rights were unalienable, "not annexed to us by parchments and seals . . . . They are born with us; exist with us; and cannot be taken away from us by any human power without taking our lives. In short, they are founded on the immutable maxims of reason and justice."[15]

Jefferson and the other Founders meant it. They fought for this principle—the principle of individual rights—not only against monarchies and theocracies, but against democracy and unlimited majority rule.

After listing the basic Natural Rights of man, Jefferson explained the proper nature and function of government, which is "to secure these rights." He then gave the moral justification for altering or abolishing a government, which is when government "becomes destructive," rather than protective, of the rights of man.

---

[14] Quoted in Peikoff, *Parallels*, 110.
[15] Quoted in *ibid*, 110.

He followed this with a list of the reasons for the separation from Great Britain, which he calls a "long train of abuses." Understanding these grievances is necessary to understand how certain things in the Constitution are to be understood. The Declaration lists the problems; the Constitution offered the solutions.

Jefferson says the action of independence wasn't entered into lightly, as the Americans had spent most of the last century trying to heal and correct their ties to Britain.

JOHN TRUMBULL'S *DECLARATION OF INDEPENDENCE*,
PLACED IN THE U.S. CAPITOL ROTUNDA IN 1826.

"We, therefore, the Representatives of the united States of America, in General Congress, Assembled, appealing to the Supreme Judge of the world for the rectitude of our intentions, do, in the Name, and by Authority of the good People of these Colonies, solemnly publish and declare, That these united Colonies are, and of Right ought to be Free and Independent States, that they are Absolved from all Allegiance to the British Crown, and that all political connection between them and the State of Great Britain, is and ought to be totally dissolved; and that as Free and Independent States, they have full Power to levy War, conclude Peace, contract Alliances, establish Commerce, and to do all other Acts and Things which Independent States may of right do.—And for the support of this Declaration, with a firm reliance on the protection of Divine Providence, we mutually pledge to each other our Lives, our Fortunes, and our sacred Honor."

Those delegates, who then signed this document, literally did pledge their lives, fortunes, and honor to the cause of liberty. In a figurative sense, they signed their names in their blood. If the American colo-

THOMAS JEFFERSON

nies had lost the war, the signers of the Declaration of Independence would have been rounded up and charged with treason. The penalty at that time, if convicted, hadn't changed in centuries: "To be hanged by the head until unconscious. Then cut down and revived. Then disemboweled and beheaded. Then cut into quarters. Each quarter to be boiled in oil. The remnants were scattered abroad so that the last resting place of the offender would remain forever unnamed, unhonored, and unknown."[16]

"Of those 56 who signed the Declaration of Independence, nine died of wounds or hardships during the war. Five were captured and imprisoned, in each case with brutal treatment. Several lost wives, sons or entire families. One lost his thirteen children. Two wives were brutally treated. All were at one time or another the victims of manhunts and driven from their homes. Twelve signers had their homes completely burned. Seventeen lost everything they owned. Yet not one defected or went back on his pledged word. Their honor, and the nation they sacrificed so much to create, is still intact.

"And, finally, there is the New Jersey signer, Abraham Clark. He gave two sons to the officer corps in the Revolutionary Army. They were captured and sent to the infamous British prison hulk afloat in New York harbor known as the hell ship "Jersey," where 11,000 American captives were to die. The younger Clarks were treated with a special brutality because of their father. One was put in solitary and given no food. With the end almost in sight, with the war almost won, no one could have blamed Abraham Clark for acceding to the British request when they of-

---

[16] Skousen, *America*, 31.

fered him his sons' lives if he would recant and come out for the King and parliament. The utter despair in this man's heart, the anguish in his very soul, must reach out to each one of us down through 200 years with his answer: 'No.'"[17]

In this chapter, we have seen that the common flaw in historical forms of government has been the failure to recognize and protect rights.

We have seen that the distinction between Right and Left, when not defined in terms of freedom and force, has only furthered confusion about what form of government is best, and instead confines the discussion to which form of tyranny is best.

We have seen that America was the first country in modern times to break this trend because it was based on the philosophical idea of freedom. Liberty is based in reason. Through America's governmental structure and declaration of rights, the Founders sought to preserve freedom. We will now examine a portion of how they attempted to establish this through the Constitution of the United States.

THE CONSTITUTION OF THESE UNITED STATES

The Constitution of the United States of America represents man's best attempt in modern times at securing for every individual their human rights. It encompasses the work of some of the brightest minds to ever apply themselves to the practical questions of government, and while it is not a perfect document, we owe those men gratitude. Because of the freedom afforded by the Constitution, America rose to be the world's greatest power. It is because of our deviation from its principles—implied and explicit—that we are declining in many ways.

The preamble to the Constitution is an introduction—it is not the law, but a commentary on why the law was made. That is important because many people try to justify government programs by saying that it "promotes the general welfare." Having free ice cream would promote the general welfare, so should we do that? It is the protection of individual rights which will "establish Justice, insure domestic Tranquility, provide for the common defense, promote the general Welfare, and secure the Blessings of Liberty to ourselves and our Posterity . . ." No amount of

---

[17] Limbaugh, Jr., Rush H. "The Americans Who Risked Everything." Online. usff.com/usff/sacredhonor.html. Accessed 27 Apr 2011.

government programs can do this if they are done at the expense of, and in contradiction to, human rights and freedom.

There are loopholes built into this impressive document which have been the "Achilles Heel" of America from its inception. By failing to completely define and protect human rights, it left the door open, ever so slightly, for them to be trampled on. Another problem is vague language describing the powers delegated to the Federal Government, such as the Commerce Clause which has been used to justify endless overreach into private business and the rights of the States.

Scene at the Signing of the Constitution of the United States, by Howard Chandler Christy, 1940, Displayed in the Capitol Building

The main body of the Constitution lays out the framework of establishing a federal government with its proper separations of power and jurisdiction. A study of this is not necessary or possible to include in this book. See Appendix B for some recommended books to assist in a study of the Constitution. We will move on to discuss some amendments to the Constitution, since they pertain directly to individual rights.

THE BILL OF RIGHTS

The Bill of Rights, comprising the first ten amendments to the Constitution, addresses some concrete extrapolations of rights which the federal government cannot infringe upon. These amendments do not, however, identify the underlying principle beneath the concrete examples. Remember that the three basic human rights are life, liberty, and property. We can identify the foundational rights implied behind these amendments:

LIFE

Ninth Amendment: *The enumeration in the Constitution, of certain rights, shall not be construed to deny or disparage others retained by the people.*

The source of your rights is your human nature, not your government or constitution.

Tenth Amendment: *The powers not delegated to the United States by the Constitution, nor prohibited by it to the States, are reserved to the States respectively, or to the people.*

The people of the States delegate authority to the federal government. By virtue of their existence, those people retain all rights not expressly delegated to the Federal Government, and should govern themselves on a local level as much as possible to increase accountability in the stewardship of the government officials.

Notice that the Ninth and Tenth amendments make it very clear that rights are not bestowed by government, but exist only with the individual. They take pains to say that just because something isn't included in these amendments doesn't mean that it doesn't exist and is therefore "retained by the people."

The Tenth Amendment is, of course, consistently violated by the Federal Government, especially since the Civil War, which now leaves to the States only those powers it chooses to grant.

LIBERTY

First Amendment: *Congress shall make no law respecting an establishment of religion, or prohibiting the free exercise thereof; or abridging the freedom of speech, or of the press; or the right of the people peaceably to assemble, and to petition the Government for a redress of grievances.*

We have liberty of conscience. We have freedom of speech protected from government censorship, a press free from government coercion, freedom to assemble peaceably, and freedom to work to protect our freedoms.

PROPERTY AND LIBERTY

Fourth Amendment: *The right of the people to be secure in their persons, houses, papers, and effects, against unreasonable searches and seizures, shall not be violated, and no Warrants shall issue, but upon probable cause,* *supported by Oath or affirmation, and particularly describing the place to be searched, and the persons or things to be seized.*

You have the right to keep your property and liberty against any government infringements not based on probable, objective evidence of wrongdoing.

Second Amendment: *A well regulated Militia, being necessary to the security of a free State, the right of the people to keep and bear Arms, shall not be infringed.*

You have the right, by nature of your existence, to both own arms and use them in the furtherance of your life.

PROPERTY

Third Amendment: *No Soldier shall, in time of peace be quartered in any house, without the consent of the Owner, nor in time of war, but in a manner to be prescribed by law.*

You have the right to control your property as you see fit.

LIFE, LIBERTY, AND PROPERTY

Fifth Amendment: *No person shall be held to answer for any capital, or otherwise infamous crime, unless on a presentment or indictment of a Grand Jury, except in cases arising in the land or naval forces, or in the Militia, when in actual service in time of War or public danger; nor shall any person be subject for the same offence to be twice put in jeopardy of life or limb; nor shall be compelled in any criminal case to be a witness against himself, nor be deprived of life, liberty, or property, without due process of law; nor shall private property be taken for public use, without just compensation.*

There is only one proper definition of "just compensation": whatever the owner will agree to voluntarily. Anything else is unjust.

Sixth Amendment: *Trial by jury and rights of the accused; Confrontation Clause, speedy trial, public trial, right to counsel. In all criminal prosecutions, the accused shall enjoy the right to a speedy and public trial, by an impartial jury of the State and district wherein the crime shall have been committed, which district shall have been previously ascertained by law, and to be informed of the nature and cause of the accusation; to be confronted with the witnesses against him; to have compulsory process for obtaining witnesses in his favor, and to have the Assistance of Counsel for his defense.*

Seventh Amendment: *In suits at common law, where the value in controversy shall exceed twenty dollars, the right of trial by jury shall be pre-*

served, and no fact tried by a jury, shall be otherwise re-examined in any court of the United States, than according to the rules of the common law.

Eighth Amendment: *Excessive bail shall not be required, nor excessive fines imposed, nor cruel and unusual punishments inflicted.*

Amendments Five through Eight relate specifically to protocols to be followed after there has been an alleged violation of a law. They are procedural guidelines to ensure that the defendant's rights are not unduly wronged as alleged guilt is assessed. These amendments are a check against the use of force in executive and judicial action after a crime has been allegedly committed.

In America, a man is innocent until proven guilty; his rights should not be taken away until there is objective proof of law-breaking. Because the government holds the monopoly on retaliatory force, these amendments are vital. Otherwise, we would have situations where rights are suspended upon the first accusation of malfeasance. These amendments are legal rights which were identified in order to protect human rights.

Imagine being accused of a crime you didn't commit, and before the trial you are locked up indefinitely and you are forced to give up all your property. Couldn't happen in America, right? During World War II, President Franklin D. Roosevelt approved that thousands of American citizens with Japanese heritage should have their property confiscated and be sent to live in camps. And, no, they didn't get all their property back after the war.

You see the problem? Nowhere in the Bill of Rights among the delineated legal rights are the three core individual rights specifically outlined. Within these amendments there are protections for individual rights based on specific problems contemporary to the time of the Founders, but rather than stating the principle plainly where there would be little need for judicial interpretation, only specific and particular applications of individual rights were given. How often have you worried about having to quarter a soldier in your home? The right to control your property is the issue at hand; being forced to put up a soldier in your home is just one of a thousand ways your right to property could be violated. Rather than try to list every conceivable way property rights could be violated, it would be much more effective to state the right to property as a principle—the right to keep, control, or dispose of one's property shall not be infringed. Written as a general principle, the law would then have universal application and could better protect against every conceivable violation of the right without having to predict or list them.

Because of the catastrophic oversight of failing to explicitly protect freedom in a country founded implicitly on the idea of freedom, abuses have been able to occur throughout America's history, slowly shackling freedom. With no firm moorings in our founding documents, the belief, philosophy, and protection of freedom have been eroded under the constant waves of progressive attack.

Abraham Lincoln suspended the writ of habeas corpus during the Civil War. That means when you are thrown in jail, on what may be bogus charges, you don't have the right to request to see a judge so you can be let out. It protects you from being held indefinitely.[18]

John Adams decided that free speech and freedom of the press were too threatening when he passed the Alien and Sedition acts, making it illegal to speak out against the administration. By virtue of these laws, twenty-five men, most of them editors of Republican newspapers, were arrested, fined, and imprisoned (one of Jefferson's first acts as President was to pardon them and restore their fines with interest).

Andrew Jackson signed the Indian Removal Act in 1830 causing the forced removal of tens of thousands of Native Americans from their lands in what is now known to history as the Trail of Tears.

Woodrow Wilson passed his Espionage and Sedition Acts of 1917 and 1918, respectively, leading to the arrest of war-protesters. These laws again suppressed free speech and led to Americans being imprisoned for having exercised their right of free speech.

George W. Bush's Patriot Act allows for you to be held in prison indefinitely if you are declared an enemy combatant (Military Commissions Act of 2006).

Barack Obama's approval of the National Defense Authorization Act for Fiscal Year 2012 allows any American who is considered belligerent against the U.S. in a time of war to be held "without trial, until the end of the hostilities."[19] This is in addition to controversy surrounding his administration's use of drone strikes, NSA surveillance of the American population, arming Mexican drug cartels, and IRS persecution of political enemies.

Even with these amendments clearly protecting the legal rights of citizens in case of an alleged or suspected crime, without specific mention of individual rights, the government will frequently ignore them in an

---

[18] PBS Civil Liberties and National Security Timeline.
pbs.org/now/politics/timeline.html. Accessed 27 Apr 2011.
[19] Wikipedia description of the National Defense Authorization Act for Fiscal Year 2012.
en.wikipedia.org/wiki/National_Defense_Authorization_Act_for_Fiscal_Year_2 012. Accessed 24 Jun 2012.

"emergency" or for the "greater good." As Senator Lindsey Graham said in 2011, "Free speech is a great idea, but we're in a war."[20]

ADDITIONAL AMENDMENTS

The amendment process has been considered by many as rapidly becoming the only recourse of a free people to rein in an abusive Federal government. It's difficult to get the Constitution amended, but it has been done, most of the time for the better—but not always.

Fourteenth Amendment: This is primarily a good one—it recognized every man's right to life and the property of his own body by abolishing slavery. It was soon followed by the **Fifteenth Amendment** which allowed men of any ethnicity to vote and have representation in their government.

Sixteenth Amendment: The Congress shall have power to lay and collect taxes on incomes, from whatever source derived, without apportionment among the several States, and without regard to any census or enumeration.

This was a huge backslide delivered at the height of the Progressive era in 1913. This amendment denies property rights and discourages production by giving Congress the power to collect taxes in any amount and on incomes from any source.

The history of this amendment dates to the Civil War when direct taxes on incomes were first levied and upheld by the Supreme Court. Another income tax law in 1893 was found unconstitutional. In the early twentieth century the Progressive idea to "soak the rich" began to take deeper root among people. Democrats introduced bills to tax the rich—bills which were defeated by more conservative members of the Republican party. Democrats used this as evidence to make accusations that the Republicans were the "party of the rich" and should be removed from power. These accusations made President Taft, a Republican, concede in political speeches that the income tax might be all right "in principle," but he opposed it![21]

The conservatives lost ground not because they disagreed with the Progressives. They lost because they agreed! They had no principles of their own to guide their judgments. They were reduced to "me-tooing"

---

[20] "Lindsey Graham." en.wikipedia.org/wiki/Lindsey_Graham. Wikipedia. Accessed 5 May 2014.
[21] Skousen, *America*, 738.

the Progressive movement, only arguing about the degree of changes to be made. The conservatives ceded the moral high ground (if they ever had it in the first place) and had no argument to defend the empty vacuum that used to house principles of proper government and free markets. The amendment was approved by the Senate with a unanimous vote of 77 to 0! The House had a vote of 318 to 14.

The Sixteenth Amendment necessarily violates the rights provided in the Fourth Amendment—the privacy of home, business, personal papers, and affairs. The government cannot verify that everyone has paid the correct amount of taxes without inspecting the private papers, private business, and personal affairs of individual citizens.

T. Coleman Andrews, upon resigning as Commissioner of the IRS, said: "Under the Sixteenth Amendment Congress can take 100 percent of our income anytime it wants to . . . The income tax is fulfilling the Marxist prophecy that the surest way to destroy a capitalist society is by 'steeply graduated' taxes on income and heavy levies upon the estates of people when they die . . . I believe that a better way to raise revenue not only can be found but must be found because I am convinced that the present system is leading us right back to the very tyranny from which those, who established this land of freedom, risked their lives, their fortunes and their sacred honor to forever free themselves."[22]

While some claim this is impossible, Dr. Skousen, in his book *The Making of America*, listed some interesting ideas to go about the process of repealing the Sixteenth Amendment and restoring America to a fiscally balanced government:

1. Pass the Balanced Budget Amendment, which would outlaw deficit spending in peacetime, and not allow an increase in taxes to cover deficit spending.

2. Pass a "Sunset Law," which would eliminate every government agency or federal expenditure which exists outside the Constitution and cannot survive an amendment to justify its continuance.

3. Pass a Fiscal Reform Amendment which would raise required revenue indirectly by a temporary consumer tax (federal sales tax, or fair tax), and simultaneously repeal the Sixteenth Amendment.[23]

This would, in Skousen's view, serve as a "nicotine patch" to a country in withdrawals from its spending addiction. It should also in-

---

[22] Quoted in *ibid*, 742.
[23] *ibid*, 743.

clude a mandatory expiration date. There would be no exceptions or exemptions to such a simple tax. This would only be a temporary measure to help guide the country towards a completely voluntary method of government funding (see Chapter 22 for more on this subject).

Seventeenth Amendment: The Senate of the United States shall be composed of two Senators from each State, elected by the people thereof, for six years; and each Senator shall have one vote.

Ratified in 1913, this amendment delivered a crippling blow to the republican system of government set up by the Founders, stripping the states of an essential check and balance of power, all in the name of democracy. Senators are now elected by popular vote, rather than by their respective state legislatures.

"That doesn't sound so bad," you say. "I'd like to pick my Senator. That's democracy! The rule of the majority!"

Unfortunately, your Senator wasn't meant to represent you individually, or even your state's citizens collectively. And as we discussed previously, this country wasn't supposed to be democracy, it was supposed to be a republic.

At the Constitutional Convention there was great debate on the best form of representation. In a historic compromise it was decided to have the population represented in the House of Representatives, and the states equally represented in the Senate. **Senators were appointed by their state legislators *to represent the state* and see that its rights and interests were protected.**[24]

Senators now represent the people of the state "at large" and there is no one appointed in Washington D.C. to watch over states' rights and sovereignty. Senators were not originally meant to represent the views of the people—that is the function of the congressmen. The Senators were originally meant to represent their state as a sovereign entity, holding a veto power over any legislation which violated the Tenth Amendment.

Why did the Founders want to do it that way at all? Let's have them tell us in their own words:

William Davie: "The senators represent the sovereignty of the states." "It was in the Senate that the several political interests of the states were to be preserved, and where all their powers were to be perfectly balanced."[25]

---

[24] *ibid*, 258.
[25] Quoted in *ibid*, 295

John Dickinson: "The sense of the states would be better collected through their governments than immediately from the people at large."[26]

James Madison: "The state legislatures also ought to have some means of defending themselves against the encroachments of the national government."[27]

James Iredell: "The Senate is placed there for a very valuable purpose—as a guard against any attempt of consolidation . . . in order to preserve completely the sovereignty of the states."[28]

The repeal of the Seventeenth Amendment would go far in wresting power from Washington, D.C. and returning local sovereignty to the states as originally designed. (Repeal would not have to come from Congress. The Constitution allows for amendments to be made by three-fourths of the states, without Congress's approval.)

Eighteenth Amendment: This prohibited the "manufacture, sale, or transportation of intoxicating liquors." This is a statute of law, rather than a principle of government as the rest of the Constitution had been. Prohibition was a foolish move, delivered by the Progressive movement, which denied a basic right of liberty to drink whatever you want and however much you want until your liver fails and you die. What it actually ended up doing was creating a black market protected by violence.

A little-known story from this era was how the government, to prevent bootleggers from using industrial ethyl alcohol to produce illegal beverages, ordered the poisoning of industrial alcohols. In return, the bootleggers then "hired chemists who successfully renatured the alcohol to make it drinkable. As a response, the Treasury Department required manufacturers to add more deadly poisons, including the particularly deadly methyl alcohol . . . . As many as ten thousand people died from drinking denatured alcohol before Prohibition ended."[29]

Heavy profits from illicit liquor also led to the corruption of judges and police. This amendment was repealed by the **Twenty-first Amendment**, though its lessons have yet to be applied to the War on Drugs or immigration.

The **Nineteenth Amendment** finally recognized women as full citizens with a personal vote in their governance, not merely "represented" by the vote of the men in their family. While this doubled the number of

---

[26] Quoted in *ibid*, 296

[27] Quoted in *ibid*, 297.

[28] Quoted in *ibid*, 301.

[29] Wikipedia. "Prohibition in the United States." en.wikipedia.org/wiki/ Prohibition_in_the_United_States. Accessed 26 Jun 2013.

people entitled to a vote, it did little at the time to alter the morality in politics or shift political thinking drastically one way or the other.[30]

The **Twenty-sixth Amendment** extended voting rights to all citizens eighteen years and older. The government presumed to draft young men into military service at the age of eighteen and the point had been raised that if these men were old enough to fight and die for their country, they were old enough to vote about it.

The U.S. Constitution laid the groundwork for the freest nation that had ever existed in modern history; and although it's not perfect, it's the best that's been done so far. Urgent updates are needing to reign in Federal overreach: requiring the states to approve any increase in the national debt; term limits on Congress; limiting Federal overreach by returning the Commerce Clause to its original meaning; limiting the power of Federal regulations by giving an easy congressional override; require a super majority for federal taxes and repeal the 16th amendment, give the States (by a 3/5 vote) the power to abrogate any Federal law, regulation, or executive order; require Congress to remain in their districts near their constituents and away from centralized lobbyists, and conduct business via telecon.

The proper role of a government is to protect the individual rights of those within its given geographical area. We have detailed the principles of good government set up in the founding of the United States of America. We next turn our attention to economic and social theories.

---

[30] Skousen, *America*, 750.

REVIEW

Q1: What is the philosophical foundation of America?

Q2: Why is the typical left-right dichotomy of government inaccurate?

Q3: What is a more accurate spectrum of government?

Q4: What form of government was America founded as?

Q5: What were the three types of freedom central to the founding of America?

Q6: When the Declaration of Independence says all men are created equal, to what is it referring?

Q7: What did the Bill of Rights fail to do?

Q8: What are two ways a constitutional amendment can be passed?

Q9: Should any parts of the Constitution be repealed or replaced in your opinion? Which ones and why?

Q10: Are there any new amendments you would like to see passed? What effects would this have?

CHAPTER 7

THE PROPER ENVIRONMENT FOR MANKIND

"A man was either free or not free. And where it had formerly been assumed that men were not fit for freedom, it was now thinkable that nothing but freedom was fit for men."[1] - Isabel Paterson

We've discussed the nature of man and what he requires to sustain and maintain his life. We've discussed two crucial concepts most commonly avoided in any modern discussion of politics—rights and the proper role of government. But what sort of environment is optimal for mankind's prosperity and happiness? Is there a particular social system that would best guarantee man's life and pursuit of happiness? Or is any system good as long as it is "democratically" chosen?

The former Secretary of Agriculture, Ezra Taft Benson, described an essential question of life. In speaking about how the republican system established by the Founders cannot endure long without its fundamental principles, he said, "Momentum is gathering for another conflict . . . This

---

[1] Paterson, Isabel. *The God of the Machine* (Originally published in 1943. Qualiteri eBook, 2009), Chapter 7.

collision of ideas is worldwide . . . The issue is . . . will men be free to determine their own course of action or must they be coerced?"[2]

The question: **Is man free?**

John Locke identified freedom as man's natural state, "To understand political power right . . . we must consider what state men are naturally in, and that is a state of perfect freedom to order their actions and
dispose of their possessions and persons, as they see fit, within the
bounds of the law of nature; without asking leave, or depending upon the
will of any other man."[3]

Freedom begins with what some Founders referred to as "liberty of
conscience." It is the unalienable right to a free mind. Men can choose
what they value and prefer, and cannot force their value judgments on
others.

Why is liberty the optimal state for man's prosperity and happiness? Because we must rely on our minds to sustain our lives. To rely on
our mind requires that we be free from coercion that would keep us from
acting in our rational self-interest.

Freedom means freedom from the force of others. Freedom is the
ideal environment for mankind to thrive, be happy, and prosper. Freedom in a social environment does not mean, and has never meant, anarchy. An environment of freedom must also include a viable method for
the protection and maintenance of rights. Unfortunately, most social systems in history have had a much different basic premise at their foundation.

A major argument in favor of freedom is that the number one killer
of humans in the twentieth century was oppressive governments. An estimated 262 million people were victims of political mass murder between 1900 and 2000. That is six times the number that was killed in
wars! Professor Rudolph Rummel concludes that, "The more power a
regime has, the more likely people will be killed. This is a major reason
for promoting freedom. Concentrated political power is the most dangerous thing on earth."[4]

Then which social system, if any, is best?

---

[2] Benson, Ezra T. "The Constitution—A Heavenly Banner." Available online.
speeches.byu.edu/reader/reader.php?id=6985. Accessed 27 Apr 2011.

[3] Locke, John. "Second Treatise on Civil Government." Online. constitu-
tion.org/jl/2ndtr02.htm. Accessed 9 Aug 2011.

[4] Rummel, Rudolph. Wikipedia bio. en.wikipedia.org/wiki/Rudolph_Rummel#
Democide. Accessed 8 Aug 2012.

A social system is a "set of moral-political-economic principles embodied in a society's laws, institutions, and government, among men living in a given geographical area."[5]

Two primary questions to determine the nature of any given social system are:

1. Does it recognize individual rights?
2. Does it ban physical force from human relationships?

Is man a sovereign individual who owns his own life, person, mind, work, and its products, or is he the property of the state, society, or collective?

Does man have a right to live for his own sake, or is he born a slave to be disposed of as or used as others see fit?

Remember that if force is not banned, rights are not protected. The answer to question number two is also the answer to number one. A society that does not ban force, including legal plunder, but claims to stand for rights is deceived.

This is the basic question of life: Is man free?

In all of mankind's history, capitalism is the only social system that answers, "Yes!"

Let us see why.

---

[5] Rand, Ayn. *Capitalism: The Unknown Ideal* (New York: Signet, 1967), 18.

REVIEW

Q1: What is a social system?

_____

Q2: What are the necessary requirements for a moral social system?

_____

Q3: Why do humans require freedom?

_____

Q4: What was the number one killer of humans in the twentieth century?

_____

CHAPTER 8

CAPITALISM

"[Here] a man is allowed to thrive and flourish without having a penny taken out of his pocket by the government; no visits from tax collectors, constables, or soldiers."[1] - John Doyle, Irish immigrant to America, 1818

If you had to name the single, foundational idea that has made the United States different from every other nation on earth, what would it be? What idea lies at the heart of the American Dream, its entrepreneurs, and unparalleled prosperity? Is it faith, hard work, or liberty? Is it self-reliance or respect for the rule of law? What idea is the cause of these things? What was it that made America so unique?

We can find the answer in the Declaration of Independence. America was founded on the idea that all men are created equal and have certain unalienable rights.

The bright, shining light at the source of all that is good in America is the principle of individual rights. America is the dream; it is the place where dreams may exist. It is the place that, unlike so many others at the

---

[1] Schweikart, Larry. and Michael Allen. *A Patriot's History of the United States: From Columbus' Great Discovery to the War on Terror* (New York: Penguin, 2004), 253.

time of its founding, allowed people to have dreams in the first place. The place where citizens may dare to hope and work for a life better than their fathers had. America is the place where they had the freedom to consider such a thing. The American Dream is not, as some politicians would have you believe, merely owning a home or having more stuff than your parents or neighbors. It is to have the freedom to pursue whatever dream you have without coercive interference from others.

This answer leads us to the social system set up by the Founding Fathers implicitly, but never explicitly explained by them—capitalism. This is the only social system that recognizes the principle of individual rights.

What is capitalism? Is it greed? Exploitation? Worship of profits? Government influenced by Big Business? Monopolies? Imperialism? Institutionalized Racism? Slavery and oppression? Class warfare?

If you answered "yes" to any of the above, you have been the target and are now the end result of a long, strategic, and widespread campaign to both distort and hide the moral foundation of capitalism, to rewrite its history, and in fact completely reverse its essential meaning. So what is it then?

Many sources define capitalism primarily as an economic system, not a philosophical system or even a social system. For example, a dictionary definition might read: "Capitalism is an economic system where the means of production are privately owned; wage labor is predominant; supply, demand, and price are at least partially determined by markets; and profit is distributed to owners who invested in the business."

This definition is true, but not complete. For a more complete understanding of what this definition means, what its essentials are, and what it looks like in practice, we must ask some additional questions. Let's take what we know from definitions like this one and identify the implications through the following questions. Take some time to answer these as specifically as possible:

- *What kind of society* is one where property and the means of production are privately owned? (Completely—all property and all business is private.) What principles of governmental and private action does this imply must exist?
- *What kind of society* is implied in that definition? What conditions must exist for prices, including wages, to be freely decided by those involved, and for profits to be given to those who invested time, talents, creative thought, human life value, and capital to produce them?

- *What kind of society* recognizes that man must be left free to live according to his own conscience and exercise his own agency for choice and responsibility? Think about this in areas of education, health care, business, home ownership, retirement, etc.
- *What kind of society* recognizes that it should pass no laws restricting freedom of trade and production?

The kind of society, or social system, which would make these things possible, must be based on the recognition and protection of individual rights. Then we must ask:

- *What are the essential features* of a social system based on individual rights?
- What are rights and how they are violated?

After these are answered completely, and we have resolved any contradictions in our ideas, we will understand the *broader philosophical, social, and political* meaning of capitalism, rather than merely its narrow economic meaning. We will come to understand that capitalism is a social system based on the recognition of individual rights, including property rights, in which all property is privately owned, and in which no one may initiate the use of force against others.[2]

A social system that protects rights necessarily banishes the initiation of physical force from human relationships. The only function of government in a capitalistic society is protecting its citizens from physical force, acting as the agent of man's right of self-defense. A capitalist society places the retaliatory use of force under objective control. All human relationships in such a society are voluntary. We can all persuade, cooperate, discuss, and contract freely, or choose not to.

(Unfortunately, hearing capitalism's principles described clearly like this does not automatically dispel all misconceptions associated with it. Typically, the false ideas have to be removed one by one, which we will work on later in this book.)

JUSTICE AND FREEDOM

The justice capitalism claims as its ruling principle is simple: the justice of reality. Justice means seeking and granting only what is

---

[2] This definition is drawn primarily from Ayn Rand. See "Capitalism." The Ayn Rand Lexicon. Online. aynrandlexicon.com/lexicon/capitalism.html. Accessed 14 Sep 2012.

earned—good or bad, success or failure, honor or guilt. Justice means granting respect to those who have earned it by being honorable. It means granting a good grade to a good learner, and a poor grade to a poor learner. It means being distrustful of someone who has earned a false respect by lying. It means refusing to do business with someone who has cheated you.

Equality under capitalism means what it meant to the Founders—equality of rights. All men are created equal, not in things, talents, genetics, or circumstance, but equal in what matters most: equal in the protection of their life, property, and liberty of conscience. Equality does not mean that if one person has a private jet, everyone should have a private jet. Equality means that a white man and a Black man get the same prison sentence for the same crime.

In his historic book, *The Naked Communist*, Dr. Cleon Skousen identified four specific freedoms that a capitalistic system protects:

- The Freedom to Try
- The Freedom to Sell
- The Freedom to Buy
- The Freedom to Fail

The **freedom to try** is one of the most essential ingredients in a healthy economy. If a man wants to be a professional rock climber, he is free to try it. In a free country a man can develop a new mousetrap, an improved screwdriver, or a faster computer. When he is through, no one may wish to buy his product, but he is still free to try and sell it if he can.

If men are to be left free to use their inventive and creative genius, they must also be left **free to sell** their product for a profit. "Of course," says Dr. Skousen, "some new product might make a whole industry obsolete, temporarily throw thousands out of work and require numerous economic, social, and political readjustments."[3] Such new industries have included the cotton gin, printing press, DVDs, airplanes, and microchips. This is one of the keys to success in a free enterprise economy. Selling is not to be curbed unless it involves products or services that criminally threaten others.

The public must also have the **freedom to buy**. Price controls and restrictions create shortages, black markets, and a depressed economy. Taxes, duties, and fees all inhibit the free choice of a consumer to buy a

---

[3] Skousen, W. Cleon. *The Naked Communist* (Salt Lake City, Utah: Ensign Publishing Company, 1960), 276.

product, especially when they can't afford or don't want to pay the higher price caused by the tax.

The "golden secret" of all capitalist economies is the **freedom to fail**. Every businessman must continually study his operation, improve products and services, increase efficiency and customer service just to keep from failing. Failure is a lesson to be learned about your performance, and it is the constant threat of failure which keeps businesses focused on being better at customer service, less expensive, and more efficient than their competitors. These benefits come because of the natural incentives not to fail. But when natural incentives are removed, people behave differently. If a company cannot make a profit and is subsidized by tax dollars, the company receives an incentive for their inefficiency. No lesson is learned. If the choice to fail is not followed by failure, this encourages businesses to invest more time in pleasing government officials rather than their customers. The very thing which spurs a company to succeed is the possibility of failure.

Saying, "This company is too big to fail!" implies that because it's a large company (or more likely because it has active lobbyists), it's more important than the protection of individual rights. Property is then expropriated either directly through taxation, or indirectly through inflation, to "bailout" the failed company for the "good of Main Street." There is always some evasion or rationalization to accompany it. During his Presidential campaign, Senator John McCain was asked how he could support such "socialistic" bailout programs. His response was, "It's not socialism, it's necessary." In other words, he likes to make decisions not on principle, but on apparent expediency. A social system is rapidly losing any connection with capitalism when the freedom to fail is suspended.

The **basic moral code** of capitalism is founded on the premise *that every man is an end unto himself, not the means to the ends of others*, and on the premise that men must deal with each other voluntarily as traders, through mutual choice and benefit.[4] As Isabel Paterson put it, "Capitalism is the economic system of individualism."[5]

We've defined capitalism, but to help clear any additional false ideas about it, we will study some economic principles as well as collectivist

---

[4] Some phrasing for this idea comes from Ayn Rand. See "Introducing Objectivism." Aynrand.org. aynrand.org/site/PageServer?pagename=objectivism_intro. Accessed 19 Sep 2012.

[5] Paterson, Isabel. *The God of the Machine* (Originally published in 1943. Qualiteri eBook, 2009), Chapter 19.

social systems, and then move on to addressing common attacks against capitalism.

REVIEW

Q1: Why must capitalism be viewed not only as an economic system, but also as a philosophic system and a social system?

_____

Q2: What is the most fundamental characteristic that sets capitalism apart from every other social system?

_____

Q3: What is the only means by which rights can be violated?

_____

Q4: What premise is the moral code of capitalism is based on?

_____

CHAPTER 9

PRINCIPLES OF ECONOMICS

FREEDOM OF CONSCIENCE

"When politics and religion ride in the same cart, the whirlwind follows."
- Frank Herbert, *Dune*

The phrase "the separation of church and state" came from a personal correspondence of Thomas Jefferson. But what does it mean?

Government should not pass any laws which foster or suppress any religion, nor should it proscribe what we believe. Religion and government have no reason to ever be mingled together by earthly men and should absolutely be separated because when they're not, tyranny can abound, and our freedom of conscience may be violated.

What are the consequences of failing to separate religious opinions from government? Just look at countries with Islamic Sharia law. In such places, government becomes religion's police force to punish citizens who break religious commandments, where women can't drive, can't vote, and must wear all black abiyahs in the scorching sun, where gays and adulterers are stoned to death, and apostates are hanged.

There are less extreme, but still problematic examples in America. The constitutions of some states has prevented Catholics and atheists from holding public office. In 2012, with 54% of the vote, the predominantly Mormon residents of Highland, Utah, passed legislation forcing businesses to remain closed on Sundays, claiming they have a right to establish values.[1] There is no qualitative difference between forbidding women to get educations and forcing a business to close on Sunday. Each is motivated by "values" and traditions, but neither is based in reason or respect for the rights of other humans. Freedom of conscience is often destroyed by non-objective religious laws. An educated woman behind the wheel or a store being open on your holy day does nothing to violate your rights. It is abominably evil to use government to force others to live your religion.

Economy and state should be separated, as Ayn Rand put it, "in the same way and for the same reasons as the separation of state and church."[2]

The primary reason is freedom of conscience. What is the difference between the government telling us we have to pay a tax to support a specific church, and telling us we have to pay a tax to bail out or subsidize a certain company?

What is the difference between the government telling us we must support a particular creed, and telling us we are required to pay social security taxes whether we agree with it or not?

What is the difference between the government suppressing our religion and the government regulating, taxing, and suppressing our business? The same violation of freedom of conscience happens when we are forced by the state to buy specific products, pay certain wages, and bail out certain companies, as occurs if we are forced to pay tithes, change our beliefs, or attend any church.

In economy, as in religion, governments have no proper or moral role—whether national or local—except, as always, to guard against physical violence, violation of contract, fraud, and other infringements of rights. When a government acts outside of its moral scope, its actions violate principle, and will therefore cause problems.

---

[1] Warnock, Caleb. "Highland Voters Reject Sunday Business Opening." Daily Herald. 7 Nov 2012. heraldextra.com/news/local/north/highland/highland-voters-reject-sunday-business-opening/article_5e115376-dbae-5fa4-8fbd-8980b69a5995.html. Accessed 4 June 2014.

[2] Rand, Ayn. *The Virtue of Selfishness* (New York: Signet, 1964), 33.

Why must we have freedom of conscience? Man's tool of survival is his mind, and he must be free to act on his own judgment. It is for the sake of man's survival and prosperity, as well as of justice and fairness, that we must keep the government separate from things that fall outside its proper purpose. A government exists to protect the rights of all its citizens universally. It must not do anything which cannot be done universally, such as promote one religion over another or one business over another. Such actions do not universally benefit the general welfare, but suppress the welfare of some for the supposed benefit of others. Such circumstances need never exist.

Everyone has the right to choose their destiny, to follow their passion, and to prosper, or fail, according to their own will and labors; and a social system which recognizes this truth, and protects it, is the best-suited for men's happiness and prosperity.

ECONOMICS 101

"We have abundant reason to be convinced that the spirit of trade which pervades these states is not to be restrained; it behooves us, then, to establish just principles."[3] - George Washington, 1785

You may have noticed that you often hear a journalist or a politician quote a supposed "expert economist" on a given subject. You may also have noticed how an "expert" can seem to be found to support or contradict any idea or proposal. Some of these experts have admitted as much and more. Consider what one of the most "successful" economists, John Perkins, of the late 1970's had to say: "The fact was that I never thought of myself as a bona fide economist . . . My status as chief economist and as manager of Economics and Regional Planning could not be attributed to my capabilities in either economics or planning; rather, it was a function of my willingness to provide the types of studies and conclusions my bosses and clients wanted."[4] With that in mind, it's probably best if we learn to use economic principles ourselves, then we won't have to worry about what an alleged expert wants us to believe.

---

[3] Allison, A., Parry, J., and W. Cleon Skousen. *The Real George Washington* (Washington D.C.: National Center for Constitutional Studies, 1991), 721. Emphasis added.
[4] Perkins, John. *Confessions of an Economic Hit Man* (New York: Penguin Group, 2004), 161.

You may have heard the phrase, "There are lies, damned lies, and statistics." Statistics can be used to paint any picture and prove any point. All the difference is made by what details are left out. The truth about the economy contains millions of data points. To have a complete understanding of the whole economy would require you to know about every single part and how they each interact and fit together.

In the figure below, notice that there is an upward trend. But if we made a graph that only showed the area in the circle, we would all reach the opposite conclusion—that the trend was downward. The truth in the context of the small area is that there is a downward trend.

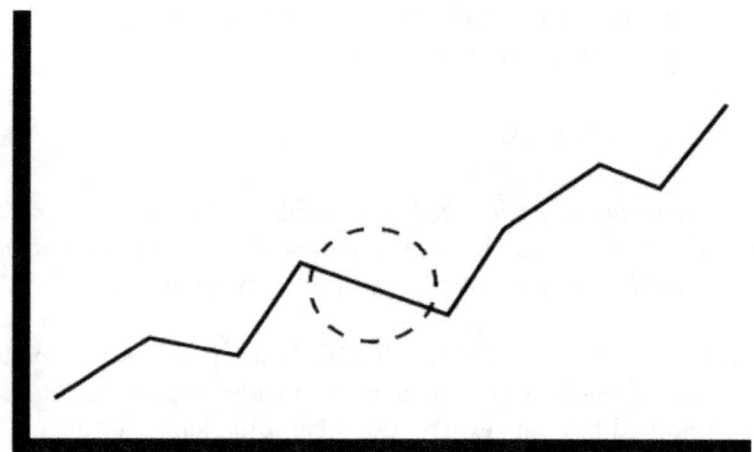

The truth in looking at the larger graph is that there is an upward trend. Perhaps if we zoomed way out of the big graph, we would find that our upward trend is actually just a small blip in what is an overall downward trend. These truths are in opposition to each other, but they do not contradict each other because they are each placed in their proper context. If we remove the context, we destroy the truth. We must never forget that there is no truth without context. Anytime we see a graph or statistic, we must remember it is a small part of the whole and consider the context we do not see.

We have an ocean of information to make sense of. There's no possible way we could sort through it all. It isn't viable for us all to get doctorate degrees in economics. We can listen to the experts, but which ones? How do we know who is right when there is so much contradiction? Here again is the value of principles. If we understand the overarching laws of causality that govern economics, we can have firm footing in our understanding and decisions.

We must keep in mind that there are very broad principles and very specific ones. Specific principles, governing cause and effect on smaller scales can act as exceptions in specific contexts, and be factors which alter, delay, or change outcomes from what the general principle would predict. The more principles we know, the more confident we can be in our decisions. Having a broad outline of the main principles involved can be an effective guide to keep our actions in line with reality.

Economics is essentially the study of human interaction: how people exchange with and relate to one another and in doing so produce, distribute, and consume goods and services. One of the first basic principles that governs economics has to do with why these interactions happen in the first place. As the authors of Freakonomics simply put it, "Economics is, at root, the study of incentives: how people get what they want, or need, especially when other people want or need the same thing."[5]

Human beings respond to incentives. There is always some reason why we do what we do. Ignoring the role of incentives creates waste and inefficiency. There have been many well-intentioned laws and programs designed to change human behavior that have failed because they did not consider the actual incentives. For example, the DARE program is an antidrug program used in many schools. But research shows that it is not effective.[6] Why? Because one of the premises DARE operates on is that kids use drugs because they don't understand the risks. The problem is, kids don't use drugs because they are ignorant of the consequences. People use drugs as a coping mechanism. If DARE wants to keep kids off drugs, they need to address anxiety, depression, and coping skills.

---

[5] Simon, Scott. "Freakonomics: Musings of a 'Rogue Economist.'" NPR.org. 9 Apr 2005. npr.org/templates/story/story.php?storyId=4583937. Accessed 17 Sep 2013.

[6] Hanson, David, J. "Drug Abuse Resistance Education: The Effectiveness of DARE." Online. Alcoholfacts.org/DAREhtml. Accessed 26 Jul 2014.

Another basic principle of economics is illustrated by Henry Hazlitt in his book, *Economics in One Lesson*: "The art of economics consists in looking not merely at the immediate but at the longer effects of any act or policy; it consists in tracing the consequences of that policy not merely for one group but for all groups."[7] If we understand the role of incentives in driving behavior and have the ability to consider systemic and long-term effects, we will likely see things experts and public officials do not.

HENRY HAZLITT

It is not within the scope of this book to examine and disprove every economic fallacy. The aim of this book is to help the reader identify true principles and to apply those principles to any issue. We will give a few brief examples of how to understand economics and how this applies to your life.

PUBLIC WORKS MEANS TAXES

"Everything we get, outside of the free gifts of nature, must in some way be paid for."[8] - Henry Hazlitt

It is important to always remember that, however much our elected officials and professional lobbyists evade the matter, all government expenditures in our current system must eventually be paid for through taxation (and inflation is merely a form of taxation).

For example, Hazlitt offers a $10 million bridge project. It is easy to observe the two hundred employed bridge workers, and the bridge itself. These are obvious. What is not obvious is what we cannot see: that for every job created on the bridge, a private job was destroyed somewhere else. There are two hundred fewer employees to work on other things. Yes, we will have more bridge-builders, but fewer clothing makers, elec-

---

[7] Hazlitt, Henry. *Economics in One Lesson* (New York: Three Rivers Press, 1979), 17.

[8] *ibid*, 31.

tronics engineers, and dance instructors. What we don't see are all of the products, services, and jobs that would have existed had the taxpayers been allowed to spend their money in the places of their own choosing. That $10 million left in the pockets of those who earned it would have been used in thousands of transactions, acting as fuel to the economic engine. This would have equated to greater prosperity as more jobs, products, and services were created. Now, instead of paying for dance classes for your daughter, you pay taxes for a bridge worker. Instead of replacing your old television or paying off your car, you pay taxes for a bridge worker.

Taxing everyone to create jobs, doesn't create more overall jobs—at best, it merely shifts them from industries the public would choose to industries the government chooses. This violates the freedom of conscience of the public in choosing where to spend its own money, and it decreases the incomes of all businesses and people to whom that money would have been freely exchanged for goods and services.

TAXES DISCOURAGE PRODUCTION

Taxes inevitably affect the actions and incentives of those from whom they are taken. If a business must be responsible for 100% of its losses, but through taxation only gets to keep forty cents of every dollar it earns, its policies are affected. It will expand more slowly taking on considerably less risk (risks such as new locations, new employees, and new products). Would-be entrepreneurs who recognize this may be discouraged from starting their own new enterprises. Improved machinery comes about more slowly than it would otherwise. Consumers are prevented from getting better and cheaper products than they otherwise would.[9] A small business owner may decide to do more work himself rather than hire another assistant.

The opposite is also true if taxes are lowered or removed. If you have a greater potential to gain from an endeavor, you will work harder, think harder, and try longer, because your successes will pay off better.

---

[9] *ibid*, 38.

GOVERNMENT MONEY DIVERTS PRODUCTION

Government assistance rewards bad or failing companies, and penalizes good or profitable ones. For example, the housing and mortgage crisis that began around 2007 and crashed the economy was both preventable and predictable. It's always possible when one knows true principles. Here is Hazlitt's explanation from 1946 which eerily sounds like it applies, not decades ago, but today:

"Government-guaranteed home mortgages, especially when a negligible down payment or no down payment whatever is required, inevitably mean more bad loans than otherwise. They force the general taxpayer to subsidize the bad risks and to defray the losses. They encourage people to 'buy' houses that they cannot afford. They tend eventually to bring about an oversupply of houses as compared with other things. They temporarily over stimulate building, raise the cost of building for everybody (including the buyers of the homes with the guaranteed mortgages), and may mislead the building industry into an eventually costly over-expansion [known as a 'bubble']. In brief, in the long run they do not increase overall national production but encourage malinvestment."[10]

Yes, a simple look at cause and effect not only predicted the 2007 economic crisis sixty years early, but could have prevented it. Principles get violated through greed, ignorance, a denial of reality, ambition for power, or even a misguided desire to help; and we all suffer the consequences. Even after the consequences are seen and exposed, politicians have shown that they care more about assigning blame and seizing more power than in learning and correcting the true causes of the disaster.

Here is more recent proof that the housing market crash of 2007-2008 was both foreseen and preventable when one thinks according to principle. Read what U.S. Representative Ron Paul predicted two years before the crash, in 2005:

"The connection between these government sponsored enterprises [GSE] and the government helps isolate their management from market discipline. This isolation from market discipline is the root cause of the recent reports of mismanagement at Fannie Mae and Freddie Mac. After all, if Fannie and Freddie were not underwritten by the federal government, investors

---

[10] *ibid*, 47.

would demand assurance that Fannie and Freddie follow accepted management and accounting practices. Ironically, by transferring the risk of a widespread mortgage default, the government increases the likelihood of a painful crash in the housing market.

"Despite the long-term damage to the economy inflicted by the government's interference in the housing market, the government's policy of diverting capital into housing creates a short-term boom in housing. Like all artificially created bubbles, the boom in housing prices cannot last forever. When housing prices fall, homeowners will experience difficulty as their equity is wiped out. Furthermore, the holders of the mortgage debt will also have a loss. These losses will be greater than they would have been had government policy not actively encouraged over-investment in housing.

"[This bill] further distorts the housing market by artificially inflating the demand for housing through the creation of a national housing trust fund. This fund further diverts capital to housing that, absent government intervention, would be put to a use more closely matching the demands of consumers . . .

"Perhaps the Federal Reserve can stave off the day of reckoning by purchasing the GSEs' debt and pumping liquidity into the housing market, but this cannot hold off the inevitable drop in the housing market forever. In fact, postponing the necessary and painful market corrections will only deepen the inevitable fall. The more people are invested in the market, the greater the effects across the economy when the bubble bursts."[11]

Government incentives diverted production and capital into a housing market where, if such incentives had not been in place, the free market would have spread such productivity to other safer and more profitable ventures.

---

[11] Paul, Ron. "The GSE Crisis." 27 Oct. 2005. Available Online. lewrockwell.com/paul/paul282.html. Accessed 29 Apr 2011.

Production Grows the Economy

In response to a troubled economy, President George W. Bush issued "stimulus" checks to most people in America. The idea was to spend it, thus driving the economy forward through (false) consumption and demand. What happened? Things got worse.

President Obama's stimulus, which didn't go to the American people, but to big failing businesses, also failed in its aims. Giving out a stimulus check is artificial and useless because it is a false and temporary increase in demand. There is no ability to continue to consume at that level. It is an unsustainable bubble. When it bursts, everyone is worse off than before.

A basic principle was ignored. Economist Peter Schiff stated it simply, explaining that economies don't grow because people consume more—people consume more because the economy grew.[12] Only by increasing supply can people get more of what they demand.

While consumption and production is a reciprocal cycle, this is not a case of the chicken or the egg. There is a definite beginning because people cannot consume what does not exist. A thing must be created before it can be sold. An iPad must exist before a buyer even knows he can demand one.

In the beginning of this cycle, a producer must sacrifice, work harder, go without, and/or take out loans so that they can raise the level of their productivity. If they are producing goods that others find valuable, they will be able to trade and be successful. The increased amount of production lowers prices and allows for greater consumption. How? In general, every product is in competition with every other product in the marketplace. Because consumers have finite amounts of money to spend, they must choose which of all the options they would like to purchase the most. If you spend your money on a round of golf, that may mean going without the 40 oz. porterhouse steak. Production is what gives people a greater ability to consume collectively and individually. Greater production means greater wealth. As people create and trade more, their wealth increases, in turn giving them the ability to consume more. As long as production lags, so does income.

There are certainly other factors that influence production however. The uncertainty that you will be able to sell more goods might very well be enough to discourage more production. When there is a recession, when confidence is low, or when the future looks uncertain, con-

---

[12] Schiff, Peter. and Andrew Schiff. *How an Economy Grows and Why It Crashes* (Hoboken, New Jersey: John Wiley & Sons, Inc. 2010), 21.

sumers tend to save more and spend less. And reciprocally, this causes production to slow. In this way, markets can enter self-perpetuated downward spirals until something interrupts the circuit and causes a change.

The solution to uncertainty in a market? Remove the most uncertain element—arbitrary government interference (which means: actions that do not protect individual rights). Aside from bureaucratic meddling, the only other real threat to long range planning, production, and prosperity is natural disaster (assuming of course that the government is doing its job in protecting rights). But even natural disasters can often be mostly mitigated through proper insurance. Unfortunately, there is no insurance policy that can protect against government seizures.

Ludditism: The Belief That Technology Creates Unemployment

"There are some structural issues with our economy where a lot of businesses have learned to become much more efficient with a lot fewer workers. You see it when you go to a bank and you use an ATM; you don't go to a bank teller. Or you go to the airport, and you're using a kiosk instead of checking in at the gate."[13] - Barrack H. Obama, his reason for high unemployment

The belief that technology creates unemployment, when examined logically, leads to pretty crazy conclusions. Taken to its logical extreme it means that cavemen first started creating unemployment when they invented the wheel. While new machines may put a few people temporarily out of work, they open up entire new fields of labor full of employment opportunities.

Consider farming. Before any technology greater than the scythe, flail, and winnowing fan, farmers had a tremendous amount of back-breaking reaping, threshing, and winnowing to do by hand. All that work was just to have grain, not to mention all the time and effort required to further process the grain. The amount they were able to produce, even working sixteen hour days was not very far above bare subsistence, especially if they had no children to help them.

---

[13] Jamaal, D.K. "Obama Blames Unemployment on ATMs." 15 Jun 2011. Online. examiner.com/post-partisan-in-national/obama-blames-unemployment-on-atms. Accessed 30 Jul 2011.

With the invention of labor saving devices like the combine harvester, what used to take weeks of toil now only took hours. This increase in productivity, along with other equivalent advances, had the effect of making food abundant and cheap. Instead of a large portion of a town having to farm to survive, with food more available, a greater division of labor was possible. Where before those who would prefer to be bakers, artists, tailors, carpenters, and barbers had to farm, now they or their children were able to give up farming entirely and work in their chosen fields of labor. Having so much labor opened up to specialization meant increasing the availability and affordability of goods and services for everyone.

The gift of technology is time—our very lives. With our time freed up by the diminished requirement for labor, we have the option of engaging in other activities—productive and recreational. Prosperity is eternally bound to productivity; it is thanks to labor-saving technology that the western world enjoys the opulence it does.

New technology may cause short term unemployment as the economy adjusts to the changes, but these growing pains are wholly positive. The automobile may have crushed the horse-and-buggy industry much as airplanes nearly crushed the railroads, but how many hundreds of thousands are now employed in these new industries? How many more industries has mankind yet to explore? When men are free to work and create, they will invent new products which not only will provide new areas of employment, but will also raise the aggregate quality of life for all. Those put out of business by the invention of the car were now freed up from antiquated and less-effective labors in order to work somewhere else which would be more productive. As machines and new inventions make life easier for everyone, man's productive capability is free to be put to better uses.

Yet, this idea is ignored in the creation of hundreds of make-work rules by unions: electricians who refuse to install equipment made out of the state unless it is disassembled and reassembled at the job site; plumbers who insist on cutting the pre-threaded ends off pipes and re-threading them themselves; theater unions insist on the use of scene shifters even in shows in which no scenery is used; postal workers who can't clean up the equipment used by others of a different craft because it isn't part of their job, etc.

Nobel Prize-winning economist Gunnar Myrdal opposed the introduction of labor-saving machines in underdeveloped countries on the grounds that they "decrease the demand for labor"![14] Mr. Myrdal might be pleased, it seems, with a remote Amazonian or African tribe where employment is 100%, from sunup to sundown.

There is an anecdote told of an American businessman who visited China. He approached a work site with hundreds of people hard at work with shovels, moving earth to build a dam. The man approached the foreman and said, "If you employed the use of a tractor to move this earth, you could have done in a day what it will take these men three weeks to accomplish."

The foreman was stunned and sputtered, "But think of all the unemployment that would cause!"

"Oh, I'm sorry," the American responded. "I thought you wished to build a dam. If it's employment that you want, take all their shovels away and make them use spoons."

All those men were wasting hundreds of hours of labor doing something inefficient. If they did bring in a tractor to do the work, what could those men be doing instead? Instead of one dam, maybe two? Maybe an entirely different line of production making life better for all? If they hadn't been wasting their time there, they could have accomplished so much more, and more production means better quality of life— cheaper goods and services of a higher quality and in greater abundance. Production grows the economy.

GOVERNMENT PRICE CONTROLS

"Let vigorous measures be adopted, not to limit the price of articles, for this I believe is inconsistent with the very nature of things and impracticable in itself."[15] - George Washington, 1779

There's always a "well-intentioned" reason for government price controls. If prices are to be kept artificially low, it's because government officials want to "protect" the public from price gouging and exploitation. If prices are to be kept artificially high, it's to make sure the producers get "fair" market value.

---

[14] Hazlitt, *Economics*, 53.

[15] Allison, A., Parry, J., and W. Cleon Skousen. *The Real George Washington* (Washington D.C.: National Center for Constitutional Studies, 1991), 720.

According to the principle of supply and demand, the "natural" price of an item on the open market fluctuates constantly depending on a few factors.

SUPPLY: How much of a product is available? Is it plentiful or scarce? Is it easy to produce? Or is it difficult or costly with lots of time, skill, or resources involved? Is it a unique and hard to find item, or are there hundreds available to compete and bring the price down? An item will tend to cost less the more there is of it and the easier it is to come by. People may refuse to buy it when they know they can get it easily elsewhere for less.

DEMAND: How much do people desire and value the product? Is it rare?

The phenomenon of eBay is a great study in the law of supply and demand. It is easy to see how much an item is valued by people looking for it at any given time. They get to set the price themselves, and the item justly goes to whoever valued it most during the auction time.

What happens if government keeps prices artificially low? An almost immediate shortage results. People's demand increases as the price drops, people buy more than they normally would—more than they can utilize effectively. Demand soon exceeds the supply and then the government decides it has to institute rationing. Producers no longer want to produce an item that may not have a sufficient profit margin anymore to make it worthwhile. The government then tries to subsidize the producers for the difference. So in essence, the government is taxing all the people to make prices lower for the few who purchase the product.

How can a government keep prices artificially high? The government has been known in the past to intentionally decrease the supply of an item to raise its value. One such time was when farmers in the late 1930's such as Roscoe Filburn, who had grown more wheat than the law allowed, were ordered to destroy their crops and pay a fine because the government was trying to raise and "stabilize" the price of wheat.[16] People were lined up for food at soup kitchens and our government was burning food to make sure that it wasn't "too cheap."

Another method to keep prices high is by taxing the item to make it more expensive. A major consequence to this is that black markets grow to the extent that an item is made more expensive through taxes. A black market is an "underground" market that operates outside the confines of the law. The most famous black market in U.S. history occurred during

---

[16] Wikipedia. Wickard v. Filburn. en.wikipedia.org/wiki/Wickard_v._Filburn. Accessed 26 Jun 2013.

the era of Prohibition when alcohol was made illegal. Unfortunately, people like alcohol. The result was bootleggers, mobsters, crime lords, just as today's prohibition against drugs has created cartels, gangs, kidnappings, trafficking, and murders.

Now what if the item itself isn't illegal, but just discouraged and made expensive through excessive taxation? You still get a black market to avoid paying the tax and obtain the desired item for less. See New York's cigarette industry for proof. As of this writing, there's more than a $4.00 per pack tax on cigarettes in New York. But, people still smoke, and the crazy part is, they buy their cigarettes somewhere cheaper. According to one article in 2007, one in three packs were purchased via untaxed Indian smoke shops (resulting in a loss of nearly $1 billion in potential tax revenue).[17] The New York Times reported that one legitimate vendor saw his sales in 2002 decreased 75% after the recent tax increase.[18] The USPS also put a ban on shipping cigarettes in large quantities through the mail, presumably to help cut down the black market sources.[19]

After World War II, some countries in Europe saw their black markets grow at the expense of the legally recognized markets until the former became, essentially, the market. Everyone used it. But, you can't suppose no harm was done merely because the black market was widely used. The harm was both economic and moral. Not only were goods on the black market generally inferior and dishonest, but the long-established "honest" firms suffered economically, and demoralization spread into all business practices.

PRICE GOUGING

What about "price gouging"? That's charging "too much" for something, right? Consider the following story reported in May 2006 by John Stossel and Gena Binkley for ABC News:

---

[17] Guevara, Marina, Walker. and Kate Willson. "Big Tobacco's New York Black Market." 19 Dec 2008. Online. publicintegrity.org/articles/entry/1098. Accessed 29 Apr 2011.

[18] O'Grady, Jim. "Neighborhood Report: New York Smoking; Shared Misery: Newsstands Feel the Tax's Pinch Too." The New York Times. 18 Aug 2002. Online. nytimes.com/2002/08/18/nyregion/neighborhood-report-new-york-smoking-shared-misery-newsstands-feel-tax-s-pinch.html. Accessed 29 Apr 2011.

[19] Markham, Jen. "House Bans Cigarette Sales Through U.S. Mail." 17 Mar 2010. buffalo.ynn.com/content/all_news/499108/house-bans-cigarette-sales-through-u-s--mail/. Accessed 29 Apr 2011.

Mississippi Attorney General Jim Hood announced a crackdown on gougers after Hurricane Katrina.

John Shepperson was one of the "gougers" authorities arrested. Shepperson and his family live in Kentucky. They watched news reports about Katrina and learned that people desperately needed things.

Shepperson thought he could help and make some money, too, so he bought 19 generators. He and his family then rented a U-Haul and drove 600 miles to an area of Mississippi that was left without power in the wake of the hurricane.

He offered to sell his generators for twice what he had paid for them, and people were eager to buy. Police confiscated his generators, though, and Shepperson was jailed for four days for price-gouging. His generators are still in police custody.

So did the public benefit? Here's the real question: What is the best way to deal with shortages after a natural disaster?

"Any time there is a natural disaster, or a hurricane, an earthquake, the price of the things that people desperately want to have—batteries, flashlights, generators, water or milk—they go up. Or they disappear," said economist Russ Roberts.

If sellers don't raise prices, supplies vanish. Anxious buyers line up and often buy more than they need, just in case. Those not at the front of the line may get nothing.

"More people want to buy it than there is stuff available . . . What do you do? How do you solve that problem? And how do you find out who should get those scarce items," Roberts asked.

The answer is you allow people to raise prices—even to "gouge"—because only people who REALLY need them will cough up the money. Gouging also encourages greedy entrepreneurs to rush in with much-needed goods, or to look for more supplies.[20]

A man was arrested for using his creativity to try and make a profit by supplying sorely desired products to people. In the interest of "protecting" the public, the government both stopped him from providing the generators and confiscated them so that no one could utilize them. His crime: trying to make a profit doing what the government was unable

---

[20] Stossel, John. and Gena Binkley. "MYTH: Price-Gouging is Bad." 12 May 2006. Online. abcnews.go.com/2020/Stossel/story?id=1954352&page=1. Accessed 29 Apr 2011.

to do even at a loss—providing needed goods and services to a disaster-ravaged populace.

If you were in line waiting anxiously to obtain a generator so your family could have some electricity, would you have been happy to see the man arrested knowing you would now have to go back to a dark home? Or would you be angry that the government, after failing to help you in the first place, was now making matters worse by trying to tell you how much you should value an item—that if they thought it was too expensive, they were going to prevent you from buying it at all?

There are many prices that governments attempt to control and they all have unintended consequences, whether it's gasoline, food, rent, utilities, or one of the most controversial: wages.

MINIMUM WAGE LAWS

"Wage" is merely a special name given to the price of something: the **price of labor**. It is unfortunate that is has been given a different name and thus assumed by many to operate under different laws.

When a law is passed that no one shall be paid less than $5/hour, the first effect is that anyone who is not worth $5/hour to an employer will not be employed at all. He is deprived of the right to use his abilities and skills and earn the amount that he is able. The community is also deprived of the moderate services he could have provided. For a low wage, we now substitute unemployment or black-market employment.

To see if an idea is ridiculous, take it to its logical extreme. For example: If government can create jobs, then why doesn't it hire every citizen? Because it can only collect taxes to pay those employees from people who are actually producing goods and services. In the case of minimum wage laws, what would happen if Congress passed a law raising the minimum wage to $200/hour? What happens next? Where will employers get the money to cover wages? Assuming any business could actually sustain such a cost, do you think business owners would be willing to pay for that out of their own pocket? If their costs are higher, then their prices must be as well. This means a Happy Meal is now $82. Every business must adjust its wages up and pay for them by an equivalent rise in prices. Has anything actually changed? Sure, you're making $8,000 a week, but one gallon of gas is now $100. Actions have consequences, and any coercive meddling in markets will only cause problems. Any arbitrary increase in wages will be balanced out by an equivalent rise in prices. Minimum wage laws are the equivalent of taking water from the deep end of the pool and pouring it in the shallow end in an attempt to raise the water level.

As prices rise to accommodate the increased wages and the cost is shifted to consumers, what will happen? A higher price may drive consumers to buy less of the higher priced item, or to buy nearly equivalent imported products. On the other hand, if prices are not raised and the difference taken from the profit margin instead, marginal producers in the industry may be driven out of business altogether resulting in less production and more unemployment. In addition to these consequences, the man who is now unemployable may choose to seek out welfare rather than to increase his skills, knowledge, and relationships—his human life value. He is incentivized to remain unemployed.

THE MORALITY OF ECONOMICS

It is important to remember in all these economic issues, to never ignore or evade the moral issues underlying them all. Many will attempt to argue specific facts, causes and effects, etc. They will also always attempt to take the moral high ground in defense of government bailouts, minimum wage laws, tariffs, taxation, etc. *"Don't you want people to earn enough to have a good living? Don't people deserve a living wage? Don't you care about people? There isn't any other way."*

It is imperative to never concede the moral high ground in the battle for liberty. Identify the core principles involved and the individual rights at stake. Minimum wage laws are immoral because they violate the right of personal conscience and preference, the right to enter into agreements with others without outside coercion, and the right for both the employer and the employee to determine how much they value each other in the exchange. The violation of the economic principles in this chapter by the government is immoral first and foremost because it is an initiation of force.

DEBT, DEFICIT, AND LIABILITIES

The Federal Deficit is the difference between the amount of money spent by Congress and the revenue collected by the IRS in a given year. (A difference of $590 billion in October of 2016). This budget deficit must be made up by either printing more money or borrowing more money—inflation or debt.

The National Debt is the amount that is owed to investors by the Federal Government. ($19.6 trillion in October of 2016).

The United States' Unfunded Liabilities is all money promised to be paid at a future date, such as Social Security, Medicare, and Prescription Drugs (Medicare Part D). This amounted to over $103 trillion in October of 2016 according to usdebtclock.org.[21] The total wealth of the entire planet that is produced in one year (the global GDP) is about $70 trillion. In other words, you could tax every person on the planet at 100% for an entire year and not be able to pay off the United States' unfunded liabilities.

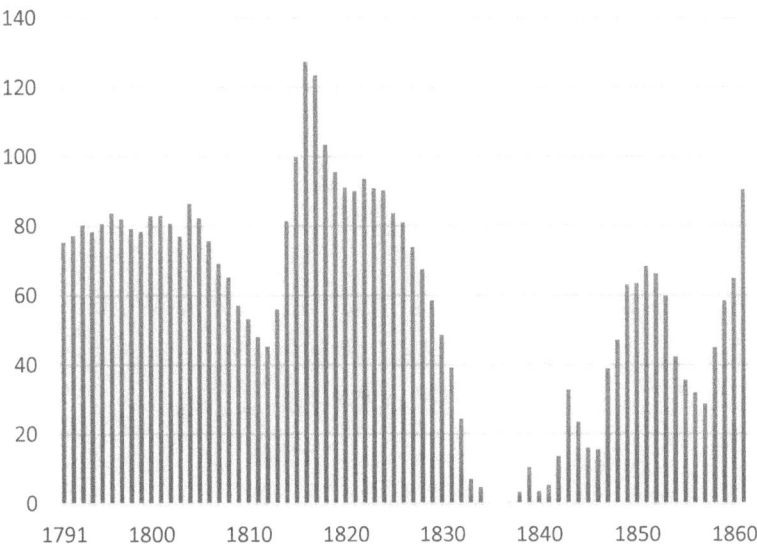

Debt in Millions 1791 - 1861

The above chart shows the national debt up until the Civil War.

[21] US Debt Clock. Online. usdebtclock.org/index.html. Accessed 12 Oct 2016.

The next chart shows the jump of the Civil War through 1911:

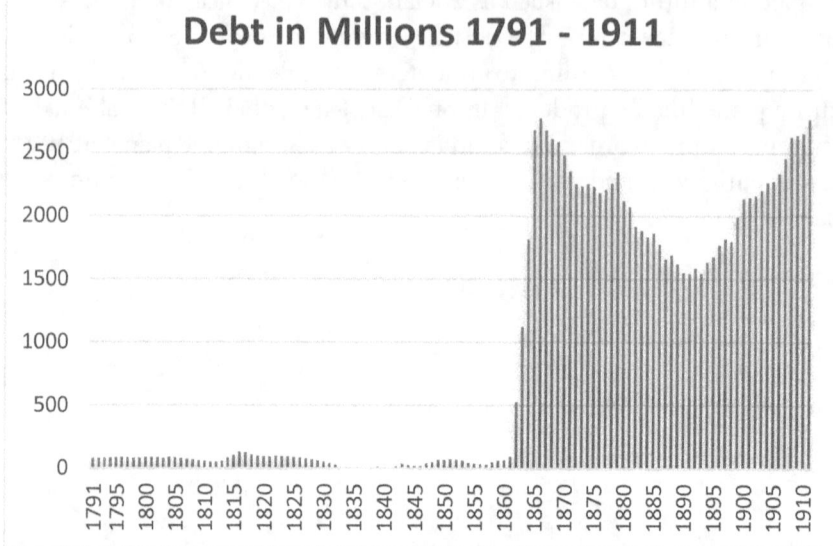

Now compare that to the jumps that occurred for the World Wars:

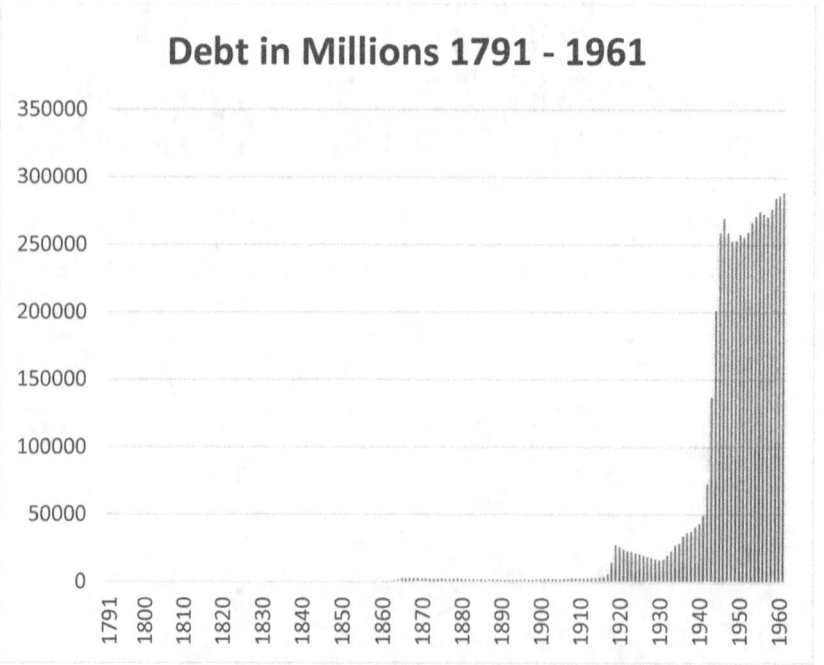

Now here is the full chart through 2020, in which the previous jumps all but disappear as inconsequential. It's sometimes hard to visualize a trillion. It's a million millions:

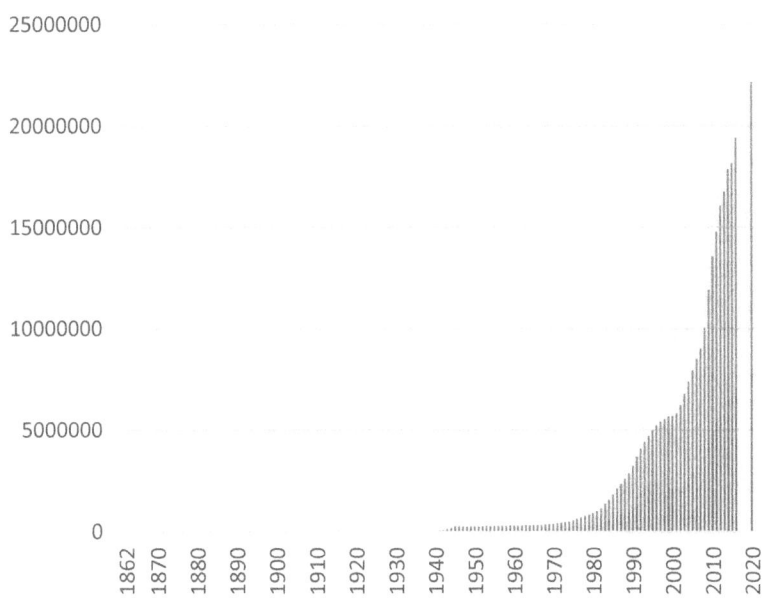

Debt in Millions 1862 - 2020

One thing should be obvious here: the direction these figures are heading is unsustainable. Barring some major changes to the financial trends of the U.S. government and its entitlement programs, catastrophic financial collapse is inevitable. Historically, this has often included massive inflation and hyperinflation as governments desperately try to print enough money to pay their debts, followed by civil unrest when this fails.[22]

---

[22] "US National Debt by Year." Source: US Dept of Treasury.
http://www.polidiotic.com/by-the-numbers/us-national-debt-by-year/. Accessed 10/13/2016.

INFLATION

"The crucial test of private property is the attitude of government toward money. Devaluation of currency is outright expropriation."[23]
- Isabel Paterson

It may seem logical that if the government were to simply print a lot of money and give it to everyone, we would all be a lot richer, right? All but the most naive instinctively feel that statement is wrong, but many don't know why. Others, less naive, sense there must be a catch somewhere and so they would limit the amount of additional money the government would issue to only what is "needed."

Still others recognize the fact that an increase in monetary supply will result in inflation, and that is exactly why they want it. They think it will improve the condition of poor debtors if the money they owe is worth less. They think it will stimulate exports or cure an economic depression.

Economist Peter Schiff described inflation as "simply a means to transfer wealth from anyone who has savings in a particular currency to anyone who has debt in the same currency."[24] In other words, those who are saving money hate inflation because it decreases the value of their savings, while those who are borrowing money love inflation because it makes the money they owe worth less.

It is a mistake to try and use one set of financial principles for your family and another for your nation. If your family were experiencing a financial depression—decreased cash flow and increasing liabilities and debt—would it make sense to tell yourself that you are just going to "spend your way back into prosperity" and run up your debt just to get your money flowing again? Would you give further loans to people who owed you money with the hope that they would pay you back so you could then pay your creditors? Not at all! You would decrease your superfluous expenditures, sell unnecessary assets, and attempt to increase your productivity. Instead, we are told by politicians that it's because they care, that it's for our own good, that it's just an emergency, or that we're too dumb to understand what's at stake while they are raiding our wallets.

---

[23] Paterson, *Machine*, Chapter 6.
[24] Schiff, *Economy*, 220.

When the Republic of Zimbabwe was established in 1980, so was the Zimbabwe dollar, which began its life as more valuable than the U.S. dollar. In its early years, Zimbabwe experienced strong growth and development. The wheat and tobacco industries were thriving. Things were going so well (despite some modest inflation) that the government decided it could afford to try and "fix" some other things.

From 1991–1996, the Zimbabwean government of president Robert Mugabe embarked on an Economic Structural Adjustment Program, designed by the IMF and the World Bank. It should be unsurprising to you by now, dear reader, that this had serious negative effects on Zimbabwe's economy.

"In the late 1990s, the government instituted land reforms intended to redistribute land from white landowners to black farmers to correct the injustices of colonialism. However, many of these farmers had no experience or training in farming." Food production plummeted and the banking sector collapsed. Farmers could no longer obtain loans for capital development, and unemployment rose to 80%. The government began printing nearly infinite amounts of currency to cover its expenses.

During the height of inflation from 2008 to 2009, it was difficult to measure the hyperinflation because the government of Zimbabwe stopped filing official inflation statistics.

However, the highest month of inflation is estimated at 6.5 sextillion percent in mid-November 2008, or about 80 billion percent a month. That means that a loaf of bread that cost $1 in October, cost $80,000,000,000 in November. Prices had to be adjusted upwards several times a day and money received was immediately exchanged for foreign currency to avoid catastrophic loss.

"In 2009, Zimbabwe abandoned its currency. As of 2013, Zimbabwe still has no national currency; currencies from other countries are used."[25]

Still, some argue that the national economy is multi-faceted and complex, and that the complexity and lifespan of a nation's finances make it different than the financial rules of a single household. Despite the differences, in the end we still have to earn income and pay bills. The current strategy is to cover our unsustainable spending addiction by taking on future debt to pay the current creditors, all while increasing our spending every year. It is a revolving door of borrowing, like getting a new credit card every year to roll the old balance over while adding to the debt.

Perhaps it is the naive belief of some economists that more debt now will buy us the necessary time to get our financial house in order. Perhaps these economists believe that somehow Congress will be wiser, more restrained, less power-hungry, and more willing to work together in the future (stop laughing). Perhaps they believe Social Security and Medicare costs will eventually decline and then we will be able to be financially disciplined. Or perhaps they are simply looking to pass the buck to the next unfortunate generation, and not caring if we last that long. Such a policy of deferment only snowballs the problem—we are destroying our future for momentary comfort. The painful withdrawals of stopping this spending addiction will only worsen, perhaps to fatal levels the longer we wait to quit. There comes a point when investors look at your income-to-debt ratio and realize you will never be able to repay them, and so they stop lending you money. But when that happens to a government they simply print more money, resulting in inflation—which means everyone just got poorer.

Thomas Jefferson said there have been nations who have had the belief or tradition "that a father might sell his child as a slave." "We acknowledge that our children are born free," he went on. But though "we act as if we believed that . . . an individual father cannot [enslave] . . . his son" we legislate as if all the fathers could enslave all their sons together and "oblige them to pay for all the enterprises, just or unjust, profitable or ruinous, into which our vices, our passions, or our personal in-

---

[25] "Hyperinflation in Zimbabwe." Wikipedia entry.
en.wikipedia.org/wiki/Hyperinflation_in_Zimbabwe. Accessed 13 Sep 2013.

terests may lead us." Jefferson considered passing debt on to the next generation to be a horrible "stage of degeneracy."[26]

Inflation is actually a form of taxation. However, it is more pernicious and dishonest than direct taxation. Instead of expropriating our money directly under a written law we can read and repeal, the government merely prints more money for its purposes. It is taxation without representation or recourse. Inflation still takes our money from us because the purchasing power of our money is now less—we essentially have less money than before. We might have more dollars but can buy less with them. Instead of taxing us now, we are being taxed in a slow creep that is only apparent down the road—at least until hyperinflation sets in.[27]

Representative Pete Stark from California illustrated how the concepts of debt and inflation are distorted and disconnected from reality for most politicians. This is from his interview with Jan Helfeld:

Stark: The national debt measures how wealthy we are.

Helfeld: So, the more you owe the more you're worth?

Stark: In Federal account, in the national scheme of things, that's quite right.

Helfeld: So should we borrow another trillion next year?

Stark: I'll say it slowly, you are trying to make an enemy . . . out of the concept of debt, which for a nation is different than debt for an individual.[28]

(When confronted with the contradiction in his thinking, Rep. Stark soon got belligerent and left the interview.)

Ayn Rand warned us to watch money as a sign for when a society will vanish. Whenever "destroyers appear among men, they start by destroying money, for money is men's protection and the base of a moral existence. Destroyers seize gold and leave to its owner a counterfeit pile of papers."[29]

Principles do not change with size or with the entity involved. Schiff stated it simply, "Just as the principles of mathematics don't

---

[26] Allison, A., Maxfield, M., and W. Cleon Skousen. *The Real Thomas Jefferson* (Washington D.C.: National Center for Constitutional Studies, 2009), 395-96.

[27] For more on inflation, its causes, and the problems it causes, read *End the Fed*, by Ron Paul.

28 Helfeld, Jan. The Bottom Line. Online. jan-helfeld.com/shop/interview/stark/. Accessed 5 Mar 2011.

29 Rand, Ayn. *Atlas Shrugged* (New York: Signet, 1957) 387-91.

change with the size of the problem, basic economic principles do not change with the size of the economy."[30]

The principles and morality of a free market are essential for the student of freedom to understand. The morality of a free market lies in how it leaves each man free to act on his own judgment. As Rand said, "Intellectual freedom cannot exist without political freedom; political freedom cannot exist without economic freedom; a free mind and a free market are corollaries."[31] A system of private ownership and private property is the only moral economic and social system, because it is the only system that recognizes the role of man's mind and his moral agency and personal responsibility for his own life.

REVIEW

Q1: Why should the economy and the State be segregated?

Q2: What effect do taxes have on production, and why?

Q3: What are the effects of government assistance to private companies?

Q4: How are economic bubbles created?

Q5: What are the effects of controls on prices, including wages?

Q6: Define the following: National Debt, National Budget Deficit, Unfunded Liabilities.

Q7: What do you think will happen if we stay on our current course?

Q8: What caused our current financial course? Can it be changed? How?

---

[30] Schiff, *Economy*, 87.
[31] Rand, Ayn. *For the New Intellectual* (New York: Signet, 1963), 25.

CHAPTER 10

COLLECTIVISM

"The greater the good, the harder the blow."
- Stephen Sondheim, *Into the Woods*

INTRODUCTION

The evil seeds that became the Nazis of World War II were planted decades earlier, before the Third Reich. The Weimar Republic Germans in the 1920s and 30s heard over and over that there were to be "no more private Germans," that there was another entity whose will determined the course of their lives. This entity was the nation, the whole, the group, the volk (people). These citizens were mentally bombarded every day with the concept that has been used by dictators everywhere as a justification for their tyrannies—collectivism.

In order to completely understand capitalism, the social system of the free individual, it is necessary to understand its antithesis. We need to understand not only the true principles of a free society, but the pernicious falsehoods of an unfree society that can infect our thoughts—mostly unnoticed—until we train ourselves to recognize and eradicate them. If we cannot clearly identify what we fight against, we will never be able to advocate effectively for freedom.

Collectivism comes in many names and flavors. But like the selection at your local ice cream parlor, a change of flavor doesn't alter the foundational ingredients of the ice cream. (The metaphor ends there, however. Collectivism, in any form, is not full of cool, creamy goodness.) Now, before learning to identify the many flavors, we must first learn the basic ingredients found in all forms of collectivism. Unlike the language of capitalism, which is simple, direct, and honest, the language of collectivism is consistently and historically couched in vagueness, cloaked in euphemism, and characterized by deception; this is done on purpose because if it were not sugar-coated in deception, people could more easily identify it as the poison it is.

Collectivism is the moral, political, or social ideology which holds that the individual is property of the collective, that the individual's interests, values, goals, and rights are subordinate to the group. Collectivism's alleged aim is for the "good" of the society and community, emphasizing the interdependence of every human in a group. The cardinal difference between capitalism and collectivism concerns the recognition and protection of man's most valuable attribute, which is an individual attribute—his creative mind.

Capitalism is based on the recognition of individual rights and the sovereignty of the individual human being, on man's life as an end to itself, and his happiness as its only moral purpose.

Collectivism is the exact opposite. It is based on the recognition of the group as sovereign over the individual, that man's life is a means to the good of the whole, and that the happiness of others is his purpose. It holds that in human affairs the collective—society, community, nation, race, class, party, etc.—is the "unit of reality and the standard of value."[1]

THE GREATER GOOD

According to collectivist thought, the individual has no value, except as part of a group and only so far as he serves its purpose. It includes the nebulous concept of the "greater good" or "public interest," and the sacrifice of individual rights to "collective rights."

The "common good," or greater good, is an indefinable concept as commonly used today. There is no such entity as a tribe or "society" or "the public." Society is only a number of individuals. This concept is

---

[1] Peikoff, Leonard. *The Ominous Parallels* (New York: Penguin, 1982), 17.

meaningless unless it refers to the good of all the individuals involved. In this case, it is a meaningless term morally because it doesn't answer the question of what is good for the individuals. Usually this term is used because it is vague and mystical and is seen as something separate and superior to the good of individuals. It means, as Rand observed, that "the good of some men takes precedence over the good of others, with those others consigned to the status of sacrificial animals."[2]

The terms "greater good" and "common good" imply the "good of the majority" rather than of a minority or individual. Even this is a deception, since the violation of one individual's rights means the effective potential loss of everyone's rights.

THE CITY OF OMELAS

Some try to define the "greater good" as the most good for the greatest number of people. Ursula Le Guin's short story, "The Ones Who Walk Away from Omelas," tells of a beautiful utopia, a city with towers, gardens, green fields, tree-shaded avenues, parks, and harbor, all set against majestic mountains. It was a city filled with a happy, yet complex people who enjoyed a society without the clamor and stress of modernity that we know, without war, and without guilt. "They were mature, intelligent, passionate adults whose lives were not wretched." Their joy was a "boundless and generous contentment, a magnanimous triumph felt not against some outer enemy but in communion with the finest and fairest in the souls of all men everywhere and the splendor of the world's summer: this is what swells the hearts of the people of Omelas, and the victory they celebrate is that of life."

But this beauty and perfection came at a price. In a dark cellar with no window, there was a naked, starved child. "The child used to scream for help at night, and cry a good deal, but now it only makes a kind of whining . . . and it speaks less and less often. It is so thin there are no calves to its legs; its belly protrudes; it lives on a half-bowl of corn meal and grease a day. It is naked. Its buttocks and thighs are a mass of festered sores, as it sits in its own excrement continually." The child, "who has not always lived in the tool room, and can remember sunlight and its mother's voice, sometimes speaks. 'I will be good,' it says. 'Please let me out. I will be good!'" The child receives no answers. The only visitors who ever come are silent, they only kick or gawk at the child with disgusted eyes.

---

[2] Rand, Ayn. *Capitalism: The Unknown Ideal* (New York: Signet, 1967), 20-21.

All the people of Omelas are aware of the child. "They all know that it has to be there. Some of them understand why, and some do not, but they all understand that their happiness, the beauty of their city, the tenderness of their friendships, the health of their children, the wisdom of their scholars, the skill of their makers, even the abundance of their harvest and the kindly weathers of their skies, depend wholly on this child's abominable misery . . . They would like to do something for the child. But there is nothing they can do. If the child were brought up into the sunlight out of that vile place, if it were cleaned and fed and comforted, that would be a good thing indeed; but if it were done, in that day and hour all the prosperity and beauty and delight of Omelas would wither and be destroyed. Those are the terms. To exchange all the goodness and grace of every life in Omelas for that single, small improvement: to throw away the happiness of thousands for the chance of the happiness of one: that would be to let guilt within the walls indeed."[3]

In Omelas, the greatest amount of good was achieved for the greatest number of people. The cost was negligible. What is the misery of one child compared to a perfect and happy society? The title of the story refers to those citizens of Omelas who decide to leave, rather than live at the cost of another's sacrifice. This story is an extreme example, but it accurately portrays the principle of collectivism and shows it taken to its logical conclusion. Some would argue that in our world there is no cosmic whipping child, and our society (which is far from the perfection of Omelas) requires only the small sacrifice of some of the liberty and property of the citizens; the burden is minor, and widely shared. But this difference is only one of degree not of kind.

Collectivism's moral code holds that man has no right to live for himself, and service to others is the only justification of his existence. Just like the child, but applied to everyone.

The basic theory was explained perfectly by one of its most faithful adherents this way:

> "It is . . . necessary that the individual should . . . come to realize that his own ego is of no importance in comparison with the existence of his nation; . . . that above all the unity of a nation's spirit and will are worth far more than freedom of the spirit and will of an individual"

---

[3] Le Guin, Ursula. "The Ones Who Walk Away From Omelas." San Diego State University Online. rohan.sdsu.edu/faculty/dunnweb/rprnts.omelas.pdf. Accessed 30 May 2012.

"This state of mind, which subordinates the interests of the ego to the conservation of the community, is really the first premise for every truly human culture . . . By this we understand only the individual's capacity to make sacrifices for the community, for his fellow men."[4]

Those statements were made by Adolf Hitler, describing the moral philosophy underpinning National Socialism. Yet how often have you heard similar sentiment expressed in American classrooms, homes, and State of the Union addresses? Whether or not it is expressed as clearly and explicitly as stated here, it is the underlying philosophy of many Americans. (We do not quote Hitler or others like him in this section in order to give them credence. On the contrary, we quote them to identify the source of their evil and make sure their ideas haven't seeped into our own philosophies.)

ANTI-MIND AND ANTI-LIFE

Collectivism is anti-mind because in valuing the group over the individual, it denies the source of wealth and man's tool of survival—his mind. There is no such thing as a "collective mind" and in denying man's tool of survival, collectivism is anti-life. Isabel Paterson observed in *The God of the Machine*, that "Thinking is an individual function. Therefore the collectivist, to attain his objective . . . seeks the . . . political agency which is directly prohibitory and must tend to stop men thinking."[5]

Auguste Comte denied that individual achievement was even possible, instead attributing success to collective action. "We are not to encourage the foolish and immoral pride of modern capitalists, who look upon themselves as the creators and sole arbiters of their material power," he wrote, "the foundations of which are in reality due to the combined action of their predecessors and contemporaries. They ought to be regarded simply as public functionaries, responsible for the administration of capital and the direction of industrial enterprise."[6]

Producers were to be regarded as lever-pulling, pencil-pushing functionaries whose minds did not create anything new and must merely administer what they were lucky enough to be in charge of. This is denial

---

[4] Quoted in Peikoff, *OP*, 13.

[5] Paterson, Isabel. *The God of the Machine* (Originally published in 1943. Qualiteri eBook, 2009), Chapter 14.

[6] Lenzer, Gertrude, ed. *Auguste Comte and Positivism* (New Brunswick, New Jersey: Transaction Publishers, 2006), 386.

that the human mind can do anything or create anything—anti-mind. The same ideas are seen today in such statements as Barack Obama's comment to business owners, "If you've got a business—you didn't build that. Somebody else made that happen."[7] However, a whisper of the truth seems to disturb Comte as he warns us that, "At the same time we must be careful not to underrate the immense value of their function, or in any way obstruct its performance." Why leave producers alone if they do not create anything and merely direct industrial work? No answer. The role of man's mind must be evaded in all collectivist sentiment.

Even Adam Smith, in his deepest moral philosophy, succumbed to collectivism, writing that, "The wise and virtuous man is at all times willing that his own private interest should be sacrificed to the public interest . . . He is at all times willing, too, that the interest of this order or society be should be sacrificed to the greater interest of the state . . . he should, therefore, be equally willing that all those inferior interests should be sacrificed to the greater interest of [all beings]."[8]

We are told an individual must sacrifice himself to the collective because that is what is right. Why?

Immanuel Kant answers that such "moral" action (sacrifice) is an end to itself, not a means to an end. Virtue must have nothing to do with the pursuit of any rewards or man's happiness, he tells us. In Kant's view, the "principle of one's own happiness is the most objectionable of all" because it seeks to incentivize morality which thus destroys its "sublimity." Kant and all his collectivist followers hold that man's purpose is not his "preservation . . . welfare, [or] happiness . . ."[9] Man's purpose is his duty to others, and his morality is in the performance of that duty with no hope of reward, whether physical or spiritual. Kant began with, "You are nothing." Hitler finished with, "Your people (volk) are everything." Kant began with, "Sacrifice for others." Karl Marx finished with, "Sacrifice all to all."

Now we will turn to an examination of the various flavors of collectivism that we encounter today. These groups may all disagree on particulars, but not on the fundamental principles that unite them. After reading the following pages you will be able to define and identify the most common forms of collectivism, in philosophies and governments,

---

[7] Obama, Barack. "Remarks by the President at a Campaign event in Roanoke, Virginia." 13 Jul 2012. whitehouse.gov/the-press-office/2012/07/13/remarks-president-campaign-event-roanoke-virginia. Accessed 9 Aug 2012.
[8] Quoted in Peikoff, *OP*, 73.
[9] *ibid*, 74.

and also be able to identify the underlying ethic that ties them all together. Since thought precedes action, and philosophy precedes a political system, we will begin with the collectivist philosophies in "The Philosophy of Evil" chapter, and end with collectivist politics in action in "The Politics of Evil" chapter.

CHAPTER 11

THE PHILOSOPHY OF EVIL

PART 1: THE COLLECTIVISTS' CODE OF ETHICS

Among all the various weaves of collectivism that we will discuss, there will be a common ethical thread running throughout this tapestry. See if you can identify it in the following quote:

"This self-sacrificing will to give one's personal labor and if necessary, one's own life for others is most strongly developed in the [American]. The [American] is not greatest in his mental qualities as such, but in the extent of his willingness to put all his abilities in the service of the community. In him the instinct of self-preservation has reached the noblest form, since he willingly subordinates his own ego to the life of the community and, if the hour demands, even sacrifices it."[1]

---

[1] Hitler, Adolf. Ralph Manheim, trans. *Mein Kampf* (Houghton Mifflin: New York, 1999), 297.

Again, that quote is from Adolf Hitler, only he was speaking of the Aryan people, not the American. One of history's most evil men used a

AUGUSTE COMTE

"moral" argument to further his diabolical agenda. His speeches and writings abound with this constant theme which unifies all the evils of these various "-isms" we will discuss into one organic and ethical whole. That moral fabric is the morality of selflessness, i.e. altruism.

This last term is attributed to French philosopher Auguste Comte who advocated a social system (called Positivism) based entirely on the subjugation of the individual to the collective. He rejected individual rights and advocated social duties; he sought after a Religion of Humanity administered by the State which would discourage outbreaks of "personality."

"Alter" is Latin for "Other"; the word altruism literally means other-ism. It is simply the ethical imperative to live for others.

Dictionary.com defines altruism as:

1. The principle or practice of unselfish concern for the welfare of others;
2. The philosophical doctrine that right action is that which produces the greatest benefit to others.

Altruism should not be confused with merely being helpful or kind or giving service, though it is often mistakenly used to mean such. Bill Gates would probably not be called altruistic by most people, charitable activities aside, even though he has made more people wealthier, and helped and served more people on the planet than almost anyone else. He will not be called that because he did it by trade for profit. The core meaning of altruism is that service for others must be done self-sacrificially—at a cost to you, not at a benefit.

Immanuel Kant was another leading philosophical father of altruism. He taught that an act is only moral if we have no desire to perform it, and we do not receive any benefit from it whatsoever, whether material or spiritual. Read that last sentence again.

If we want to help someone because we like them and we would be happy to see them be helped in some way, that is not moral at all, says Kant. "To be beneficent when we can is a duty [he does not explain why this is a duty, it just is]; and besides this there are many minds so sympa-thetically constituted that, without any other motive of vanity or self-interest, they find pleasure in spreading joy around them and can take delight in the satisfaction of others . . . . [This] lacks the moral import, namely, that such actions be done from duty, not from inclination."[2]

The fact that we get any enjoyment out of it means that it was self-interested, not altruistic, and thus immoral in Kant's view. Altruism holds that we must serve others because we do not want to—it is a matter of duty, rather than choice. There must not be any ulterior motive in serving others, we are told. The help we give must not be as a trader, giv-ing value for value, with everyone going away wealthier. The help must be self-sacrificial, only being considered moral if the other benefits from your loss. For altruists like Kant, "An action done from duty must wholly exclude the influence of inclination and . . . I should follow this law even to the thwarting of all my inclinations."[3] Happiness and prosperity are not the purpose of man's life, he tells us, "our existence has a different and far nobler end, for which, and not for happiness, reason is properly intended . . ."[4] What is the end he proclaims? We asked this question at the beginning of this book. Now is time for the answer: man's purpose, according to altruists like Kant, is a duty to sacrifice for others.

In addition, it is astounding to consider that Kant was clear in pro-claiming that this altruist ethic has no basis or reason for its existence! He considered moral laws to be separate from and even contrary to the laws of reality. "But it is otherwise with moral laws. These, [are] in contradis-tinction to natural laws."[5] We cannot base our moral principles on our life experiences, he says. Those are only practical matters, not moral. "Conceptions and judgments regarding ourselves and our conduct have no moral significance, if they contain only what may be learned from ex-perience."[6] Reality has no relevance to morality, he proclaims.[7] "Moral principles are not based on properties of human nature, but must subsist a priori [independent of experience] of themselves . . ." and ". . . it is this

---

[2] Kant, Immanuel. *The Critique of Pure Reason, The Critique of Practical Reason and Other Ethical Treatises, The Critique of Judgment* (Chicago: Encyclopedia Britannica, 1978), 258.

[3] *ibid*, 259.

[4] *ibid*, 257.

[5] *ibid*, 387.

[6] *ibid*, 387.

[7] *ibid*, 254.

purity of their origin that makes them worthy to serve . . ."[8] The fact that altruism has no good reason "in heaven or earth" is what makes it sublime.[9] Virtue, he says, is morality that has been stripped of "sensible things and of every spurious ornament of reward or self-love."[10] This is the anti-self-interest ethic, and what is anti-self is also anti-life.

The link between altruism and collectivism can be seen when we ask the question, "Which other should I serve?" Altruism gives no answer to you, because it doesn't matter who is served as long as it is not you. The good is not found in the action or in the receiver; the good is found intrinsically in the fact that you sacrificed.

Collectivism, however, provides the answer: it is society, or the collective, that must be served. Collectivism also provides the means to such service: the State. Since sacrifice for others is held a moral imperative, the altruist-collectivist ethic holds that it is therefore moral to force others to do the proper sacrificing.

John Stuart Mills wrote that the foundation of morality is "the greatest happiness principle" which holds that "the standard of what is right in conduct is not the agent's own happiness but that of all concerned."[11]

But, there is one question which the ethics of collectivism has never answered and never will: "Why?"

Why must I live for others?

Why is that the good?

Why is my own life the standard of evil?

Why is it moral to serve the happiness of others but never my own?

There has never been a rational reason for it, though there have been many ugly distortions of philosophy and religious doctrine to try and cover for that failure.

While this is not a book designed to treat religious issues, we can address two of the most common Christian altruistic fallacies based on the following:

---

[8] *ibid*, 263.

[9] *ibid*, 270.

[10] *ibid*, 271.

[11] Mill, John, Stuart. *Utilitarianism* (Indianapolis: Hackett, 2001), 17

1. The Golden Rule:
Do unto others as you would have them do unto you.

2. Love thy neighbor as thyself.

The altruistic distortions of these mantras are self-contradictory at best, and blatantly evil at worst. The standard of value found in both of these proverbs is individual life and happiness. Whose life and happiness is the standard used for the measurement? Yours.

How are we told to love others? As ourselves. Our self-love is the standard. We can't love them until we love ourselves. What is the standard given to judge how to treat another person in both of these phrases? Our rational self-interest.

In order to love another, whom must you first love and know the best way to love? Yourself.

The only rational interpretation of these proverbs is that one must have a moral code using individual rights to guide your own actions and the actions of others towards you. The alternative is a whim-based subjective code where each person treats another according to their feelings or demands. Self-interest, or self-love, is the true standard behind these maxims, yet altruism would have you believe that these must be interpreted as "Do unto others as they would have done unto them, regardless of the cost to you," and "Love Thy Neighbor More Than Thyself."

THE CRUSADE AGAINST THE SELF

The collectivist ethical crusade to destroy the concept of self-interest is widespread and active, both consciously and unconsciously, among today's "intellectuals." Professor Zygmunt Bauman passively states that, "It is true that objectively good—helpful and useful—deeds have been time and again performed out of the actor's calculation of gain . . . these deeds, however, cannot be classified as genuinely moral acts precisely because of having been so motivated."[12] He makes no attempt to explain this view, to explain why personal gain is anathema to the concept of morality. He takes, as a given, that altruism is morality, that help-

---

[12] Bauman, Zygmunt. *Does Ethics Have A Chance In A World of Consumers?* (Cambridge, Massachusetts: Harvard University Press, 2008), 62.

ing people out of a desire for personal gain is immoral, and that morality consists in serving others self-sacrificially.

Despite clear descriptions of the altruist code, coming from St. Augustine, Kant, Comte, Hitler or modern presidents and legislators, this code is consistently mistaken by many as meaning kindness, charity, and helping others. Gary Morsch and Dean Nelson, in their touching book, *The Power of Serving Others*, characterize altruism as "acting for the welfare of others as well as oneself."[13] As we have seen, altruism is not meant to be helping others "as well as oneself," but at a self-sacrificial cost.

Self-interest is the principle that is violated by the creed of the altruists for no other reason than that it does not sacrifice. It was one of Hitler's common insults to hurl at the Jews, that "The Jew is led by nothing but the naked egoism of the individual."[14]

The philosophical attack against individualism and self-interest is relentless. Your bread is not moral in your own belly, you are told, but only in the bellies of others. It is immoral to earn money, but not to give it to others who did not earn it. The basic altruist principle here is that man does not have the right to exist for himself, but only to exist as a means to the ends of others, whether those others are the proletariat, the State, society, or the world. The code of altruism does not care which "others" are referred to, but only that the self is denied as a matter of moral duty. This is the cause of the bloodshed and tyranny wreaked by history's tyrant-altruists.

John Stuart Mill wrote in *Utilitarianism* that, "It is a part of the notion of duty in every one of its forms that a person may rightfully be compelled to fulfill it. Duty is a thing which may be exacted from a person, as one exacts a debt."[15] If altruism is our moral duty, then we may be rightfully compelled to self-sacrifice.

The belief that we must serve others self-sacrificially is the root cause of many misguided government policies, from financial and mortgage policies mandating that the taxpayer pay for defaulted loans of those who otherwise would not have qualified, to military policy which demands that American soldiers hold the lives of enemy civilians above their own safety, to financial bailouts of foreign nations at the altruistic expense of American citizens.

---

[13] Morsch, Gary. and Dean Nelson. *The Power of Serving Others*. (San Francisco: Berrett-Koehler Publishers, 2006), 3.

[14] Hitler, *Kampf*, 302.

[15] Mill, *Utilitarianism*, 49.

Ayn Rand put it most strongly when she said, "Since nature does not provide man with an automatic form of survival, since he has to support his life by his own effort, the doctrine that concern with one's own interests is evil means that man's desire to live is evil—that man's life, as such, is evil. No doctrine could be more evil than that. Yet that is the meaning of altruism."[16]

(For an excellent explanation of how altruism doesn't just ruin nations, but individual romantic relationships as well, see *The Selfish Path to Romance: How to Love with Passion and Reason*, by Edwin A. Locke and Ellen Kenner.)

PART 2: PRAGMATISM

"There is no such thing as truth, either in the moral or in the scientific sense."[17] - Adolf Hitler

As a philosophy, "pragmatism" does not simply mean doing what works best. Pragmatism (with a capital "P") is an American-based philosophy that surfaced in the late 19th century and flourished among intellectuals, professors, Progressives, and liberals. It is responsible for much of the collapse of any possible philosophical, intellectual, principled, or moral approach to modern political discussions. Early pragmatists included C. S. Pierce, William James, and John Dewey.

It is difficult to define concretely because it is not so much a set of doctrines as a way of thinking. It is a "big tent" theory that seeks to include a host of conflicting beliefs and ideologies. It is a method of thinking that consists of determining the meaning of truth based on "practical consequences." It gives no method for answering, "Which consequences? How are we to measure consequences? What is the standard of practicality? Which ends are desirable to advance?"[18]

Pragmatism holds that there is no permanent truth, no absolute principles, no objective reality, and that collective subjectivism identifies truth. It is the doctrine that philosophy must be "practical" and the truth is whatever "works."

---

[16] Rand, Ayn. *The Virtue of Selfishness* (New York: Signet, 1964), ix.
[17] Peikoff, *OP*, 59.
[18] Smith, Tara. "The Menace of Pragmatism." *The Objective Standard*. Fall 2008. Online. theobjectivestandard.com/issues/2008-fall/menace-of-pragmatism.asp. Accessed 30 Apr 2011.

JOHN DEWEY

This doctrine quickly leads to relativism, if it is not already underpinned by it, which holds that an idea is only judged as true or false according to its utility in a particular situation, that what works today may not work tomorrow, and thus there are no principles in any field, no absolutes.

For the Pragmatists there is no ready-made reality. We create reality, they say. Thus there are no absolutes, no facts, no laws of logic, and no certainty. What must be done away with, James said, is "truth independent; truth that we find merely; truth no longer malleable to human need." The "true," he said, "is only the expedient in the way of our thinking, just as 'the right' is only the expedient in the way of our behaving."[19]

Tara Smith, professor of philosophy at the University of Texas, masterfully distilled the Pragmatist style of thinking into four succinct features:

1. A short-range perspective. Pragmatism involves range-of-the-moment thinking. The measurement of truth is what works, and that "since reality has no definite, enduring nature, what works today may be quite different from what works tomorrow." The here and now is what is most important.
2. The inability (or refusal) to think in principle. "Pragmatism rejects principles and erodes its practitioners' ability to grasp principles, let alone apply and be governed by them."
3. The denial of definite identity. "The pragmatist characteristically resists identifying things by their essential nature. Whatever the subject of inquiry, each thing is regarded as sort of this and sort of that." "To name things—to clearly identify or define an entity, an event, a policy, or any phenomenon—would be unrealistically constraining."

---

[19] Quoted in Peikoff, *OP*, 58.

4. The refusal to rule out possibilities. "When it comes to decision-making, the pragmatist's inclination is to keep all options open—indefinitely. Whether he is negotiating differences with others or making a solitary, primarily self-regarding decision, nothing is ever off the table. After all, there is nothing that might not be 'expedient' someday."[20]

Author Leonard Peikoff identified Pragmatism as being one of the two core doctrines of the Nazis (the other being dogmatism).[21] Hitler latched onto Pragmatism very soundly, stating in Mein Kampf that the standard for ideas is not logic or fact, but the idea's usefulness (i.e. practicality) to the Volk. "The needs of the state . . . are the sole determining factor. What may be necessary today need not be necessary tomorrow," Hitler said. "That is not a question of theoretical suppositions, but of practical decisions dictated by existing circumstances. Therefore, I may—nay, must—change or repudiate under changed conditions tomorrow what I consider correct today." And as his Minister of Propaganda, Joseph Goebbels, said, "Important is not what is right but what wins."[22]

Another of Pragmatism's earliest advocates was John Dewey, an American philosopher and education reformer. He said, "If we start from reason alone, we shall never reach fact."[23] Using Pragmatism as the moral impetus for statism and Progressivism proved very effective. Dewey advocated the "use of unchecked state power to control the future through shaping the thought, action, and character of its citizens." Pragmatism "provided the moral dexterity" necessary to Marxist politicians, offering a philosophy that translated questions of moral value into "problems of strategy" and defined principles as "the expedient within a given set of social circumstances."[24] Metaphorically, Pragmatism is the railroad track that takes the train of statism on its journey.

As long as Pragmatism thrives either consciously or unconsciously in America, personal liberties will continue to be trampled as government expands. People will have no political principles to base their decisions on, believing that no such things are possible or desirable. As Dewey said, the chief characteristic of the Pragmatic notion of reality is precisely "that

---

[20] Smith, "Pragmatism," Online.

[21] Peikoff, *OP*, 54.

[22] *ibid*, 59.

[23] Quoted in Westbrook, Robert. *John Dewey and American Democracy* (Ithaca and London: Cornell University Press, 1991), 27.

[24] Westbrook, *Dewey*, 186.

no theory of reality in general . . . is possible or needed."[25] This describes the root of the Pragmatic line of thinking—that there is no way to know about reality and no point to knowing anyway. The only thing that matters is whatever seems to work to help you accomplish a certain aim—knowing why it works, or how to interpret a principle for long-range planning is impossible and unnecessary.

SUBJECTIVISM

Implicit in Pragmatism is the doctrine of subjectivism—which holds that feelings create facts and therefore man's primary tool of knowledge is feelings. If men feel it, that makes it so. Recall that subjectivism may be divided into two kinds: personal and social.

Personal subjectivism is the idea that truth and morality are creations of the mind of the individual—or "matters of personal opinion." Its slogans are "Who's to say what's right?" and "What's true for you may not be true for me." The personal subjectivist values whatever he feels like valuing and does whatever he feels like doing. Taken to an extreme, he is seen as a follower of hedonism—which holds that morality is acting in whatever manner gives you pleasure. (See "Rational Self-Interest" in Chapter 3 to review how hedonism is not to be confused with self-interest.)

Social subjectivism is the notion that truth and morality are creations of the mind of a collective—or "matters of social convention."[26] The consensus of the majority is the source of all truth for the social subjectivist.

The important key to understand in respect to these ideas is that they hold the belief that truth and morality are created by man, rather than discovered.

The foundational morality of social subjectivism is that you don't place yourself, your own judgment and values, above those of the group, or "common good." You must subordinate your interests to the whole, of which you are merely a part.

---

[25] Menand, Louis, ed. *Pragmatism: A Reader* (New York: Vintage Books, 1997), 223.

[26] Biddle, Craig. *Loving Life: The Morality of Self-Interest and the Facts That Support It* (Richmond, Virginia: Glen Allen Press, 2002), 7.

THE MIXED ECONOMY

The economic system that is the result of subjectivist/Pragmatist philosophy is that of the mixed economy. Today's economy in America and many other countries cannot be considered capitalist. To distinguish between what we have today and what is actually capitalism, many use the term "laissez-faire" capitalism, but that is merely redundant. Only an economy completely laissez-faire (hands-off) is capitalism; anything less is a mixed economy, meaning a mixture of freedom and controls, choice and coercion, individualism and collectivism.

This type of economy has no principles, rules, or theories to guide it. The introduction of controls into an economy always necessitates further controls. It is an unstable mixture which can only go one of two ways—the controls can be repealed towards freedom, or they can be compounded towards dictatorship. A mixed economy will always slide one way or the other.

No one's interests are ultimately safe in a mixed economy. It breaks a country into enemy camps fighting, looting, and draining the productive elements of the society. As Ayn Rand described it, "A mixed economy is rule by pressure groups. It is an amoral, institutionalized civil war of special interests and lobbies, all fighting to seize a momentary control of the legislative machinery, to extort some special privilege at one another's expense by an act of government—i.e. by force."[27]

A mixed economy gives rise to the dominance of lobbying. Lobbying is attempting to influence legislation by privately influencing legislators. This activity is the spawn of government-by-pressure-groups whose methods range from social courtesies and luncheons to threats, bribes, and blackmail. Professional lobbying is an activity which naturally stems from the Pragmatic idea that there are no principled reasons for doing anything, and the only way to get ahead is to squeeze concessions and favors out of those with the guns—i.e. the government. A mixed economy is built on the foundation of Pragmatism and subjectivism.

HOW TO FIGHT PRAGMATISM

Pragmatism denies the concept of unalienable rights. Jeremy Bentham described the idea of natural rights as "nonsense." He saw rights

---

[27] Rand, Ayn. "The New Fascism: Rule By Consensus." *Capitalism: The Unknown Ideal* (New York: Signet, 1967), 206-7.

merely as instruments to be used in the pursuit of certain objectives.[28] We've shown that rights are moral principles to guide man's conduct in a social context. Pragmatists deny this and use rights only insofar as they help to achieve a desired end. If it seems that the end would be best accomplished by abrogating those rights, instead, then so be it. It is this line of thinking that leads governments, such as China, to deny any rights to achieve a desired aim. For example, they deny the liberty-based right to reproduce in favor of the Pragmatic goal of population control.

Combating the destructiveness of Pragmatism can be difficult. To do so, we must know what principles our thinking is founded on and what objective proof we have of their correctness. Still, Pragmatic opponents can be hard to get a grip on because they shift so quickly. It is difficult to argue with a method of arguing—especially one that denies the possibility of a correct method of arguing! Normally, as Professor Smith points out, "when a doctrine is mistaken, a rational argument can demonstrate that its conclusions do not follow from its premises or that its premises are false; one can point out faulty logic. Pragmatism, however, corrupts people's understanding of what logic is."[29]

She also offers a few tips on resisting pragmatism. First, is to identify it when you see it and name its failures, helping others to realize that Pragmatism is not actually practical.

Second, she encourages us to vigilantly police the meaning of words. Definitions are the first line of defense against irrationality.

Third, defend idealism and demonstrate the practical value and success of a devotion to ideals.

Smith also offers the counsel to avoid illegitimate compromise in the face of complexity. Do not give up trying to sort out a complex issue, but keep working to resolve it by using relevant principles.

---

[28] Sen, Amartya. *Development as Freedom* (New York: Alfred A. Knopf, 2000), 211.

[29] Smith, "Pragmatism," Online.

PART 3: PROGRESSIVISM

"Government does not stop with the protection of life, liberty, and property, as some have suggested; it goes on to serve every convenience of society."[30]
- Woodrow Wilson

Progressivism is a particularly virulent form of statism which appeared in America starting in the late 19th century and has been carried forward in varying degrees by most politicians since that time.

It is an outgrowth of Pragmatic philosophy. Historian Arthur Ekirch, Jr. identified Pragmatism as "the philosophy of the progressive movement," and that "pragmatists and progressives alike looked to the national state as the means of attaining their goals."[31] Theodore Roosevelt, Woodrow Wilson, FDR, John Dewey, Ted Kennedy, Hillary Clinton, John McCain, Barack Obama, and George W. Bush, are just a few examples of political figures who have had Progressivism deeply rooted in their political philosophy. Both major political parties currently hold Progressivism as an ideal, the only difference being in degree.

Progressivism, with statism as its main premise, aims for particular roles for the government to be achieved progressively over time. In effect, modern Progressives are just really patient dictators.

Ekirch, in his book *The Decline of American Liberalism*, described the Progressive movement as "not primarily a liberal movement . . . . In contrast to former American efforts at reform, progressivism was based on a new philosophy . . . which emphasized collective action through the instrumentality of the government." "Progressivism," he goes on, "[sought] greater concentration and centralization of political and economic power in the Federal government."[32]

John Dewey described the aim behind these Progressive statist reforms. To him, freedom was "individuality operating in and for the end of the common interest." He believed that everyone should be provided with equal opportunity, equipment, and resources to "enable him to put his powers thoroughly at the service of society . . . to give to society the

---

[30] Bell, H.C.F. *Woodrow Wilson and the People* (Garden City, New York: Doubleday, Doran, and Company, 1993), 60.
[31] Ekirch, Jr., Arthur. *The Decline of American Liberalism* (Oakland: The Independent Institute, 2009), 182.
[32] *ibid*, 171.

full benefits of what is in him."[33] The *professed* aim of Progressive ideology is to create good citizens and productive members of society, i.e. good servants of the collective. The *actual* aim of Progressive ideology is to seize control of every facet of human life.

Progressive goals historically included the following:

- The direct election of U.S. Senators;
- Women's Suffrage;
- Prohibition;
- Nationally directed "progressive" education;
- Trust busting;
- Child Labor Laws;
- Conservationism (National Parks, Wildlife Refuges, etc.);
- Work safety standards;
- Minimum Wage laws;
- Social Security;
- Unionization;
- Supervision and Regulation of Wall Street;
- Centralized banking and control of currency;
- Government-run health care;
- Amnesty and citizenship for illegal immigrants.

We can easily identify the explicit statism contained in Progressive theory. The following is an excerpt from a letter written to a friend by one of the titans of Progressivism, Woodrow Wilson: "Now the world is going to change radically, and I am satisfied that governments will have to do many things which are now left to individuals and corporations. I am satisfied for instance that the government will have to take over all the great natural resources . . . all the water power; all the coal mines; all the oil fields, etc. They will have to be government owned."[34]

Here are some statist principles from the Progressive Party platform of 1912:

- "It is time to set the public welfare in the first place."
    - o [In first place over what? Individual welfare.]
- "Up to the limit of the Constitution, and later by amendment of the Constitution, if found necessary, we advocate bringing

---

[33] Westbrook, Robert. *John Dewey and American Democracy* (Ithaca and London: Cornell University Press, 1991), 93.
[34] Bell, *Wilson*, 433.

under effective national jurisdiction those problems which have expanded beyond reach of the individual States."

- o [The States are not guaranteed to be Progressive enough. Bump everything up to the national level, disregarding the 10th Amendment and Jefferson's warning that we ought to "[support] the state governments in all their rights as the most competent administrations of domestic concerns."][35]
- "The supreme duty of the Nation is the conservation of human resources through an enlightened measure of social and industrial justice."
  - o [Humans aren't individuals; they are resources. See social justice under "Liberalism" later in this chapter.]
- "We demand that the test of true prosperity shall be the benefits conferred thereby on all the citizens, not confined to individuals or classes, and that the test of corporate efficiency shall be the ability better to serve the public; that those who profit by control of business affairs shall justify that profit and that control by sharing with the public the fruits thereof."
  - o [Serve better according to whose standards? Justify the profit to whom? This is a direct attack on the individual freedom of businessmen through vilification and confiscation of profits. The crucial issue evaded by Progressives is the difference between the earned and the unearned.]

The Administration of Woodrow Wilson advanced Progressive changes in government faster and more radically than any President prior and most since. He said, "I am a progressive. I do not spell it with a capital P, but I think my pace is just as fast as those who do."[36]

Some of the radical actions during his administration included establishing the Federal Reserve Bank, passing Sixteenth Amendment authorizing direct income taxes, establishing the Federal Trade Commission to regulate business practices, the Espionage and Sedition Acts to suppress anti-war protests, establishing the propaganda and censorship Committee on Public Information, instituting the first military draft since the Civil War, and taking over the railroads.

---

[35] Safire, William, ed. *Lend Me Your Ears: Great Speeches in History* (New York: W. W. Norton & Company, 1992), 727.
[36] Bell, *Wilson*, 351.

Why did he do all this? His political philosophy was drastically different than that of the Founders. Wilson's policies came to be known as the New Freedom. "New," in this case, is used to identify the Progressive concept of freedom as different from that of the "Old," or that of the Founders. Wilson described it this way, "[M]ust not government lay aside all timid scruple and boldly make itself an agency for social reform as well as for political control?"[37]

WOODROW WILSON

Compare these views with Thomas Jefferson who described the "Old Freedom" in his first inaugural address: "A wise and frugal government, which shall restrain men from injuring one another, shall leave them otherwise free to regulate their own pursuits of industry and improvement, and shall not take from the mouth of labor the bread it has earned. This is the sum of good government . . . . Equal and exact justice to all men, of whatever state or persuasion, religious or political."[38]

This is why Tara Smith urges us to protect the meaning of words. Notice how the concept of freedom is destroyed and how language is corrupted by Pragmatic Progressivism. Freedom is to be unhampered by the force of others, to make choices according to one's own will. "New" freedom removes the ability to make one's own decisions and instead imposes governmental force against citizens—the exact opposite of freedom. In other words, to quote George Orwell's *1984*, "Freedom is slavery."

Ekirch also identified how Progressivism was deeply rooted in collectivism, explaining how "Progressives [argued that] society in the future would have to be based more and more on an explicit subordination of the individual to a collectivist, or nationalized, political and social order."[39]

Such a subordination of the individual was also apparent in other Progressive administrations. Theodore Roosevelt's "New Nationalism" and "Square Deal" expressed the "need to rise above material desires in

---

[37] Bell, *Wilson*, 60.
[38] Safire, *Great Speeches*, 727.
[39] Ekirch, *Liberalism*, 180.

order to serve a transcendent national purpose."[40] FDR's "New Deal" programs escalated these progressive experiments in a "planned economy." Lyndon B. Johnson's "Great Society" initiated major new spending across education, medical care, and other areas, allegedly aiming to eliminate poverty and racial injustice, but in fact increasing both.

Progressive ideas continue to permeate all major areas of today's political arena.

PART 4: NATIONALISM

"An intimate coupling of nationalism and a sense of social justice must be implanted in the young heart."[41] - Adolf Hitler

This is the collectivism which holds that the nation, not mankind as a whole, or the majority, or the race, or the class, is the favored group and the standard of value. The individual is held as of no value, except in relation to his service to the nation-state. Theodore Roosevelt described his New Nationalism as putting "the national need before sectional or personal advantage," and regarding the "executive power as steward of the public welfare."[42]

Nationalism has most notoriously been seen as a core belief of the National Socialist German Workers' Party—or Nazis. It was used by them as a counter to the Marxist view of an international socialism. In early days, the party was called the Nazis-Sozis, in reference to their belief in both Nationalism and Socialism. The Socialism was eventually dropped as redundant since, for the Nazis, Nationalism meant Socialism in practice. This nationalism, according to Hitler, meant the power of the nation over the individual in every aspect of life, including economics. It was also closely combined with racist and genocidal policies because of the view that the nation of Germany should only be composed of the race of Germans.

Nationalism can usefully be differentiated from patriotism. A patriot is proud of his country's virtues and seeks to correct its faults. A nationalist claims his country to be the greatest, regardless of its deficiencies and is aggressively contemptuous towards other nations. The patriot rec-

---

[40] Bell, *Wilson*, 351.

[41] Hitler, *Mein Kampf*, 427

[42] Roosevelt, Theodore. "The New Nationalism." 31 Aug 1910. theodore-roosevelt.com/images/research/speeches/ trnationalismspeech.pdf. Accessed 1 May 2011.

ognizes what the nationalist does not: that a country need not be great, only good.

PART 5: POLITICAL PARTIES

"If I could not go to heaven but with a party, I would not go there at all."[43]
- Thomas Jefferson

Political parties encourage collectivism on a sweeping scale. A "party" is a group of individuals who decide to designate themselves as holding a particular set of ideas and principles about the philosophy of government, usually designated in a platform. This is all well and good and the right of free citizens.

However, the various parties take their strategy beyond the mark by advocating decisions based on membership and loyalty to a group—rather than encouraging the consideration of an individual candidate's views and beliefs. "The good of the party" is touted as the highest good, and even a disagreeable candidate is supported as a "lesser evil" to the choice offered by a rival party.

"Vote for me," we are often told. "Not for who I am and what I believe, but because I have a (D) or an (R) next to my name." The power of a political party, as Hitler pointed out, is not found "in the greatest possible independent intellect of the individual members, but rather in the disciplined obedience with which its members follow the intellectual leadership."[44]

To correct this, to get past the false two-party system that is handed to us, requires something very simple—vote your conscience. Vote for principles, not party; donate to people, not party; don't ever vote for the lesser of two evils—it is still a vote for evil. Vote for a third party or write in another candidate if you must, even if you think it will change nothing. Never vote for an increase in political power, only for an increase in character and principle.

---

[43] Peterson, Merrill, ed. *The Political Writings of Thomas Jefferson* (Annapolis Junction, Maryland: Thomas Jefferson Memorial Foundation, 1993), 88-89.
[44] Hitler, *Mein Kampf*, 457.

PART 6: LIBERALISM

Liberalism is a broad term with an interesting history. As its name implies, it is an idea founded in liberty and equality. It can best be understood in America today if divided into two distinct categories—classical liberalism and social liberalism.

CLASSICAL LIBERALISM

This is a political ideology that developed over the course of several centuries in England, Western Europe, and the Americas. It is committed to the ideal of liberty of individuals and limited government, and includes freedom of religion, speech, press, assembly, and markets. Classical liberals included John Locke, Thomas Jefferson, and Frederic Bastiat. This theory was revived in the 20th century by such people as Ronald Reagan, Ludwig von Mises, and Friedrich Hayek.

In the latter part of the 19th century, however, and in the early decades of the 20th century, the term "liberalism" came to mean something else entirely. In America today, "liberalism" most often means Social Liberalism.

SOCIAL LIBERALISM

This is the belief that liberalism should include "social justice." It differs from classical liberalism in that it recognizes a role for government in addressing economic and social issues such as unemployment, health care, and education while simultaneously expanding government-granted privileges.

Social liberalism is a self-contradictory ideology which takes the root of liberalism—the liberty of individuals—and bastardizes it as a spawn of collectivism. To understand this claim we must examine the concept of "social justice."

Justice is a concept of moral rightness based on ethics, natural law, and equity; it is granting that which has been earned. America was founded on the implicit concept of "equal justice"—which means equal rights, protections, and treatments under the law for all individuals. Men are created equal and are thus guaranteed equal protection of their rights.

What happens when we add collectivist theory to the mix? Then we consider men as not having merely the right of life, liberty, and property, but the right to various other things. Men must be provided with health care, housing, swimming pools, and internet service. Essentially, men are not sovereign individuals, but ignorant cattle to be taken care of as resources of the nation—as a rancher would care for his herd. Therefore, men must have the right to employment, medication, education, housing, a living wage, retirement income, etc. This means the role of government—under social justice—is to provide those rights.

This is a violation of principle. Remember, there is no such thing as a right which must be provided by someone else. Here is where the advocates of social liberalism and social justice reach a mental wall—a blank-out. The government must provide those "rights," which means someone must be forced to provide them. This is contradictory to the historical root of liberalism which is equal individual rights. "Social justice" is a gross perversion of the concept of justice. It is, in fact, the exact opposite.

The concept of social justice assumes one of two things. First, these rights are to be provided miraculously out of a vacuum from the all-powerful, magical force of Government. Second, it asserts that the rights of some groups are more important and supersede the rights of other groups. Everyone is equal, but some are more equal than others.

Sometimes, the term social justice is used to describe the movement towards a "socially just" world. It is a movement to create not a level playing field, but the complete equality of players, and this is done by draining the resources of one to give to another. In this context, social justice is achieved through progressive taxation, income redistribution, or even property redistribution. Justice, in this perverted sense, is only achieved when all people have equal things, not equal rights.

Modern liberals differ from socialists not in theory, but in degree of practice, as they will likely try to limit government actions at the point where they feel a decent quality of life is guaranteed for the poor. A major problem here, though, is that the more their policies are put into effect, the greater the hardships that the poor experience, so they are always advocating for more "fixes" to the ever-escalating difficulties. Modern liberals are less likely to approve of the nationalization of industry than are socialists. Liberals tend to favor statist, or even fascist solutions to issues (terms we will discuss), looking to government to provide their desires rather than innovation, persuasion, and cooperation.

In the alleged interest of protecting rights, social liberals (closely linked with Progressives) have flipped 180 degrees from the original liberal ideas of free markets and limited governments; and now, regulated markets and expanding government controls are the order of the day. Unfortunately, it's not much different for their more conservative counterparts.

PART 7: CONSERVATISM

This political and social theory promotes the maintenance of traditional institutions and to "conserve" or "preserve" things as they are or even return them to what they were. American conservatives have historically differed from those in Europe by never advocating aristocracy or monarchy. Modern conservatism holds views closer to that of classical liberalism than of classical conservatism. They are in many ways attempting to conserve and preserve the old ways of classical liberalism. However, in other ways, they are not.

There are a few basic conservative principles among most factions of conservatism:

- Respect for the U.S. Constitution and the rule of law on which it is based;
- Respect for life as a natural, inherent, and unalienable right for all individuals at all stages;
- An insistence of "limited" government so as to minimize conflict with each individual's rights and freedoms;
- Personal responsibility—the idea that the individual is accountable for all of his actions.

The U.S. Constitution is held as the ultimate standard for traditional conservatism—it is the core foundation on which to base all the conserving and preserving. As we have seen, it is a fine, albeit imperfect, document with many loopholes and imprecise language that has been thoroughly taken advantage of or even outright ignored over many decades to bring us where we are today. While an earlier stage of our cancer may be desirable in that we would have a better chance to beat it, it still means we have cancer. Conservatives generally accept the philosophy that too much cancer is bad, but that we still have to have a little to get by.

Conservatives mostly claim to base their political philosophy, not on a defined set of principles, but either on tradition or the Constitution. In this way, they substitute a reference to a legal or traditional framework in place of an understanding of the proper role of government. A major drawback to this line of thinking is that in answer to a "Why?" the conservatives will have little reason beyond an impassioned, "It's unconstitutional!" That can often be a good legal reason, but as a moral reason it fails to say why something should or shouldn't be in the Constitution in the first place.

Modern American conservatism can sometimes best be understood in three groups: fiscal conservatism, social conservatism, and compassionate conservatism.

FISCAL CONSERVATISM

Fiscal conservatives support limited government, limited taxation, and a balanced budget. They argue that competition in the free market is more effective than the regulation of industry. Like liberals, they have a self-contradictory ideology which supports some taxation and some social programs, failing to recognize that "limited" government is different than "proper" government. A small tyranny is acceptable to those unable to quite identify the correct purpose of governmental force. They support free markets on practical or traditional grounds, not moral grounds. The free market is desirable because it is what works best, they say. They will run for public office pledging to do away with "excessive" regulation of small business and "excessive" taxation, not perceiving that this is an impossible concept to define. What is excessive? To whom? Why is a larger degree of fascism less desirable than a smaller degree? Fiscal conservatives accept the philosophical premises of the liberals they claim to oppose. They merely want to advance those ideas to a lesser degree and by alternative methods.

SOCIAL CONSERVATISM

Social conservatives defend social norms, values, and local customs. They strongly identify with American patriotism, supporting the military and police, and they emphasize traditional views of social units such as family and church. Social conservatism has also been infected with statism, and many conservatives now seek to use federal power to block local state actions they disagree with. Thus came the "No Child Left Behind" educational program, support for a Constitutional amendment opposing same-sex marriage, and support for federal laws attempting to overrule states' attempts for legalized marijuana or assisted suicide. They have no problem using the force of government to uphold their idea of public morality concerning everything from gambling to doing business on Sunday to dress codes. They do this while ignoring the true morality of advocating change without force—such as through persuasion, education, and voluntary boycotts.

The challenge with conservatives is that most don't have political principles so much as political issues. On some issues they are the lone force for good, but without principles they cannot chart a straight course.

They are like rock climbers attempting to free climb with no safety gear: their footing slips and they have nothing to catch them.

COMPASSIONATE CONSERVATISM

In 1999, George W. Bush began to frequently use this term to describe his views. This conservatism includes the moral philosophy that we, in partnership with our government, have a duty to serve the needs of the sick, homeless, poor, and the aged. "Compassion" refers to desiring to relieve the pain and suffering of others.

Compassionate conservatives fully accept the liberal notion that we have a duty to help the poor; they merely differ from social liberals on how to help them. As soon as they substitute duty for desire, compassion becomes compulsion.

These conservatives say the Federal Government is inefficient and unfair in its management of the welfare state and that these services should be outsourced to community, civic, and church groups who are closer to the problems and can better and more equitably manage them.

As writer C. Bradley Thompson explains, compassion is a sub-rational moral guide. It processes political topics emotionally through a "no-fault" morality, saying, "Don't judge people, just accept their plight and help them." This denies the Law of Causality, asking you to ignore what caused the jobless person to be jobless, what caused the elderly to have saved nothing for retirement, or why those with coastal homes did not have insurance—you just need to give them a job, a retirement, and a home. (We can be charitable and voluntarily help others, but why shut off our minds and ignore the causes of why they need our help in the first place?)

Compassionate conservatism accepts the collectivist premise that man must live for the needs of others; solving the problems of the poor is the duty of society as a whole, and some people must be sacrificed for the greater good.[45]

Liberals are actually more consistent with their ideology. In holding statism as the primary means to a compassionate end, liberals are willing to go whole hog, while conservatives uncomfortably follow along, wanting to reach the same destination, just not quite as fast.

---

[45] Thompson, C. Bradley. "The Decline and Fall of American Conservatism." *The Objective Standard.* Fall 2006. Online. theobjectivestandard.com/issues/2006-fall/decline-fall-american-conservatism.asp. Accessed 11 Aug 2011.

This is why the national debt soared up by $4 trillion under President George W. Bush, and President Barack H. Obama beat that in half the time.[46]

The basic premises of compassionate conservatism are as follows:

- The needs of others constitute a moral claim on our lives and property;
- We, the taxpayers, have a duty to love and support the poor;
- The federal government must coerce our love and compassion by taking our wealth and giving it to private organizations that will use it to serve.

The Heritage Foundation, allegedly conservative in its views, resisted President Bush's prescription drug entitlement program, not on any principled grounds, but on the grounds that it cost too much, was too restrictive, and didn't give seniors enough choice. "There is no debate," they wrote, "over the need to assure that all seniors should have access to prescription drug coverage . . . The danger is that Congress will enact badly designed Medicare prescription drug benefits that end up dumping senior citizens out of the coverage they do have into a government program that will be plagued by explosive costs and constrained by regulatory restrictions on the availability of high-quality prescription drug coverage."[47]

In other words, conservatives agreed with the liberal welfare state in principle, and merely disagreed as to the means by which policies should be implemented. Thus we see that compassionate conservatives are merely thinly veiled social liberals.

---

[46] Knoller, Mark. "Bush Administration Adds $4 Trillion to National Debt." CBSNEWS. 29 Sep 2008. cbsnews.com/8301-500803_162-4486228-500803.html. Accessed 6 Mar 2011.

[47] The Heritage Foundation. "Time For a Sensible Medicare Drug Benefit." 23 Jul 2002. heritage.org/research/reports/2002/07/time-for-a-sensible-medicare-drug-benefit. Accessed 12 Aug 2011.

PART 8: RACISM

"Like every other form of collectivism, racism is a quest for the unearned . . . [for] automatic knowledge . . . [and] unearned self-esteem."[48] - Ayn Rand

Racism is the lowest and crudest form of collectivism, in part because we are biologically primed to mistrust that which is different. Racism usually refers to the belief that the collective group of one particular genetic ancestry is better/worse inherently than the collective group of another—that a group's skin, blood, race, or nationality somehow makes that group more/less human or more/less deserving. This collectivist thought is based in fear, ignorance, and inadequate self-esteem, resulting in the belief that one has value only in regard to one's race.

Peikoff observed that, "Every central doctrine of the Nazi politics, racism included, is an expression or variant of the theory of collectivism," and that the collectivism of the Nazis was more racist than nationalist, but they "were able to combine the two doctrines easily, by the device of holding that Germany contains the purest Aryan blood."[49]

A favorite idealist of the National Socialists was J. G. Fichte, who claimed the "individual life has no real existence since it has no value of itself, but must and should sink to nothing; while, on the contrary, the Race alone exists, since it alone ought to be looked upon as really living."[50] We can see here that collectivism has a literal, metaphysically different view of existence than that of individualism. Collectivists such as Fichte and Dewey described the collective as an actual living entity in reality, and denied that individuals really even exist by themselves! Somehow, they manage to miss the fact that for groups to exist, individuals must exist first.

Racism has more than one definition and is a much larger concept than how it is typically used in common discourse. Explicit racism—open antipathy for those of different ethnic and racial backgrounds as exemplified by the Nazis and KKK—is easy to see. But there is another kind of racism of which most people are completely unaware.

Implicit racism is unconsciously held beliefs and prejudices which create a social system that offers advantages and privileges for those of

---

[48] Rand, Ayn. and Peter Schwartz, ed. *Return of the Primitive: The Anti-Industrial Revolution* (New York: Penguin, 1999), 181.
[49] Peikoff, *OP*, 40-41.
[50] Quoted in *ibid*, 42.

lighter skin. Generally, when white people talk about racism, they usually mean the explicit kind—hating others based on race. But, when Black people talk about racism, they're usually referring to the more complex definition of implicit racism that involves the social structure.

Believing "racism" to only have one definition causes misunderstanding and can further racial tension. Have you ever been outraged to hear someone say, "Black people can't be racist"? Likely you wondered how someone could be so out of touch with reality. It's not that they were out of touch, they were simply referring to implicit racism—something most whites are ignorant of.

Racism is not merely prejudice. It is not merely thinking one race superior to another. It is a social system which rewards those with lighter skin and punishes those with darker skin. Please notice the word "system." In America, people with lighter skin have historically held more social and economic power and influence. As the majority culture, whites have driven the social ethos, and through millions of individual actions and decisions, a system is in place where discrimination exists. The only people with the power to discriminate on a meaningful scale are those on the top. Since the social system is based on skin color, those with dark skin are at the bottom of the social pecking order. In this system, therefore, Black people can't be racist in the implicit sense. They might explicitly hate those with lighter skin, but they have no power to oppress or discriminate on any significant scale.

There's a good chance you've never heard this topic discussed in such a way before. How can this be? It is because of socialization.

Socialization (in the non-political sense) is the process by which we unconsciously learn from our parents, friends, neighbors, and culture. We pick up the beliefs, attitudes, and philosophy of the culture we grow up in without knowing it. In this way, people are much like computers. Computers run on a basic operating system such as Microsoft Windows. The programming of the operating system determines how the computer works.

As people, we have an "operating system" that is made up of our core beliefs about the world. These core beliefs affect how we think, what we value, and how we make decisions. But our operating systems are not something we consciously created; the majority of our programming is written by the people around us and our culture long before we're ever old enough to realize it. The good news is we don't have to believe everything we were taught; the bad news is we can't change something we're unaware of. We do not have the option to decide what to keep and what to discard if we are ignorant of our beliefs and their roots. In order to change, we must become consciously aware of our beliefs, and through a process of rational deliberation, decide what to keep and what to reject.

Before you read this book, it's likely you'd never explicitly noted your collectivist beliefs. Unless someone pointed it out to you in the past, you had probably never questioned the idea that you must sacrifice your own good for others. You'd been raised to unquestioningly accept that we have no choice but to support the elderly with government programs. If you had been raised in ancient Egypt, you would have believed that the Pharaoh was a god on earth. If your father was a plantation owner in the 1800's you may have accepted slavery as normal and moral. If you were born in the Korowai tribe of New Guinea, you would think cannibalism was perfectly acceptable. We accept the beliefs and assumptions we are raised with. Even when people rebel it's still usually within the dichotomous set of choices offered by society. Children raised conservative become liberals, and vice versa. Heads and tails may seem separate and distinct, but they're still part of the same coin.

Society trained you with a philosophy that it never named or pointed out. As children, we accepted all of it. It's incredibly hard to discover our implicit beliefs because they are the lens through which we see the world. Just as light passes through the lens of our eye and is bent to focus on our retina, so our beliefs influence our very perception, and we can't exactly remove our eyes to get an objective view of how they work. In the same way we can't see the back of our own heads without a mirror, so we cannot see our worldview without external help.

The dominant culture has its own narrative that is written from its own perspective. For example, in most states the Civil War is called "The Civil War." But in some places in the South, it is still referred to as the "War of Northern Aggression." The victors write the history books, and they don't trouble themselves with understanding the perspective and motivations of the conquered. In the same way, the white cultural narrative doesn't incorporate the culture and perspective of minorities.

Our worldview is tied to our sense of identity. It provides an organizing framework by which we make sense of the world. Humans crave stability and security. Anything that shakes our worldview shakes our sense of self. We have a lot of psychological defense mechanisms that our unconscious mind uses to protect our conscious awareness from information that would challenge what we already believe.

Confirmation bias is one of these cognitive distortions we use to avoid the anxiety of questioning ourselves. Whenever we are exposed to information that supports our beliefs, we seize on it (usually taking it out of context) and remember it. Anything that challenges our beliefs is ignored. We have a tremendous capacity for self-deception, and are no different in this regard from the emperor with his new clothes. The most disturbing part is how insidious defense mechanisms are, not only do they avoid conscious detection by being primal, automatic, and instinctual, but they deny their own existence when challenged! It is pure arrogance to think we are unaffected by these universal human frailties.

A major factor in the creation of our worldview is our ethnicity and the culture we grow up in. A Black kid in the projects of Harlem is going to have a very different worldview than a white kid from Staten Island.[51] Their ethnicity will provide them a large portion of their identities and philosophy about life. The Black kid will face prejudice and racism. The white kid, as a member of the majority culture, will not face persistent, generalized discrimination. As a member of the dominant ethnicity, the white kid likely won't think of himself as having a specific culture, but will instead see white people as the normative status quo, the default, the standard by which all other things are judged. The white kid will assume his experiences have universality and likely never have to face what it means to be white.[52]

A PRO-RACIST IDEOLOGY

Why all this talk of worldview and the socialization process? Because racist tendencies have some biological predisposition and are unwittingly reinforced by the process of socialization. While most Americans find racism a horribly evil and ignorant ideology, even the most well-meaning of us may accidentally and unknowingly act in ways that support the superiority of whites. These unconscious, unintentional ac-

---

[51] While capitalizing "Black" goes against the typical standard used by media outlets and the AP Stylebook, we have chosen to capitalize in this book out of respect for the opinions of many Black authors who prefer to use it. Here's how one author explained his choice: "I have chosen to capitalize the word "Black" and lowercase "white" throughout this book. I believe "Black" constitutes a group, an ethnicity equivalent to African-American, Negro, or, in terms of a sense of ethnic cohesion, Irish, Polish, or Chinese. I don't believe that whiteness merits the same treatment. Most American whites think of themselves as Italian-American or Jewish or otherwise relating to other past connections that Blacks cannot make because of the familial and national disruptions of slavery. So to me, because Black speaks to an unknown familial/national past it deserves capitalization." Online. dcentric.wamu.org/2011/10/when-to-capatalize-black-and-white/index.html. Accessed 18 Jul 2014.
[52] Vice, Samantha. "How Do I Live in This Strange Place?" *Journal of Social Philosophy* (Wiley Periodicals, 2010), 41(3), 323-342.

tions and beliefs are known as a pro-racist ideology. A pro-racist ideology falls under the category of implicit racism and unconsciously supports a system of rewards and opportunities based on skin color and can also be manifested through tolerating and refusing to challenge racist conditions.[53]

Remember, we are born knowing nothing which means ignorance is our default condition. Unless we have specifically learned something, then we remain ignorant of that thing. You can't know anything until you learn it. Unless you have taken a graduate level class on cultural competency, you've likely never been exposed to these ideas in any depth. Unless you've taken time to consider and allowed yourself to be challenged, you likely remain ignorant of these issues. Hearing that you have a pro-racist ideology is likely making you feel angry, defensive, and perhaps like dismissing this book as hippie nonsense. If you're feeling challenged, that's an indication that you have some new information to thoughtfully consider. Keep in mind that having a pro-racist ideology doesn't mean you are an intractable, hate-filled bigot. It simply means that no one is exempt from the process of being socialized by the culture they grow up in. Like any other false indoctrination, these hidden beliefs and ways of acting need to be brought to light and eliminated.

Most white people never question their assumptions about race, let alone realize they even have assumptions about race. Having a pro-racist ideology is the automatic consequence of being unaware of how race shapes life and our everyday reality. The ability to completely ignore, remain unaware and unaffected by racial issues is one of the privileges of being white. And the ability to ignore racial matters means the assumed superiority of whites goes unchallenged within us.

There are hundreds of small and unnoticed ways we might exhibit a pro-racist ideology. For example, did you notice that the last few paragraphs make the implicit assumption that you, the reader, are white? Part of being the majority culture is viewing your race and culture as the normative standard. This would mean assuming the author is white and the audience will be too. Someone sensitive to racial issues would have noticed the slant immediately.

Just as fish don't know they're wet because they haven't experienced air, so white people do not know what it means to be white. Whites in America don't have the experience of growing up as a minority to pro-

---

[53] Hardy, Kenneth V. and Tracey A. Laszloffy. *The Dynamics of a Pro-Racist Ideology: Implications for Family Therapists*. Revisioning Family Therapy/ (2008) Guilford Press. New York, NY.

vide a contrast. Because whites don't face the negative effects of racism, they can remain blissfully unaware of its existence. Minorities do not have that option. Minorities are brought face to face with discrimination, prejudice, and implicit racism on a regular basis. They don't have the option to ignore racial issues. Even if a white person grew up as the only white in their neighborhood and was picked on, they are still connected to the majority culture, and it will be part of their identity.

Talking about race can be an uncomfortable experience for white people, especially for fear of being accused of being racist. Anxiety leads to defense mechanisms, which are often justified considering how often conservatives are accused of racism simply for disagreeing with a policy. One common defense mechanism is to deny racial issues exist. A variant of denial is to minimize the importance of racial issues. If you have found yourself being dismissive as you've read this section, you are refusing to consider racial topics with an open mind. If you are upset or emotionally reactive to this subject, it indicates you feel threatened by it.

Of course, part of denial is denying you're upset. There are other easy-to-see defense mechanisms. Have you ever caught yourself saying, "I don't see color"? Unless you're visually impaired, you see color. Whether you fixate on it is another matter. What about, "I have Black friends"? Having Black friends does not mean you're free from implicit biases. When faced with stories of racism, do you respond with examples of prejudiced minorities to prove it can go both ways? The fact that anyone can be prejudiced does not change or negate the reality of racism. When you've been told you have advantages and privileges because of white skin, have you responded with stories of your own struggles, how you worked hard for what you earned, and how nothing was handed to you on a silver platter? These responses are a reaction to the perception that you are being viewed as racist. To argue against statements like this implies that the issues don't exist or aren't important. If any of these examples have applied to you, it is an indication you have not fully explored your racial identity and your racial sensitivity could use work.

I, (Kenneth) was born well after Martin Luther King, Jr. was murdered. When I came on the scene, the Civil Rights movement was just something in the history books that seemed as far removed from me as World War I or the Wild West. I knew that the KKK and white supremacist groups still existed, but knowing only of explicit forms of racism made me think it wasn't really a large issue. I wondered to myself, "Why are we still talking about this? It's been more than a hundred years since the Emancipation Proclamation, and segregation ended before we even had color TV! Why can't we just move forward?"

At this point in my life, I was unaware of implicit racism, and largely unaware of how we can believe one thing consciously, but believe something completely different on a deeper level. Social psychologists have called this the "dual attitude system." This is how it is possible for a person to consciously reject racism while implicitly holding a pro-racist ideology. Again, we are not consciously aware of ideas we hold implicitly. I was unaware of how implicit beliefs translate into attitudes and behaviors.

On a very primitive level when humans see other entities, they make instinctive classification of "self" and "other." That which is not like us is the "other," and we have a visceral distrust and unease with that which is different. If they're not part of our tribe, they're an unknown, and thus a possible threat.

One expert explained how "different brain regions are involved in automatic and consciously controlled stereotyping. Pictures of outgroups that elicit the most disgust (such as drug addicts and the homeless) elicit brain activity in areas associated with disgust and avoidance. This suggests that automatic prejudices involve primitive regions of the brain associated with fear, such as the amygdala, whereas controlled processing is more closely associated with the frontal cortex, which enables conscious thinking. We also use different bits of our frontal lobes when thinking about ourselves or groups we identify with, versus when thinking about people that we perceive as dissimilar to us."[54]

Birds of a feather do not simply flock together; they also keep other species at a distance. This well-established behavior is called the in-group, out-group bias, and it is based on our attitudes and thoughts. We are biologically predisposed and society reinforces those beliefs. How can behaviors spring from implicit beliefs?

Here's some evidence as an example,

"1,115 identically worded emails were sent to Los Angeles area landlords regarding vacant apartments. Encouraging replies came back to 89 percent of notes signed 'Patrick McDougall,' to 66 percent from 'Said Al-Rahman,' and to 56 percent from 'Tyrell Jackson.' Other researchers have followed suit. When 4,859 U.S. state legislators received emails shortly before the 2008 election asking how to register to vote, 'Jake Mueller' re-

---

[54] Myers, David, G. *Social Psychology* (McGraw Hill, 2010), 310. Online. seospecialoffers.com/docs/highered__mheducation__com--sites--dl--free--0078035295--969688--mye35295_ch09__pdf.html. In-text citations have been removed. Accessed 3 Oct 2014.

ceived more replies than 'DeShawn Jackson,' though fewer from minority legislators. Likewise, Jewish Israeli students were less likely to alert the sender to a misaddressed email that came from an Arab name and town ('Muhammed Yunis of Ashdod') rather than from one of their own group ('Yoav Marom of Tel Aviv')."[55]

As this small example shows, our in-group, out-group biases make us treat people differently based on whether they're "one of us."

WHITE PRIVILEDGE

You've probably heard the expression "white privilege." Among other things, white privilege is comprised of benefits and advantages which minorities lack. In the previous example, the privilege of being white was manifested by being more likely to be responded to, which can translate into having an easier time finding housing, or receiving information. White privilege is partially the privilege of not having to face discrimination based on skin color.

Because whites have been in the majority in America, they are in a position to sustain the implicit belief that whites are superior. Since the pro-racist ideology is implicit, the greater cultural power of whites was a fait accompli.

Consider the legacy of slavery in America. Slaves were social pariahs from the beginning, but after emancipation, they now had the responsibility of finding work among people that hated them in a land they didn't choose to come to. What would life be like for their children and grandchildren who may have had to work as sharecroppers? What would it have been like to grow up where there was a constant threat of being raped, beaten, or lynched and there was nothing that could be done about it? What sort of educational opportunities would have been possible, what chances for upward mobility? How possible would it be for someone in this situation to advance economically or socially? Consider on the other hand those who used slave labor to amass great wealth and power. Their children would have started life well up the social and economic ladder. They would have had many opportunities for advancement.

Of course there are exceptions, not all whites were rich, landowners, not all owned slaves, and there were Blacks who managed to get

---

[55] *ibid*, 316. In-text citations have been removed.

out of their impoverished conditions. In America we tend to have a pull-yourself-up-by-the-bootstraps mentality. We tend to attribute success and failure to character alone and ignore contextual factors. This is called the fundamental attribution error. For example, if someone cuts us off in traffic, we assume it's because they're an idiot, but if we accidentally cut someone off, we don't conclude we're idiots—we blame the sun in our eyes or a dirty windshield.

Our American "Can Do" spirit tends to blame people in poverty as being lazy and unambitious. We ignore failing schools, gang violence, broken homes, addiction, and lack of opportunities. Not to mention the learned helplessness that can come from being socialized in such an environment. With no examples or role models, without ever being encouraged, without friends and family who moved up and out, it is extremely unlikely a person would ever even entertain the possibility that they would be able to achieve and escape poverty. This would obviously go for people of any ethnicity, but even whites born into poverty start life with higher social standing than minorities in the same conditions. Regardless, the effects of racism are still reverberating through America's social and economic fabric.

The aggregation of prejudice from the majority's pro-racist ideology translates into discrimination on a systemic level. The universal human proclivity for people to stick with what is familiar, paired with power being largely concentrated among whites, means minorities will face barriers and challenges that whites will not. In this way, personal prejudice becomes institutionalized. For example,

"To test for possible labor market discrimination, M.I.T. researchers sent 5,000 résumés out in response to 1,300 varied employment ads. Applicants who were randomly assigned White names (Emily, Greg) received one callback for every 10 résumés sent. Those given Black names (Lakisha, Jamal) received one callback for every 15 résumés sent."[56]

Again, minorities can be prejudiced, they too can hate people based on ethnicity, but what they do not have is the power to discriminate on a systemic level. Currently, only whites have that power in America. Only those with lighter skin have privileges and advantages that minorities do not. It is not intentional; it is merely a consequence of millions of individual positions, decisions, and perceptions in aggregate.

---

[56] *ibid*, 313. In-text citations have been removed.

Perhaps in reading this section you may wonder if it is racist to make generalizations about race. Keep in mind it is one thing to acknowledge cultural differences exist; it is quite another thing to reduce a person to a racial stereotype. Understanding group differences does not mean treating people as drones of a homogenous collective.

How does all this talk of groups apply in a book that is fundamentally about the individual? A person's culture is an integral part of who they are as an individual. To refuse to see cultural attributes in a person is to remove them from the context they exist in. To truly "see" an individual implies seeing every bit of what makes them who they are. Explicit racists will deny individual differences exist and see people as stereotypes. On the other side of the coin, those with a pro-racist ideology will often ignore race for fear that noticing it would mean they are racist. When you have examined your own identity and feel comfortable with differences, it is only then you can see the person more completely. You cannot appreciate the uniqueness of an individual if you deny the major components of their identity that come from their race and culture.

Being culturally sensitive does not mean thinking that every member of a given ethnicity is the same. It does not mean treating people according to your assumptions, stereotypes, or previous interactions with others like them. Each person has their own "culture," so to speak. Each person is a unique blend of their personal beliefs and values and those they gained from their socialization process and racial identity. Being culturally sensitive means acknowledging and respecting people's racial background; it means asking them how they define themselves and prefer to be treated.

It is a great undertaking to deconstruct and come to understand one's ethnic identity and cultural assumptions. As strange as it sounds, in order to pursue individualism and treat everyone we meet according to their character, we have to be aware of their identity in the group they come from. We have to understand the role that culture and racial experience plays and consciously learn to see past biases we may not have even known we have. We have only briefly touched on the major points of this common blind-spot and hope everyone will make it a topic for further inquiry. A pro-racist ideology is a subtle form of collectivism and must be transcended if we desire to be fully rational humans.

THERE OUGHT TO BE A LAW!

The government is not the answer to racism, prejudice, or discrimination. Many of the modern government remedies to correct discrimination use discrimination itself to combat the issue. For example, the policies of Affirmative Action encourage decisions to be based, not on individual merit, but on an individual's race or membership in a social group. This well-meaning legislation was designed to circumvent the power differential of whites and minorities, but what ends up happening is employers are forced to hire individuals not for their skills, but to meet a quota of diversity. Sadly, Affirmative Action is the opposite of someone being judged on the content of their character.[57] So much for Dr. King's dream.

A student group at Texas A&M asked other students why they would support Affirmative Action's policies in academics and the workplace, but not want to sign a petition to apply the same "racial consideration" policies to the sports teams. Some answers were very enlightening, "No, that should be based on talent." The contradictory thinking had many students stumped for a response.[58] If you are trying to put an end to racial discrimination by racially discriminating, you are doing it wrong.

Many cry, "But if we don't have laws there will be discrimination; we would still have segregation!"

Actually, "segregation" was enforced by law. The solution was freedom, i.e. repealing those laws. Freedom never came with the promise of a perfect world. Even though new Civil Rights laws accompanied the least racist America we have ever seen, the means, such as Affirmative Action, cannot be justified. Undoubtedly, without those laws there would still be bigots who would refuse to do business with anyone other than their own ethnicity, but there are anyway.

As stupid as that is and as much as we disagree with them, we still can't morally force them to change their actions in regard to their own property and their own conscience. All we can do is try to educate them to remove their hatred, and refuse to do business with them until they do; we can use peer pressure to coax them into doing good. We can help create in them a proper self-esteem so they won't seek a false substitute in racist activity. Having more freedom means having more responsibility to

---

[57] Quoted in Safire, *Speeches*, 499. "I have a dream that my four little children will one day live in a nation where they will not be judged by the color of their skin, but by the content of their character."

[58] "Affirmative Action for Athletic Teams Petition—Texas A&M." campusreform.org. 23 Feb 2012. YouTube.
youtube.com/watch?feature=player_embedded&v =gxCEKaKCXec. Accessed 23 Aug 2012.

do the right thing. Racism is evil. It is vile. But the only thing the government can (should) do about it is what it should do for every individual—protect him or her from physical force.

REVIEW

Q1: What is collectivism?

Q2: What is the moral code of collectivism?

Q3: What are the four main features of Pragmatism?

Q4: Why is subjectivism evil?

Q5: What are the features of a mixed economy?

Q6: What defines Progressive thought?

Q7: Describe the difference between nationalism and patriotism.

Q8: Describe the differences between classical and social liberalism.

Q9: Why are all forms of conservatism inherently unprincipled?

Q10: Why is racism based in collectivism?

Q11: How is having a pro-racist ideology different from being a racist?

Q12: Why is starting with a pro-racist ideology inescapable if you are part of the majority culture?

Q13: What are some ways you have unconsciously supported the superiority of whites? Or, if you are Black, what are some ways you have seen others unconsciously support a pro-racist ideology?

Q14: What is altruism? Why is it evil?

CHAPTER 12

THE POLITICS OF EVIL

PART 1: STATISM

"[Americans] do not wish to curtail the activities of this government; they wish, rather, to enlarge them."[1] - Woodrow Wilson

"Ask not what your country can do for you, ask what you can do for your country."- John F. Kennedy, Inaugural address

All the collectivist theory we've discussed, when applied to the philosophy of politics, leads to only one possible outcome: statism. Statism is the philosophy of collectivism applied to politics, guided by the policy of concentrating extensive social, economic, and political controls in the state at the cost of individual liberty. Statism is a large tree: its roots are collectivism, and its many branches include theocracy, absolute monarchy, National Socialism, fascism, communism, democratic socialism, democracy, Progressivism, and authoritarianism. These differ only in

---

[1] Bell, H.C.F. *Woodrow Wilson and the People* (Garden City, New York: Doubleday, Doran, and Company, 1993), 274.

form and tactics—not ideology. Regulations, taxes, controls, and other governmental coercions are manifestations of the basic principle of statism which is that man's life belongs to the state.

Statist policies and tendencies can be identified because they look first and foremost to the State, whether federal or local, to address issues and find solutions. Solutions to be found through private entities, free-markets, persuasion, or simple freedom are disregarded completely.

Franklin D. Roosevelt illustrated the statist mentality perfectly, saying, "It may be that an unprecedented demand and need for undelayed action may call for temporary departure from the normal balance of public procedure . . . I shall ask Congress for . . . broad executive power to wage a war against the emergency, as great as the power that would be given to me if we were in fact invaded by a foreign foe."[2]

Every emergency, whether real or imagined, is an excuse for a power-grab. Statism designates concentration of power in the state at the expense of individual liberty, with the state having power over every sphere of human activity.

As Ernst Huber, an official Nazi party spokesman said in 1933, "The concept of personal liberties of the individual as opposed to the authority of the state had to disappear . . . . There are no personal liberties of the individual which fall outside the realm of the state and which must be respected by the state . . . . The constitution of the nationalistic Reich is therefore not based upon a system of inborn and unalienable rights of the individual."[3]

George W. F. Hegel, one of Germany's most prominent philosophers, stated the fundamentals of statism thus, "A single person . . . is something subordinate, and as such he must dedicate himself to the ethical whole. Hence if the state claims life, the individual must surrender it."[4] He didn't stop there, however. To Hegel, the State wasn't merely a secular entity, but a manifestation of God, "the Divine Idea as it exists on earth." Thus, the purpose of the State is not the protection of its citizens, because it is not the means to any human end. The State is an "absolute unmoved end in itself" with supreme right against the individual!

---

[2] Safire, *Speeches*, 782.
[3] Quoted in Peikoff, *OP*, 16.
[4] *ibid*, 35.

Hitler wrote that, "The state must act as the guardian of a millennial future, in the face of which the wishes and the selfishness of the individual must appear as nothing and submit."[5]

Leonard Peikoff, writing on what he called, "Hitler's war against reason," observed that "statism and the advocacy of reason are philosophical opposites. They cannot coexist—neither in a philosophic system nor in a nation."[6] Such a contradiction is the primary source and cause of today's political and economic woes. Those problems come when a freedom-loving nation is clamoring to be chained down by statist ideology.

American leaders have been openly statist for over a century, as Woodrow Wilson clearly showed us when he said, "I am perfectly sure that the state has got to control everything that everybody uses."[7]

Slowly, Americans have been led to believe that men should not deal with one another as free agents via persuasion, but that the only way men can deal with one another is through physical force wielded by an elite government. The heart of totalitarianism is that the collective holds all rights, and the individual has none.

We will now move on to a discussion of the collectivist philosophies as applied to the political systems of Communism, Socialism, Fascism, and Democracy.

PART 2: COMMUNISM

"Remember the Roman Emperor who said he wished humanity had a single neck so he could cut it? People have laughed at him for centuries. But we'll have the last laugh. We've accomplished what he couldn't accomplish. We've taught men to unite. This makes one neck ready for one leash. We found the magic word. Collectivism." - Ayn Rand, *The Fountainhead*

Communism is a social structure in which classes are abolished and property is commonly controlled, as well as a political philosophy and social movement that advocates and aims to create such a society.

"Pure Communism," in the Marxist sense, refers to a classless, stateless, and "oppression-free" society where decisions on what to produce and what policies to pursue are made democratically, allowing every

---

[5] Hitler, Adolf. Ralph Manheim, trans. *Mein Kampf* (Houghton Mifflin: New York, 1999), 404.

[6] Peikoff, *OP*, 45.

[7] Bell, *Wilson*, 511.

member of society to participate in the decision-making process in both the political and economic spheres of life.

(In Communist literature, "bourgeoisie [means] the class of modern capitalists, owners of the means of social production and employers of wage labor . . . . Proletariat [means] the class of modern wage labourers who, having no means of production of their own, are reduced to selling their labour power in order to live.")[8]

The founders of modern Communism, Karl Marx and Friedrich Engels, decided it was man's duty to remake the world in a fashion that would best preserve mankind. They accepted the fact that this would be a cruel and ruthless task, involving the destruction of all who opposed it. With a clean sweep, Communist leadership would gradually introduce a society of perfect harmony for all future ages.

However, Marx and Engels also realized that they would have to develop a new view on morality and ethics for their Communist followers. As Lenin said, "Our morality is wholly subordinated to the interests of the class struggle of the proletariat."[9] To the Communist, whatever pragmatically works to bring about the Communist ideals is morally good; whatever does not is morally bad. It is not wrong to lie, steal, cheat, or even kill if it is for a "good" cause. In *The Communist Manifesto*, Marx and Engels stated plainly that Communism "abolishes eternal truths, it abolishes . . . all morality."[10]

A twentieth century American Marxist, William Foster, said it this way, "With [the Communist], the end justifies the means. Whether his tactics be 'legal' or 'moral' or not, does not concern him, so long as they are effective pragmatically. He knows that the laws as well as the current code of morals are made by his mortal enemies . . . Consequently, he ignores them insofar as he is able, and it suits his purposes. He proposes to develop, regardless of capitalist conceptions of 'legality,' 'fairness,' 'right,' etc., a greater power than his capitalist enemies have . . ."[11]

HISTORY'S ONE EVIL

The Marxists have a special interpretation of history. They try to explain all human progress in terms of class struggle. They apply a pair-

---

[8] Marx, Karl. and Frederich Engels. *The Communist Manifesto* (London: Verso, 1998), 34.
[9] Skousen, W. Cleon. *The Naked Communist* (Salt Lake City, Utah: Ensign Publishing Company, 1960), 38.
[10] Marx, *Manifesto*, 59.
[11] Quoted in Skousen, *Naked Communist*, 305.

ing of opposites to their version of history. All past societies, according to Communist theory, have been a combination of opposite forces or classes—"freeman and slave, patrician and plebian, lord and serf, guildmaster and journeyman, in a word oppressor and oppressed."[12]

KARL MARX

There was one evil which was responsible for all past conflicts and will be the cause of one last great and terrible class struggle. All selfishness, jealousy, struggle, and war were traced to one root cause—private property. Marx called this "the leading question," and said that, "the theory of the Communists may be summed up in the single sentence: Abolition of Private Property."[13] If you could get rid of that, he contended, as well as "that single unconscionable freedom—free trade," there would be no more fighting because there would be nothing to fight over![14] (Marxists fail to distinguish between the right of private property and the abuse of private property.)

They were also wrong about the causes of war. Private property has never been the issue. The cause of war is linked to a belief which is still vibrantly infectious today, and one which Communists hold dear—the belief that the initiation of physical force is acceptable.

Marx considered material possessions to be anathema to the fulfillment of human nature. He wrote that the "enemy of being is having," that "the less you eat, drink and read books; the less you go to the theatre, the dance hall, the public house; the less you think, love, theorize, sing, paint, fence, etc . . . .—The greater becomes your treasure which neither moths nor dust will devour . . . . The less you are, the more you have; the less you express your own life, the greater is your . . . life."[15]

---

[12] Marx, *Manifesto*, 35.

[13] *ibid*, 77, 52.

[14] *ibid*, 38.

[15] Thompson, C. Bradley. "Why Marxism? Evil Laid Bare." *The Objective Standard.* Vol. 7, No. 2. Online. theobjectivestandard.com/issues/2012-summer/why-marxism.asp. Accessed 10 Aug 2012.

COMMUNIST GOALS

The *Communist Manifesto* states ten goals to be accomplished in the progress towards pure Communism. These are important to recognize, both to identify the progress Communists have made in these areas in all countries of the world, and to identify why these things will further the movement to abolish private property. We have included them here as a reference:

1. "Abolition of property in land and application of all rents of land to public purposes."
2. "A heavy progressive or graduated income tax."
3. "Abolition of all rights of inheritance."
4. "Confiscation of the property of all emigrants and rebels."
5. "Centralization of credit in the banks of the state, by means of a national bank with state capital and an exclusive monopoly."
6. "Centralization of the means of communication and transport in the hands of the state."
7. "Extension of factories and instruments of production owned by the state; the bringing into cultivation of waste lands, and the improvement of the soil generally in accordance with a common plan."
8. "Equal obligation of all to work. Establishment of industrial armies, especially for agriculture."
9. "Combination of agriculture with manufacturing industries; gradual abolition of all the distinction between town and country by a more equable distribution of the populace over the country."
10. "Free education for all children in public schools. Abolition of children's factory labor in its present form. Combination of education with industrial production, etc."[16]

Communism not only denies the right of private property, but as we can see in point 8, above, "Equal obligation of all to work," it also denies explicitly the right to liberty. In theory and in practice, Marxism/Communism denies all individual rights. *The Principles of Communism*, by Engels, advocated further measures against the evils of private property:

---

[16] Marx, *Manifesto*, 60-61.

1. "Limitation of private property through progressive taxation, heavy inheritance taxes, abolition of inheritance."
2. "Gradual expropriation of landowners, industrialists, railroad magnates and ship-owners, partly through competition by state industry, partly directly through compensation in the form of bonds."
3. "Confiscation of the possessions of all emigrants and rebels against the majority of the people."
4. "Organization of labor or employment of proletarians on publicly owned land, in factories and workshops, with competition among the workers being abolished and with the factory owners, insofar as they still exist, being obliged to pay the same high wages as those paid by the state."
5. "An equal obligation on all members of society to work until such time as private property has been completely abolished. Formation of industrial armies, especially for agriculture."
6. "Centralization of money and credit in the hands of the state through a national bank with state capital, and the suppression of all private banks and bankers."
7. "Increase in the number of national factories, workshops, railroads, ships; bringing new lands into cultivation and improvement of land already under cultivation—all in proportion to the growth of the capital and labor force at the disposal of the nation."
8. "Education of all children, from the moment they can leave their mother's care, in national establishments at national cost. Education and production together."
9. "Construction, on public lands, of great palaces as communal dwellings for associated groups of citizens engaged in both industry and agriculture and combining in their way of life the advantages of urban and rural conditions while avoiding the one-sidedness and drawbacks of each."
10. "Destruction of all unhealthy and jerry-built dwellings in urban districts."
11. "Equal inheritance rights for children born in and out of wedlock."

12. "Concentration of all means of transportation in the hands of the nation."[17]

THE FAMILY AND PRIVATE PROPERTY

Point 8, above, demands government education of children from an early age. What does the education of children have to do with the abolishment of private property? Engels claimed that the institution of marriage was exploitation and Communists should aim to abolish "the dependence rooted in private property, of the women on the man, and of the children on the parents." Marx decried the "exploitation of children by their parents."[18]

We've shown that all property rights are linked with ownership of your own body. Observe in the following excerpt the fruits of the abolition of all private property, including that of your body. Marx claimed that the Communists would abolish private property to its fullest logical extent when he described how he desired to introduce "an openly legalized community of women."[19]

"Community," in this sense, is the term applied to all communal property under Communism. Some Russian Communists initially attempted to live as true Marxists and in some places mandated that all women were common property. An excerpt from a decree of the Soviet of Saratov (a soviet is a popularly elected legislative assembly) illustrates this and is worth quoting at length to get some sense of the Communist mindset:

> "Beginning with March 1, 1919, the right to possess women between the ages of 17 and 32 is abolished . . . By virtue of the present decree no woman can any longer be considered as private property and all women become the property of the nation . . . All women thus put at the disposition of the nation must, within three days after the publication of the present decree, present themselves in person at the address indicated and provide all necessary information . . . .
>
> "Any man who wishes to make use of a nationalized woman must hold a certificate issued by the administrative Council of a professional union, or by the Soviet of workers, soldiers or peas-

---

[17] Engels, Frederich. *Principles of Communism*. 1847. Online. marxists.org/archive/marx/works/1847/11/prin-com.htm. Accessed 11 Aug 2011.
[18] Marx, *Manifesto*, 56.
[19] *ibid*, 57.

ants, attesting that he belongs to the working class . . . . Every worker is required to turn in 2% of his salary to the fund . . . . Male citizens not belonging to the working class may enjoy the same rights provided they pay a sum equivalent to 250 French francs, which will be turned over to the public fund . . . . Any women who by virtue of the present decree will be declared national property will receive from the public fund a salary equivalent to 575 French francs a month . . .

"Any pregnant woman will be dispensed of her duties for four months before and three months after the birth of the child . . . . One month after birth, children will be placed in an institution entrusted with their care and education. They will remain there to complete their instruction and education at the expense of the national fund until they reach the age of seventeen . . . . All those who refuse to recognize the present decree and to cooperate with the authorities shall be declared enemies of the people . . . and shall suffer the consequences."[20]

Another decision handed down by a Soviet official said: "There is no such thing as a woman being violated by a man; he who says that a violation is wrong denies the October Communist Revolution. To defend a violated woman is to reveal oneself as a bourgeois and a partisan of private property."[21]

ECONOMIC DETERMINISM

One irreducible feature the Marxist view of history was called "determinism," which denied that man had free will, or agency, to make choices. He was believed to have no choice because his actions were determined by his nature. In the *Communist Manifesto*, it was proposed that men could not choose whatever form of society they wanted, but only one which promoted the prevailing mode of production. Your society makes your ideas, they said, not you. "Your very ideas are but the outgrowth of conditions of your bourgeois production and bourgeois property, just as your [system of law] is but the will of your class, made into law for all, a will whose essential character and direction are determined

---

[20] Quoted in Skousen, *Naked Communist*, 72-73.
[21] Quoted in *ibid*, 73.

by the economic conditions of existence of your class."[22] In *Poverty of Philosophy*, Marx said, "Are men free to choose this or that form of society? By no means."[23] He claimed that man's ideas, views, and consciousness changed with every change in his material existence.

Applied to history and economics, this theory is Economic Determinism, which is the belief that economic laws determine the course of men and thus of history. Marx described how he believed that "the mode of production in material life determined the general character of the social, political, and spiritual processes of life."[24]

Marx and Engels felt they had discovered something vitally important to human welfare. Closely associated with economic determinism is a sort of personal determinism. If they could somehow force on mankind a highly-perfected system of economic production it would automatically produce a higher type of human being!

In other words, as Dr. Skousen put it in *The Naked Communist*, "they would reverse the Judaic-Christian approach which endeavors to improve humanity in order to improve society."[25]

Economic determinism assumes that if you change things outside of a man this automatically compels a change on the inside, that the only way to improve humanity was a change in economic structure. It fails to recognize that environment only conditions man;

FRIEDRICH ENGELS

it does not change his very nature, or remove his agency.

This is an important concept because it identifies how Communists arrive at such a violent, often genocidal, materialism that disregards individual human life, personal agency, and potential.

---

[22] Marx, *Manifesto*, 35.

[23] Quoted in Skousen, *Naked Communist*, 46.

[24] Skousen, *Naked Communist*, 46.

[25] *ibid.*

PEOPLE ARE ASSETS

Communists have a very particular philosophy of value. They believe that material things have intrinsic value that should be determined by one group and imposed on everyone else. Businessman and author Garrett Gunderson explained the results of such a view, saying, "In our normal everyday relationships, imposing our value determinations on other people is a form of subtle tyranny; when it becomes a full-blown economic theory, supported by the force of government, it literally becomes a machine for oppression, destruction, and death."[26]

Communists value things not people. That idea is exactly backwards from the true principle that people have value, things do not.

Marxists believe that people lie, cheat, steal, and kill because they don't have enough "stuff." If we could only give them food, clothing, houses, and whatever else they "need" (according to economic determinism), then they wouldn't do all those bad things. Things are important, they proclaim. If everybody only had enough stuff, then we would all live in harmony. To quote Marx again, "Man's ideas . . . [change] with every change in the conditions of material existence." He believed we could get people to be good if we gave them things, rather than trying to help them become good and allowing them to obtain the things they desire.

The strange thing is most Communists like to say they value people and that it is the greedy capitalists who only love money and "things." Such materialism, however, is an explicit foundational tenet of Communism. On the other hand, you might hear a smart capitalist realtor say something like, "Houses don't write checks; people do." That realtor recognizes the fact that the value isn't in the house—it's in the person that values the house.

Answer this question quickly as a test: How much is your house worth?

Are you sure? How much would your house be worth in a different city? On a road near a dog food plant? In a different state? How about in the middle of the Sahara Desert? It changes, doesn't it? The value is not intrinsically in the house. Most people recognize this principle implicitly, but fail to identify it in words. If your house were intrinsically worth $100,000, then how could its value change with location or over time? The only time the question, "How much is something worth?" is a useful question to ask is when it includes the caveat, "To whom and for what?"

---

[26] Gunderson, Garrett. and Stephen Palmer. *Killing Sacred Cows* (Provo, Utah: Decade Media, 2007), 30.

The correct answer to the question "How much is my house worth?" is "Nothing!" It has no value unless a there is a person to value it for a specific purpose. What good would that pile of bricks and lumber you call your house be on the moon? The words value and worth can be changed to be use and utility.

Suppose I have a candy bar. I offer to sell it to you for $1. You agree, and we make the exchange. How much was the candy bar worth?

"A dollar!"

That is exactly wrong.

We don't exchange a value for an equal value. There would be no point; we would just keep what we had in the first place. Why would you go to the trouble of the business transaction if you didn't want one thing more than the other? You exercised a preference, a choice. I preferred to have the dollar more than the candy bar. So what was the candy bar worth to me? Less than $1. How much less? You don't know. All you can infer from this is that if I preferred the dollar to the candy bar, then I valued the candy bar less. It could have been one cent less or ninety cents less.

Now, how much was the candy bar worth to you? More than $1. We know this because you also exercised a choice and preferred to have the candy bar more than the dollar.

This equation applies to non-monetary values as well. Suppose you decide to buy a lemonade from a little girl on the sidewalk for $1. You don't value the watery lemonade more than a dollar, but you do value the feeling of helping the little girl be successful in her initiative and work. Even when engaged in charity we receive more in value than we paid.

Marx and Engels would disagree with this idea. They claimed that the value was in the object and that it was valued at whatever it cost to make it. As Engels put it in *The Principles of Communism*, "Price . . . is . . . always equal to its cost of production."[27] He believed that if anyone valued anything differently than its intrinsic value, then they were either being exploited and deceived, or they were the ones doing the exploiting.

---

[27] Engels, *Communism.*

It is tyrannical to say the candy bar has a "correct" value and price—that would be forcing your values on others.

"You must like this candy bar!"

"But I don't like chocolate!"

You deny the right of the parties involved to decide how much they value it themselves.

Communism was partially the result of this idea that things have a certain value that must be enforced. It follows that if things have an intrinsic value, then to make everybody happy we have to make sure they all have enough of those valuable things. If we can't provide them ourselves, it becomes our moral duty to take it from those who have "too much" and give it to those that don't.

Communists believe that resources are finite and that their intrinsic value should be asserted through price controls and centralized redistribution of resources so that people don't get exploited by high prices. Such a belief violates the principle that people must be allowed to choose their own value determinations. Communism denies basic human individuality and worth. They also deny that a worker's time can be any more or less valuable than the time of someone else with different experience or skills. Everyone must be paid the same, no matter the job, in a Communist world.

What good is a pile of gold to a starving man in the desert? What good is a pile of paper money if an earthquake has shut down all the grocery stores and you have no food storage? Of what value is a house that no one wants to live in or utilize?

Individual people are the only things that have value, and the only reason "things" can ever be considered valuable. Value is in the minds of people; the people are the creators of the value.

AN EXERCISE IN COMMUNISM

Let us imagine an application of the Communist creed, "From each according to his ability, to each according to his need," and see if we can identify some fundamental flaws in it, especially when confronted with human nature.

In a well-known example, imagine you are a high school teacher and announce to your class a new grading rule—the new law of your classroom. You explain to them that to get a passing grade they need a 75. So, if any of them earn a 95, you will take off 20 points and give it to someone who earned 55.

Which students would think this was a grand idea? The brighter, hard-working students or the less studious ones?

In the long run, none of them would like it. Here's what would happen:

First, the highly productive students would lose all incentive to produce. Why strive to make a great grade if part of it is taken and given to someone else?

Second, the less productive students wouldn't have to produce at all, at least for a while. This would continue until the high producers had sunk or been driven to the level of the low producers—having nothing left to offer.

At that point, in order to even survive, the "authority," that means you, would have to begin a system of forced labor and punishments against even the low producers. The entire class can't be allowed to fail. Something must be done.

STATUE OF MARX AND ENGELS, BERLIN

These same unintended consequences would occur in any setting—industrial, commercial, or even in your own home. When the principle of self-interest as a primary motivating factor is removed, punished, or even just ignored, all production collapses.[28]

Communism's premise is fundamentally flawed and its methods are evil. If human nature was motivated and served by self-sacrificial (i.e. altruistic) concern for the welfare of others, then the brutal and bloody agenda of communism would be unnecessary. Because self-interest is the inseparable motivation of every rational individual, Communism can never achieve its ends; it is an impossible dream (more of a nightmare).

Author C. Bradley Thompson delivered this scathing summary of his analysis of Marxism which deserves to be quoted at length:

"There is nothing noble or attractive about Marxian socialism. Marxism is, by definition, totalitarian and genocidal by motive, design, practice, and result. The political goal of com-

---

[28] Retold from Skousen, *Naked Communist*, 82-83.

munism is to annihilate freedom in all realms of life—economic, social, and intellectual.

"By philosophic design, Marxism in power must always use force to achieve its ends. Any government that expropriates and redistributes private property, any government that seeks to control the economy, any government that violates the rights of its citizens on a daily basis, any government that seeks to reconstitute human nature will and must use force as a matter of course. Thus the theory of socialism necessitates the use of coercive force in practice . . .

"Marxism is a philosophy of malevolence and hatred. It is, from beginning to end, a criminal activity. It begins with theft (literally) and ends with murder (literally) . . .

"In conclusion, we must say this about Marxism: first, it is the single worst blight to have affected human life over the course of man's entire history; and second, those who advocate it represent the very definition of human evil and must be openly judged and condemned accordingly."[29]

PART 3: SOCIALISM

"We must move as a . . . loyal army willing to sacrifice for the good of a common discipline . . . We are, I know, ready and willing to submit our lives and property to such discipline, because it makes possible a leadership which aims at a larger good."[30] - Franklin Delano Roosevelt

Socialism is characterized by state ownership of land and all means of production and distribution of resources. It comes in many varieties and degrees, and they all have the same basic premises and philosophy. The varieties differ only in application and method.

All Communists are also socialists. But not all socialists are Communists. Both share the same collectivist roots in theory, but historically differ in two important aspects in actual practice.

---

[29] Thompson, "Marxism."
[30] Safire, *Speeches*, 781.

FRANKLIN DELANO ROOSEVELT

First, the socialists have maintained from the beginning that centralized control of all land and industry can be achieved by peaceful legislation. Communists hold out for revolution—violent, if necessary. As Marx said, Communists "openly declare that their ends can be attained only by the forcible overthrow of all existing conditions."[31] Socialists aim to change society through evolution, Communists through revolution.

Second, the endgame of the socialists is state control as the means to "common" control of industry and property. Communists believe state control is only a transitory phase on the way to decentralized control by all of mankind communally, without the force of an organized government.

Joseph Goebbels, the Nazi propaganda specialist, recognized the implicit collectivism found at the heart of socialism. "To be a socialist," he said, "is to submit the I to the thou; socialism is sacrificing the individual to the whole."[32] William Walling, a socialist journalist who cofounded the NAACP, observed in 1912 that socialism was not created for how man is, but for how socialists think man ought to be, saying, "It remains for the Socialist movement to supply the principles and the force required to create a new type of man and society."[33]

Note: Unless someone is a self-proclaimed Communist or Socialist and understands all the implications that such a thing entails, it is usually counter-productive to label that person as such. A more productive, honest, and accurate appraisal would involve labeling some of their ideas as socialistic or Communistic, followed by an explanation of why that is. Label only the ideas, unless the individual has already labeled himself. Using terms people don't understand often comes across as inflammatory buzz-words in their minds. For example, a President or Mayor or Sen-

---

[31] Marx, *Manifesto*, 77.
[32] Peikoff, *OP*, 19.
[33] Westbrook, Robert. *John Dewey and American Democracy* (Ithaca and London: Cornell University Press, 1991), 190.

ator might not claim to be or consider himself a socialist. However, if we are clear on our concepts, we can identify certain policies of theirs as socialistic simply by reference to the definition of socialism. We might ask ourselves, for instance, does national health insurance constitute a distribution of resources by the State? If so, then it is, by definition, a socialistic measure.

Sometimes, socialist ideas and practices can creep into our ideas and actions if we haven't developed the ability to think by principle. Economic destruction always results. Chelsea Nelson tells of how this happened at one of her first jobs:

> When I was eighteen, I got a job at a café-type eatery. It was a small place, but the boss was excited because he had bought into this new franchise that he was sure would pay off big and make him rich pretty quick. My job was to stand behind the counter, greet customers as they entered, then take their order, roll out a crepe, fill it, fold it, ring it up, and hand it over.
>
> The grand opening was a great success, and word of this place seemed to spread. We were busy from morning to night. I really enjoyed it! There were rules about everything, of course, like how many strips of chicken we were allowed to put in, and how much milk to make the perfect foam in the cappuccino. But the boss seemed like a pretty nice guy and encouraged us to have fun, communicate, and build a "team atmosphere."
>
> Soon, the other girls that worked there discovered that I was a little more outgoing than they were. Nothing wrong with that, of course; it just meant that they preferred me closer to the door because I wasn't afraid to yell out a friendly, "Hello!" whenever a customer came wandering in. We had been told it was part of our job to welcome every person who came into the café.
>
> I had noticed, through trial and error, that this was the best way to greet people. A simple "Hi!" often got lost in the noise, and a more formal, "Welcome!" seemed to put people off. Before long, I was being offered tips on a regular basis. At first, I was surprised at the offers, but am not one to turn down gratitude for my smiles. I made sure it was okay with the boss, who was pleased as punch when I asked him, and then accepted the tips.
>
> I began to get more tips. Other girls asked me to teach them how to get tips, which I did. A few of them started getting tips,

though by now I had a few regulars and the girls were still pretty shy.

One day we get called into a meeting and I am told that I am not allowed to greet the guests with "Hello" anymore, because the boss felt it was too formal. I already knew "Hi" didn't work so I tried out "Howdy" as it almost always brought a smile to the incoming faces. Not three days later, I was taken aside and told that I couldn't say "Howdy" because he didn't want people to become confused that they had walked into a BBQ joint. So I asked what he wanted me to say. He told me to say "Hi." I did what I was told and two days later he was upset because he felt I wasn't making the customers welcome in his café. I explained that "Hi" got lost in the noise and asked what he'd like me to say. He threw up his hands and said he didn't care as long as I didn't hog all the greetings.

That same day he seemed to notice that I was walking away from a shift with three times as many tips as any other girl. The next morning, he instituted a "tip jar" where all tips would be split—equally—between everyone who worked the entire day (including him, though he didn't work with the customers). He told us it was because we were a team and he didn't want anyone to feel bad.

The change was quick and drastic. The tip jar went out and when a customer would offer me a tip I'd indicate the jar and invariably a puzzled look came onto their face. They'd look at the other girls who had not helped them and say, "How do I know you are going to get this?"

"We'll split it equally at the end of the night." I'd answer. "We're a team."

They'd smile at me like I was perhaps a little slow and say, "You were the only one who waited on me. I hope you don't mind, but if this tip isn't going to go just to you, I'd rather not leave it."

The smile I'd return would show them I understood all too well and I'd reply, "I understand completely. Thank you for your gratitude."

They'd look a little sad and a little impressed and put the tip back in their wallet. My regulars rarely came back.

Four days after this, my boss told me I wasn't allowed to tell customers that the tips would be split. And we were to put fewer strips of chicken in the wraps. But the prices were going to remain the same. He thought it would make him more money and maybe they'd order more because the first one wouldn't fill them up like it used to.

I quit about a week later, and the café closed shortly thereafter as well. I see tip jars at many registers nowadays, and the employees are resigned to that situation. If someone does a good job, they all get to split it at the end of the night; I rarely see any money at all in those tip jars.[34]

As Chelsea discovered, socialist ideas don't have to just be about the government, but can creep down into very seemingly small aspects of our lives.

Many people point to the Scandinavian countries as examples of how socialism "works." Prime Minister Fredrik Reinfeldt of Sweden openly blamed high taxes and welfare state policies for the problems of his nation's economy, "At the beginning of the 1970's Sweden also had the fourth highest GDP per capita measured in purchasing power parity. Sweden was blooming." Thanks to Swedish socialism, Reinfeldt said, the wealth that "took a hundred years to build was dismantled in twenty-five years." "Growth fell off. Unemployment rose. The quality of welfare declined."[35] This is from the country touted as a "success" in socialism. To claim these countries are proof of the validity of socialist theory is to ignore the myriad of suppressed freedoms of the populace and to view a slow decay as "living."

Of course, when people must justify their existence to the collective, it is not long until the violence begins, however much the socialist may claim pacifism. A famous literary socialist, George Bernard Shaw, was well ahead of the Nazis (and possibly influenced them) when he called for the development of a "deadly" but "humane" gas for the purpose of killing, many at a time, those unfit to live. In a 1931 interview, he said,

"Just put them there and say Sir, or Madam, now will you be kind enough to justify your existence? If you can't justify your existence, if you're not pulling your weight in the social boat, if you're not producing as much as you consume or perhaps a little more, then, clearly, we cannot use the organizations of our society for the purpose of keeping you alive,

---

[34] As told to the authors by Chelsea Nelson.
[35] Quoted in Forbes, Steve. and Elizabeth Ames. *How Capitalism Will Save Us* (New York: Crown Business, 2009), 23.

because your life does not benefit us and it can't be of very much use to yourself."[36]

Such is the brotherly love and equality of the socialists.

PART 4: FASCISM

"We have buried the putrid corpse of liberty."[37] - Benito Mussolini

This concept is one that is widely referenced but rarely used correctly. As George Orwell pointed out in 1946, "The word Fascism has now no meaning except insofar as it signifies 'something not desirable.'"[38]

Fascism comes from the Italian fascio meaning "bundle, group"— even its origin has collectivist roots.

Fascism is a governmental system with strong centralized power, permitting no opposition or criticism, which, while not having ownership of the means of production, nevertheless plans and controls the economic affairs of the nation.

Historians Larry Schweikart and Michael Allen describe Mussolini's fascism as "a hybrid of state corporatism, nationalism, and socialism."[39] They explain that the, "Fascists' economic doctrines lack any cohesion except that they wedged a layer of corporate leaders between state planning and the rest of the economy. There was no operation of the free market in fascism, but rather the illusion of a group of independent corporate leaders who, in reality, acted as extensions of the state and were allowed to keep impressive salaries as payroll . . . The Italian state bought large stock holdings in the major banks and other companies, making it the leading stockholder in ventures controlling 70 percent of iron production and almost half of all steel production. It was as close to communism as one could get without collectivizing all industry . . ."[40]

---

[36] "George Bernard Shaw." Wikipedia.org. Accessed 29 May 2014.

[37] Safire, *Great Speeches*, 121.

[38] Orwell, George. "Politics and the English Language." *Why I Write* (New York: Penguin: 2005), 109.

[39] Schweikart, Larry. and Michael Allen. *A Patriot's History of the United States: From Columbus' Great Discovery to the War on Terror* (New York: Penguin, 2004), 577.

[40] *ibid.*

There has been a long and consistent campaign to whitewash and disguise the true nature of fascism and equate it with some sort of nationalistic capitalism. It is sometimes called state capitalism or crony capitalism. This campaign places fascism on the opposite end of the political spectrum from Communism. This effort is to distort economics, rewrite history, and eliminate the possibility in the minds of people for the existence of a free country and uncontrolled economy. The distinguishing feature of fascism in the minds of most people is some vague concept relating to authoritarianism and ultra-nationalism. Racism is often mistakenly cited as a defining characteristic, though it is not—Hitler's fascism was racist, Mussolini's was not.

Both socialism and fascism are concerned with power over the use and control of property. Socialism negates property rights altogether, vesting control in the community as a whole, which means in the state. Fascism leaves nominal ownership in the hands of private individuals, but transfers control of property to the government.

Ownership without control is a contradiction, of course. Under fascism, the citizens retain the responsibility of property ownership with none of its benefits.

Apply this new knowledge by asking yourself, "Which ideology is more prevalent in America today?" Remember, a system in which the government does not nationalize the means of production, but merely assumes control over it, is fascism. Wealth redistributionists have rarely claimed socialism as their goal. They do not intend or advocate the socialization of property, they want to "preserve" it—with government control of its use and disposal. That is exactly the defining characteristic of fascism. Such a system of nominal private property with extensive government controls is not capitalism, but fascism.

However, a concerted effort continues by Marxists to portray capitalism as a system of government controls serving some privileged class. They want to form the vague concept in our minds that governments are the tools of economic class interests.

They love the traditional Left-Right spectrum which assigns us a choice between Communism on the Left and Fascism on the Right. How are two social systems, whose defining characteristics include totalitarianism and tyranny (whether by one or many), supposed to be opposites? Yet, this doctrine is accepted and leaves everyone groping blindly for some sacred middle ground in avoidance of "extremes," without ideals, principles, or conviction, sacrificing all to "Compromise and Moderation." If tyranny reigns at both "extremes," we are told, the safest ground is the center.

As we discussed in Chapter 6, it is much more accurate and truthful to use a spectrum of government based on essentials—tyranny and rights-violators to the left, liberty and rights-defenders on the right. This is why fascism, socialism, and Communism would all be located at one extreme end—not opposites at all!

Let's cement the essentials of fascism in our heads by letting its originators explain it to us. Mussolini laid out some defining characteristics of his fascism in 1928: "The citizen in the Fascist State is no longer a selfish individual who has the anti-social right of rebelling against any law of the Collectivity. The Fascist State with its corporative conception puts men and their possibilities into productive work and interprets for them the duties they have to fulfill."[41]

BENITO MUSSOLINI AND ADOLF HITLER

As Hitler's Nazi party adapted fascism to its policies beginning in 1933, he defined his version of fascism clearly, saying: "The state should retain supervision and each property owner should consider himself appointed by the state. It is his duty not to use his property against the interests of others among his own people. This is the crucial matter. The Third Reich will always retain its right to control the owners of property."[42]

Fascism is alive and well in today's world; just not exactly how many people would imagine it to be.

---

[41] Mussolini, Benito. *My Autobiography* (New York: Scribner's, 1928), 280, emphasis added.

[42] Barkai, Avraham. *Nazi Economics: Ideology, Theory, and Policy*. Trans. Ruth Hadass-Vashitz (Oxford: Berg Publishers Ltd., 1990), 26–27.

PART 5: DEMOCRACY

"Democracies . . . have ever been found incompatible with personal security or the rights of property; and have in general been as short in their lives as they have been violent in their deaths."[43] - James Madison

"There are few things more democratic than a [lynch mob], where everybody is satisfied except a small and insignificant minority of one."[44]
- Thomas Nixon Carver

We've already discussed democracy in some detail in our section on the American system of government. While our system of government does contain some democratic principles in action, it is not a democracy. Democracy is not what we should advocate, it is not what we should fight wars for, and it is not how our country was founded. It is not the ideal.

Democracy is government by the people—specifically, the rule of the majority. It has been humorously described as two wolves and a sheep voting on what to eat for dinner. Yet infringements against minorities have done little to make most people question the moral foundation of democracy. This is because they have learned no other way to discover what is right or wrong beyond an appeal to popularity.

America was not founded as a democracy. A group of representatives (i.e. a republic) met and formed the framework of our nation on a written system of principled law. It is this foundation of principles that determines which new laws may be enacted and which are unconstitutional. A majority vote by the people does not generally decide new policies or bills. This is for the best because a comparison of a new law to a principled foundation is the only way to adequately protect the rights of minorities, regardless what the majority desires—and we must remember that the smallest minority is an individual. The people may alter the Constitution through a very difficult process, thus adapting slightly the foundational framework used for all other laws, but this should be rare and carefully considered.

Democracy is purely collectivist in principle and violates the individual rights it claims to esteem. There is little that can be more collectivist or evil than the doctrine of the sanctity of the "Will of the People" tak-

---

[43] Quoted in Peikoff, *OP*, 111.
[44] Ekirch, *Liberalism*, 219.

en as a majority ruling, disregarding all principles, and sacrificing minorities to the coercive power of the gang in charge.

Writer Isabel Paterson denied that democracy has any unique moral authority, saying, "If one man has no right to command all other men—the expedient of despotism—neither has he any right to command even one other man, nor yet have ten men, or a million, the right to command even one other man, for ten times nothing is nothing, and a million times nothing is nothing."[45] If one man has no inherent right to be a tyrant, then a million men also do not have that right.

> "*The difference between democracy and socialism is not an essential difference, but only a practical difference.*"[46] - Woodrow Wilson

There is not some vague, indefinable concept such as a "social contract" that gives the majority the authority to rule the life of the individual. It is not the price of living in a society to give up our lives and property to the ruling majority. The only rational and moral "social contract" is that of individual rights. I can't violate yours, and you can't violate mine.

CONCLUSION

When SS Captain Josef Kramer was asked at the Nuremberg trials what his feelings were as he stripped and gassed eighty women, he replied, "I had no feelings in carrying out these things because I had received an order to kill the eighty inmates . . . That, by the way, was the way I was trained."[47]

Yes, he was trained that way; down to his deepest core, his philosophy. This shows the practical results of the philosophy of collectivism.

Altruism is a creed of sacrifice for the sake of sacrifice. Egoism and its social system, capitalism, is a creed of the individual's right to live for his own sake. It based on the trader principle where no one has any claim to the unearned.

Each creed of collectivism identifies who must be altruistically sacrificed for the good of whom. Communism sacrifices the producers for the sake of the consumers. Socialism sacrifices the rich to the poor. Fas-

---

[45] Paterson, Isabel. *The God of the Machine* (Originally published in 1943. Qualiteri eBook, 2009), Chapter 12.
[46] Bell, *Wilson*, 60.
[47] Peikoff, *OP*, 95.

cism sacrifices the businessmen to the state. Democracy sacrifices the minority to the majority. Racism sacrifices one ethnic group to another. Pragmatism leads to a mixed economy where pressure groups vie for control in deciding who gets sacrificed next. Capitalism calls for the sacrifice of no one and lets each man achieve and earn whatever he is able, to the best of his abilities, and demands that the individual rights of all must be protected. No other system does that.

It is no exaggeration to say collectivism is evil—it is an understatement. Collectivism is a creed of death, misery, and destruction preached as a moral ideal, for it elevates the immolation of the individual for the good of others. Which others? Anyone but you. Collectivism tells you that anything that builds you up is bad, and anything that tears you down to feeds others is good.

What is the ultimate goal of collectivism? Not merely to feed you to the cannibals—to make you want to feed yourself to the cannibals. Its foundational meanings are hidden, evaded, lied about, and distorted because its ultimate message is that human life has no value.

REVIEW

Q1: What does Communism primarily seek to abolish?

Q2: What is economic determinism?

Q3: Explain the principle "People Are Assets."

Q4: What are the differences and similarities between Communism and socialism?

Q5: What is fascism? How is that different than what it is commonly understood to mean?

Q6: What is statism? In what ways is it evident today?

Q7: Why are democracy and freedom incompatible?

CHAPTER 13

PROSPERITY PRINCIPLES

WHAT IS MONEY?

The concepts of "money" and "currency" are essential to understanding a principle-based approach to life, politics, prosperity, and economics. In attacks against capitalism and freedom, money itself is attacked, distorted, vilified, and even deified. A correct understanding of this important tool is essential to a cognitive defense.

Money

- A *concept* referring to value created or the potential of value creation.

Currency

- The *physical representation* of that value, given as a *receipt* for value given or expected to be given.

Money is a concept; currency is a physical concrete such as dollars, yen, or precious metal coins.

THE MORALITY OF MONEY

Money is merely an idea. It is not intrinsically evil or good. It is a tool. A hammer in an experienced builder's hand can create great value for everyone. In the hands of the ignorant or foolish it can be very destructive.

In morality, money itself is value-neutral. It doesn't corrupt or purify; instead, it serves as a magnifier or revealer of the character of the individual who has it. It will not provide or destroy virtue or change the character of its owner for better or worse. Money will merely make the character of the person who controls it more obvious. Are they generous, kind-hearted, disciplined, and wise? Money will magnify those qualities and make them more readily visible to others. Is a man mean-spirited, shallow, miserly, and foolish? Give that man a large sum of money and you will find out.

Money is a tool of exchange. Money represents the principle that men must deal with one another by trading value for value, not by looting or mooching.

Where does such a principle come from? Consider a microchip or flat screen television and try telling yourself that they were made by unthinking cavemen. Try to grow food without the knowledge left to you by others who discovered it. Man's mind is the root of all the goods produced and all the wealth that has ever existed on earth. Man's mind is the root of money.

In *Atlas Shrugged*, the character Francisco d'Anconia gives his famous "Money Speech." He asks,

"But you say that money is made by the strong at the expense of the weak? What strength do you mean? It is not the strength of guns or muscles. Wealth is the product of man's capacity to think. Then is money made by the man who invents a motor at the expense of those who did not invent it? Is money made by the intelligent at the expense of the fools? By the able at the expense of the incompetent? By the ambitious at the expense of the lazy? Money is made—before it can be looted or mooched—made by the effort of every honest man, each to the extent of his ability. An honest man is one who knows that he can't consume more than he has produced . . ..

"To the glory of mankind, there was, for the first and only time in history, a country of money—and I have no higher, more reverent tribute to pay to America, for this means: a country of reason, justice, freedom, production, achievement. For the first time, man's mind and money were set free, and there were no fortunes-by-conquest, but only fortunes-by-work, and instead of swordsmen and slaves, there appeared the real maker of wealth, the greatest worker, the highest type of human being—the self-made man—the American industrialist.

"If you ask me to name the proudest distinction of Americans, I would choose—because it contains all the others—the fact that they were the people who created the phrase 'to make money.' No other language or nation had ever used these words before; men had always thought of wealth as a static quantity—to be seized, begged, inherited, shared, looted, or obtained as a favor. Americans were the first to understand that wealth has to be created. The words 'to make money' hold the essence of human morality."[1]

WEALTH AND PROSPERITY

Webster's *New World College Dictionary* defines wealth as "much money or property; great amount of worldly possessions; riches; the state of having much money or property; valuable products; everything having economic value measurable in price; any useful material thing capable of being bought, sold, or stocked for future disposition."[2]

Is anyone surprised at that definition? What usually comes to mind at the word wealth? Money.

This is strange, however, considering the etymology of the word. In Middle English, it was welthe, meaning "happiness," or wele, meaning "a sound, healthy, or prosperous state; well-being."[3] Wealth was originally synonymous with happiness and health. Many people who have lots of money are miserable, and many people with lesser financial means are very happy. It should be apparent that if you are not happy then you aren't prospering, regardless of the amount of money you have.

Happiness is the state of consciousness that comes with the achievement of your values—not a whim, or momentary pleasure. This feeling is a profound, guiltless self-esteem and pride in your achievements. It is the enjoyment of life.[4] Included in the principles governing the achievement of happiness is the principle of personal choice. To a

---

[1] Rand, Ayn. *Atlas Shrugged* (New York: Signet, 1957) 387-91.

[2] "Wealth." Quoted on Yourdictionary.com. yourdictionary.com/wealth.

[3] "Wealth." Memidex Online Dictionary. memidex.com/wealth#etymology.

[4] Rand, Ayn. *For the New Intellectual* (New York: Signet, 1963), 123.

very real extent, we can choose to be happy from moment to moment. Long-term joy, however, requires that we pursue and achieve life-serving values. For example, choosing to be happy will not work if it is in contradiction with our actions. We may try to have a positive attitude but if we also choose drug addictions, abusive relationships, or dishonest professions, we will not attain lasting or meaningful happiness. To ignore or distract yourself from the things you have the power to change is an evasion of reality and will only bring more anxiety.

Prosperity is having every resource that an individual must utilize in order to fulfill and accomplish their values. This is synonymous with the concept of wealth, although, as the modern dictionary showed us, being wealthy now generally places emphasis on access to the material things that make life enjoyable. To be wealthy is the state of having the power to obtain what you rationally desire; having the power to rationally act in your self-interest.

As we have discussed, a value is "that which one acts to gain and/or keep."[5] It assumes an answer to the question, "Of value to whom and for what?" Individuals need to achieve values for the furtherance of their existence, and for the fulfillment of their happiness. Correct values (e.g. honest and productive careers and relationships, a healthy body, etc.) result in happiness and life. Incorrect values (e.g. dependence on government, addictions, dysfunctional relationships, etc.) result in misery and death.

Prosperity and wealth refer to all areas of a man's life which affect his well-being:

- Physical prosperity—Includes physical health and fitness, material comforts and resources, and the freedom to use them. To prosper physically one must be a producer and a steward— produce more than you consume, and take personal responsibility.
- Social prosperity—Refers to healthy relationships, both familial and otherwise, communication skills and resources, social skills, and respect for and from others.
- Mental prosperity—Includes adequate mental faculties for life on earth, access to sources of knowledge, reasoning abilities, and freedom as much as possible from deception, coercion, and ignorance.

---

[5] Peikoff, Leonard. *Objectivism: The Philosophy of Ayn* Rand (New York: Penguin: 1993), 208.

- Spiritual prosperity—This refers to a proper (i.e. rational and life-serving) moral code, a rational philosophy consisting of reason, purpose, self-esteem, and other virtues, and the fulfillment of rational and life-serving goals and ideals.

All these areas are required for true prosperity. Money is only regarded as an aid to achieving some aspects of physical prosperity—not a source of happiness and certainly not an end in itself.

The nature of happiness makes it impossible to find in the pursuit of irrational whims. There are rules governing the pursuit and achievement of happiness—rules that govern how man is to achieve a joy of living that agrees with his nature. Principles govern everything—the key is discovering them and living by them. We do so by consciously integrating our moral code with reality. We may think freedom means living however we want without consequences. This won't help us live in reality. Instead, we must come to understand the law of causality and decide which consequences we want and then act appropriately.

Capitalism is the only social system that properly protects man's life and property. Man requires the use of private property in his pursuit of his values—family, career, religion, hobbies. In achieving proper values, he will experience the reason for his existence: happiness. We will now discuss some guiding principles in your pursuit of happiness and prosperity.

EXCHANGE CREATES WEALTH

"Both parties to an economic transaction benefit from it, provided the transaction is bi-laterally voluntary and informed."[6] - Milton Friedman

Skousen illustrated in the following scenario that both buyer and seller in a transaction make a profit:

"Take a man who wants to buy a used car. He has a certain amount of money or credit. When he offers this money to the dealer it means that he would rather have the car than that amount of money—the value of the car is greater to him than the value of the money. If the dealer agrees it means that the

---

[6] Friedman, Milton. *Capitalism and Freedom* (Chicago: University of Chicago Press, 2002), 13.

dealer would rather have the money than the car. In fact, he won't sell the car unless the price he gets is of greater value to him than the value of the car."[7]

Who profited in this scenario?

Both parties went away wealthier. Both men exchanged something they valued less for something they valued more—that is the definition of profit.

Marxists would say that if the dealer sold it for more than it cost him to make or obtain it, then he was exploiting the customer. What Marxists fail to understand is the following principle:

> There is no exploitation without deception or coercion.

Take candy bars (again) as an example. They seem to really go up in price at airports, theaters, and sporting events. Why? Are we being deceived about what it cost the vendors to provide the candy bars? We know how much we can get them for at the store down the street. It's horrible to charge $3 for one at the movies, isn't it? Not really. Are we being forced to buy one? No, we can eat something else or buy nothing at all. We may sometimes get pretty angry at the movie theater, staring at a $6 bag of popcorn that cost five cents to make. Are we being exploited? Karl Marx would say, "Yes," but it is not so.

Sometimes, it is worth it to us to buy the popcorn at the theater, or the hot dog at the ballpark. Sometimes, however, it might not be. We can choose to not buy it. (If enough people refused to buy the popcorn at $6/bag the price would drop.) It is obviously worth $6/bag in that place and situation to enough people to make it worthwhile. No one is forcing us to do anything. If we value our money more than the popcorn, then we don't buy it, and we don't grumble that we chose what we preferred. We cannot have our popcorn and our money, too.

Here is a concept maybe a little closer to home—your wage.

Sometimes we (or our co-workers) might think, "My boss doesn't pay me enough, he just doesn't know how much I'm really worth."

Recall that a wage is just a fancy name for the price of labor. Let's ask the same questions as we did of the car purchase. If we agree to work

---

[7] Skousen, W. Cleon. *The Naked Communist* (Salt Lake City, Utah: Ensign Publishing Company, 1960), 274.

for $15/hour, how much do we value our time? How much do we value one hour of our life at that time and place? (Don't say $15!)

We value it less than $15. This is obviously true because if we valued it more, we would find someone else to pay us what we think we're worth, or we would use that hour for ourselves. We value our hour less than $15 because we constantly trade our hour for that amount. It is our choice to continue to work for $15/hour, we are perfectly free to seek higher-paying employment (and many people do).

How much does our employer value our time and labor? Not enough? They actually value it more than we do! They would prefer to have our hour of labor more than the $15, therefore they value our labor more than that amount of money. How much more? We can't know—maybe fifty cents more, maybe forty dollars more.

The principle remains that both parties involved in a free exchange profit and grow wealthier. Under capitalism, the employer, the employee, the distributor, the manufacturer, and the customer all benefit and grow literally wealthier as they exchange with each other voluntarily.

Now apply this in non-financial situations. Everyone profits from exchanges of knowledge, of personality, of love and friendship, of familial associations. It's the entire reason for individuals to want to live near and interact with one another rather than live as hermits. Sometimes we may choose to do a service for someone without getting paid. Why? Because we value seeing that person get help, or we value how service makes us feel, or what we learn from it. What we get out of an exchange doesn't always have to be measured in dollars. Yet, voluntary exchange, of anything, makes us wealthier.

DOLLARS FOLLOW VALUE

*"A free market . . . demands the best of every man
and rewards him accordingly."*[8] - Ayn Rand

Q: If I want more dollars in my control, where do I get them? Where are they currently?
A: In the pockets and bank accounts of other people.
Q: How can I persuade others to give those dollars to me?

---

[8] Rand, Ayn. *Capitalism: The Unknown Ideal* (New York: Signet, 1967), 25.

A: Create value. Provide a value in the form of a good or service that those people value more than the dollars in their pockets. They will then want to exchange those dollars with you.

In a world of cause and effect, value creation is the cause and dollars are the effect. For a moral individual who does not want to cheat or steal, the only way to increase the amount of dollars he or she has is to find out what value other people want and provide it for them in exchange for currency.

What about begging? This is also an exchange, though not a physical one. The alms-giver may receive the goodwill of the beggar, or the satisfaction of helping someone else. Don't make the mistake in assuming that because nothing of physical value was given for the dollars that value wasn't exchanged.

A highly underrated President, Calvin Coolidge, observed that, "Large profits mean large payrolls." Profit is a good thing! "In no land are there so many and such large aggregations of wealth as here; in no land do they perform larger service . . . . Don't expect to build up the weak by pulling down the strong."[9] He understood that you can't help those in need by attacking those who are doing the helping, and it is profit that makes it possible for anyone to help anyone else.

It is not within the scope of this book to train the reader on specific strategies for wealth creation; the aim of this book is to teach principles, not issues, number-crunching, or financial-advising. But, in order for any form of wealth-creation strategy to produce fruit, it must be rooted in this truth: dollars follow value.

PROFIT

"If profit is denounced, it must be assumed that running at a loss is admirable."[10] - Isabel Paterson

A DIRTY WORD

To socialists, profit is an "overage." Marx called it surplus value—an unnecessary "overage" over the "actual" price of a product.

---

[9] Safire, William, ed. *Lend Me Your Ears: Great Speeches in History* (New York: W. W. Norton & Company, 1992), 56.

[10] Paterson, Isabel. *The God of the Machine* (Originally published in 1943. Qualiteri eBook, 2009), Chapter 19.

To him, there was no such thing as good profit. Socialists view these "unnecessary" overages as lacking utility, purpose, or value.

Marx described this idea with his Labor Theory of Value. Basically, he said that the value of an item is equal to how much it cost to produce it. This is figured in "labor units"—somewhat like estimating the average skill of everyone on the planet and dividing it by how long it takes to produce an item.

Marx believed that value was intrinsic in things. He said that if a business owner sells a product for more than it cost to make, and he doesn't give that "overage" to his workers, then he is exploiting them of what is rightfully theirs. We have shown that collectivism is anti-mind—well, here is an example. Marx is ignoring and evading the truth that the genius of the human mind and tons of hard work is required to invent an item, start a business, hire workers, and keep a company profitable enough to continue to pay them. Profit is not evidence of exploitation, but a validation of proper business practices. There is no exploitation without force or deception.

Isabel Paterson made an astute comparison. "The objection to profit," she wrote, "is as if a bystander, observing the planter digging his crop, should say, 'You put in only one potato and you are taking out a dozen. You must have taken them away from someone else; those extra potatoes cannot be yours by right.'"[11]

Profit is income minus expenses. It means you produce more than you consume. The idea that profit, or even "excessive" profit, is evil has been a bitter poison that has slowly seeped throughout the philosophy of America for over a century.

Profit is the proper and moral consequence for the courage, thought, initiative, and effectiveness of the movers of an economy. Profit shows that decisions and actions have been a success. Loss represents failure. The amount of profit is an indication of how much customers value something. A loss shows that customers are not valuing it. Because profit is thus a moral value, the only means by which the public may morally curtail corporate or personal profits is this—the public's refusal to buy. Using government force to curtail profits is as obscenely evil as using government to curtail religion.

---

[11] *ibid.*

AN IMPORTANT TOOL

To be used as a helpful principle to guide our actions, profit is best considered as a tool of validation.[12] What does it validate? It validates to us that our activities are valued by other people. If our activities are valuable to others, then they will willingly trade with us for them.

Yet, we are asked to "bail out" companies that fail to make a profit. That a company might be "too big to fail" is a blatant deception. There is no private company, occupation, institution, or government program that is such a necessary and natural part of reality that it is to be protected at all costs. The fact that a company is not turning a profit is proof that it indeed is big enough to fail, and should. Every company has ups and downs, but without long-term sustainable profits, the company has proven that whatever product or service it provides is not valuable enough to its customers to continue its current activities. Giving a bailout is forcing the minds and wallets of all taxpayers to support a business that they may not agree with and may not patronize.

Providing a company with a false source of profit incentivizes the poor behavior that resulted in the problems in the first place—it creates a false demand for an unwanted product or service in the marketplace. The same principle applies in our families. If we reward poor behavior in our family or friends, we are offering no incentive for change—the poor behavior will continue, as will the demand for further reward.

For example, you may have seen a child screaming and throwing a fit in the grocery store because they want candy. The parent tells the child "no" time after time and even threatens punishment when they leave the store. But the child won't stop making a scene, and being embarrassed and too stressed to continue the battle of wills, the parent relents and buys the candy to stop the tantrum.

What has the child learned in this situation? They have learned that their parents are not to be respected or obeyed, that their word means nothing, and that their means to getting what they want in life is disobedience and annoyance. They've also seen that escalation in their bad behavior brings about the results faster. They have learned that emotion is their weapon for extorting others. They may have learned a lesson in perseverance, but unfortunately they learned perseverance in emotional terrorism rather than in reason, persuasion, and value creation. If this behavior is not corrected, they will later take these maladaptive behaviors

---

[12] Koerber, Rick and Israel Curtis, prod. "Lecture Series on the Principles of Prosperity." FreeCapitalist Radio. (May 19-June 26 2008). iTunes Podcast.

into their other relationships with children, spouse, friends, and coworkers and attempt to wreak similar havoc.

If you agree that profit is necessary for prosperity and progress, but that everyone should only be allowed to keep some of their profit, you are still missing the moral issue. Suppose a company had in its mission statement that they believed in earning a "reasonable profit." What is reasonable? How much is too much? Is $500 too much, or $1 million? Is a 2% profit margin reasonable or 200%? If we answer "yes" to any of these questions, then we only want people to value everything in the world the same way we do. Why does Bill Gates have more money than most people? Because he created more value than most people and his profit is the evidence of that.

Income
- Evidence of value created for someone.

Profit
- Evidence of valid behavior in a larger context including income and expenses.

Profit is a tool which can be used to see if certain actions are valid in the context of value creation for others, and the longer the time period we examine, the more accurate our assessment will be. Profit is proof that what we did was valuable to someone else. What does this imply about loss? If profit is evidence of valid behavior, loss is evidence of invalid behavior. It is invalid because consuming more than we produce is unsustainable behavior—for individuals, families, communities, and nations.

THEORIES OF VALUE

How people consider value can be divided into three basic belief systems. We've discussed the first belief system espoused by Marx—the intrinsic theory. This holds that value—or the good—is inherent in things and actions regardless of any context or consequences, of any benefit or injury that may be had by any party involved. It is also this theory which Kant applies to the collectivist ethic—the belief that self-sacrifice is intrinsically good regardless of any good or bad consequences.

The second is the subjective theory which holds that value bears no relation to reality and is to be found only in man's consciousness, created by whims, feelings, opinions, and desires. To quote Shakespeare's *Hamlet* on this one: "There is nothing either good or bad but thinking makes it so." As we've discussed, this subjectivism can be based on personal whims, or the whims of a collective.

Value is not intrinsic in things, not even in the most stable of value-retaining materials such as diamonds or gold. Nor is value found exclusively in each person's subjective preferences since sometimes those preferences are not based on the facts of reality.

No, what we must understand is that value is objective. The objective theory holds that "good" is "an aspect of reality in relation to man."[13]

How much is this book you're reading worth? The correct answer is "nothing!" Things have no value! The question, to be valid, must include the implied modifiers, "To whom and for what?" Remember another word for "value" is "utility."

How much is this book of value (i.e. of use) to whom and for what purpose? A textbook may be worth (i.e. used as) nothing but kindling to a stranded hiker or a homeless person. A textbook may be worth much to a college student who doesn't have one and wants to use it to study for an important exam the next day. It might be worth little to someone who has twenty of them on their shelf and sells them to people for a living.[14] As you can see, it is not just the opinion of the individuals that determines the value, but a consideration of the context of that person's life and to what use they would put it.

My (Caleb's) brother-in-law once won a carousel horse on The Price is Right. It certainly had a retail price assigned to it. But it was worthless to him because he had no use for it.

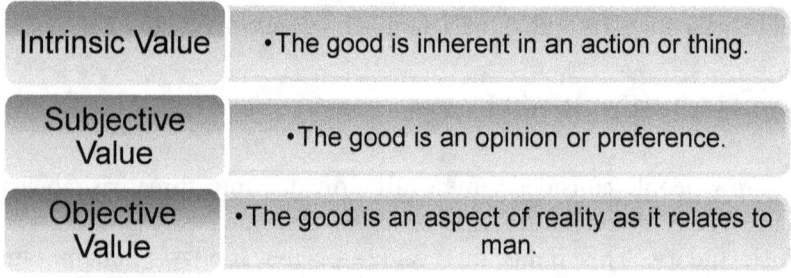

Intrinsic Value	• The good is inherent in an action or thing.
Subjective Value	• The good is an opinion or preference.
Objective Value	• The good is an aspect of reality as it relates to man.

---

[13] Rand, *Capitalism*, 21-22.

[14] Koerber, Rick and Israel Curtis, prod. "Lecture Series on the Principles of Prosperity." FreeCapitalist Radio. (May 19-June 26 2008). iTunes Podcast.

Value must always be ascertained objectively within a context of a man's life, needs, goals, and knowledge. Under capitalism, wrote Leonard Peikoff, "Men are left free to judge the worth of various products, the worth to them; each judges in accordance with his own needs and goals as he himself understands these to apply in particular context. Market value thus entails valuer, purpose, beneficiary, choice, knowledge."[15] The essential question is always, "Of value to whom and for what?" This is the meaning of valuing things objectively.

HUMAN LIFE VALUE

This next prosperity principle borrows an old term from the insurance industry. Life insurance companies hire full-time underwriters whose job, as strange as it may sound, is to determine the economic value of someone's life. They look at a variety of factors including age, income, profession, etc. to determine the amount of insurance to issue to someone. They call this Human Life Value.

For our purposes, Human Life Value is everything we are without our material possessions. It is our unique combination of talents, abilities, perspective, thoughts, character, virtues, relationships, and education.

As a principle: Human Life Value is the source and creator of all property value.[16] This means that any material wealth in the world is created by, and/or is the effect of, someone's human life value (e.g. skills, relationships, passions, abilities). "If we find ourselves in a situation where we have less currency than we want," explained businessman Garrett Gunderson, "the way out of that situation is to share our Human Life Value with people. Do research for others, make phone calls, educate yourself on real estate acquisitions and help someone get out of a bad situation with a house, turn your hobby into a business, call one of the busiest people you know and offer your services to help get some things off their plate—the possibilities are endless. None of the things I mentioned require you to have currency in order to make currency. They require YOU. They require your creativity and your initiative. They require your ability to . . . see and fulfill the desires of other people . . . Human

---

[15] Peikoff, *Objectivism*, 397.

[16] Koerber, Rick, ed. *The FreeCapitalist Project Primer* (Provo, Utah: FreeCapitalist Project, 2007), 25.

Life Value is the cause; currency is the effect. Focus on the cause and the effect naturally and inevitably follows."[17]

This idea is closely related to Dollars Follow Value. What we specifically identify with this principle is where the value originates. The good news is that no matter how much you use it, your Human Life Value will never decrease as long as you use it well. It is yours. You get to do with it what you want. You can increase it by living according to true principles; it will even change as you age or progress, giving you incentive to constantly reevaluate what personal resources you have. Economist Amartya Sen called this "Human Capital" which individuals can increase through education, learning, skill formation, and become more productive and capable over time.[18] You can also deplete your human life value by violating principles (e.g. dishonesty, theft, violence, addiction, etc.).

"You were given a simple piece of wood," wrote businessman Rick Koerber to illustrate this principle, "It's just a log to everyone; no one wants it. However, if you know how to use a chisel and a hammer and use that knowledge to sculpt a beautiful image into the wood, that simple piece of wood then becomes a sculpture. You could sell the beautiful sculpture for $1 million, $1,000, or even a $100. You created value, and it's not because the wood had value; rather, it's because you had value and exercised your talent on a physical thing to create value for someone else. All property value is created by human life value."[19]

It doesn't take money to make money. It takes you, and when you exchange the products or services of your Human Life Value with others, all become wealthier.

PERSPECTIVE DETERMINES ACTION[20]

This principle describes how our actions and reactions are based on what we know or think we know. Different information or assumptions may change our paradigms—or the pattern of our perspective that we impose on the world.

A story related in *Mind Over Mood* illustrates this:

---

[17] Gunderson, Garrett. and Stephen Palmer. *Killing Sacred Cows* (Provo, Utah: Decade Media, 2007), 112.

[18] Sen, Amartya. *Development as Freedom* (New York: Alfred A. Knopf, 2000), 292.

[19] Koerber, *Primer*, 81.

[20] Koerber, Rick and Israel Curtis, prod. "Lecture Series on the Principles of Prosperity." FreeCapitalist Radio. (May 19-June 26 2008). iTunes Podcast.

"Sally was at home with the flu and asked her 7-year-old daughter, Barbara, to play quietly while she rested. An hour later, Sally walked into the kitchen to get a drink of water and was distressed to see crayons spread all over the floor, shredded colored paper and an open bottle of glue on the table, open scissors in the wastebasket, and a half-drunk glass of milk on the counter next to the refrigerator.

"Furious about the mess, Sally went hunting for Barbara and found her sleeping soundly in front of the television in the living room. On the cushion near Barbara's head was a large, brightly colored card, covered in hearts, that read, 'I love you, Mom! Please get well soon!' Sally shook her head slowly and smiled. She tucked a blanket around Barbara's shoulders and returned to the kitchen to get her water."[21]

The authors go on to demonstrate how thoughts determine one's feelings and moods, and a change of evidence can sometimes change one's perspective. That perspective shift can either be drastic, as in Sally's case, or sometimes lead to a more "balanced perspective."[22] This principle can help in both personal and political affairs.

Personally, it can lead you to examine the perspective of others, rather than assuming you completely understand their situation, motives, and thoughts, which can lead to misunderstandings and unnecessary conflict. It can help you examine your own beliefs—with practice you can even examine them down to your very core beliefs. You can discover why you feel a certain way and learn to compile and use evidence to give you a more balanced grasp of any issue.

Politically, this principle will help you understand others' points of view, as well as your own. The perspective with which one views the world determines how one will act. Knowledge is power because knowledge expands viewpoints and allows a person to see what couldn't be seen before.

Why do some people strap dynamite to their chests and blow themselves and other people up? Because of the ideas in their head. If you want to change someone's behavior, don't outlaw dynamite; that will not change anything. If you want to change the behavior of drug-addicts,

---

[21] Greensberger, D., and C. Padesky. *Mind Over Mood* (New York: The Guilford Press, 1995), 89.
[22] *ibid*, 94.

don't outlaw drugs; that will not change anything but make them criminals. To influence someone's behavior, assist in changing their perspective.

When we view the world from a new perspective, our behavior changes. Steven Covey's book, *7 Habits of Highly Effective People*, discusses this principle and calls it a paradigm shift. As we grow in knowledge and ability, our perspective changes in relation to how we act.

FREEDOM VS. SECURITY

Sociology professor Zygmunt Bauman lamented what he perceived as the human predicament of choosing between the responsibility of freedom and the freedom from responsibility. He said freedom was exhilarating, but, "Soon after freedom settles in . . . a new kind of horror, the horror of responsibility . . . makes the memories of past sufferings pale. Nights that follow days of obligatory routine are filled with dreams of freedom from constraints. Nights that follow days of obligatory choices are filled with dreams of freedom from responsibility."[23]

Dr. Bauman is describing the very understandable, yet childish wish to be free from the demands of existence, and to evade the requirements of reality; to get our cake for free, simultaneously have it on our plate and in our stomach, and not get fat in the process.

Freedom and security are opposites in some ways and related in others. Personal freedom, when used wisely in conjunction with the other prosperity principles we've discussed, leads to the truest and most lasting security, since it is based on personal ability and stewardship.

However, when security is sought from an outside source, such as a government, and exceeds the principle of protection of rights, security then begins to erode freedom. As government programs are established and bureaucracies engaged to provide us with more and more things and take care of our needs, our corresponding freedoms are restricted. Instead of the security of liberty, it becomes the security of a prison.

Our proper place in this world is as a thinking adult who confronts the requirements of existence head-on, as ones who use our human life value to be productive, to obtain the necessities and comforts of life, and to find joy in existence. To desire some sort of security beyond a protection of rights is essentially a desire to abdicate our minds and our identity

---

[23] Bauman, Zygmunt. *Does Ethics Have A Chance In A World of Consumers?* (Cambridge, Massachusetts: Harvard University Press, 2008), 46-47.

as rational humans. It is the desire to be shielded from real life—to live, as it were, rent-free in nature's basement.

VICTIM VS. STEWARD

This comparison is sometimes useful to assist us in contrasting two opposing attitudes and perspectives we can choose to cultivate.

Do we make our own choices or do we allow ourselves to be controlled by outside circumstances? This concept is referred to as an internal locus of control as opposed to an external one. Do we believe we are in control of our life, choices, and thoughts, or do we think we are at the mercy of what happens to us? Scientists have found that having an internal locus of control is the number one contributor to happiness![24]

We can choose to act and to shape our destiny, or we can relinquish responsibility for our lives, believing we cannot influence external events, viewing ourselves as pieces of driftwood in an ocean of chance, or as pawns in an arbitrary universe of random happenstance, prey at the mercy of every predator.

The steward is marked by action, drive, achievement, and dreams.

The victim is marked by stagnation, complaints, and seeing themselves as powerless.

Stewards spend their time and energy concentrating on what they can do while victims spend their time and energy making excuses and wishing things were different.

The victim says, "It's not my fault."

The steward says, "It's my responsibility."

The victim says, "It's not my job."

The steward says, "How can I help?"

The victim says, "I wish things would change."

The steward says, "What can I do to change things?"

The victim says, "I wish I had more."

The steward says, "How can I better use what I have?"

---

[24] Salmansohn, Karen. "The Number 1 Contributor to Happiness." *Psychology Today.* Online. 30 Jun 2011. psychologytoday.com/blog/bouncing-back/201106/the-no-1-contributor-happiness. Accessed 19 Jun 2014.

PRODUCTIVITY IS THE STANDARD[25]

While profit works as our tool to validate that our actions have value in the marketplace and to provide us with the means to achieve our goals, it is not the standard by which we ought to gauge our activities. That standard is productivity.

Productivity is the result of a continual self-evaluation seeking to answer and then apply the answer to the question: Is this the best use of my time, talents, and resources?

Why is this principle important? So we don't mistake profit as the standard of our lives. As we discussed, profit can be used as a tool to demonstrate that our actions are valuable to others. But only you, as sovereign of your own life, are able to evaluate how productive you are in your progress and journey in achieving your values and desires—in achieving happiness (although other people, such as a mentor, may be helpful in pointing out blind spots of which you are not aware).

If you use profit as your standard you may fall victim to the mistake of not using your talents to produce the most value possible in the world. You might see your profit margins and net worth increase, but still feel restless and dissatisfied because you are not using your unique abilities to the fullest.

For example, are you an entrepreneur who profitably takes a product, service, or idea to a few dozen or a few hundred people? What if a new focus and direction could expand your effectiveness to thousands or even millions of people? Could you be more productive if you delegated jobs and responsibilities? What if you even changed careers, freeing yourself up for the things for which only you are best suited or most passionate?

Producing more than we consume is being profitable; producing the most and best possible is being productive. Thus productivity, not profit, is our most appropriate standard. This involves questioning our actions and choices in terms such as, "Is that the best use of that resource which I control?" This question applies on any level, "Is this the best use I have for the $10 in my pocket, or the $100, or the $1,000, or the $1 million?" "Is this the best use of my artistic talent?" "Is this the best use of this hour of my day?"

---

[25] Koerber, Rick and Israel Curtis, prod. "Lecture Series on the Principles of Prosperity." FreeCapitalist Radio. (May 19-June 26 2008). iTunes Podcast.

Using productivity as our standard, rather than profit, is also useful in measuring the long-term value of our actions. It is possible to turn a profit month after month and suddenly fail in the next because a long-term violation of principles hadn't caught up with us yet. The failure of the housing market bubble illustrates this perfectly. It was profitable to sell risky mortgages incentivized and backed by government agencies. Inflated housing prices created many jobs and lots of artificial wealth and net worth. Eventually, the violation of principle in these matters collapsed in destruction. When the government got involved it suspended productivity as the standard. It demanded instead that loan qualification requirements be lowered to provide the dream of a home for every American family. This diverted funds, both public and private, from other, more productive, uses to which they would have gone. The standard for the government was need and popularity and power, instead of productivity.

The question, "Is this the best use of my time, talents, and resources?" also implies that the meaning of the word best will rely on a reference to a hierarchy of values. One must have criteria and a method to determine what is best.

HIERARCHY OF VALUES

"The cause of most of man's unhappiness is sacrificing what he wants most for what he wants now."[26] - Gordon B. Hinckley

As long as we choose to continue living, and as long as we want life to be meaningful, we have to choose and pursue rational goals in all areas of our lives—romance, work, friendship, recreation, and family.

First, it is important to choose goals that are compatible with each other. It does no good to hold family as a value and then choose a career that takes you away from it. It does no good to choose a hobby you can't afford, or form relationships you don't have time to pursue.

---

[26] Hinckley, Gordon, B. Quoted on Motivatingquotes.com. Online. motivatingquotes.com/happiness.htm. Accessed 30 May 2012.

Next, these goals should be organized around the central major purpose of your life. This is your primary long-range goal, for which any number of short-range goals are organized to achieve. Having such a purpose saves you from pointless inner conflicts of indecision. What you choose as a major purpose should necessarily involve productive work, since you cannot continue to live (unless as a parasite) without it.

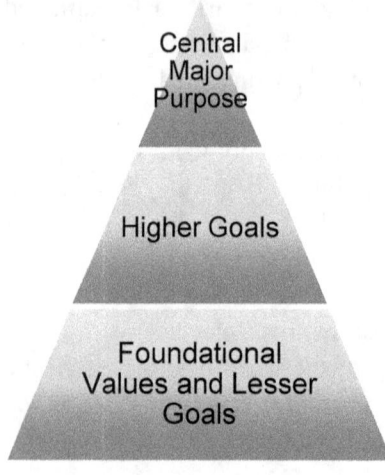

The values of your life are formed in a hierarchy, from least to greatest. You may also wish to view these values in somewhat of a pyramid shape, with foundational values and goals being placed to build up to the primary long-range purpose as the capstone.

Most people's values are chosen unconsciously and valued sporadically. Consciously chosen values, numbered and arranged according to importance will give the best results. The purpose of utilizing such a hierarchy in decision-making is to do your utmost to never seek a lesser goal at the expense of a higher value. In fact, the key to a moral life is learning to never sacrifice one of your higher values for a lesser.

(Altruism will teach you the opposite—that to be moral you must sacrifice all the values you hold dear to the needs of others. The collectivist ethic will try and disguise this, of course, and try to persuade you that the needs of others should be your highest value, with your own needs considered as lowest on the scale and as expendable in their service.)

Let's see how a proper hierarchy of values would function. For example, you may rationally hold the virtue of honesty as a value in life. You have seen the value of not faking reality in any way, and have committed to practicing honesty in your dealings with others and with yourself. Should honesty be practiced at all times and in all circumstances regardless of the results?

Suppose you own and run a small market. One night, a robber comes in with a gun and demands all the money from your cash register. You comply in order to save your own life. The robber then asks if there is any more money anywhere in the store. You know you keep a safe hidden in the back with much of your savings in it. You have no reason to believe that the robber knows anything about it. What do you do? Will you bow to your commitment to honesty and inform the robber of the additional cash reserve? Wouldn't it be considered moral to tell the truth like that? If you were an altruist, would you not have to consider his needs and wants above your own?

What if, instead, you lie to the robber, telling him that you have no more money? Is it immoral to lie like that, knowing that statement is untrue?

How do you decide if lying is moral in this situation? A look at your hierarchy of values will help to determine the answer. Which is your highest value, to be honest, or to have a happy life? If your life is your highest value, you will need to have many other lesser values that will support, and help you to enjoy it to its fullest. Such values include reason, self-esteem, friendship, as well as honesty. All these lesser values are subordinate to the highest value of your happy life; they exist to serve and achieve it.

What if you reverse those values and place honesty as the highest one? You could tell the robber about the safe and thus live according to your value hierarchy, but what will the result be? You will be broke and probably not very happy. We choose to be honest because it helps us achieve our overarching goal of a happy life. We do not live for the purpose of being honest. To do so would be to place the cart before the horse.

In this case, lying to the robber is an action that rationally supports both your life and your central major purpose. You sacrifice the lower value of honesty in order to uphold and protect the higher values of your life and livelihood. This must be considered a rational and moral decision. On the other hand, if you chose to sacrifice your savings and future productivity, your progress in your career, and much of your means to support your own life, in preference for the lower virtue of honesty, that could be considered an immoral and irrationally self-destructive decision.

Remember, the art of living morally consists of learning to never sacrifice your higher, life-serving values in favor of any lower values. Rationality consists in learning how to accomplish this in your life with consistency and without contradiction.

Philosophy is important because it guides the way we live. It teaches us what to value, how to interact with the world and people around us, and what goals to seek. It is vital to do our best to live our lives without contradiction.

In matters of truth, there is no room for ego. One thing most lacking in the world is intellectual humility. By humility we do not mean capitulation and uncertainty, only commitment to truth at the expense of conceit. It is a very rare thing to find someone willing to admit that they don't know something, or that their opinions have not been thought out, or that they have never bothered to question their beliefs. Most people feel threatened by questions to their belief structure because their sense of self, and self-worth, is tied to those beliefs. It takes emotional stability to be able to admit you were wrong, or don't know something. A person's ability to recognize and accept truth is most often tied to their level of emotional maturity.

Because there are no contradictions, and because truth does not change, neither do the demands of our lives, nor the actions we must take to further our lives. This means that there will never be a time or circumstance in which we will need to give up a greater value for a lesser one (i.e. choose evil). There is no such thing as a necessary evil or a justification for taking an immoral action. This is true in every decision we will ever make as long as we are freely using our uncoerced agency.

REVIEW

Q1: What is money? How is that different than currency?

Q2: What does it mean to be wealthy, happy, and prosperous?

Q3: How does exchange create wealth?

Q4: What is Human Life Value and how does it create property value?

Q5: How does our perspective determine our actions?

Q6: How is money earned?

Q7: What does profit validate?

Q8: Why should productivity be the standard of your actions?

Q9: How can you use a Hierarchy of Values in your life?

Q10: What is your central major purpose?

Q11: Contrast victim and steward, freedom and security, producer and consumer.

Q12: Explain the theories of value.

CHAPTER 14

THE ATTACK ON CAPITALISM

"The United States cannot claim to be exempt from manifestations of economic slavery, of grinding the faces of the poor, of exploitation of the weak, of unfair distribution of wealth, of unjust monopoly . . . and of a preference of the material over the spiritual."[1]
- James Fullarton Muirhead, 1898

Why do we need to discuss and answer attacks against capitalism? Because widespread attacks on the liberty of the individual and the rights of man are escalating. To overcome an opponent, we must first understand what they are saying, and that means being able to articulate the position of the opponent so clearly that they agree with us, saying, "Yes, that's what I believe!" To stand for something, we must also understand its opposite.

We may be sold on the concept of capitalism, but soon we will be confronted with difficult questions, "What about depressions, monopolies, child labor, corporate welfare, and the elderly?" To be effective, we must have the answers, especially since there are many who would agree

---

[1] Quoted in Croly, Herbert. *The Promise of American Life* (LaVergne, Tennessee: Book Jungle, 2010), 24.

with the moral idea of capitalism, but mistakenly think that morality and practicality are somehow disconnected.

The entire political philosophy of capitalism is built on observable facts and the observable requirements of life. It doesn't depend on anything invisible or unprovable. It has a foundation rooted in the bedrock of existence, and brick by brick, each proposition is rationally built on the preceding principle.

Before we dive into critiques of capitalism, let's review briefly what we have already learned about it. It has been demonstrated that existence exists, and that the only way to gain knowledge is by integrating your perceptual information through reason.

The moral purpose of your life is to be happy and is achieved by pursuing your rational self-interest.

To do this, you must be able to follow your own judgment and to keep and dispose of the property you create and acquire.

To enjoy your life, liberty, and property you must be kept free from the forceful interference of others.

To best be kept free from the force of others, there must be an objective government whose sole job is the protection of rights.

This government must hold a monopoly on the use of retaliatory force, only acting to protect individual rights of those within its borders.

With its scope thus defined, government will have no dealings in the economy except to prosecute any initiation of force and violation of contract.

In such a system, all citizens are free to buy and sell whatever and with whomever they want so long as they do not deceive or coerce. They are free to try, fail, buy, sell, and to accomplish and earn as much or as little as their desire and capability allows. This is capitalism—unfettered freedom to rationally pursue your own life.

MORAL VS PRACTICAL

One of the lies about capitalism is that it works in principle but not in practice. This contradiction is called the moral/practical dichotomy. It is a false pairing of alleged opposites.

To call something practical you must first define what it is you wish to practice.

Since the proper standard of value is man's life, then to be considered practical an act must be objectively seen to further and protect that life. That which is objectively moral is always practical. Since the definition of morality is that the "good" is that which is proper to human life (i.e. for its existence and happiness), then, by definition, that which is moral must be practical in furthering that life.

Some people might see the morality vs. practicality argument another way. They may see that the theory is sound but they think the majority will not accept or comply with it. They are letting morality be held hostage by circumstance. They are saying that they will not try to do the right thing because not everyone will accept it. This line of thinking is dangerously close to the logical fallacy "Appeal to Consequences"—rejecting the moral premise because the consequences may not be desirable. Letting the projected consequences determine what you do and believe means you don't have integrity. As comedian Jon Stewart put it, "If you don't stick to your values when they're being tested, they're not values—they're hobbies. You know, one of the genius moves of The Founders was not writing The Bill of Rights on the back window of a dusty van."[2]

The Founders pledged their sacred honor and their lives for the truth, and many of them paid a steep price for their beliefs. If people never fight for their values when the odds are against them, then our world is truly doomed.

Recall how Pragmatism denies the existence of truth, but only focuses on what seems most effective at the moment. Those who claim to be "pragmatic," even without knowing about the philosophy of Pragmatism, share its fatal flaw of short-term thinking. Pragmatists do not see the big picture and generally accept the options before them at face value. They fail to consider alternatives. One common example is Presidential elections. Many Republicans do not like the Republican candidate very much (e.g. John McCain), but vote for him anyway because "he's better than a Democrat." This is an example of the long term blindness of Pragmatism, as well as the weakness of Sensors (see Chapter 1) who only focus on concrete facts in the present.

1. They know they don't want a Democrat in office.
2. They know they don't agree with the Republican either.
3. They know the third-party candidate who most closely represents their values might have little chance of winning.
4. They feel if they vote their conscience, they may end up with the Democrat.

---

[2] "Fox News Fear Imbalance." The Daily Show. thedailyshow.cc.com/videos/ol3px4/fox-news-fear-imbalance. 22 Jan 2009. Accessed 19 Jun 2014.

Therefore, they make their choice based on the likely effects rather than on their values.

This scenario played out in the 1992 election that brought Bill Clinton into office. Many Republicans were livid that Ross Perot split the vote, citing that if Perot voters had chosen George Bush, we could have avoided Clinton. What the Republicans fail to consider is the long-term consequence of continually backing someone who doesn't share your values. As we have shown, despite any apparent differences, Republicans and Democrats both share the same belief in statism which denies individual rights. Year after year, we vote for the ideology of statism, and the assault on our rights has advanced. In the battle for our liberties, it doesn't matter whether a Republican or Democrat is in the White House—either way our rights continue to be eroded. Those accustomed to voting for the lesser of two evils will soon learn that the difference between the two has lost all meaning.

There is a story told of men cutting down trees. Some of the lumberjacks noticed that one man was often sitting down, not cutting any lumber, but instead sharpening his saw. They scoffed at this seeming waste of time, only thinking of all the work he was not getting done while he sharpened his saw. But at the end of the day, the man was able to cut down more trees than the other lumberjacks who worked steadily with their dull tools. To the casual observer, sharpening the saw looked like a step backwards. Yet moving forward relied on it. When it comes to elections, Conservatives have been furiously sawing without taking a break. The once sharp teeth have become dull and useless. The teeth are now no more than rounded, ineffectual nubs. Though the nubs are doing nothing, they still seem better than using the back of the blade. One may be marginally better than the other, but in the end, it is not enough and will make no difference to our lost freedom.

Some Pragmatists are willing to sell out principles for the illusion of safety. For example, Conservative parents want to reduce the risk to their children as much as possible, so they support laws that make drugs illegal. They will support these laws even though they deny the right to liberty. On the other hand, Liberal parents want to reduce the risk to their children as much as possible, so they support laws that make guns illegal. What is the difference? There is no difference. Both ideologies throw rights under the bus because of Pragmatic concerns which destroy safety and liberty for the fleeting promise of security.

Doing the right thing sometimes requires hardships in the present. Doing the right thing might not produce immediate results. Doing the right thing might mean uncertainty, danger, or less than satisfactory living circumstances for a time. Doing the right thing means thinking about long-term consequences and not holding values hostage to momentary concerns. Doing the right thing may mean splitting the vote until enough people are fed up with two horrible choices to do something truly different. The Founding Fathers chose to suffer in the present for the hope of a better future, are we willing to do the same?

TRADITIONAL ATTACKS ON CAPITALISM

Almost all attacks on capitalism are straw-men—they misconstrue essential meanings, ascribe a characteristic which capitalism does not possess, and then attack the misconception.

Ironically, almost every attack on capitalism made by a statist actually amounts to an attack on statism itself!

Most attacks are usually not made against pure capitalism but its mongrel statist hybrid—the mixed economy. America and every other semi-free nation on earth have mixed economies in varying degrees.

Most of the alleged evils of capitalism are actually the results of statism. Historian Leonard Peikoff examined some of these alleged evils and identified their actual statist causes:

ECONOMIC DEPRESSIONS

A depression is a sustained downturn in economic activity across a large geographic area.

The only way a financial system can become unsound and cause a depression is through overextension of credit and paper currency. The only thing able to cause this would be an agency with nationwide power. The only agency with nationwide power to affect currency is the government—specifically, through the Federal Reserve system. This is done principally by manipulating the money supply. Lending money too easily or cheaply gives incentive to spend irresponsibly. The suspension of cause and effect (dollars follow value; failure follows non-value) makes possible market bubbles and quickly collapsing business sectors. But often a normal market fluctuation will persist even longer because of tax policy, fear of more tax policy, fear of government intervention, and actual government intervention.

Also thrown in is the fact that incentives of character have been removed with the introduction of the "I'm-property-of-the-state" victim mentality.

One common Progressive/statist response is to decry all economic problems as the results of too much freedom, and look to regulations and controls for the solutions. It has been one of the primary methods used by statists to destroy capitalism: establish controls that make businesses unable to solve their problems, and then cry that freedom has failed and stronger controls are required. It is also a deeply entrenched part of human history that we tend to seek more power over others, rather than relinquish it.

Isabel Paterson examined the history of depressions and recessions in America before the 1930's. She observed that during several heavy depressions in America, the government did practically nothing. "There was rock-bottom poverty, men tramping the country looking for work, and living on handouts or soup-kitchens. But prices of commodities were so low, being allowed to go down as far as they would, that very little money sufficed for subsistence. When the credit collapse had been liquidated, recovery was so rapid that the change seemed fabulous in retrospect."[3] After the Second Bank of the United States led directly to the Panic of 1819, nothing was done to stop it, and the panic ended peacefully. Jefferson wrote that the flood of paper money had exaggerated prices and produced "fictitious" capital, which the ensuing panic wiped out while also deflating prices.

Such rapid recoveries do not exist when government rides to the rescue and tries to keep prices from falling naturally. There have been more than twelve major recessions since the 1930's. Facing this page is a chart showing the annual inflation rate of the U.S. marked with historical events and banking panics.[4]

As you can see, for about 150 years, the inflation rates changed dramatically and often quickly, and there were several banking panics spanning the years. However, this self-correction of the market kept consumer prices relatively stable during this time. From the Revolutionary War up until the Federal Reserve System was established in 1913, prices rose sometimes and then fell back to original rates. Many things cost the same 1776 as they did in 1900! However, once the Fed started manipulating interest rates and inflation, and especially when the U.S. partially and then completely dropped the gold standard, they never let the prices correct themselves to lower levels. Each year, things cost more than they did

---

[3] Paterson, Isabel. *The God of the Machine* (Originally published in 1943. Qualiteri eBook, 2009), Chapter 19.

[4] Graph is from visualizingeconomics.com. Accessed 15 Aug 2014. visualizingeconomics.com/blog/2008/05/27/us-inflation-annual-percent-change-1774-2007

before. We will discuss more about the gold standard and consumer prices later in this chapter.

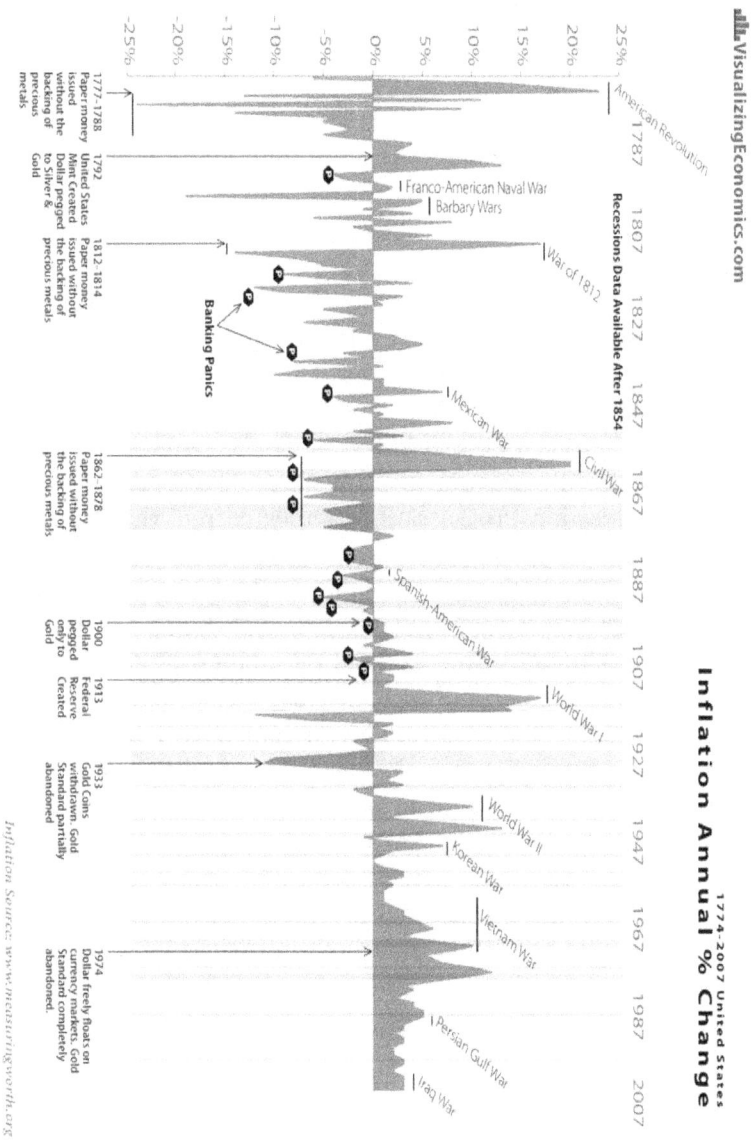

CHILD LABOR

What is needed to raise the standard of living across a broad range of people? Not laws or redistribution of wealth, but production. Before people can consume anything, it must be produced. For much of history, nothing could be produced beyond a bare subsistence.

Mercantilism helped amass large quantities of capital, and the Enlightenment helped free people somewhat politically and economically. What resulted? The heavy machines of the Industrial Revolution. Such increased production with its divisions of labor made many of the modes of production from the Middle Ages obsolete. This increase in production also helped increase population exponentially, as well as the overall standard of living since more goods were available that were cheaper to produce and thus cheaper to buy.

What about horrific working conditions and child labor? Such labor was due to inherited poverty from the feudal systems. This sort of labor was prevalent throughout most of mankind's history. The Child Labor Public Education Project says that the "current causes of global child labor are similar to its causes in the U.S. 100 years ago, including poverty." They estimate that of "215 million child laborers around the globe: approximately 114 million (53%) are in Asia and the Pacific; 14 million (7%) live in Latin America; and 65 million (30%) live in sub-Saharan Africa."[5] If freedom and capitalism cause child labor, it would be logical to assume that the freest and most capitalistic countries would suffer from it the most. As we can see, this is far from the truth.

Child labor was wiped out in the United States, not primarily by laws and unions, but by capitalism's productivity which slowly made such labor unnecessary for a family's survival and prosperity. This increase in productivity slowly started providing for people's needs without them having to resort to such heart-breaking methods for survival. Keep everything in context and you will see that capitalism did not cause such things, but eradicated them in all but the most statist of modern countries.

---

[5] The Child Labor Education Project. Online. continue-tolearn.uiowa.edu/laborctr/child_labor/about/what_is_child_labor.html. Accessed 4 Jul 2012.

SLAVERY

The founding principle of America—individual rights—contradicted the established institution of slavery, which had existed since the earliest recorded histories. That principle paved the way to a Civil War and eventually eradicated legalized slavery from America and from the earth.

Abraham Lincoln claimed that a higher law superseded the statutory laws of slavery and found them in violation of a "nation conceived in liberty and dedicated to the proposition that all men are created equal." As author Jean Elshtain observes, "Lincoln could not have made such a claim if he lacked the principles from which to challenge the abhorrent practice he condemned. Slavery was not a founding American principle. It was a repulsive practice that clashed with our principles and was therefore doomed."[6]

Lincoln said that the Black man was "entitled to all the natural rights enumerated in the Declaration of Independence, the right to life, liberty, and the pursuit of happiness . . . . In the right to eat the bread, without leave of anybody else, which his own hand earns, he is my equal and . . . the equal of every living man."[7]

George Washington foresaw that the existence of slavery, a European tradition that the Americans would have to wipe away, would threaten the future existence of the union: "I can clearly foresee that nothing but the rooting out of slavery can perpetuate the existence of our union, by consolidating it in a common bond of principle."[8]

Slavery in America only survived as long as it did, say historians Schweikart and Allen, because of political machinery put in place to protect it: "Ultimately slavery could exist only through the power of the state. It survived because political forces prevented the typical decay and destruction of slavery experienced elsewhere."[9]

The adoption of capitalism wiped out slavery in matter and in spirit.

---

[6] Elshtain, Jean Bethke. *Just War Against Terror* (New York: Basic Books, 2003), 28.

[7] Schweikart, Larry. and Michael Allen. *A Patriot's History of the United States: From Columbus' Great Discovery to the War on Terror* (New York: Penguin, 2004), 289.

[8] Allison, A., Parry, J., and W. Cleon Skousen. *The Real George Washington* (Washington D.C.: National Center for Constitutional Studies, 1991), 623.

[9] Schweikart, *History*, 260.

POOR FOOD/DRUG QUALITY

A seller relies on his reputation to achieve long-term profits. Poor quality will send his buyers elsewhere, and fraudulent representation has always been illegal and is one of the reasons we need the protection of government. Goods never achieved such high quality in such a short period of time on earth as they did under capitalism's partial reign.

Quality slowly declines in a mixed economy. The public is lulled into thinking that since inspectors from the government are checking everything that their own judgment is unnecessary. Furthermore, once businesses have met a minimum standard set by government, they often have no incentive to produce higher quality products. Nor is the government capable of guaranteeing the safety and health of products in the first place, as can be seen in numerous cases of harmful drugs and contaminated foods that were approved or completely missed.

POLLUTION

"The word 'pollution' implies health hazards, such as smog or dirty waters."[10] "As far as the issue of actual pollution is concerned," Ayn Rand explained, "it is primarily a scientific, not a political, problem. In regard to the political principle involved: if a man creates a physical danger or harm to others, which extends beyond the line of his own property, such as unsanitary conditions or even loud noise, and if this is proved, the law can and does hold him responsible. If the condition is collective, such as in an overcrowded city, appropriate and objective laws can be defined, protecting the rights of all those involved—as was done in the case of oil rights, air-space rights, etc."[11]

It is well within the proper scope of government to protect people against harm from pollution.

Unfortunately, it is a fact of our existence that you can't make the delicious omelet which is our prosperity without breaking a few eggs. Industrial waste is an inescapable, yet minor side effect of industrialization. The only alternative is primitivization, where pollution is actually worse!

The World Health Organization found that the amount of harmful "small particles" in the air of a hut where solid fuel is being burned is 12.5 times greater than even a roadside in Bangkok. Children and adults living

---

[10] "Pollution." The Ayn Rand Lexicon. Online. Quoted from "The Left: Old and New," *Return of the Primitive: The Anti-Industrial Revolution.* aynrandlexicon.com/lexicon/pollution.html. Accessed 26 Aug 2012.

[11] *ibid.*

in such primitive conditions have an incredibly high risk of developing, and dying from pulmonary and respiratory problems.[12]

Statism is the cause of ongoing pollution problems. Despite decades of EPA regulations, pollution still occurs in significant amounts. "Regulations regarding sewage treatment have proven similarly impractical. Since 1972, the federal government has forced water utilities to spend billions of dollars upgrading water treatment facilities, and yet, during the past four years, record numbers of beaches have closed due to pollution from sewage. And the EPA predicts that by 2016 American rivers will be as polluted by sewage as they were in the 1970's."[13]

Government controlled "public land" does away with the concern and responsibility that comes with the stewardship of owning private property. If waterways were privately owned, overfishing would not be the problem that it is today because the owners would have the incentive to act sustainably to insure their long term survival and prosperity.

As with so many other problems caused by statism, pollution can be greatly reduced by protecting rights. The only entities with the finances, technology, and willpower to clean up are free and unfettered businesses, empowered by the restoration of stewardship and strengthened by the removal of crippling taxes.

WAR

This is a product of dictatorships which survive by looting others. Free countries seek to trade with others, unfree countries seek to dominate and leech resources from others. Free countries only attack to defend against objective threats.[14]

GOVERNMENT CORRUPTION

Business has no power to influence politics in a free market. Business and politics are only mingled in statist governments where the economy isn't guided by principles. In capitalism, private business does not

---

[12] World Health Organization. www.who.int/en/. "Household Energy, Indoor Air Pollution and Health." who.int/indoorair/publications/fflsection1.pdf. Accessed 26 Aug 2012.

[13] Phillips, J. Brian. Germani, Alan. "The Practicality of Private Waterways." *The Objective Standard.* Spring, 2020. Online. theobjectivestandard.com/promo/gyu937bis936kyd917hst562/tos-v5n1.pdf. Accessed 26 Aug 2012.

[14] Peikoff, Leonard. *Objectivism: The Philosophy of Ayn Rand* (New York: Penguin: 1993), 409.

hold the monopoly on the retaliatory use of force—only government does. Therefore, any coercion against the public must, by definition, originate in government.

Isabel Paterson asks, "Is it wrong to produce something or to process or exchange the products? No. Then it cannot impart corruption to anything else. Is it wrong to restrain, obstruct, or seize the goods of another? Yes. It is always wrong if done by initiating action . . . The potential corruption then lies in politics, not in business . . . . Now the sole remedy for the abuse of political power is to limit it; but when politics corrupt business, modern reformers invariably demand the enlargement of the political power."[15] The Progressive solution to government corruption is to expand government control and power, rather than limiting it.

CONTRADICTORY ATTACKS

The contradictions among the most common attacks on capitalism are rarely used together in the same argument and are really quite embarrassing to see together as a dichotomy—an opposite pairing.[16] That is, it's embarrassing for anyone seeking to use reason as their guide. Many of these attacks are completely self-cancelling opposites, both sides of which are entirely false. Simply put, detractors will state A=B and then claim somewhere else that A≠B. Pragmatism tells them these contradictions are okay to use as long as they are effective. Let's turn over the rocks and expose these fallacies to some sunlight.

---

[15] Paterson, *Machine*, Chapter 16.
[16] Peikoff, *Objectivism*, 409. The contrasted attacks discussed in this section were identified by Peikoff.

> **ATTACK #1**
> Capitalism Results in Coercive Monopolies
> VS.
> Capitalism Results in Cutthroat Competition

When people talk about monopolies, they usually mean coercive monopolies—monopolies which have such power as to bar any new entrants into the market, thereby being the only company providing a specific good or service, and the only place where consumers may go for that product.

Despite all you have been taught to believe, it is impossible for a coercive monopoly to form or exist in capitalism. Such monopolies are only created, and have only ever been created, by governmental influence, mandate, subsidies, and intervention. In America, which has never known pure capitalism, there has never been the formation of a nongovernmental coercive monopoly for any significant period covering any significant geographical area.

What about AT&T? For much of its history, AT&T and its Bell System functioned as a legally sanctioned, regulated monopoly. Essentially, when AT&T was broken up, the government broke up its own monopoly.[17]

What about Northern Securities? It was neither coercive nor lasting for any significant period. Competitors were still free to enter the marketplace.

What about Standard Oil? It doesn't qualify as coercive either. "The fact that Standard Oil faced such stiff competition and was driven to expand output and lower prices ever further demonstrates the myth of Rockefeller's 'control' of the market," Alex Epstein, founder and director of the Center for Industrial Progress, explains,

> "Markets are not possessions that one can acquire or control. They are dynamic, evolving systems of voluntary association, in which competing producers have no ability to force customers to buy their product, nor any ability to prevent others from offering their customers superior substitutes. The expression 'control a market share,' translated into reality, means simply that at a given time one has persuaded a given group of

---

[17] AT&T. corp.att.com/history/history3.html. Accessed 12 Jan 2012.

individuals to buy one's product—a state of affairs that can quickly change if someone offers a superior substitute.

"Standard Oil enjoyed high market share because it produced a highly desirable product and offered it at a price that the vast majority of people were willing to pay. If someone else had made cheaper kerosene or a better illuminant than kerosene, or if Rockefeller had lowered his standards or raised his prices significantly, his customers would have purchased their goods elsewhere. Such is the nature of the so-called 'monopolist's' control. And such is the nature of economic power."[18]

Contrary to popular belief, a free monopoly would be good thing. Keep in mind, we mean a monopoly in pure laissez-faire capitalism, not in any mixed economic system. Since a free-market monopoly has never existed, we can't point to one as an example, but we can perform a thought experiment and exercise our brains on a conceptual level in order to see what one would be like.

A FREE MONOPOLY:
EXCHANGE, EMPOWERMENT, EFFICIENCY

In a free market no one is forced to buy or sell anything. In such a case, how would a monopoly form without government influence? The only way would be if everyone, of their own free will and choice, decided to do business with a certain company, so exclusively and for such a long time, that all competitors dropped out.

Why would people do that? What would cause people to be so fiercely loyal to one company? In a free market, the reasons range from the best price, to the highest quality, to the best service, to the most convenient, to the newest product. In other words, in a free market, a monopoly only exists if it is producing products or services less expensively, better, and more abundantly than its competitors. The only way for a company to get to the top and stay there is to consistently please its customers and do so better than competitors.

The chances of such a situation ever occurring are infinitesimally small. It would be nearly impossible to be so superlative that no other companies could stand against you with comparable goods and services.

---

[18] Epstein, Alex. "Vindicating Capitalism: The Real History of the Standard Oil Company." *The Objective Standard*. Summer 2008. Online. theobjectivestandard.com/issues/2008-summer/standard-oil-company.asp. Accessed 22 Jan 2012.

Even if a company made great, affordable products, was ethical and responsible, even if they did everything right, what are the chances that a super majority would do business with them exclusively enough to sink the competition? But even if this were the case, this monopoly would still have no power to stop anyone from trying; anyone could go into business for themselves and compete against them.

So what happens if this number one company, now with no real competition decides to raise prices, decrease quality, reduce wages, and cut the benefits of their employees? Just what you would expect to happen—employees will quit and alienated customers will go elsewhere for the product or not buy it at all. Start-up competitors would spring up, eager to carve out a share of the market.

In a free market there are no government safety nets. Those who want to continue to make a living must continue to provide products and services that people want at a price they will pay.

"But without regulatory agencies wouldn't we get scammed by people trying to make a quick buck?" While there have been fly-by-night operations and scammers throughout history, they have been the self-destructive exception rather than the rule.

Such scammers are rare because to act in such a way is ultimately self-destructive, stressful, and requires a lot more work than to make an honest living—at least in a free society. In general, business deals work well, transactions are ethical, people sell good products and get honest paychecks, and getting scammed is a rarity. This is not because government watchdogs are constantly foiling evil plots, but because it is naturally in people's best interest to be honest and well-informed. After the success of the iPod, when it was time to roll out the next generation, did Steve Jobs trick us all and fill the insides of iPod 2.0 with sawdust and then flee with his billions to his secret, palatial moon base? No, Apple continues to make awesome products we think we can't live without, and they continue to laugh all the way to the bank. Everyone wins.

Despite all the regulatory agencies we currently have, the government is still unable to prevent fraud and crime. Even with the watchful and intrusive eyes of the Securities and Exchange Commission and their $906 million budget, Bernie Madoff was still able to commit eleven federal felonies and pull off the largest Ponzi scheme in history.[19] One, we should note, federal investigators believe began as early as the 1970's. De-

---

[19] Securities and Exchange Commission 2008 Annual Report. "SEC Snapshot and Financial Performance." Online.
sec.gov/2008annual/SEC_2008annual_financial.htm. Accessed on 31 Jul 2011.

spite the regulatory agencies, there are still private companies like Consumer Reports and Angie's List because we value knowing which people are worth doing business with. We have seller reviews and buyer feedback on Amazon and Ebay. The government can't help us decide who to trust.

Why would a world without governmental economic regulations be better? First, it is a matter of principle—freedom is moral. Not infringing on people's liberties is the right thing to do. Anything less is tyranny. That is the really the only justification capitalism needs. However, because it is morally in line with reality, there are naturally positive benefits that flow from such a situation, such as empowerment.

Think about the psychological effects on the minds of people who don't have to use their own judgment, who don't have to rely on their own decision-making skills but instead have a paternalistic nanny-state to tell them what to do. It weakens the individual. It teaches them to be dependent, ignorant, uncritical, to not take responsibility for their lives and choices.

How would we act differently without an FDA to tell us what to eat and what drugs were safe, without a Department of Commerce to tell us what to buy, without a Department of Consumer Protection to tell us who to trust, with no Department of Education to tell us what and how to teach our children, no FCC to censor our media, no licensed barbers to tell us who can cut hair well, no licensed Realtors to show us houses, and no EPA to tell us which light bulbs to buy? We would have to fully embrace our personal sovereignty. It would force us to rely on ourselves, to become educated. We'd be more careful. We wouldn't just buy the first thing we saw. If we were wise, we would make sure that the company we were thinking of dealing with was trustworthy and had a track record of excellence. We might consult a private consumer ratings organization or go to a website where consumers gave reports on businesses they had interacted with. We would consider the recommendations of people we knew and trusted. We would be wary of new companies, we would make them earn our trust, and they would have to fight hard to do so. Proven excellence would be our standard of judgment, not the blithe acceptance of a seal of a government approval—a seal which ensures companies must only meet minimum requirements and takes away their incentive to surpass it.

Yes, there would still be ignorant citizens who make poor choices, buy poor quality products, and get scammed—but that happens with the regulations! Millions of dollars a year are still sent to email scams like the infamous Nigerian Prince. Laws can't make us less naïve or less greedy.

There is nothing a government can do to help an economy grow (other than protecting rights). Every action government takes is an interference and a brake on the engine of prosperity. Government creates nothing; it can only establish a safe climate for business and trade. But even its necessary functions are a drain on the economy as the money which goes to support it is diverted from production. Of course, this is a proper and necessary expenditure considering military, police, and courts provide the foundation of law and order which allow prosperity to flourish in the first place. But beyond these things, all a government can do to help an economy is leave it alone. An economy is a self-regulating mechanism like a heart. We don't have to worry about micromanaging ventricular contractions, the timing of valves, and the rate of blood flow. All we have to do is make sure we set up the right conditions of diet, exercise, and sleep, and the heart takes care of itself.

Because freedom is moral, natural, and in conformity with reality, it is therefore also practical. That means without market regulation, things would work. They would go much more smoothly than we are used to. Ups and downs in the stock market would be less drastic and of much shorter duration. Investor confidence wouldn't be pegged to something so arbitrary and ridiculous as the Federal Reserve's interest rate, or the next Presidential press conference.

There would be no bailouts and safety nets, no allowance made for poor performance. Everyone and every company would stand or fall on their own merits and abilities and be judged by the marketplace. There would be no insulation from the most prestigious of universities: the School of Hard-Knocks. People would be empowered by the knowledge that they live in a world of consequences, and can choose the consequences they want by their actions. People would be taught that success requires relying on themselves, that they must take action and claim full responsibility for their lives and choices. These requirements of survival are the most effective check against immoral action.

Yet for those to whom the requirements of survival are insufficient motivation, a free market would still have objective laws to punish those who cheat and defraud. Legal punishments would act as deterrents to crime just as they do now. We've already seen that laws have no power to prevent crime; they may only punish it, just as natural causality does.

Through more than two hundred years of government intervention in the market, we have seen that the state is helpless to avoid disasters and prevent calamity. Problems caused by regulations cannot be fixed with more regulations. When a doctor confuses poison for the cure, the result is death. It would be better to let natural laws and incentives drive the marketplace, while we become informed and cautious consumers and only give our trust to the trustworthy. When we occasionally fail in our vigilance, we will still have done much better than the government regulators. To prevent fraud and deception, let the laws be strong enough to discourage even the vilest opportunist from considering a breach of trust.

How would things continue to work without market regulation? Suppose an inventor comes along and creates an industry. It won't be long before competitors arise and begin producing the same sorts of products in the same price range, with only minor variances for quality and the like (the smart phone, for example). Because the products are more or less made in the same way, and with the same materials, the cost of production of these products will remain fairly static across the board.

One way for this equilibrium to change is innovation. When a company innovates, it has an edge in the market. Because it has found a way to cut costs, it can undercut the competition and charge less for the same thing while maintaining a workable profit margin. If competitors fail to follow the industry leader and cut their costs with the same or other innovations, they will most likely go out of business. Because it is in their self-interest to remain in business, most companies will adopt the innovations. This permanently lowers the price of the good or service for the consumer and frees up capital to be put toward other more productive ends. Innovation may also lead to a better product with different features which would attract interested consumers to prefer it over the competition's version.

At this point we still have multiple competitors in the market. How can a coercive monopoly arise out of this situation? How could one company capture the full market share? They couldn't. Nothing about America is one-size-fits-all. The company could offer higher quality or better service, but not everyone wants that. There will always be those who prefer low price over high quality or good service over low price.

Let's turn to some real world examples of these principles in action. The objective here is to give a detailed historical example to show all the ways capitalism works in an economy, and to show how true principles actually work. Having a concrete example of principles in action dispels the doubt that principles don't work or aren't practical.

"MONOPOLIES" IN HISTORY

In 1798, the state of New York had granted a thirty-year steamboat monopoly to Robert Fulton and Robert Livingston.[20] That meant that it was illegal in the Land of the Free to start your own steamboat company to compete with Fulton! The predictable inevitability occurred—with no competition, the prices were artificially high. Prices were set by the whim of the company that had coercive monopoly power backed by the government.

Working for Thomas Gibbons based in New Jersey, Cornelius Vanderbilt began to run steam ships in defiance of the monopoly and offered lower prices. Eventually, the Supreme Court struck down the monopoly in 1824 in Gibbons vs. Ogden. Within two years of that ruling, steamboat traffic quadrupled on the Ohio River. By creating a monopoly in the "public interest" the government was guilty of restraint of trade. They limited the number of options for the consumers and in this way forced every steamboat consumer to pay higher prices than if government had not meddled in the first place.

With the salt now removed from the economic soil, the market was free to flourish. With new companies competing, innovation soon followed as it inevitably does. Competition and technological advancements allowed the operation costs to drop, and therefore the prices as well. As soon as the monopoly was struck down, prices dropped from $7 to $3.[21] Fulton couldn't compete and soon went out of business.

In the 1830's Vanderbilt began competing against the Hudson River Steamboat Association (HRSBA), the largest steamboat company in the country, which had informally tried to fix prices. On the New York to Albany line, Vanderbilt cut prices from $3, to $1, to 10¢, and finally to nothing![22] How did he manage that? By selling food on the boats and making a profit on that. Remarking on this incredible situation, a newspaper of the day said, "Times must be hard indeed when a traveler who wishes to save money cannot afford to walk."

---

[20] Folsom. Burton, W. Jr. *The Myth of the Robber Barons* (Virginia: Young America's Foundation, 2007), 2.

[21] *ibid*, 3.

[22] *ibid*, 3.

CORNELIUS VANDERBILT

Vanderbilt so vexed his competitors, that the infuriated steamboat association finally bought him out for $100,000, and an annuity of $5,000 a year for ten years. Vanderbilt brought the HRSBA to its knees with only two boats to their ten. Despite being up against the largest company, David was able to take down Goliath. With this deadly precedent set, a slew of competitors followed, many of which also got buyouts from the HRSBA. Vanderbilt took his money and moved on.[23]

This was no isolated event. Vanderbilt went on to compete in the trans-Atlantic steam boat industry. A man named Samuel Cunard managed to get a massive subsidy from the British government to run passenger ships and deliver mail. Not to be outdone, Edward Collins went to the American Congress and also got a subsidy to compete against Cunard.

Because Collins had not earned the money he got from the government, he spent it haphazardly. Without having to face the demands of reality—to be profitable or go bankrupt—Collins had no reason to be wise or efficient with his free money. He built four huge, opulent ships filled with the finest trappings. These lumbering ships used double the amount of coal that his British competitors did. When Vanderbilt went to congress offering to do what Collins did for much less and was rebuffed, he decided to take down Collins without any help.

As always, Vanderbilt was innovative and creative in the ways he competed. Vanderbilt's ships needed far less upkeep than Collins' leaky clunkers, and they were captained by competent men whose expertise allowed Vanderbilt to do without the cost of insurance. He also sold second and third class tickets to draw a larger volume of passengers. Despite all this, after one year of fierce competition, Vanderbilt was barely making it. Once again, his interest in new technology helped give him an edge. He built the largest steamship to ever sail the Atlantic which he

---

[23] *ibid*, 3.

equipped with the newly invented Vertical Walking Beam engine. This engine was not only more efficient than the conventional Crosshead design, using less wood and cutting fuel costs, but it was also smaller which would allow for more passenger space.

Half of Collins' unseaworthy fleet sank, and his huge new vessel to replace them was built so poorly that it could only make two trips before it was mothballed and sold at a nearly $1 million loss. Finally, Congress admitted their debacle and cut off funding to Collins.

This is an instance of one of the unintended consequences of government interference: the stagnation of technological advancement. With no competition as incentive to innovate, older and inefficient technologies lasted much longer than they naturally would have. Dr. Burton W. Folsom, Jr. observed that "Cunard and Collins both used their monopolies to stifle innovation and delay technological changes in steamship construction. Several English steamship companies experimented with iron hulls and screw propellers in the 1840's, but Cunard thwarted this whenever he could."[24]

Vanderbilt's exploits in the world of steamboats is just one of many examples in history of how true principles will always work when applied properly, and how breaking them inevitably brings problems. To summarize the principles covered in this historical example:

- Governments are the only entity with the power to create a coercive monopoly;
- Innovation and technology reduce costs and provide greater prosperity;
- Because government monopolies suspend the demands of reality, the need to be efficient is removed, waste abounds, innovation is stifled, costs remain high, and labor is squandered.

The question statists avoid is, if they claim to be against man's "dependence" on a large, centralized economic entity in the form of a "free market" monopoly, why do they then say that the solution is that everyone be forced to deal with a large, centralized economic entity in the form of the government, knowing that this form includes the added monopoly on the use of force to enact its interests? A supposed free market monopoly could never, by definition, FORCE anyone to do business with it—the government can and does.

---

[24] *ibid*, 9-10.

THE "ROBBER BARONS"

"Well, I obviously have made a decision to make sure the economy doesn't collapse. I've abandoned free market principles to save the free market system."[25]- George W. Bush

Another way capitalism has been eroded is by the absurd belief that the government must restrict free trade in order to preserve free trade. How can something that is restricted, mandated, or controlled be considered free? That's like your doctor saying, "We're going to abandon the principles of healthy living to save your health;" then he injects a Twinkie straight into your brain.

Opponents of capitalism typically make the assumption that complete laissez-faire capitalism used to exist in America and then point to so-called "robber barons" which exercised unjust dominion over the working class. Their main contention is that, before the benevolent government regulated the industries and put checks against the corporate greed, America was a nightmare of tyrannical businesses oppressing the lower classes. They contend that without regulation, these "robber baron" types would establish coercive monopolies which would bar new entrants to the market, gouge consumers, enslave workers, and hurt everyone. This view is victim to three main fallacies, with a host of other implicit ones about how capitalism works.

  ➤ First, America has never known a truly free market.
  ➤ Second, none of the prominent titans of the industrial revolution fit the description of "robber baron." Those who claim these tyrants existed rarely bother to name their specific crimes. We are merely meant to feel that somehow they were bad and the world is better off without them.
  ➤ Third, coercive monopolies cannot exist in a free market. Such monopolies are only created, and have only ever been created, by governmental influence, mandate, subsidy, and intervention. The alleged power of a robber baron can only be obtained by government sanction.

The term "robber baron" makes reference to the feudal lords of medieval Europe who had special privileges, land, and power granted by the King. These lords reigned over serfs who were in servitude under

---

[25] Bush, George. W. 16 Dec 2008. google.com/hostednews/afp/article/ALeqM5jyyKrPjYt 7VhpS8G8DrRkr18B0hA. Accessed 2 May 2011.

their authority. The earliest reference of this term was made by the preacher Henry Ward Beecher, who, in speaking of the low quality of goods in his day said, "It is the attempt of the more shrewd to take advantage of the less shrewd. It is the attempt of the strong to oppress the weak. It is the old robber baron in his castle descending, after men have planted their crops, and stealing them. It is the grasping king that appropriates the earnings of his subjects."[26]

Under capitalism, no one has authority to appropriate the property of another—no single person or group of people. Any form of fraud or theft is immoral, condemned by, and punishable by objective law. In American history, no business owner had the ability to seize earnings of others—that is, except one special class of businessmen that Folsom calls "political entrepreneurs."[27] These political entrepreneurs arose as a result of statism in a mixed economy. They cannot exist in a free market. Political entrepreneurs use (bribe, buy, pressure) legislatures to seize the earnings of others through taxation in the form of subsidies, bailouts, tax exemptions, and grants. Political entrepreneurs lobby for special favors, laws, tax breaks, subsidies, or any other governmental action that will give them an advantage over their competitors.

What Folsom calls "market entrepreneurs," in contrast to the political ones, seek success by using their own judgment, competing in the market, providing products and services that other men find valuable enough to trade for by their own free choice. They rely on no special favors from politicians; they sink or swim solely on their ability to please their fellow men.

Who in this scenario is the true robber baron? The one that must give superior products and services to survive? Or the one who lobbies for plunder from your pocket?

The profit motive is the self-interested force which drives innovation and wealth creation. It is what has raised many parts of the world from starvation and squalor to a level of commonplace and seemingly indispensable luxuries. How wonderful it is to have television, microwaves, refrigerators, cars, planes, iPads, and computers; even chocolate, once a luxury for nobility, is now ubiquitous and inexpensive. Things are so good now in America that our primary cultural concern is trying not to eat ourselves to death! What a contrast to world history! What a change from the ancient cultures that associated corpulence with high

---

[26] Beecher, Henry, Ward. "Truthfulness," 1871. Online Etymology Dictionary. etymonline.com/index.php?term=robber. Accessed 3 Aug 2011.
[27] Folsom, *Robber Barons*, 1.

social status! What we call poverty, ancient people would call opulence; 91% of Americans have a cell phone.[28] Even the poorest Americans are often overfed. This prosperity we enjoy today directly results from our level of economic freedom. As good as things are now, think of how much better they'd be if the trillions of dollars squandered by Congress every year were in the hands of productive people, interested in improving life for all and making a profit on it.

---

[28] Foresman, Chris. "Wireless survey: 91% of Americans use cell phones." arstechnica.com/telecom/news/2010/03/wireless-survey-91-of-americans-have-cell-phones.ars. Accessed 3 May 2011.

> **ATTACK #2**
> Capitalism Debases Men by Creating Hunger
> VS.
> Capitalism Debases the Morality of Men by Creating Riches

"The United States is the only country on record that has never had a famine since it became a nation."[29] - Isabel Paterson
(Fact check: We don't know if it is still the only country, but it is true it has never had a famine since its founding, with the contextually meaningless exception of some Eskimos on an island in the "Department of Alaska" shortly after its acquisition from Russia around 1880.)

POVERTY

Which is it? Does capitalism create poverty or riches? Or is the problem that it creates wealth for some and not for others? Both statements in these attacks are false. Even the poorest of Americans live like kings, not only compared to the poor in other countries, but compared to actual kings of a hundred years ago or more. Ask yourself which life would you rather lead—that of King Louis XIV of France or of a poor American? What has capitalism given the poor American that a king didn't have? Indoor plumbing, phones, television, internet, cars, deodorant, advances in health care and dentistry, fast food, grocery stores, and on and on. You eat more chocolate than ancient kings; their cushiest chair was nothing compared to your recliner.

No one in America who actually has a need, barring the prideful or mentally disordered, ever has to go without shelter or food.

GREED

"Those greedy capitalists—all they care about is money!"

"They don't really need that big house/car/toy. Don't they know how much good they could be doing with the money it cost to buy that?"

"Why would she spend that much on that! I wouldn't do that."

"It's immoral to make that much profit."

"That's highway robbery!"

---

[29] Paterson, *Machine*, Chapter 7.

If you've ever heard or said any of the above sentiments, you've experienced a pretty slippery mental mistake that many good people get caught up in.

To be greedy is usually defined as being "excessively desirous of acquiring or possessing, especially wishing to possess more than what one needs or deserves."[30]

Are there any problems in that definition? Let's start with the word "needs." According to whom? Who gets to decide how much another person needs, deserves, utilizes, or wants? Who gets to dictate what values another chooses to pursue?

It would be a better definition to say that greed is placing more value on objects than people. Greed is the violation of the principle that People are Assets, and is entirely different from the concept of rational self-interest discussed in the first chapters.

What about the claim that it is immoral to be affluent? Why? There is no clear answer given. Did money corrupt a moral man, or did an immoral man corrupt his money? Money is a neutral idea and currency is an inert object; they are neither good nor bad. The only effect money has is to magnify and make more obvious the qualities its owner already possesses. Money earned honestly is a product of virtue, achieved by trading your best for the best others have to offer. Dollars are the result of value offered to the world. Profits are the result of producing more than you consume. These are all important concepts when examining morality.

---

[30] "Greedy." The Free Dictionary. Online. thefreedictionary.com/greedy.

ATTACK #3
Capitalistic Greed Causes Inflation
VS.
The Gold Standard (or any limit on an increase in money
supply) Leads to Inadequate Credit and Money

INFLATION

"Inflation is a symptom of the terminal stage of that social disease which is a mixed economy."[31] - Ayn Rand

The expansion of fiat money, unmoored to any actual value in the marketplace (not even the reputation of a private bank), is the direct and only cause of inflation. Fiat currency derives its value from mandate rather than from a physical commodity. Inflation has a direct correlation to the degree of statism in a nation.

It would require an entire book to explain and evaluate the harm done to our monetary system by the Federal Reserve System that was instituted in 1913 by the Wilson Administration under the influence of powerful banking magnates. Use the basics here as a starting point for further research. The chart on the next page shows the inflation history of the U.S. set against a line showing the price of goods. As you can see, while inflation was very volatile before the creation of the Federal Reserve, prices remained fairly stable. Consistent inflation since after the early 20th century has caused prices to skyrocket. Capitalism didn't cause this.

If the correlation seems fishy, you are on to something. Then again, annual inflation rate is one thing—that only compares it to the previous year. The cumulative inflation rate from 1913 to 2014 is 2307.5%! That's right, what only cost your grandparents $100 now costs you $2,407.[32] Write a thank you letter to the Treasury Secretary and the Federal Reserve Chair if that thought makes you feel warm and fuzzy.

A stated goal of the Fed is to keep inflation in place. Purportedly, this is to prop up employment, debtors, and the speed of buying and sell-

---

[31] Rand, *Reason*, 274.
[32] See usinflationcalculator.com to compare inflation changes between other years.

ing. They fear people will stop buying things and start saving money if it starts gaining in value. For some reason, they consider that a bad thing.

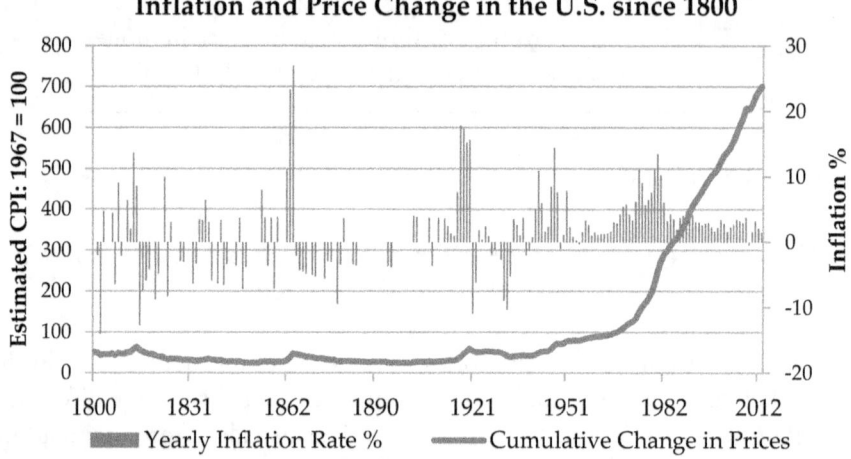

THE GOLD STANDARD

It is absurd to claim that to have money backed by an objective standard of value, such as gold or silver, leads to an inadequate supply of money or credit. For a few centuries from the early 1700's, money often increased in value, and prices often deflated. This was accompanied by the boom of the Industrial Revolution. This is why Benjamin Franklin's adage that "A penny saved is a penny earned" made sense literally. As people saved their money, they actually saw it increase in value—in purchasing power. Credit didn't dry up because people could actually do more with less currency. Today, inflation discourages savings because no one wants to sit on a pile of paper that will become worth less the longer it is held.[33]

The return to the gold standard isn't the only way to fix the problem. While gold has historically held its value, it is mostly only valued for its scarcity. In a famine, a gold bar is worthless compared to a loaf of bread. Gold only really has value because we decide it does because of its unique and objective properties and uses. In the same way, using only

---

[33] Graph data is from the Handbook of Labor Statistics, U.S. Department of Labor, and Bureau of Labor. Retrieved online from minneapolisfed.org/community_education/teacher/calc/hist1800.cfm. Accessed 5 Oct 2014.

paper for currency is perfectly fine so long as it is universally accepted as the medium of trade and it cannot be arbitrarily printed. In other words, with a set limit on how much currency a government or bank can manufacture (ideally, only to replace old bills and coins), artificially-caused inflation would stall dramatically. Even with the severe challenges facing the future of America, merely passing a Balanced Currency Amendment would do an incredible amount of good in stabilizing and strengthening the economy.

As you can see from the previous chart, prices remained relatively stable until the early 20th century. A penny saved was a penny earned. Today, a penny saved is most of a penny lost. This is part of why your house, your car, your education, your health care, and your groceries all cost so much.

> **ATTACK #4**
> Capitalism is Militaristic Imperialism
> VS.
> A Draft is Necessary Because No One Would Fight Even a War
> of Self-defense in a Free Society

IMPERIALISM

Is capitalism about imperialistic warmongering—sending innocent soldiers against their will to conquer foreign countries and expand its sphere of exploitation? Or is conscription necessary in a free market because no one will want to go to war even to defend their own country and lives?

This slight against capitalism, first made popular by Lenin, relies on evasion. Neither "capitalism" nor "imperialism" is ever adequately defined by those who use this attack—that is the point. "Imperialism" sounds bad. Its use is meant to imply all the evils of an expansionist, fascist Hitler or Napoleon and seeks to equate it with "a system of private property and free exchange." If we can be made to blank-out, to give up the process of conceptualizing, then we can be made to accept that somehow capitalism is bad because imperialism is bad.

Lenin attempted to explain it this way: The root of capitalism is free competition. This leads to higher and higher stages of production and wealth. (True enough. Then what?) This, he said, eventually leads to the "highest" stage of capitalism—imperialism, or monopoly capitalism. Capitalist powers then seek to annex other territories, "striving for violence and reaction."[34]

This assertion is the justification for all Communist aggression in the twentieth century: defense. In order to protect territories from capitalist imperialism and "exploitation," Communists engaged in war after war of "defense" (i.e. invade a territory to "protect" it from capitalist aggression). Observe the following official statements from the Communist Party of America:

> "In the capitalist world today, the revolutionary proletariat supports the war of defense of the proletarian state (the U.S.S.R.) against the imperialist states."

---

[34] Lenin, Vladimir. "Imperialism, The Highest Stage of Capitalism." marxists.org/archive/lenin/works/1916/imp-hsc/ch07.htm. Accessed 3 May 2011.

"Every war of the Soviet Union is a war of defense, even if it is conducted with offensive means."[35]

Lenin defined capitalism as competition and monopoly, attempting to explain this contradiction by claiming that competition is an early stage, and that monopoly/imperialism is a later stage of capitalism. However, Lenin doesn't understand the law of identity—a thing is what it is. If capitalism is free exchange and competition, as he admits, then also defining it as forced exchange and exploitative control is not capitalism. What he describes must, out of necessity of having different essential characteristics, be defined as something else (e.g. fascism, mixed economy, corruption, coercive monopoly, etc.). $A \neq B$.

CONSCRIPTION—THE MILITARY DRAFT

Of all the violations of rights put forth by a statist government, the draft is one of the worst. It is a blatant violation of the right to life, and an explicit declaration of the statist doctrine that man's life belongs to the state and may be claimed at any time by sending him into battle.

The draft is unconstitutional and falls under the category "involuntary servitude." The only proper and moral solution to national defense is an all-volunteer army (which doesn't necessarily mean "unpaid"). Would a man volunteer to fight if his country was attacked? Yes, if he values his life; and no semi-free country has ever lacked for volunteers to defend against a hostile invader. Many military personnel would also claim that a volunteer army is the most effective, and a drafted one the least effective (read Band of Brothers by Stephen Ambrose).

What if a country lacked a sufficient number of volunteers? This still would not justify a claim to the lives of those who don't volunteer. There are a few reasons that men may refuse to fight:

(1) They might be demoralized by a corrupt and authoritarian government and refuse to defend it;

(2) Their country is fighting for some reason other than self-defense and they don't understand it;

(3) They might be disabled or afraid; and

(4) They might be traitors, sympathizing with the enemy. Thus, a volunteer army is the best defense against both foreign ag-

---

[35] Quoted in Skousen, W. Cleon. *The Naked Communist* (Salt Lake City, Utah: Ensign Publishing Company, 1960), 239-40.

gression and the warlike ideologies of the army's own government. Men will defend their country in just conflicts where their freedom is clearly at risk; not many volunteer for aimless self-sacrificial and undeclared wars such as in Vietnam and Korea.

ATTACK #5
Capitalism is Fine for a Genius, but what about the Regular Guy?
(The Business Owner make more than the Hired Man)
VS.
Capitalism is Fine for the Common Man, but what
about the Genius? (The Sports Star makes more than the Scientist
or Teacher)

Remember that Dollars Follow Value. Under a system which protects individual rights, everyone is free to produce as much as they are able, and pursue values to the best of their abilities. This, in turn, lets each man live according to his own judgment and reap the rewards that he is able. A single principle determines his profits: the voluntary consent of those who are willing to trade with him in return (which is the moral meaning of the law of supply and demand).

Many people like to complain about the messed up world we live in where someone who dribbles a basketball makes millions while the noble martyr, the school teacher or scientist, lives below the poverty level. Before we quickly nod our heads and agree, let's examine the sentiment.

If this really is as immoral as they claim then the first question we should ask is, "Is there any force involved?" Are people required to watch basketball? No. People willingly watch the sport in massive numbers because they want to. The professional basketball player makes his money by doing something that people value. Dollars follow value; this means that people will spend money on what they value, and other people will pay to advertise to those people. The number of people who love basketball and the degree they value those players' skills puts those players in such demand that owners can afford to pay them millions of dollars a year. Good for them! That's a lot of value being created. Another thing to keep in mind is that there are millions of teachers and only hundreds of NBA players. Workforce wages are subject to supply and demand as well.

As for teachers, they are paid as much as they are valued. But by whom? Public school teachers' value isn't determined by the free market like the salaries of sports stars. Their value is determined in part by votes and politicians and taxation and unions. If there is anything to be upset about, it's that they don't work on the same playing field as other professions. They are kept from receiving the wage which the market would determine. Keep in mind that the "market" is the aggregate desire of the people involved in trading. There are many people out there willing to pay a lot of money to someone to provide a quality education to their children. There would be even more people wanting to do that if they weren't also forced to subsidize a school that their children were not attending. There is a very high demand for private schools and even charter schools. Great mentors are able to receive high remuneration for training and teaching.

Whether or not you think people are valuing the right things is irrelevant. Everyone is free to love and value what they want, even if it's not good for them or if there are better options they could choose. We are not responsible for the values of others, nor should we try to force others to value the same things or professions we do.

ATTACK #6

Capitalism is Impractical in the Complex Modern World

VS.

Capitalism is Impractical in Undeveloped Countries;
They are not Advanced Enough for Freedom

One argument is that capitalism and a free economy were all well and good in older times when things weren't as fast and complex and widespread as they are today. "Freedom was fine when things were simple," many say, "but today we need a more pragmatic and flexible approach to dealing with economic issues." We need some centralized planning and regulation to control and guide the "excesses" of freedom for everyone's own protection. (The same argument is used for the abrogation of freedom because of military threats, e.g. freedom was fine when the enemy lined up in bright red coats.)

On the contrary, it is impossible for government to foresee or control much of anything, and with the dismal approval numbers of Congress, one would wonder why anyone would entrust them with the country's prosperity.

Adam Smith explained the concept of the invisible hand of the market. When the combined forces of self-interest, competition, and supply/demand are left free to interact, the results are as if some "invisible hand" were guiding and directing resources to those who can put them to the best use and to those who need them most. Such perfection in the production and distribution of resources cannot be accomplished by any political leader or committee. The "hand" providing the guidance which brings such order and efficiency is no actual unseen power, but merely a result of combined decisions of people in an economy using their free judgment to pursue their self-interest. No one can run your life better than you.

In the other argument, we are told that capitalism is only meant for advanced and stable countries—countries who have the infrastructure and expanding economy necessary to support and allow the private property and other economic freedoms essential to laissez-faire policies.

In countries dealing with impoverishment and crime and more primitive conditions, we are told a more centralized planning is necessary in the early stages to lay a solid foundation that will allow for the future uncertainties of capitalism. The poor populace can't be allowed to own and keep property because they may not use it in a way which supports the common good. Greedy risk-taking can't be allowed early in a poor country's development because a profit might be made.

This argument is exactly wrong, but we have to discuss it because some people believe it. America's major export should be the principles of capitalism which have allowed America to rise out of poverty and become the massive source of production that she is today. That would be the most charitable contribution this nation could make to any other. Freedom is the source and wellspring of six major revolutions in earth's history that resulted in exponential increases in the quality of human life: the Industrial Revolution decreased the labor required to produce; the Machine Revolution made things abundant and cheap; the Transportation Revolution; the Communications Revolution; the Energy Resource Revolution; and the current Computer Revolution.[36] These advances were not the cause of the major civilization progress in the last two hundred years, they were the result of the recognition of individual rights.

In 1848, the Frenchman Alexis de Tocqueville observed of America that, "For sixty years [they] have increased in opulence; and . . . it is found to have been . . . not only the most prosperous, but the most stable of all the nations of the earth," and that "the principles on which the American constitutions rest, those principles of order, of the balance of powers, of true liberty, of deep and sincere respect for right are indispensable to all republics."[37]

Thomas Jefferson wrote to one of his friends, "A just and solid republican government maintained here, will be a standing monument and example for the aim and imitation of the people of other countries; and I join with you in the hope and belief that . . . our revolution and its consequences, will ameliorate the condition of man over a great portion of the globe."[38] It did, and very quickly, too. "The climate of free-market economics," Skousen wrote,

> ". . . allowed science to thrive in an explosion of inventions and technical discoveries which . . . gave the world the gigantic new power resources of harnessed electricity, the internal combustion engine, jet propulsion, exotic space vehicles . . . .

---

[36] Skousen, W. Cleon. *The Making of America: The Substance and Meaning of the Constitution* (USA: National Center for Constitutional Studies, 1986), 2-3.
[37] Toqueville, Alexis de. *Democracy in America*. p. 910. Googlebooks. Online. books.google.com. Accessed 17 Aug 2011.
[38] Randall, Henry Stephens. *The Life of Thomas Jefferson: In 3 Volumes, Volume 2.* Googlebooks. p. 634. Online. books.google.com. Accessed 17 Aug 2011.

"The average length of life was doubled; the quality of life was tremendously enhanced. Homes, food, textiles, communications, transportation, central heating, central cooling, world travel, millions of books, a high literacy rate . . . surgical miracles, medical cures . . . .

"Of course, all of this did not happen just in America, but it did flow out primarily from the swift current of freedom and prosperity which the American Founders turned loose into the spillways of human progress all over the world.

"In 200 years, the human race had made a 5,000-year leap."[39]

Such advances were not happenstance or mandated by government edict. Such advances happen quickly and naturally when allowed to flourish in an environment of economic and political freedoms where rights are protected. Such principles are what today's third-world countries must have in order to join the freer countries in a leap of prosperity.

---

[39] Skousen, W. Cleon. *The 5000 Year Leap: A Miracle That Changed the* World (Washington, D.C.: National Center for Constitutional Studies, 2006), 3-4.

THREE ASSAULTS ON
THE CONCEPT OF RIGHTS

Now that we have discussed the only social system which recognizes the principle of rights—capitalism—it would be helpful to recognize and counter the common attacks on this principle, since any victory over the concept of rights constitutes a victory over capitalism by implication.

Nobel-prize-winning economist, Amartya Sen, identified three main "critiques," from "critically demanding circles" that directly or indirectly undermine and distort the concept of rights.[40] All three of these attacks are based on a faulty understanding of rights and thus seek to undermine the principle via a straw-man argument; they set up a false idea and proceed to attack it.

Sen calls the first attack the **legitimacy critique**. This attack questions the legitimacy of rights as a pre-legal principle. It views government as the ultimate legal authority and provider of rights and that no such principles exist outside of a legal context. In this view, humans are no more born with rights than they are with clothes—rights have to be provided through the tailoring of the legislative process. As Karl Marx insisted in his pamphlet, "On the Jewish Question," rights cannot precede (but rather follow) the institution of the state.

A proper understanding of rights will quickly show the illegitimacy of this attack. Rights, you will recall, are moral principles guiding human action in a social context. To confuse these with entitlements granted by the state (which are unfortunately often termed "rights" as well) is to misunderstand the meaning and purpose of such ethical principles. When this attack is successful, individualism is destroyed and statism advances.

The second attack is the **coherence critique** which claims that rights are null and void unless listed coherently with a corresponding agency-specific duty to provide those rights. This attack claims that if *A* has a right to some *X*, then an agency such as *B* must also be recognized as having to provide *A* with *X*.

This is the stance taken by those who say that rights can only be sensibly formulated in combination with correlated duties. Someone has a right to something; and someone else has a duty to provide it. They ask, "How can we be sure a right is realized unless it is matched by someone's

---

[40] Sen, Amartya. *Development as Freedom* (New York: Alfred A. Knopf, 2000), 227-31.

duty to provide it?" Immanuel Kant called this a perfect obligation, one which it is moral to coerce from the agent responsible for the realization of the right. If no such agency exists for this purpose, the claim is then directed at anyone who can help. If health care is a right, there must be an agency created to provide that right, and the taxpayers, doctors, and insurance companies must all be coerced into it.

The problem here is that this attack holds a contradiction as a principle: that a right has to be provided by someone else. Rights, as we discussed, cannot be identified as such if someone else's rights must be violated in order to provide them. It is a contradiction to have a right to any man-made goods or services. Rights, to be a valid concept, must be universal and equal and unalienable. If the rights of some must be violated to provide education or housing or food to others, then those things are not, by definition, rights. This attack calls for a mixed economy and coercive State to provide for the supposed rights of every pressure group.

The third attack is the **cultural critique**. This view questions if rights can really be universal if they are not regarded by some cultures as particularly valuable. The moral authority of rights, in this view, is dependent on how they are accepted by a given society. This view violates the principle that collective action has no unique moral authority, and assumes that consensus determines reality. The proper conditions of man's existence are not decided by a culture or nation; they are objective requirements of the nature of man. Individual rights are the principles that recognize this and provide a proper framework for man's prosperity in all cultures, all places, and for all individuals.

In this book, we are concerned less with the concept that capitalism is practical (even though it is) and more concerned with the concept that capitalism is good, and why it is good. It is true that capitalism is practical; it is effective and efficient. Capitalism is moral; it is just and its end is happiness. Capitalism is true; it agrees with man's nature and it agrees with reality. Yet, there are many who wish to see it destroyed, both in reality and as an idea. In the next chapter, we will look deeper into the tactics of the enemies of freedom

REVIEW

Q1: What causes and cures an economic depression?

Q2: What caused and cured child labor and slavery?

Q3: When government and business are corrupted, who is at fault?

Q4: Why would a free-market monopoly be a good thing?

Q5: Why are governmental/coercive monopolies bad?

Q6: What is the traditional view of greed? What is a better definition?

Q7: Which social system has eradicated famine to the extent that it has been implemented?

Q8: Why do statist social systems cause famine?

Q9: What is the history of associating capitalism with militant imperialism?

Q10: Is capitalism too advanced or too simplistic for the modern world? Or something else entirely?

Q11: What is the "invisible hand"?

Q12: Describe and debunk the three basic assaults on the concept of rights.

CHAPTER 15

KNOWING THE ENEMY

"It is said that if you know your enemies and know yourself, you will not fear the result of a hundred battles; if you know yourself but not the enemy, for every victory gained you will also suffer a defeat. If you know neither the enemy nor yourself, you will succumb in every battle."[1] - Sun Tzu

To defeat tyranny, we have to know how it operates. We have to know explicitly why our own principles are true, and how they counter every tenant of tyranny. Some would say that tyranny is too strong a word. Let's define it for our purposes as the initiation of, or advocacy of, force.

Those who espouse tyranny fall under many labels: conservative, liberal, Democrat, Republican, even family and friend. But no matter the ideological affiliation, they all fall under a wider umbrella which has one thing in common: the denial of individual rights by advocating the initiation of force—whether directly or indirectly. Their ethical philosophy is altruism and their political philosophy is statism. (The exception to this is

---

[1] Tzu, Sun. *The Art of War.* chinapage.com/sunzi-e.html#03. Accessed 3 May 2011.

anarchists who advocate for what they call individual liberty, but deny the need for the protection of that liberty via government.)

Many collectivists believe very deeply that they are doing the right thing. The collectivist ethic holds that sacrifice for other people is the standard of moral action, and that any means to that end is right. Preventing and alleviating perceived human suffering is to be done at any cost, they believe, even the destruction of liberty, prosperity, and other requirements for human life.

Collectivism is the spirit of our times. It is the ideological ocean in which society is swimming. There is hardly one area of truth that has not been tainted and mixed with error. It is taught in schools, churches, homes, and from the halls of government. It shapes personal ethics, alters religious dogma, misinforms legislation, and directs warfare. Collectivism is ingrained into almost every child's psyche from the first stirrings of self-awareness, and reinforced in almost every step of their education. This is done through many channels and influences, and as early as children begin to understand anything at all. (This is the same process of socialization we discussed in the section on racism.) Sharing is a virtue, but where collectivism taints the concept is when parents mingle it with force—they take the property from the children and make them share whether they want to or not. This teaches the child that property is not a right, that it is okay to use force, and that anyone who makes a claim on your property is entitled to it.

Notice that these concepts are not taught explicitly, in clear words, but implicitly, with actions and behaviors. Remember, ideas that are implicit are unconscious, automatic, and unquestioned. When we learn things implicitly, they seem like basic and undeniable facts of existence. We accept the things we learn implicitly as "the way the world works," that the way things are is how they should be. "My parents did it this way, so it must be right." Thus children are primed with bad philosophy from before the time they can talk. We should not wonder why the world is plagued with violence and war when we teach our children that force is moral. Unfortunately, collectivism is the unquestioned ethos of the age.

In this war of ideas, reason is a small minority and fights an uphill battle against the inertia and tradition of the world. If collectivism and its political manifestation of statism continue unchecked, their terrible momentum will destroy the unprecedented prosperity achieved on the foundations laid during the Age of Reason.

This section will discuss what we need to know to combat the enemy—the tactics and common misconceptions which are the doctrinal pillars of statism. It is vital to know how truth will be challenged and confronted so that we can be prepared to defend it.

STATIST STRATEGIES AND LANGUAGE

"But if thought corrupts language, language can also corrupt thought."[2]
- George Orwell

"Definitions are the guardians of rationality, the first line of defense against the chaos of mental disintegration."[3] - Ayn Rand

CONCEPTUAL AMBIGUITY

Capitalism is the only political system inferred from objective truths of reality. Because it is true, it is correct. How do you form an argument or attack against something that is true? Logically, you can't, there are no errors in it which you could attack. Therefore, any attack against capitalism has to be based on a misconception of it, or a flat out denial of reality. When something is logically sound, there can be no rational attack against it; all such "arguments" brought in opposition to it will rely on misdirection, evasion, and context-dropping. The only effective weapon against truth is the distortion of thought through language, which is the tool of thought. A major area of assault on the principles of freedom has targeted the realm of ideas specifically.

"As language is the faculty which distinguishes man from the lower animals," Isabel Paterson explained,

". . . the confusion and vagueness of terms always found in collectivist theories is not accidental; it is a reversion to the mental and verbal limitations of the primitive society it advocates, the inability to think in abstract terms . . . . The verbal language of a high civilization is also a precision instrument. When words are used without exact definition, there can be no communication above the primitive level. If those who are supposed to express or influence 'public opinion,' the writers, economists, so-

---

[2] Orwell, George. "Politics and the English Language." *Why I Write* (New York: Penguin: 2005), 116.
[3] Rand, Ayn. *The Romantic Manifesto* (New York: Signet, 1975), 77.

cial theorists, and pedagogues, think in the concepts of savagery, what can be the outcome?"[4]

Ayn Rand explained how definitions do not merely state the meaning of words, but that a word is a symbol used to represent a concept. "It is not words, but concepts that man defines," she said. He does this by specifying what, in reality, concepts refer to.[5] Every word we use (except proper nouns) is a symbol for a concept. Such a concept, to be valid, must have reference to reality. For example, take the concept of a chair. The concrete reality that the concept chair refers to is every type of separate seat for a person that has ever existed or will ever exist, usually with four legs and a back rest, but not always. One cannot accurately use the symbol (word) chair as a designation of the concept of a table, even if the table has four legs and has someone sitting on it! One cannot accurately use the word equality to designate the concrete reality of a system that actually grants special privileges. When words are used in such a way as to remove any specific reference to reality, any meaningful communication is removed.

The collectivist attack against true principles consists of an attack against man's mind and his ability to understand the words he uses, completely, down to their core. Ideas have consequences and if we can be made to have sloppy, vague ideas, the battle is already won for the collectivists. If we talk of American principles, or equality, or freedom, but have no idea what we actually mean in concrete reality, then we cannot advocate effectively for those ideas because we won't know what they look like when we see them.

The strategy of the collectivists is to substitute anti-concepts for actual concepts. An anti-concept is an unusable term designed to "replace and obliterate some legitimate concept. The use of anti-concepts gives the listeners a sense of approximate understanding."[6]

The key to using anti-concepts as an attack consists in substituting words that only give an approximate meaning in place of important concepts. Here are only a few common examples of today's anti-concepts and the vague ideas they are meant to convey:

---

[4] Paterson, Isabel. *The God of the Machine* (Originally published in 1943. Qualiteri eBook, 2009), Chapter 17-18.

[5] Rand, Ayn. *Introduction to Objectivist Epistemology* (New York: Meridian, 1990), 40.

[6] Rand, Ayn. "Credibility and Polarization." The Ayn Rand Letter. Quoted online. aynrandlexicon.com/lexicon/anti-concepts.html. Accessed 27 Mar 2011.

- "Democracy," which is used to mean freedom or equality.
- rights, which is used to mean claims, entitlements, or demands.
- "Working families," which is used to mean low- and middle-class families who earn their money rather than exploit others.
- "Capitalism," which is used to mean exploitation, fascism, imperialism, a corrupt mixed economy, and greedy monopolization.
- "Altruism," which is used to mean concern for the welfare of others.
- "Extremism," which means any dangerous or uncommon ideas.

As Rand points out, the aim is to convey vague feelings without any actual meaning. Then the hearer substitutes their feelings for any actual understanding of the concept being addressed.

With this assault, the collectivists hope we will eventually accept any contradiction as necessary and natural, and the Orwellian slogans of WAR IS PEACE, SLAVERY IS FREEDOM, and IGNORANCE IS STRENGTH, will no longer seem alien and sinister, but familiar and comforting.

Paterson explained in *The God of the Machine* that this attack is characterized by "the persistent discrediting of reason, and the deliberate corruption of language, to prevent communication." Through the misuse of language, the Marxists have done the "most serious injury to intelligence . . ." They express a false concept or theory in terms which embody the error so that "thinking is blocked until the misleading words are discarded from the given context." She claims this is more serious a handicap than statements which are simply false.[7] For example, take the slogan coined by anarchist Pierre-Joseph Proudhon that "Property is theft." The concept of theft presupposes the concept of property. The statement is logically absurd.

In 2009, Barack H. Obama went on George Stephanopoulos' show, to defend his Affordable Care Act. Stephanopoulos asked how the fine imposed on those who did not comply with the individual mandate was not a tax. The President responded, "No, but George, you can't just make up that language and decide that that's called a tax increase." Stephanopoulos replied, "I don't think I'm making it up. Merriam Webster's Dictionary: Tax—'a charge, usually of money, imposed by authority on persons or property for public purposes.'" To which the President said, "George, the fact that you looked up Merriam's Dictionary, the definition of tax increase, indicates to me that you're stretching a little bit right now.

---

[7] Paterson, *Machine*, Chapter 10.

Otherwise, you wouldn't have gone to the dictionary to check on the definition."[8]

Note what happened carefully. The President claimed Stephanopoulos was making up language; Stephanopoulos gave the dictionary definition to prove that he was not; and then, being shown to be wrong, the President claimed that Stephanopoulos was "stretching." Look at what the President did here. He was using the symbol for a concept, "tax," but he was destroying the concept by denying the meaning that is tied to the word. Because he was caught in a lie, and couldn't make a rational argument against the truth, he had to shift tactics. He had to attack reason itself! Stephanopoulos was seeking for clarity, for an unambiguous definition so no equivocation or evasion could be used. But in Obama's eyes, clarity was found in making things up. The President's deception relied on keeping the concepts fuzzy and vague. Often the fastest way to end an argument is to ask the other person to define their terms. (The health care bill passed muster in the Supreme Court by being defended as a tax, regardless of what the President said.)

The enemies of freedom know the power of words and have shaped them as tools to manipulate and control. Saul Alinsky, Progressive activist and author, devoted an entire chapter to "words" in one of his books with the heading, "A Word about Words." The Progressives have monopolized and twisted a great many words to "seize power . . . to realize the democratic dream of equality, justice, peace, cooperation, equal and full opportunities for education, full and useful employment . . ."[9] They don't actually mean a single one of those buzzwords. What do they actually mean?

• "Democratic" means rule by majority, but they actually mean rule by them.

• "Equality" means equal rights before the law, but they actually mean equal stuff provided by redistributionist policies, resulting in equal misery.

• "Justice" means everyone gets what they deserve, but they actually mean the entitled get what they haven't earned while it's stolen from those who earned it.

• "Peace" means the absence of physical force, but they mean to institute these Progressive measures using the force of government.

---

[8] Stephanapoulos, George. Interview with Barack Obama. 20 Sep 2009. foxnews-insider.com/2012/06/28/read-obamas-2009-abc-news-interview-health-care-law-is-not-a-tax/. Fox News Insider. Online. Accessed 4 Jul 2012.

[9] Alinksy, Saul. *Rules for Radicals* (New York: Random House, 1989), 3.

• "Cooperation" means persuasion and voluntary participation, but they mean obedience to their laws.

• "Equal educational opportunities" means everyone is free to pursue education, but they mean that everyone is forcibly educated by the State.

• "Full employment" means every able person who wants to can find work, but what they actually mean is to expropriate money to provide everyone an income whether they can do a job or not.

What we must do is fling their words back at them and expose them as the cultural parasites they are. We must also take control of the words we use and not let the enemies of freedom tell us what to say. Instead of fighting for "Entitlement reform" we can change our words and fight for "Entitlement security." Instead of a "Flat Tax" we can advocate for a "Fair and Equal Taxation." Instead of "Immigration Reform" we must talk about "Immigration Freedom." Instead of "Free Health Care" we must fight for "Health Care Freedom." In place of "Education Privatization" we must push for "Education Freedom." We must take the "Pro-choice" language of the abortion movement and apply it across the board: Pro-Choice Education, Pro-Choice Business, Pro-Choice Taxation, Pro-Choice Health Care.

THE TYRANNY OF NEED

"Need is the deception for entitlement."[10] - Rick Koerber

"Where there is suffering, there is duty."[11] - George W. Bush

A need maintains your nature. There is actually very little that humans need to maintain their nature. Physical needs include food and shelter. Spiritual needs include rights and healthy human interaction. Thus, unless need is actually referring to one of these, it is a deception.

Today, need is used as a weapon. It is an ultimatum that allows no argument, no recourse, and no logic. If your neighbor has a need, it is

---

[10] Koerber, Rick. and Israel Curtis, prod. "Lecture Series on the Principles of Prosperity." FreeCapitalist Radio. (May 19-June 26 2008). Podcast. Available from iTunes.

[11] Bush George W. 1st Inaugural Address. 20 Jan 2001. Available online. americanhistory.about.com/od/georgewbush/a/gwbushinaugural.htm. Accessed 14 Oct 2011.

claimed, who are you to deny, on any grounds, that you must be the one to provide it?

There is no such thing as a right to man-made goods and services. Period. Yet, need is used as the weapon against those who have by those who haven't, against those who produce by those who consume, by those who seek power against the population, by those who feel against all reason.

"The city needs a trail system."

"The public needs government radio and television."

"The artists need a paycheck."

"The elderly need welfare."

"The sports team needs a stadium at public cost or on public lands."

Need is used as the final argument, the claim on an unearned guilt accepted by the productive for being good; it is their penance for the crime of achieving while others have not achieved.

> The meaning of **justice** is to seek and grant only the *earned,*
> in matter and in spirit.

The opposite of justice is to reward evil and penalize virtue. Yet, this is precisely how statists define justice. Or as it's more commonly termed, social justice—appropriating wealth from those who earned it to give it to those who didn't.

This tyranny of need is not confined to the political realm. It can be seen almost daily in personal and work relationships. The "Need Card" is played constantly to escape responsibility and to dictate the actions of others. Most often, if we examine our own use of the word need, we will find that, in reality, a more accurate word would be want or prefer.

"I need to go home guys. My wife is making me."

Why would we use that language? To escape the responsibility that leaving is our choice, to assign blame for the situation to another person, and possibly because we don't have enough confidence in our relationship with our friends to state the truth. Many of us aren't used to using responsible language, such as, "I'm getting tired, guys. I want to go home now and see my wife. That'll make her night." "I prefer to go home now, guys. My wife is expecting me."

What is usually described as a need is often not a need at all. Disregard for the seriousness of the concept of need cheapens it, and makes our actual needs blur with our perceived needs.

Dora the Explorer, a popular children's cartoon, featured a character who tries to thrive on the tyranny of need. "We need your help!" is a common refrain she used instead of, "We want to cross the river and would love to borrow your boat. What would it take for you to help us?" Even a simple, direct question, "Will you please help us?" would be preferable to asserting a claim on someone's life (i.e. time, property, ability) solely by virtue of one's need.

It might not seem important to learn to scrub our language of certain words and phrases, but watching our language is a way to train ourselves to watch our thoughts. Thoughts have consequences. Thoughts lead to actions. Actions lead to habits. Habits make up one's character. One's character determines one's life. If we can keep our language from violating principle, it becomes easier to keep our actions from doing so as well.

Need does not grant rights nor take away the rights of those who are not needy. When need is your standard of value, you are living by the Communist ideal of "From each according to his ability; to each according to his need." This is the exact opposite of capitalism, "Each may act according to his ability; to each as he earns and deserves."

The reality of this world is that life is unfair and lots of people draw short straws from nature and circumstance. Some are born with debilitating diseases, malformed limbs, brain defects, or under a totalitarian regime, or to families who can't feed them. No amount of human action can stop the inherent unfairness of real life. Such differences of birth and circumstance are not a valid reason for the coercion of those who have different circumstances. It is a valid reason, however, for education, for private charity, and for compassionate people to engage in persuasion and service.

THE SMEAR CAMPAIGN OF EXTREMISM

"I would remind you that extremism in the defense of liberty is no vice! And let me remind you also that moderation in the pursuit of justice is no virtue."[12] *- Barry Goldwater*

By itself "extremism" has no meaning. Extreme is an adjective and must be used to describe an extreme of something. To understand it one must ask, "An extreme of what?" The answer given today is, "Of any-

---

[12] Safire, William, ed. *Lend Me Your Ears: Great Speeches in* History (New York: W. W. Norton & Company, 1992), 826.

thing!" This is the proclamation that an extreme of anything is evil because it is extreme. This is absurd because it holds degree as the essential characteristic of something, not its nature. It holds the amount of something as the substance of something. It is to put emphasis on ripeness while disregarding whether the characteristic of ripeness is referring to a rotting corpse or piece of fruit. As Ayn Rand asks, "Are an extreme of health and an extreme of disease equally desirable? Are extreme intelligence and extreme stupidity—both equally far removed 'from the ordinary or average'—equally unworthy?"[13]

In a discussion about the conflict between Israel and Hamas, movie director Rob Reiner "was quite clear about his belief that Hamas must be eliminated. He then went on to compare Hamas to the Tea Party, stating, 'anytime you're dealing with an extreme group, you cannot negotiate with them, and the way to do it is to eliminate it.'"[14] He made no distinction between the "extremism" of a terrorist group who wants to wipe Israel from the map, and the "extremism" of a group who wants more constitutionalism and less taxes.

Suppose a man was engaged in the act of beating you up in the street—that is "extreme" behavior. If I came along and saw this and used force to stop the man from beating you up—that is also "extreme" behavior. Yet, would you call your attacker and defender both evil because they were both equally extreme in their actions? Or is one clearly morally superior in his actions?

As an example of this intentional and widespread campaign to paint uncompromising positions as "extreme," and thus as dangerous, naive, and stupid, take a story reported by The New York Times on March 29, 2011. Democratic Senators were caught discussing secret marching orders before a conference call with reporters. The Senators didn't realize that several of the reporters were already logged into the call, and they began discussing just how they wanted to verbally paint the GOP, House Speaker John Boehner, and the Tea Party. The article reports that, "Mr. Schumer told them to portray John A. Boehner of Ohio, the Speaker of the House, as painted into a box by the Tea Party, and to decry the spending cuts that he wants as extreme. 'I always use the word

---

[13] Rand, Ayn. *Capitalism: The Unknown Ideal* (New York: Signet, 1967), 178.
[14] Opelka, Mike. "The Director of Glenn Beck's Favorite Movie Compares the Tea Party to Hamas: It Needs to Be 'Eliminated.'" *The Blaze.* theblaze.com/stories/2014/08/15/the-director-of-glenn-becks-favorite-movie-compares-the-tea-party-to-hamas-it-needs-to-be-eliminated. Accessed 15 Aug 2014.

extreme,' Mr. Schumer said. 'That is what the caucus instructed me to use this week . . .' 'We are urging Mr. Boehner to abandon the extreme right wing,' said Ms. Boxer, urging the House to compromise on the scale of spending cuts and to drop proposed amendments . . ."[15]

What is such an anti-concept as "extremism" intended to accomplish in politics? The most important and foundational political issue today (really the only one) is freedom vs. statism. For many decades, Progressive statists have sought to implement welfare statism one step at a time, enlarging governmental power slowly, but inexorably. This program required that the concept of capitalism be wiped out of existence. Since statism cannot win in an open debate, the history, principles, and nature of capitalism had to be distorted, smeared, misrepresented, and removed from public discussion. The plan is to have statism win by default.

Two more meaningless concepts used for this purpose are rightists and leftists. Generally, these terms are used to mean those who support capitalism and socialism, or conservatism and liberalism. But, what happens when attempts are made to falsely associate racism and violence with rightists? Then we get a new spectrum (given to us as the choice since World War II); the choice between an extreme of Communism on the left and an extreme of fascism on the right. This false dichotomy perfectly serves the goals of the statists because it removes the concept of capitalism from public discourse. It removes the choice of "Dictatorship or freedom?" and replaces it with the choice of "Which type of dictatorship—that of the rich (fascism), or that of the poor (Communism)?" There is no meaningful distinction between either side because they belong to the same philosophy; both the left and right wings are attached to the same statist center.

The comparison of Communism on the left and fascism on the right is completely false because the actual issue is individual rights vs. totalitarianism, or man vs. the state, or capitalism vs. socialism. An essential characteristic of both Communism and fascism is man's subordination to the state or collective. Yet, if we accept that these are the two "extremes" to be avoided, then what is left to us as the safest course? The middle ground, we are told—that of safely undefined "moderation." This means, in practice, moderate amounts of corporate welfare and special

[15] Steinhauer, Jennifer. "On a Senate Call, A Glimpse of Marching Orders." *The New York Times.* 29 Mar 2011. thecaucus.blogs.nytimes.com/2011/03/29/on-a-senate-call-a-glimpse-of-marching-orders/. Accessed 29 Mar 2011.

privileges for the rich, moderate amounts of freedom and slavery, of justice and injustice, of security and terror, of rights and brute force.[16]

What is the sensed meaning of "extremism" when it is used? What are we supposed to feel that it means? Hatred, intolerance, bigotry, racism, calls for violence, and crazy theories. What is the actual meaning of "extremism" as commonly used? It actually means the condemnation of any uncompromising stand on anything; yet, compromise is unacceptable in morality, as any compromise means a surrender to evil. There can never be any compromise on truth or morality. Thus if the smear of "extremism" is directed at any uncompromising stand, then that smear is in truth directed at any profound conviction, any loyalty to principles, any dedication to truth, any person of integrity.

Collectivism is bankrupt as an ideology in part because it has nothing more to offer as a solution than "moderation," and no loftier ideal than that of "compromise."

THE APOTHEOSIS OF COMPROMISE

(Apotheosis—the exaltation of a subject to divine level;
in Greek apotheoun: "to deify")

True compromise is an adjustment of conflicting claims by mutual concessions. In practice, it implies a common principle unifying the two parties and the recognition that each party has both a valid claim and a value to offer the other.

In the purchase of a home, the buyer and seller may compromise, settling voluntarily on agreed terms to exchange the ownership of the home. The basic principle is trade. If the seller does not agree to sell, there can be no exchange. If the buyer does not agree to the price, there is no exchange.

There can be no compromise, however, between a mugger and his victim. Even if the mugger only wants to take a few dollars, the result is not compromise but total surrender by the victim to the use of force by the mugger. The mugger and the victim have no common unifying principle on which to voluntarily agree. There can be no compromise on the principle of individual rights—between freedom and government controls. The surrender of just "a few government controls" is not a compromise because there is no unifying principle between the parties of the

---

[16] Rand, Ayn. *Capitalism: The Unknown Ideal* (New York: Signet, 1967), 181.

government and the individual citizens; it thus constitutes the surrender of the entire principle of individual rights.

Compromise is an impossible concept when dealing with fundamental principles. How would you define a compromise between reason and irrationality, life and death, or truth and error? What if NASA decided to compromise a little on the hull integrity of its space shuttle? What if a drug manufacturer compromised a bit on the content of your medication? "Times have changed. We all have to be flexible. We can't be tied down by rigid principles," the character of Henry Rearden is told in the movie *Atlas Shrugged II*. His response is perfect: "Try pouring a ton of steel without rigid principles."

Today, when we hear of compromise in politics, in most cases it is not a legitimate concession or trade that is implied, but an actual betrayal of one's values and principles. The use of compromise in this way is immoral because it insists on substituting some subjective whim in place of basic principles.[17]

When a bill is stalled or fails to pass a branch of Congress, the first volley in the obligatory blame-game is usually moral outrage that the other party refused to compromise. Compromise is held up as the moral standard of governance; each party gives up just enough of what they want so that the other party will agree and therefore avoid gridlock. The very fact that both sides speak of compromise so frequently, betrays the fact that they have no consistent rational philosophical base; for if either one claimed to be right, then to compromise would be to sell out their beliefs. But this is not the case. At their philosophical cores, Republicans and Democrats believe in the same principle of statism. Other than on a few issues, the only way the two parties differ is by the methods they use to accomplish their Progressive goals.

The great lack of principled ideas in the modern political arena can be illustrated by looking back to a Presidential campaign debate between John F. Kennedy and Richard Nixon. In this debate, the great climax of the nation's compromising political parties can be seen in the fact that these two candidates had nothing to debate about—they agreed on almost everything!

According to Nixon, "Senator Kennedy and I are not in disagreement as to the aim . . . the question is the means." In other words, they had the same goals, and differed only in discussing how they were to compromise on the means of achieving those goals. "Whether it's in the field of housing or health or medical care or schools or the development

---

[17] Rand, Ayn. *The Virtue of Selfishness* (New York: Signet, 1964), 68.

of electric power," Nixon went on, "we have programs which we believe will move America . . . . The test of a program is how much you are spending." Nixon had no alternative to offer America other than, "Senator Kennedy would have the federal government spend more than I would have it spend . . . . Senator Kennedy too often would rely too much on the federal government." By what standard, beyond your feelings, Mr. Nixon, do we know it is too much? No answer.

  Nixon attempted a last-ditch effort to appeal to fiscal conservatives, but it was disingenuous and fell on deaf ears, "But it is essential that [the President] not allow a dollar spent that could be better spent by the people themselves."[18] (Who gets to decide which way is the best way to spend a dollar? Not its owner, of course. The government does.)

"In any compromise between food and poison, it is only death that can win. In any compromise between good and evil, it is only evil that can profit."[19]
- Ayn Rand

  Saul Alinsky recognized the importance of the word "compromise" to his Progressive activism. "To the organizer," he wrote, "compromise is a key and beautiful word. It is always present in the pragmatics of operation. It is making the deal, getting that vital breather, usually the victory. If you start with nothing, demand 100 per cent, then compromise for 30 per cent, you're 30 per cent ahead."[20]

  This idea has been used with devastating effects to erode freedom and personal responsibility. "Compromise" must come to be used in the reverse way to gain liberty back. Instead of compromising our freedom with Progressives to merely slow the advance of tyranny, we must demand that they compromise with freedom. Demand 100% freedom and when they give us 30%, we will be that much freer. Demand complete school and teacher choice, and call it a victory when more charter schools open up or students are allowed to transfer to another school that better meets their needs.

  The results of elevating the idea of compromise to such celestial heights is that, more and more, many voters are expressing hopelessness in the political process. Rather than supporting a candidate whose principles they agree with, voters are reduced to lamely trying to vote for the "lesser of two evils."

---

[18] Safire, *Great Speeches*, 285-87.
[19] Rand, Ayn. *Atlas Shrugged* (New York: Signet, 1957), 979.
[20] Alinsky, *Rules*, 59.

If we believe that individual rights can be overridden sometimes for the "good of the public" when need requires it, then we concede that rights are not unalienable, but may be removed in favor of some supposed higher cause. In other words, we believe rights are not actually rights, but merely permissions granted by government.

The source of this idea of holy compromise being held at unquestionable god-like status—its apotheosis—is the philosophy that "there is no black and white" and "no good or evil" in the realm of morality and ideas. It comes from the idea that morality is always found in a gray area.

THE ZEAL FOR MORAL GRAYNESS

To assert that in morality there are "no blacks or whites" is the assertion that there is no "good or evil"—in principle, in action, or in people.

The first problem with this view is that in order to define gray, one must recognize the existence of black and white, since every shade of gray is merely a mixture of the two in some degree. Before one can even identify anything as gray one must know how to identify black and white—or in morality, what is evil or good. And if one can determine what is good and evil in morality, one then has no excuse for choosing the evil. The evil generally arrives in the pretense that one's actions are not black, merely gray.

If a man's moral code (such as altruism) contains contradictions, is inapplicable to reality, and offers no guidance for determining his choices, then it is the moral code itself which must be evil. If a choice confronting a man is complex and he makes an honest error, he is still morally good since errors of knowledge are not evil. However, if the man avoids the necessity of having to know, if he refuses to know the facts, then he is guilty. Ayn Rand named the refusal to think as the worst sin and the source of all other evils.

Some people use their zeal for moral grayness to assert that "nobody is perfect," that all men make mistakes and are thus in the "gray area." Morality only deals with issues that involves man's agency to choose. Even if a million people choose poorly in one instance, such a thing is no guarantee that the next man won't. Collective action has no unique moral authority. In this case, that principle means that the "rightness" of something is not determined by how many people choose to do it or not. The reason many people are morally "gray" is because they hold contradictory and conflicting values, making it impossible to act in consistent accordance with true principles. The fact that people are not perfect does not invalidate the need for man to be morally good, but makes it all the more important.

Others get their zeal for moral grayness from the belief that there are two sides to every issue—and that thereby both sides are equally valid, and nobody is ever completely right or wrong. Yes, one should give a hearing to all sides of an issue, but it doesn't mean that all sides are equal in their claims to justice.

Some issues are so complex that people give up searching for a "right" answer. However, it is in these issues that extreme attention is required. Delicate and intense effort is needed to view the issue according to principle.

There is a right and wrong to every question. The challenge is learning how to find it beyond the false choices offered to us.

In the natural realm, principles are still held inviolate. Almost everyone recognizes that in any compromise between poison and food, the poison will win. Then why is it that such a compromise between good and evil is demanded today in the realm of ideas? It is for the same reason: in any compromise of morality, evil wins.

POLARIZATION THROUGH FALSE CHOICES

Democrat or Republican? Upper or lower class? Working families or businessmen? Liberal or conservative? Left or Right? Atheist or Religionist? Communist or Fascist?

A dichotomy is a division or contrast between two things that are or are represented as being opposed or entirely different.

A false dichotomy is one in which both choices presented are false, or misleading. The false dichotomy tactic can involve the use of presenting a choice which removes facts from proper context, distorts the meaning of the terms used, and evades any mention of the actual principle at stake. The result is increased polarization in public discourse, as well as an overall guiding of that discourse away from the actual issues.

Let's take an example from the beginnings of the Progressive movement from Presidential candidate William Jennings Bryan. "There are two ideas of government," he said. "There are those who believe that, if you will only legislate to make the well-to-do prosperous, their prosperity will leak through on those below. The Democratic idea, however, has been that if you legislate to make the masses prosperous, their prosperity will find its way up through every class which rests upon them."[21]

---

[21] Safire, *Great Speeches*, 771.

The two polar opposites he presents here are that government must either legislate prosperity to the rich or legislate prosperity to the poor. He intentionally leaves no room for any other view of government or its proper role or even the question of if the government can legislate prosperity at all. The problem here is that these are not opposites at all but share the same false premises: 1) that government can or should legislate prosperity to anyone; 2) that no other valid view of the concept of government can or does exist.

The goal of such a tactic is: 1) to remove the possibility of any third choice or questioning of these premises; 2) to gain power through deception.

As long as we think we must debate the effectiveness of the Common Core curriculum rather than the moral issue of government involvement in education, or that we must debate morality or merits of stem-cell research, for example, rather than stepping back and debating the morality of taxing someone to fund such research, we are following the collectivist lead nicely. This is because we have already conceded the view that the government may tax and regulate for any purpose and to any extent as long as we think it is merited, or needed, or a public service.

OPPOSITE DAY

"We dispute their numbers. We don't have hard, concrete numbers, but we dispute them."[22] – White House Press Secretary Jay Carney on Obamacare enrollments

What was once a game for children to gleefully bewilder their peers is now one of the most insidious tools of evil. It is very simple: whatever the truth is, just say the opposite. It is one of the variations of the attack on man's conceptual faculty. If ambiguity is impossible, just supplant the truth with the error, especially with access to the machinery of propaganda. Justice becomes a right to the unearned, equality becomes racist, democracy becomes freedom, fascism becomes capitalism, a President's promises become his actual record, and socialism becomes the American Way.

---

[22] Howe, Caleb. "Carney on Obamacare Enrollments: We Don't Have Hard Numbers, But We Dispute Their Numbers." Truthrevolt.org. 1 May 2014. Online. truthrevolt.org/news/carney-obamacare-enrollments-we-dont-have-hard-numbers-we-dispute-their-numbers. Accessed 3 May 2014.

This strategy is not new; more than 2,500 years ago the biblical prophet Isaiah said, "Woe to those who call evil good and good evil, who put darkness for light and light for darkness, who put bitter for sweet and sweet for bitter."[23] Can there be any better way to win an argument? Both parties can say can "freedom" and mean completely different things while actually advocating tyranny.

Wealth "Control"

At a rally around the Martin Luther King, Jr. Memorial, Lee Saunders of the American Federation of State, County, and Municipal Employees (AFSCME) said, "The richest 1 percent of Americans controls 40 percent of this country's wealth. Our work, brothers and sisters, is not done."[24]

Take special note of the word choice used here to distort the truth. To "control" wealth implies a couple of things. Notice that he offers no definition of wealth, and leads us to believe that it is some limited and predetermined quantity or entity. No mention of earning wealth, working for wealth, or creating it; it is to be controlled. This is the language of primal brutes, fighting tribe against tribe to dominate the other and "control" the limited "resources."

To the statist, wealth is a finite pie that should be divided equally (i.e. based on need). They have not ever questioned where wealth comes from; they do not understand that there is no limit to how much wealth can be produced. They see everything through the lens of collectivism with all products and resources claimed as property of the whole. Rather than seeing individuals creating wealth, they see a community chest to be divided up.

So one percent of Americans are extremely rich, relatively—how did that happen? Did they go door to door and rob every house at gunpoint? Did they rob a bank? No, they started or engaged in trade and business. Bill Gates wrote some software, and we all thought it was so great we bought enough copies to make him one of the richest men in the world. Having billions of dollars (and a trampoline room in his house!) didn't cause any children in Africa to starve. In fact, charities that help children in Africa often use his products to be more effective and effi-

---

[23] Isaiah 5:20.

[24] Keyes, Allison. "A March for Jobs in Martin Luther King's Name." *NPR.* 16 Oct 2011. Online. npr.org/2011/10/16/141389473/a-march-for-jobs-in-martin-luther-kings-name?ps=rs. Accessed 31 Jan 2012.

cient. The prosperity of one doesn't mean someone else will have to be less prosperous. He created a product; he created something of value and thus added to the aggregate value of the entire world. The principle is that more production means more prosperity.

We've discussed in this chapter some of the tactics used by the collectivists in their crusade to obliterate individual rights. They can be obvious or insidiously subtle, but as you grow accustomed to identifying them, they lose their power. The following chapter addresses what the strategy of defense must be in order to succeed against such a foe.

REVIEW

Q1: What is the definition of a tyrant?

———————————————————————————————————

Q2: What is an anti-concept?

———————————————————————————————————

Q3: Describe the tyranny of need.

———————————————————————————————————

Q4: Why is "extremism" a dangerous and meaningless concept as used today?

———————————————————————————————————

Q5: In a compromise between good and evil, who wins?

———————————————————————————————————

Q6: Explain the difference between a good compromise and an evil compromise.

———————————————————————————————————

Q7: What is a dichotomy? Give an example of a false one.

———————————————————————————————————

Q8: What is the difference between discrimination by individuals and discrimination by the government?

———————————————————————————————————

CHAPTER 16

THE BEST DEFENSE

"The battle of human history is fought and determined by those who are predominantly consistent."[1] - Ayn Rand

This chapter will discuss understanding and implementing an effective defense of freedom. In practice, this means a defense of capitalism, the only social system which recognizes and protects individual rights.

There have been many well-meaning and misguided attempts to defend capitalism by conservatives, economists, philosophers, and statesmen. But the majority of these defenses have done worse than fail. The unfortunate results are that these defenses have helped the statist attacks and conceded ground in the most vital arena—morality.

---

[1] Rand, Ayn. *For the New Intellectual* (New York: Signet, 1963), 21.

ISSUES VS PRINCIPLES

The first failed defense that we must understand is the inability or unwillingness to identify or discuss principles, and instead a fixation on issues. Recall that a principle is a general truth that describes an aspect of reality. Because principles are general truths, they can be applied to and help guide answers to a wide range of specific problems or questions. They provide a consistent foundation for decision-making and are not dependent on or changed by circumstance. See Appendix B for a list of some principles discussed in this book.

To focus on an issue is to have a limited perspective and typically accept the premise as a given. For example, an "issue" would be the Supreme Court debating the constitutionality of the individual mandate found in the Affordable Care Act. The Court focused on whether the commerce clause of the Constitution had bearing on the issue, while the real principle at question should have been whether the government forcing people to purchase a product was within the proper role of government or not.

To discuss only issues may be exciting and controversial, but it is also futile, even harmful, if done without preliminary work in understanding the principles upon which any discussion of issues should be based. It is like trying to safely drive a car without first having knowledge of how to steer, stop, start, signal, park, or obey traffic laws. We have left discussion of issues such as immigration, welfare, education, war, and the environment until the end of this book for this reason.

To think according to principles is a skill that can be learned with practice. It may be strange at first, but is the only way to bring our decision-making in line with natural law. Simply loving or studying the Constitution is not enough to save it. If we do not know how to live by principle, we will be helping to destroy our country because we will accidentally push for solutions that threaten it.

Once we can identify principles being obeyed or violated in our own actions and in the world around us, we are ready to begin our defense of capitalism in an effective manner and with the most powerful moral reasoning to support us.

FAILED DEFENSES

Over the last two hundred years, aspects of laissez-faire capitalism have been advocated and defended in varying degrees by a wide variety of individuals, from Adam Smith to Ludwig von Mises to Henry Hazlitt. They have described and illustrated, in varying degrees, the mechanics of a free market and the general perfection of capitalism. Yet, such defenses have failed to convince the world to accept capitalism. Other individuals and organizations, in a variety of ways and for a variety of reasons, have also attempted to defend economic freedom. They have done worse than fail—they have helped the collectivist cause in their efforts, and today the assault on private property and individual rights is still escalating. Here are a few of those viewpoints and why they failed:

ARGUMENT FROM PRACTICALITY

"I am a conservative Republican, a firm believer in free market capitalism. A free market system allows all parties to compete, which ensures the best and most competitive project emerges, and ensures a fair, democratic process."[2]
- Sarah Palin

One defense of capitalism comes from a "practical" perspective. Those who use this argument claim that capitalism may not be moral, but it is the best system to have in place because of its enormously good "practical" results. They claim that capitalism creates more wealth, goods, services, and inventions than any other system. They say it's more efficient than central planning and recovers faster from bumps in the economy. They say that it ensures a competitive marketplace.

All this is true, but has failed to stem the statist tide that continues to sweep capitalism away. Why? Because that tide is not fueled by cost/benefit analysis or any other practical concepts. Instead, a swelling of moral indignation has overrun the ground lost by capitalists by asking, "How can you care about profit while people are suffering?"

The pragmatic defenders of capitalism will argue for tax cuts as the best way to optimize revenue for the government and to stimulate the economy. They will not argue that it is the right of individuals to keep what they earn. They offer no principle or morality to back up their de-

---

[2] "Sarah Palin on Budget & Economy." Ontheissues.org. Online. ontheissues.org/2012/Sarah_Palin_Budget_+_Economy.htm. Accessed 14 Sep 2012.

fense, and so continue to bicker endlessly about statistics and percent-ages. Competition is not a good reason to support capitalism. Competi-tion is not the purpose of a free-market, but a by-product.

The practical defense is a failure for three reasons:

1. An argument by cost/benefit analysis will always invite a rebut-tal by another Pragmatic "expert" whose "facts" are different from yours, or who will simply lie in contradiction;

2. Even if your facts are unassailable, the fall-back position of the collectivists is that your facts may be true, but that's not how things "should" be morally—that you only care about numbers and don't care about people;

3. You concede the altruist ethic that morality is found in provid-ing goods and services to others, rather than in the protection of man's unalienable rights.

ARGUMENT FROM THE GREATEST GOOD

"The genius of capitalism lies in its ability to make self-interest serve the wider interest."[3] - Bill Gates

This argues for capitalism on the grounds that it will provide the greatest good and the greatest happiness for the greatest number of peo-ple. The argument claims that because capitalism is so productive, it is the best way to provide for the needs of everyone and achieve the com-mon good. Steven Landsburg argued that capitalism was the best way to lift large populations out of poverty. General economic growth, he said, is most effectively fostered by capitalism, and that "the primary cause of poverty is insufficient capitalism."[4] This is true, but as a defense it is inef-fective.

As economist Walter Williams observed, the goodness of capital-ism lies in its respect of "the sanctity of the individual" and how it is "rooted in voluntary relationships rather than force and coercion."[5] This is closer to what the best defense should be.

The argument that capitalism is good because it helps the most people prosper is a failure because it concedes the collectivist ethic as the

---

[3] Kinsley, Michael, ed. *Creative Capitalism* (New York: Simon & Schuster, 2008), 9.

[4] Kinsley, *Creative Capitalism*,143.

[5] Quoted in Forbes, Steve. and Elizabeth Ames. *How Capitalism Will Save Us* (New York: Crown Business, 2009), 31.

ideal. It argues that providing for the needs of others is the justification for such a social system. It is an argument to defend capitalism by using the idea that the happiness of the majority is more important and a higher moral value than the happiness of an individual.

As George Gilder mistakenly put it, "Altruism is the essence of capitalism . . . . Capitalism begins with giving . . . . The deepest truths of capitalism are faith, hope, and love."[6] Craig Biddle rightly rejects this defense as completely wrong, "Capitalism begins not with giving but with producing—and then moves on to keeping, using, and trading the product of one's efforts for other values in the marketplace. Nor is capitalism based on faith or hope; rather, it is based on reason and long-term planning, which are the means by which businessmen succeed and grow rich."[7]

ARGUMENT FROM DEPRAVITY

"It is a system designed for sinners, in the hope of achieving . . . good."[8]
- Michael Novak

This disgusting argument claims that man is too selfish and mean to live the "higher laws" required for socialism, and must therefore be allowed to wallow in capitalism until he shrugs off his corrupt ideas, or until God comes and makes everything all better. "Man should live for the sake of others," these defenders claim, "but since man is too selfish to do so, and since we don't agree with the Communists that we can have a utopia through force, we will have to make do with the lesser of two evils."

Michael Novak, who served as U.S. Ambassador to the United Nations Commission on Human Rights, attempted to defend capitalism on these grounds, saying, "While recognizing that no system of political economy can escape the ravages of human sinfulness, [capitalism] has

---

[6] Gilder, George. Quoted in Biddle, Craig. "Capitalism and the Moral High Ground." *The Objective Standard*. Winter 2008-09, Online. theobjectivestandard.com/issues/2008-winter/capitalism-moral-high-ground.asp. Accessed 5 May 2011.

[7] Biddle, Craig. "Capitalism and the Moral High Ground." *The Objective Standard*. Winter 2008-09, Online. theobjectivestandard.com/issues/2008-winter/capitalism-moral-high-ground.asp. Accessed 5 May 2011.

[8] Quoted in *ibid*.

attempted to set in place a system which renders sinful tendencies as productive of good as possible."[9]

In other words, he says capitalism taps into the creative potential of evil souls and thus achieves moral good. This is an absurd contradiction. This argument accepts the basic ethic of collectivism—altruism—and longs for the day when man can put off caring about his self-interest. Such an argument is thus a failure in its defense of capitalism. It only strengthens the statists who claim that if the good of others is the highest ethic to achieve, then it must be moral to enforce it through government action.

THE SOCIAL DARWINIST DEFENSE

Popular in the 19th century, this defense claims that capitalism entails an economic application of the laws of nature, namely, the survival of the fittest. It may not be pretty or fair, these defenders say, but it's human nature and we can't change that. Besides, in the end it makes the human race stronger.

This defense falsely claims that the aim (and effect) of capitalism is to make the "fittest" humans rise to the top as rulers in a grotesque "meritocracy." This denies and distorts the true morality of capitalism which is to protect man's freedom to act on his own judgment.

All these defenses of the social system have failed and statism has steadily gained ground for over a century in America because capitalism's alleged defenders have conceded the most important point to the enemy: the moral high ground.

THE HIGH GROUND OF THE ENEMY

"Capitalism is an evil, and you cannot regulate evil. You have to eliminate it and replace it with something that is good for all people and that something is democracy."[10] - Michael Moore, *Capitalism: A Love Story*

The "high ground" is a spot of elevated terrain that can be useful for military tactics. The statists have taken over this high ground in the

---

[9] Quoted in *ibid*.

[10] Quoted in Collett-White, Mike. "'Capitalism is Evil,' Says New Michael Moore Film." Reuters. reuters.com/article/2009/09/06/us-venice-capitalism-idUSTRE5850F320090906. Accessed 5 May 2011.

moral battle for the soul of America. With little resistance, they proclaim their goodness and moral justification for denying individual rights.

Capitalism is labeled as evil and the source of evils such as poverty, crime, unemployment, war, and drugs. The use of such words as "evil" is intended to instill an unearned guilt in the defenders of individual rights. This guilt, if accepted by those defenders, disarms any possible resistance. Jean-Francois Revel, socialist-turned-classical-liberal, put it clearly, saying, "A civilization that feels guilty for everything it is and does will lack the energy and conviction to defend itself."[11]

Many attacks on capitalism focus on the fact that it enables self-interest. For example, Congressman Jim Moran (D-MA) said that Americans must give up "this simplistic notion that people who have wealth are entitled to keep it."[12] Capitalism's enemies know the nature of capitalism, yet its defenders do not. Karl Marx explained, "The right of man to private property is, therefore, the right to enjoy one's property and to dispose of it at one's discretion, without regard to other men, independently of society, the right of self-interest."[13] Marx, for once, hit the nail on the head. It is exactly for this reason that capitalism is vilified, and it is exactly this reason that must be unapologetically endorsed—man's right to enjoy and dispose of his property, the right to a free exercise of conscience, the right of self-interest.

A primary weapon of the anti-capitalists is guilt. They direct this guilt at their intended victims. But such guilt is only effective if their victims accept it and agree with it. These statists seek to have us endorse our own martyrdom, and agree to accept—in return for our achievements—curses, robbery, and enslavement.[14]

The key to defeating the collectivists is for capitalists to have a certainty of their moral rectitude, to turn this contempt around, and aim it at the collectivist. We must take away their pretended holiness and expose them for what they are—parasites.[15] The proper defense of capital-

---

[11] Safire, William, ed. *Lend Me Your Ears: Great Speeches in History* (New York: W. W. Norton & Company, 1992), 872.

[12] Moran, Jim. "Redistribution of Wealth." youtube.com/watch?v=QJyS1WJNisM. Uploaded 31 Oct 2008. Accessed 7 Apr 2011.

[13] Marx, Karl. "On The Jewish Question." Available Online. Marxists.org. marxists.org/archive/marx/works/1844/jewish-question/index.htm. Accessed 7 Apr 2011.

[14] Peikoff, Leonard. *Objectivism: The Philosophy of Ayn Rand* (New York: Penguin, 1993), 333.

[15] Harriman, David, ed. *Journals of Ayn Rand* (New York: Penguin, 1999), 298.

ism, and the only one that will be ultimately effective in reversing the trend of collectivism, must be done first and foremost in the arena that the collectivists have monopolized for decades nearly unchallenged—the arena of morality.

SELLING CAPITALISM

"The Revolution was effected before the war commenced. The Revolution was in the hearts and minds of the people . . . This radical change in the principles, opinions, sentiments and affections of the people was the real American Revolution."[16] - John Adams, 1818

Pragmatic Progressives have been extraordinarily effective in nudging their ideas into very nearly every aspect of human life on earth. Their tactics have proven to be perfectly suited to the job of infecting and changing the culture a little at a time. Over a hundred years of baby steps have taken a once-great nation down a long journey through stagnation and decline and heading to possible destruction.

If we are to reverse the trend and get this tidal wave to change direction, we will have to change the words we use, change from a defeatist defense to an open unapologetic attack, change our aversion to propaganda (there is such a thing as true propaganda), flood our culture with true principles via various media, become better people who embrace peace and love and courage, take responsibility for self-government and family government, and most of all, reverse the unprincipled collapse of our philosophy that has taken us into agreement with the incessant Progressive onslaught.

"There is nothing so practical as a good theory." - Kurt Lewin

To figure out how we can "sell" capitalism back to mainstream culture, let us first look to how it was sold out. The Progressive movement has used some "playbooks" as guides to many of their strategies and attacks over the last several decades. One book is called *Rules for Radicals*, by Saul Alinsky. In this book, the author lays out, not a principled belief system—which he considers impossible and impractical—but several

---

[16] Adams, John. Letter to prominent journalist Hezekiah Niles. 13 Feb 1818. Available online. teachingamericanhistory.org/library/document/john-adams-to-h-niles/. Accessed 18 Aug 2013.

tactical strategy lessons for the "revolutionary radical" to get things done in any way necessary.

The first important thing to note is that the Progressives, while they have no principles, clearly recognize where the battle for their non-beliefs should be fought. As Alinsky points out in his prologue, "The Revolutionary Force today has two targets, moral as well as material."[17]

They know they must get people to accept the Progressive way of things as moral, or acceptable, if it is to be put into widespread practice in the culture. "You do what you can with what you have and clothe it with moral garments," Alinksy advises.[18] In the same breath as this moral justification comes the attack against the moral integrity of their enemies. Alinsky says that the Establishment must be "constantly pushed to live up to their own book of morality and regulations," since "no organization . . . can live up to the letter of its own book."[19] It is this line of attack that always pushes the conservatives to go along with huge entitlement and welfare programs. The Progressives merely have to ask (often with a lawsuit) why the conservatives are racist, bigoted, intolerant, selfish, or hate poor people, and the conservatives accept the premise of this attack rather than leading with their own attack against the tyranny of the Progressives.

TACTICAL RULES

Alinsky also wrote about rules of Power Tactics that prove useful to both recognize when they are being used against you and to occasionally utilize:

- "Power is not only what you have but what the enemy thinks you have."
- "Never go outside the experience of your people."
- "Wherever possible go outside the experience of the enemy."
- "Make the enemy live up to their own book of rules."
- "Ridicule is man's most potent weapon."
- "A good tactic is one that your people enjoy."
- "A tactic that drags on too long becomes a drag."
- "Keep the pressure on."
- "The threat is usually more terrifying than the thing itself."

---

[17] Alinksy, Saul. *Rules for Radicals* (New York: Random House, 1989), xiii. Emphasis added.
[18] *ibid*, 36.
[19] *ibid*, 152.

- "The price of a successful attack is a constructive alternative." (This means when the other side finally gives in and says, "Fine, what do you think we should do?" that you have an answer and are prepared to lead.)
- "Pick the target, freeze it, personalize it, and polarize it."[20] "Freeze" means single out for blame. Don't attack corporations or cities or government entities, but personalize it, he says. Put a face to the problem—attack the leaders. "Before men can act an issue must be polarized," notes Alinsky. "Men will act when they are convinced that their cause is 100 per cent on the side of the angels and that the opposition are 100 per cent on the side of the devil."[21] (This is from a book that literally honors Lucifer in its dedication.)

The Progressives already fight unapologetically to vilify those they see as a threat. Television commentator Chris Matthews referred to sitting Senator Ted Cruz as a "terrorist," saying, "I will say he's a terrorist because what the guy has done basically says, 'my goal is demolition—blow up health care, blow up the continuing resolution, bring the government to a standstill and then make us forfeit on the national debt.'"[22] The same rhetoric is never tolerated by Progressives when it is used against them—which is why it must be.

Another important tactic that can't be overlooked anymore is humor. Alinsky said, "Humor is essential, for through humor much is accepted that would have been rejected if presented seriously."[23] There is a huge political influence being wielded today by "comedy shows"—shows that, unfortunately for many people, are their only source of political news.

Making fun of the enemy is the unforgivable sin. This was poignantly illustrated in the instance of a rodeo clown at the Missouri State Fair who was banned "from ever participating again" for satirizing and wearing a mask depicting President Obama. The incident also caused the

[20] Alinsky, *Radicals*, 127-30.
[21] *ibid*, 78.
[22] Goyette, Braden. "Chris Matthews Calls Ted Cruz a 'Political Terrorist.'" The Huffington Post. 31 Jul 2013. huffingtonpost.com/2013/07/31/chris-matthews-ted-cruz_n_3685879.html. Accessed 23 Aug 2013.
[23] Alinsky, *Rules*, xviii.

state's association to declare that future cowboys and clowns must undergo "sensitivity training."[24]

This harmless satire worked the Progressive base into an indignant lather, showing the surprising effectiveness of such activities, despite an American tradition dating back to the 1960s of dressing up in masks of both current and former Presidents and other political figures.[25] A Progressive writer responded to the incident, "Silence is not an appropriate response to this 'entertainment' on grounds owned by all Missourians. I can't write anymore at how disgusting this is. All I want is some heads to roll."[26]

For a return to freedom we must first return freedom to the hearts and minds of the people in a widespread campaign. No political revolution can survive without the supporting foundation of a popular cultural reformation.

Effective Defense

In July of 2012, Viewpoint host Eliot Spitzer couldn't figure out why liberalism seemed to him to be shrinking against the continued onslaught of the fiscally conservative Tea Party movement. "Can I tell you my theory?" Spitzer asked. "We let the Tea Party steal our thunder . . . We let the Tea Party grab the anger, the animus and the venom when it should've been ours, and you know why?" he asked. "We were chicken, we were afraid, we were lily-livered, had no backbone, no spine."[27] This shows exactly the sort of results that can come from positioning our political battles and ideas in the most effective arena!

---

[24] Levs, Josh. "After Obama-mocking Rodeo Clown, Missouri Fair Requires 'Sensitivity Training." *CNN*. 15 Aug 2013. cnn.com/2013/08/15/politics/missouri-rodeo-clowns-sensitivity-training-obama-clown. Accessed 23 Aug 2013.

[25] Green, Amanda. "A Brief History of Political Halloween Masks (and What They Tell Us About the Election). MentalFloss.com. 24 Oct 2012. mentalfloss.com/article/12859/brief-history-political-halloween-masks-and-what-they-tell-us-about-election. Accessed 23 Aug 2013.

[26] MoDem. "Obama at the Missouri State Fair." Daily Kos. 11 Aug 2013. dailykos.com/story/2013/08/11/1230444/-Obama-at-the-Missouri-State-Fair#. Accessed 23 Aug 2013.

[27] Howerton, Jason. "'We Let the Tea Party Steal Our Thunder' Eliot Spitzer Can't Understand Why Liberalism Isn't 'Persuading the Public.'" 3 Jul 2012. The Blaze. Online. theblaze.com/stories/we-let-the-tea-party-steal-our-thunder-eliot-spitzer-cant-understand-why-tea-party-movement-is-outshining-liberalism/. Accessed 6 Jul 2012.

Capitalism's would-be defenders must deflate the moral superiority flaunted by those of the collectivist/altruist ethic. Nothing less will do, and indeed, anything less helps to undermine and destroy capitalism. The system of individual rights cannot be defended with guilt, by apology, or without conviction. It requires the most righteous pride of certitude. Only this way can we hope to stop, and then reverse, the steady creep of Progressive statism and change course to ascend to freedom.

Because capitalism is moral and good, writer Craig Biddle describes what the proper grounds for its defense must be and why:

"Capitalism enables everyone to act in a consistently self-interested manner. Rather than shying away from this unassailable fact, we must embrace and emphasize it. We must do so not on the pragmatic grounds that doing so will work to defend capitalism (which it will), but on the principled grounds that the selfishness-enabling characteristic of capitalism is, in fact, what makes it the only moral social system on earth . . .

"Under genuine capitalism—not the mongrel system operative in America today, but pure, unregulated, laissez-faire capitalism—the government prohibits citizens from using physical force against each other, and the Constitution prohibits the government from using force against citizens except in retaliation against those who initiate its use. Thus everyone is fully free to act on his own judgment for his own sake."[28]

That is the essence of the principled, virtuous stand against the collectivist/altruist ethic. We must gain and keep a driving passion for the good. We must love the good for being good. We must value achievement in ourselves and others and exercise a commitment to justice—refusing the unearned, in matter and in spirit.

We may oppose our nation's present course, Piekoff writes, but by ourselves we cannot change it. The taxes and the bureaucrats are merely consequences which cannot be erased as long as their source is untouched. "The people may 'swing to the right,' but it is futile, if the leaders of the right are swinging to their own . . . brand of statism . . . . To change a nation's basic course requires more than a mood of popular discontent," he goes on. "It requires the definition of a new direction for the country to take. Above all, it requires a theoretical justification for this direction, one which would convince people that the proposed

---

[28] Biddle, "Moral High Ground." Online.

course is practical and moral."[29] It requires philosophy. Philosophy changes a culture, and culture changes the country.

"The world crisis of today is a moral crisis," said Ayn Rand, "and nothing less than a moral revolution can resolve it: a moral revolution to sanction and complete the political achievement of the American Revolution. [We] must fight for capitalism, not as a 'practical' issue, not as an economic issue, but with the most righteous pride, as a moral issue. That is what capitalism deserves and nothing less will save it."[30]

---

[29] Piekoff, *OP*, 286.
[30] Rand, Ayn. *For the New Intellectual* (New York: Signet, 1963), 54.

REVIEW

Q1: Compare and contrast issues and principles.

Q2: Defend capitalism through practicality, then identify why this argument fails.

Q3: Defend capitalism through the greatest good. Why is this argument evil?

Q4: What is the high ground that must be taken from collectivism?

Q5: Look at some news headlines from today and see if you can spot some of the Progressive Power Tactics in the stories. List them.

Q6: Explain the morality of capitalism.

A Principled Look into Some Major Issues of Today:

This book is primarily concerned with principles, not issues. Many people can passionately debate issues all day long, but end up advocating evil because they never even ask themselves what principles their opinions and policies should be based on.

We hesitate to bring up specific issues for concern that the reader will focus merely on those and rather than gaining the necessary experience in identifying foundational principles and drawing correct, non-contradictory conclusions from those. However, we think it is also important to give some examples of how principled thinking can clear the clutter from the road and set the stage for true reform. For this reason, we have chosen a few issues to give an introduction into examining them in a principled manner.

CHAPTER 17

IMMIGRATION

"Whenever an issue leads to an unresolvable conflict, you will find, at its root, the violation of someone's rights."[1] - Ayn Rand

Immigration is a hotly debated and emotional topic for many people. One of the main problems is that immigration is actually composed of several separate issues. These separate issues must be kept apart in evaluation and discussion in order to progress or come to any understanding.

Immigration, as an issue, is actually composed of the following specifics:

- Illegal immigration;
- Legal immigration;
- Border security; and
- The current undocumented population in America.

But before we even address these smaller issues we have to know what principles we are going to base our decisions on.

---

[1] Rand, Ayn. *The Voice of Reason* (New York: Signet, 1990), 252.

Immigration is defined as the act of moving into a country with the intention of remaining there. There are many people who want to live in America. For centuries various peoples have uprooted their lives and families in order to be replanted on American soil. These people want to pursue what has come to be known as the American Dream. The American Dream is a concept that has become distorted and misused over the years. It does not mean home ownership or two cars in the garage. It does not mean a guaranteed job and pension. It does not mean making sure our children have more things than we did. It means being free to act on our own judgment, to make and keep and use wealth to make life better for ourselves and our families.

George Washington described the American Dream eloquently, writing that, "The bosom of America is open to receive not only the Opulent and respectable Stranger, but the oppressed and persecuted of all Nations And Religions; whom we shall welcome to a participation of all our rights and privileges, if by decency and propriety of conduct they appear to merit the enjoyment."[2]

In the early days of our Republic, America was open to receive all people to a participation of the protection of individual rights as merited by their respect for the rights of others. Today, however, while some receive special permission to immigrate, entry to most people is forbidden by law.

PRINCIPLES OF IMMIGRATION

The first question to ask is if a foreigner has the right to move to America.

The second question is if America should welcome them.

The answer to both questions is, "Yes."

The prohibition against immigration is immoral because it is in violation of the principle of individual rights. The moral alternative to this prohibition is a policy of open immigration. This does not mean that anyone can enter the country anyway or anywhere they want. It also doesn't mean that just because someone comes to America to live that they must be granted citizenship. It means that anyone is free to enter and live in America as long they come through a designated checkpoint and pass a

---

[2] Quoted in Biddle, Craig. "Immigration and Individual Rights." *The Objective Standard*. Spring 2008, Online. theobjectivestandard.com/issues/2008-spring/immigration-individual-rights.asp. Accessed 6 May 2011.

screening process. The purpose of such screening would be to keep out enemies of America, criminals, and people with certain contagious diseases. Since the proper role of government is to protect individual rights, these are the only people that a government may morally reject from entering its borders. Such a policy is both politically and morally right.

It is moral because everyone has the right to act according to their own judgment as long as they don't violate that same right of others. The use of force prevents a person from acting in accordance with their judgment. In a civilized society, no one may initiate the use of force against others. The only question that matters is if a person has a right to take make their own choices or not. If they do, they must be left free to do so.

The right to act on one's judgment includes the right to contract with others. To help ourselves achieve consistency, let's use some examples to identify the principle, then apply it to immigration.

Suppose a man in Wisconsin wanted to work at the local grocery store, and the owner of that store wanted to hire him. Should they be free to do business? Yes. No one's rights are violated by an employer hiring an employee. No rights are violated upon the firing of another employee in preference of a more desirable one (except possible breach of contract). The fired employee may still act on his judgment, seeking employment elsewhere, or increasing his skills to make himself more desirable as a worker. There is no such thing as a right to a job.

Suppose a woman in Utah wished to move to Colorado, and that a landlord in Colorado wished to rent her an apartment. Should they be free to do so? Yes, because they have the right to act on their own judgment and they are not violating anyone else's rights.

We recognize the principle; now let's slightly alter these examples.

Suppose that the man who wishes to work at the grocery store in Wisconsin is from Honduras. Suppose the woman wanting to rent the apartment in Colorado is from China. Do these people still have the right to act on their judgment and contract freely together?

It should be clear: foreigners have the right to move to America. Americans have the right to contract, hire, and associate with them by mutual consent. Laws that prohibit this violate the rights of both parties.

Geographic location and national lineage do not bestow rights. As writer Craig Biddle explains, "America's border is not properly a barrier for the purpose of keeping foreigners out; it is properly a boundary designating the area in which the U.S. government must protect rights."[3]

---

[3] *ibid.*

IMMIGRATION OBJECTIONS

Biddle astutely lists the most common objections to a policy of open immigration and compellingly explains why they are unprincipled and immoral:

1. "This is our country, and we have a right to refuse entry to foreigners."

No one owns America. It is divided into sections of "public" and private land. If private land-owners wish to allow foreigners to make use of their land, they have the right to do so. If they wish to prohibit such use, they have that right as well.

"Public" property is allegedly owned by everyone and no one in particular. There is no way to identify which portion of such property belongs to Mrs. Jones. There is no principled reason to deny the appropriate use of such property to immigrants.

2. "We Americans have a right to our culture, which immigrants erode."

This can mean three things:
    A. We have a right to the racial makeup of our culture;
    B. We have a right to our own language;
    C. We have a right to our own lifestyle choices.

Those seeking to preserve the racial makeup of their culture are following in the footprints of some sort of Nazi-like racism. This is not a valid reason.

An official language is necessary in political and legal proceedings for clarity and consistency. However, no one has the right to force another person to speak that language. Most immigrants learn to speak English out of practical necessity, especially when not sheltered from this need by the welfare state, which makes it unnecessary to compete with others. It is also easier for them to learn English when they aren't associated with the black market status of illegal aliens for which English is unnecessary.

Those who wish to pursue their own lifestyle choices in dress, cuisine, etc., are advocating the freedom to pursue one's happiness and should advocate the same right for others, including immigrants.

3. "We Americans have a right to our jobs, which immigrants take, and to our wage rates, which immigrants lower."

As we said earlier, there is no such thing as the right to a job. If a man loses his job or receives a lower wage because an immigrant is willing to do it better or for less, his rights have not been violated. He is still free to act on his own judgment, gaining more skills or seeking employment elsewhere. He has no right to have the government prevent the employer and immigrant from doing business. This is an invalid argument.

Consider the implications of saying "Americans have a right to American jobs." This is collectivist thinking, it does not see individuals, but groups, and asserts that being born in this country bestows some sort of birthright and entitlement. Seeing this issue in collectivist terms of us vs. them is a nationalism that is similar to racism, which believes some people are superior to others by virtue of their identity.

4. "Immigrants come to America to live on the public dole via our welfare programs, and we simply can't afford to support them."

Most immigrants come to America to work hard, live in relative freedom, and be self-sufficient. If some do come here for the welfare programs, that is an argument, not against open immigration, but against the welfare state.

To help address this, immigrants should be barred from participation in this coercive redistribution of wealth. This includes "free" education and "free" medical goods and services. "In order to live the good life," explains Biddle, "immigrants, like all human beings, need to develop and maintain the virtue of independence; they need to face the demands of reality and live by their own thought and effort. Precluding them from receiving the so-called "benefits" of welfare will help them to develop or maintain that virtue."[4]

To say we can't afford to pay for immigrants is actually a critique against redistributionist statism, not immigration.

5. "Statistics show that immigrants commit a lot of crime. The more immigrants we allow into the country, the more crime we will suffer."

Immigrants don't commit crimes, individuals do. Individuals have agency. Nationality and race play no part in determining what an individual will choose to do. Like native-born Americans, immigrants should be held responsible for their actions and considered innocent until proven guilty. Individuals who commit crimes should suffer the consequences.

---

[4] *ibid.*

6. **"Open immigration might be practical under laissez-faire capitalism, but it is not practical under a welfare state. We cannot institute open immigration until we've achieved laissez-faire capitalism."**

This amounts to, "We can't practice the principles of freedom until we live in freedom." Each aspect of a free society must be accomplished one step at a time, over time. You have to start somewhere.

7. **"Open immigration makes it easy for terrorists to enter the U.S.; American security requires immigration restrictions."**

The solution to terrorist attacks on America is not the violation of individual rights, but the annihilation of states that sponsor terrorism. A secure border (all 12,000 miles of it!) would merely serve to make it more difficult and expensive for people to enter the country illegally and would not serve to greatly increase our protection against terrorism.

8. **"Granting amnesty to 'illegal' immigrants would make a mockery of the rule of law, they should be held accountable for breaking the law."**

What mocks the rule of law is the existence and attempted enforcement of anti-immigration laws.

The solution with respect to over twelve million so-called "illegals" is to grant unconditional amnesty (which is not necessarily citizenship, the requirements for which is a separate matter) and a Presidential apology for the violation of their rights and the necessity of suffering "Black Market Living." It is possible to live legally in the U.S. without being a citizen.

(Note: Use of the pejorative term "illegals" is both demeaning and disingenuous. We have all broken laws before, and most of us break many every day, including traffic laws, illegally downloading music, littering, and smoking in a public place. Boston civil-liberties lawyer Harvey Silverglate titled his book Three Felonies a Day to refer to "the number of crimes he estimates the average American now unwittingly commits because of vague laws."[5] The fact that you illegally copied a music disc twenty years ago does not mean you must be subjected to having your neighbors call you an "illegal" or a "pirate" for the rest of your life.)

---

[5] Crovitz, L. Gordon. "You Commit Three Felonies a Day." 27 Sep 2009. *The Wall Street Journal*. Online. online.wsj.com/article/ SB10001424052748704471504574438900830760842.html. Accessed 5 Jul 2012.

Legality is no guarantee of morality. Would it have been a mockery of the law for German citizens to refuse to turn over Jews to the Gestapo? It was the law!

Upholding the rule of law doesn't mean supporting whatever laws happen to be on the books. It means supporting and maintaining an objective government that recognizes and protects the requirements of man's life—which means: the principle of individual rights. This does not mean you should disobey every illegitimate law; there are contexts where it is good to obey morally wrong laws because it follows your hierarchy of values and protects your life (e.g. we pay taxes to avoid going to jail).

CONCLUSION

After such a principled look at the issue of immigration, Biddle brings us to this concluding plan of action:

• Make open immigration the law and do away with quotas, visas, green-cards, etc.

• Secure the border and establish objective screening points to turn away or detain criminals, terrorists, and people with certain infectious diseases.

• Grant amnesty (not citizenship) to the current undocumented immigrant populace and apologize for the trouble our immoral and unjust laws have caused them.

• Exclude non-citizens from welfare and public schools—and exempt them from paying taxes to support these programs.

• Declare war on foreign states that threaten us. Don't wait for enemies to come to our borders. Announce that from now on we will destroy our enemies where they are.[6]

Many claim that the issue is too complex to handle, but that is no excuse. By using principle to cut through the haze of groundless emotion, we can help defend the rights of foreigners who come to America, and the rights of Americans to associate with them.

---

[6] Biddle, "Immigration," Online.

REVIEW

Q1: What smaller issues make up the larger immigration issue?

Q2: What is immigration?

Q3: What right is it based on?

Q4: What is the purpose of America's border?

Q5: What are some common attacks against open immigration?

Q6: Why are these attacks unprincipled and immoral?

Q7: Why should immigrants be barred from welfare services? What effects do you think this would have?

Q8: Should immigrants be barred from voting? Why or why not?

CHAPTER 18

EDUCATION

"I believe that the school is primarily a social institution . . . . [and that] the true centre of correlation of the school subjects is not science, nor literature, nor history, nor geography, but the child's own social activities."[1]
- John Dewey

PRINCIPLES OF EDUCATION

Is education a right? A right is a moral principle defining our freedom of action in a social context. Such a principle guarantees the freedom to continue your existence, sans interference from others. Rights protect your freedom of action. Therefore, you have a right to seek education; you have a right to trade with others to obtain education. What you do not have is a right to an education at the coerced expense of someone else.

---

[1] Dewey, John. "My Pedagogic Creed." (1897). Available online. en.wikisource.org/wiki/My_Pedagogic_Creed. Accessed 3 Oct 2014.

Remember that "free" doesn't mean without cost, it just means that someone else has to pay for it. The next question is, "Who has to pay for it?"

The government program of "free" education initiates force against its citizens by:

- Appropriating their property;
- Coercing the parents to school their children in a manner prescribed by the government, violating their right to act according to their own judgment;
- Coercing the teachers to instruct the subject matter prescribed by the government.

A government-run education program is immoral because it violates the rights of parents, children, taxpayers, and teachers.

Isabel Paterson said it best: "There can be no greater stretch of arbitrary power than is required to seize children from their parents, teach them whatever the authorities decree they shall be taught, and expropriate from the parents the funds to pay for the procedure."[2]

No one would dispute the absolute necessity of education for a happy and fulfilling life, yet to force it by government fiat remains immoral.

Note: Nothing in this section should be construed as an attack against individual teachers, many of whom are talented, passionate, inspiring, and under-appreciated. In fact, much of this section is written with the view that a principled approach to education would be more rewarding, spiritually and financially, for the great many master teachers out there. While there are many excellent teachers in our schools, they are trapped by an immoral system, perpetuated by their unions and governmental control. Many only support this system because they see no other alternative.

GOVERNMENT SCHOOLS

Public education is a misnomer. It is more appropriate to call it government education. The false dichotomy of private vs. public causes confusion and clouds the real issues. "Public" implies that these schools are open to everyone. They are not. Ever tried to get permission to attend a public school aside from the one assigned by the government? Your request will most likely get denied. People have even been sued by the government for lying about where they live in order to try and improve

---

[2] Paterson, Isabel. *The God of the Machine* (Originally published in 1943, Qualiteri eBook, 2009), Chapter 21.

the educational environment for their children. Private schools would be more aptly named "public" schools because they are truly open and available to the public. The "public" education system today is run by, paid via, and monitored through the government.

Our current system of government education violates individual rights; this causes, in its wake, a cascade of other broken principles. The effects of all these violated laws combined together give us the sorry effects we see today—ballooning debt, many poor teachers (whether in quality or pay scale), a high percentage of failing schools, and ignorant students. "In some of America's larger cities," Andrew Bernstein reports, "fewer than half the students earn a high school diploma; in Detroit, only one quarter do. Roughly one million children drop out of school each year. Forty-five million Americans are marginally illiterate. Twenty-one million cannot read at all."[3]

Let's be specific about the effects of the violation of principle. By having a system which claims responsibility and authority to educate children, many parents feel little responsibility for educating their children.

Market safeguards are also removed by making education a government entity. A free market protects consumers in a number of ways. First, under government supervision quality is curtailed. In a free education market, quality would soar, the range of options would increase, competition would abound, and prices would steeply drop. There would be new kinds of educational options which don't exist yet. In a free market there would be more available products.

There would be an increase in the number of different types of schools which teach critical thinking skills, specific trades, or used a non-Progressive teaching philosophy such as the Montessori method. Total school time could be reduced by years (there are school children who have their high school diplomas as young as fourteen years old[4]).

Schools could offer specializations to cater to the needs of families. Does your child need special education for exceptional needs or handicaps? You would be able to "shop" around to find the school that provided what you needed. Do you want flexible hours to better fit your work schedule and avoid hiring a sitter? Looking for an inexpensive alternative

---

[3] Bernstein, Andrew. "The Educational Bonanza in Privatizing Government Schools." *The Objective Standard.* Winter 2010-11: 21-34. Print.

[4] Chung, Lori. "14-year-old Set to Graduate from Monticello High School." 8 Jun 2010. YNN. hudsonvalley.ynn.com/content/news/507410/14-year-old-set-to-graduate-from-monticello-high-school/. Accessed 25 Sep 2013.

to college to increase your skills for a specific career? The market would provide these specializations and services and many more that we can't even conceive of. Many companies currently offer daycare as a benefit to employees. What if they also offered school? In addition to babysitters, they could hire private teachers for the children of employees! No one knew they wanted an iPad until it was invented. There would be innovative educational opportunities we currently can't imagine, and they would become available for all price ranges.

Many families cannot afford to send their children to private schools, especially while paying taxes to also support government schools. They don't have the means to pay for education twice.

Many truancy laws require students to attend school until a certain age. These factors make the issue of education one of coercion, where families are being forced to attend public schools.

Remember that most of all, regardless of any cost/benefit analysis of government-run education; it is immoral because it violates the property rights of taxpayers, and the rights of parents and teachers to freely act on their own judgment and enter into contract for mutual benefit.

THE SOLUTION

The fix to the problems in state-run education is the same fix for every other problem caused by statism: the removal of forceful violation of rights and a shift to privatization.

A fully private school system would recognize and protect the rights of everyone involved—educators, taxpayers, students, and customers. Before we deal will some possible ways such a school system should come about, let's briefly address some major objections to such a system.

One major objection is that parents don't value their children's education enough to pay for it. However, the great majority of parents do value their children's education. Education will not be a priority for everyone, and some people will choose to spend their money on cigarettes instead of tuition. That is their choice, and they will have to live with the consequences of their actions. Unfortunately, so will their children.

The good news is that children are not mindless copies of their parents. As they grow into adults they can make very different choices than that of their parents. They will be free to pursue whatever educational options they desire. The United States had one President who didn't learn the basics of grammar, reading, or math until he was married and earning a living at age seventeen.[5] However, the parents of these children should be socially ostracized, and, when appropriate, prosecuted for child neglect; but, the existence of such people does not constitute a valid reason to violate the rights of the rest of Americans. There are also many parents who, under the public school system, care little for their children's education. A change to a private system would not increase that number, but may, in fact, decrease it. Isabel Paterson observed that, "The practical skill by which the average man gets a living is not learned in school. There is no reason to suppose that children would remain untaught."[6]

Another objection is that if taxpayers were not forced to fund the educational system, some families would be unable to afford quality education. Ironically, "the coercively funded and operated government schools are precisely what make it impossible for customers to receive quality education," answers Andrew Bernstein to this objection,

"[And] with the government monolith slain, the property, income, and sales taxes that had been levied to sustain it could and should be repealed. With their tax burden substantially diminished, families would retain more of their income and be fully free to spend it on their children's education . . . In a full private market for education, competition among private schools, teachers, and tutors would increase dramatically. This inevitably would drive prices down, making education increasingly affordable.

"As for those families that somehow in a free market for education still could not afford to pay for any education for their children, observe that even today many private schools offer scholarships to worthy students who cannot meet the tuition. In a fully free market for education, such scholarships would increase and abound. Private schools are highly competitive with one another, and they all seek to showcase the value and superiority of their product. Consequently, it is in their rational self-interest to attract students who will make them shine. Scholarships are a crucial means of doing so."[7]

---

[5] Miller Center, University of Virginia. "American President: Andrew Johnson." Online. millercenter.org/president/johnson. Accessed 31 Jan 2012.

[6] Paterson, *Machine*, 21.

[7] Bernstein, *Bonanza*. Online.

Scholarships and lower costs, in addition to billions of dollars already currently given annually to educational charities, would make for very few families who could not afford a quality education. (We will deal with those few shortly.) Also, the removal of government credit and intervention in schools would decrease the costs because, as in the housing market, government incentives and subsidies have created an educational market bubble where costs continue to rise. One reporter observed that "Any serious policy reform has to start by considering a heretical idea: Federal subsidies intended to make college more affordable may have encouraged rapidly rising tuitions."[8] A major symptom of the problem is that this idea is considered "heretical."

There are several viable means of privatizing the government educational system. The most straightforward would be an auction of the schools and properties to the highest bidder. A transition period of some years would be necessary to give due notice to government-dependent families and time to adjust to a free market.

Another possible method is more feasible in the near future, since a widespread auction would also require widespread recognition of the propriety of a private education system. Such recognition may not exist for quite some time yet. This other method involves the method of school choice which allows parents to choose how and where to spend their education dollars. There are two main categories of the school choice movement: school vouchers, and educational tax credits.

School Vouchers

School vouchers consist of government giving each child a specified amount to be used to pay for their education. The parents are free to spend this amount at a school of their choice, provided that school meets certain government standards.

While vouchers do offer some choice to parents and add some competition to an otherwise stagnant monopoly, this method poses some serious problems. The main principle is still the same for vouchers as for public schools: government is footing the bill and approving the decisions made with the money. Far from freeing the educational system from the coercive arm of government, this method extends that arm deeper into the private school system.

---

[8] Postrel, Virginia. "U.S. Universities Feast on Federal Student Aid." Bloomberg Businessweek. 12 Dec 2011. Online. businessweek.com/news/2011-12-09/u-s-universities-feast-on-federal-student-aid-virginia-postrel.html. Accessed 31 Jan 2012.

For an example, let's look to Sweden, which instituted a nationwide voucher program in 1991. These were the results reported by the Fraser Institute: "[Sweden's] public vouchers have made independent schools dependent on public funding, and consequently, have given elected officials the power to make independent schools submit to public controls. The problem is not that the regulations imposed so far on admission of students and fees have impinged on the educational quality of many schools. Rather, the danger is that these central controls, which were minimal at first in Sweden, continue to multiply so that eventually independent schools are absorbed into the centrally controlled system."[9]

The result was that the private schools became, essentially, like the charter schools in America. Whoever is paying the bills sets the terms; in this case it's the government. What we need in our transition to a private system is a school choice program where government plays no part in the financing of education.

EDUCATION TAX CREDITS

A tax credit is a reduction in what a person owes in taxes to offset a certain expense—in this case, education. For example, Mr. Smith receives a tax credit of $2,000 for his child each year, and spends $5,000 for private school tuition. He would receive a $2,000 deduction in that year's tax liability, could send his child to a private school costing $5,000 per year, pay the school $5,000, and receive a full $2,000 reduction in that year's tax liability. (This is different from a tax deduction, which only lowers the taxpayer's taxable income.) The important part here is that the government never gets to touch the tuition dollars and cannot mandate how or where that money is spent.[10]

Under this system, all taxpayers (parents, guardians, corporations, people without children) could claim tax credits for the purpose of funding the education of one or more children in grades K-12 for that year.

The amount that could be retained as a credit would be determined by two figures:

---

[9] Quoted in LaFerrara, Michael, A. "Toward a Free Market in Education: School Vouchers or Tax Credits?" *The Objective Standard*. Spring 2011:21-33. Print.
[10] LaFerrara, "School Vouchers or Tax Credits?" 21-33.

ETL - Education Tax Liability
• What you would otherwise pay in education taxes.

AAC - Average Attendance Cost
• The amount the government would have spent on the student.

The first is their Education Tax Liability (ETL), which is the amount of money the government would otherwise take from the taxpayer for use in the government-run schools. This amount includes income taxes, property taxes, and any other feasibly calculable taxes that apply.

The second is their Average Attendance Cost (AAC), which is the amount of money that would have been spent on the student in a government-run school that year.

The program would be optional and any taxpayer who wished to participate could retain as much of their ETL as they choose and apply it to the educational expenses of any child in any school where that child is accepted. The limit on how much of the ETL could be used would be the child's AAC. The taxpayer would be free to contribute to more than one child, up to their ETL; and the child could accept contributions from more than one source up to their AAC.

Thus, a low-income couple with an ETL of $1,000 could find several friends and relatives willing to contribute their tax credits to make up the tuition cost of a particular private school. Parents could also claim tax credits for home schooling.

The only role for government in such a program would be to calculate ETL and AAC, and continue funding government schools with such tax money as it receives. The government would have no say in which schools could accept the money or what constitutes a legitimate education expense.

Private organizations and corporations could establish scholarship funds with their ETL's. Any unused funds in such programs would be turned over to the government school system at the end of the year.

A program of education tax credits would place control of education back where it belongs—with parents. With the increase in new customers and the lack of regulation, the private education sector would expand rapidly. The public sector would shrink—while remaining properly and proportionately funded. It would put America on track for a fully free educational system. It would lay the foundation for the separation of education and state, which must exist in the same way and for the same reasons as the separation of church and state. It would lead to the cessation of the violation of the rights of all taxpayers in this regard.[11]

REVIEW

Q1: Is education a right? Why or why not?

_____

Q2: Why is free education not free?

_____

Q3: What problems arise from a government monopoly on education?

_____

Q4: What challenges would exist in a fully free market for education?

_____

Q5: Describe the Education Tax Credit program.

_____

---

[11] We could not devote space in this book for a treatment of the harm that the National Education Association and its leadership is doing to the education of children in the United States. If interested, begin your own study of how teachers' unions and the Department of Education put their own power and politics before the teaching of children.

CHAPTER 19

WELFARE AND CHARITY

THE PRINCIPLES

We've already identified the principles that government-run welfare violates throughout this book. The alleged need of some people does not constitute a valid claim on the rights of others. Welfare is not a right. Retirement is not a right. Rights are not entitlements to the products and services produced by others, but are principles protecting our prerogative to freedom of action. It is a violation of the proper role of government to take what belongs to one citizen for the purpose of redistributing it to another citizen.

Some attempt to justify statist welfare through altruistic guilt, claiming it is our duty to love our fellow man. Coerced charity is immoral; involuntary charity is a contradiction and cannot be considered a moral virtue.

When that doesn't work, they will attempt to appeal to our "self-interest," saying that it is better for us to submit to the minor demands of a screaming horde of cannibals, otherwise they will have us for breakfast. This is not a rational appeal to self-interest, it is a threat. An appeal to self-interest must be done by persuasion and education, since if it is truly good for us it must be possible to persuade us to do it without force or deception. Force is the thug's way out—an argument for the person who has no rational argument to offer.

The reality is that America has been violating these principles for a long time, and before progress can be made to a free, rights-respecting society, the consequences of such government action must be dealt with. Many people have come to expect and rely on government aid. The government has made promises to them upon which they have based major life decisions. Thus, a transition period would be necessary (as we saw in the previous section on education) in order to phase out the government programs and move towards a full separation of charity and state.

In a free society, every individual is responsible to provide for their needs and wants to the best of their abilities and ambitions. But what about those unable to help themselves—the poor, the disabled, and the helpless?

In reality, the truly needy are an extremely small number of people. Most are able to support their life, and if capable, have a moral responsibility to do so.

How would the poor, the disabled, and the helpless fare under capitalism?

THE POOR

"Poor" is a subjective term relative to culture and time period. In many periods of history being poor meant having one change of clothes, sleeping outside, and getting one meal a day if you were lucky. Much of the poor in America today live in at least a trailer or apartment with electricity, plumbing, television, and may even struggle with obesity; this is absolute luxury compared to the thousands of years that preceded it.

There is assumption in our culture that no one should be poor. This belief is flawed for a few reasons. First, since "poor" only refers to the lowest class of society, this is by definition impossible; in the future, being poor might mean having only one gold-plated rocket pack. Second, as long as someone is able to meet their own needs, there is nothing inherently wrong with being poor. While it would be preferable to be able to meet one's wants as well as needs, it is only our materialistic culture that makes us believe possessions are the secret to happiness. While some studies have shown that having a certain level of income makes it easier to be happy, happiness is not dependent material goods.

Capitalism leaves everyone, including the poor, free to think, work, and earn as much as they are able. No other social system does this. If someone wants to work their way out of poverty they are free to do so; countless poor people have done so. If they don't want to, they don't have to. Many find great fulfillment and satisfaction in life while earning very little, but doing what they love.

Some would argue that because of racism, sexism, and other discrimination, minorities aren't truly free to excel. There are very real barriers to success because of discrimination. But what free means in the context of capitalism is that all people are equally protected under the law, and that no one will be able to use force to prevent anyone from succeeding. Education, experience, and exposure will help change cultural values and help make sure everyone acts with justice and decency.

An individual seeking the charity of others, however, must rely on voluntary charity, in which America excels. In 2010, during a recession and after having their earnings plundered by government, Americans still gave $290.89 billion to charity.[1] That was even an increase from the previous year which was also during the recession.

The Disabled

Capitalism leaves the disabled free to compensate for their disabilities in any way they can. Many disabled individuals use their remaining abilities to support and further their lives. For instance, a deaf person might choose to pursue a career in genetics, maintenance, architecture, or accounting. A blind person could choose to pursue a career in music or psychology. A paraplegic might pursue a career in law, education, computer programming, or writing. And with today's technology, even a quadriplegic can learn to support himself; he might pursue a career in finance, economics, science, or radio broadcasting.[2]

Richie Parker was born without arms, but every day (as of this writing) he drives to work at Hendrick Motorsports, a NASCAR racing organization, where he works as an engineer designing vehicles. To go to work, he opens his car door with his chin and shoulder, starts up the engine by turning the key with his toes, and then at his desk he works a key-

---

[1] Pavlich, Katie. "Despite Recession, Americans Give to Charity in 2010." 20 Jun 2011. Online. townhall.com/tipsheet/katiepavlich/2011/06/20/ despite_recession,_americans_give_to_charity_in_2010. Accessed 5 Feb 2012.
[2] Biddle, Craig. *Loving Life: The Morality of Self-Interest and the Facts That Support It* (Richmond, Virginia: Glen Allen Press, 2002), 126.

board and mouse with his toes.[3] There are many individuals who lead inspirational lives such as this.

THE HELPLESS

Very few people fall into this category. Most people are capable and have untapped potential for great accomplishments. Here we are talking about those "who are severely [intellectually disabled], have a totally debilitating disease, or are injured to the extent that they are unable to support themselves by any means."[4] Capitalism leaves every individual free to offer these people as much charity as they are able and willing.

We may often hear the knee-jerk response, "What if no one voluntarily helps the truly helpless?" (A completely absurd premise.) The free-market and free-conscience response to this is, "If you want to help them, no one will stop you."[5] In a free society, everyone pays their own way and provides for themselves. Anyone unable or unwilling to do so must rely on private charity. Widespread callousness for the plight of the helpless did not exist in early America, does not now, and is possible on a large scale only when people are crushed into poverty and powerlessness by statism.

We must also examine what it means to be helpless. It means that a person is incapable of creating life-serving values, i.e. taking care of themselves and earning a living. Life-serving values can only be produced by able people. Able people can only produce those values if they are left free to do so—free to act on their own judgment, free from the initiation of force. If the able are not free to live and produce, who then is left to help the helpless? Thus, the survival of the helpless is dependent on the freedom of the able. It is only by the charity of the able that the helpless subsist, and life-serving values must be produced abundantly in order to offer the means of charity.

Production must come before charity, if only for the reason that there must first be something produced before it can be used or given. Without production there would be nothing to give. Capitalism lets men produce as much as they are able, and give as much as they desire.

In capitalism, everyone is free to produce as much wealth as they are willing and able, and many people become very rich. Truly self-

---

[3] Rinaldi, Tom. "Ritchie Parker: Drive." ESPN. 23 Jul 2013. youtube.com/watch?v=qiLDMBDPCEY. Accessed 23 Jul 2013.

[4] Biddle, *Loving Life*, 123-25.

[5] Rand, Ayn. "Collectivized Ethics." *The Virtue of Selfishness* (New York: Signet, 1964), 80.

interested people care about human life and many astonishing acts of charity exist, even in this tax-and-inflation-strapped nation.

Rational, self-interested individuals most assuredly see the benefit of helping others. They see only two options. They can either help the helpless or not. The self-interested person must ask himself, "Which environment do I think is in my best interest: one in which genuinely helpless people suffer and die in the streets, or one in which I voluntarily contribute some small fraction of my time, effort, or money to give them a hand?"[6] If someone thinks that helping others is in their best interest, they are free to act accordingly. If not, no one will force them; and many people do care about helping others. In capitalism, no one would be allowed to stop them.

IS IT MORAL TO ACCEPT GOVERNMENT WELFARE?

The statists often ask the student of capitalism if it isn't hypocritical to decry widespread, costly, and invasive government programs while at the same time benefiting from scholarships, food stamps, unemployment benefits, Medicare, school vouchers, etc. The student of freedom may often wonder himself if it is indeed moral to do so or not. Is it moral to accept government help and services, or accept a government job or research grant, while at the same time fighting against the immorality of such programs?

The answer is, "Yes." However, this answer requires a certain contextual application to be true.

It is only moral if the recipient actively opposes all forms of welfare statism and regards the benefit (a scholarship, for example) as a restitution of taxes that have been forcibly taken. If you oppose such programs, you may morally accept them; yet, if you support such things and demand them as your entitlement, you may not morally do so.

The defenders of freedom are not required to accept a "self-inflicted martyrdom" in their fight for individual rights, while their statist adversaries exploit the spoils of legal plunder for themselves.

The victims of legal plunder do not have to become martyrs and let the looters only distribute the money to those that demand it. Whenever welfare-state laws offer some restitution to their victims, it should be taken.

---

[6] Biddle, *Loving Life*, 126.

Since social security payments and unemployment insurance is taken from us by force, receiving payments of that kind can be considered as receiving back the money that was forcibly taken. Those who support such laws are culpable and often demand them as a right. Those who oppose such laws have a right to get their own money back. The cause of freedom is not helped when its advocates leave their money unclaimed for the welfare state to exploit.[7]

For example, suppose you see the many problems inherent in the government school system and the violation of rights that funding such a system involves. You would like to remove your own child from such a system but are unable to afford a private school. Would it be moral for you to accept a government voucher to help you pay for tuition?

Yes.

First, because you are attempting to decrease the amount of educational welfare you receive (from 100% in government schools to a partial percentage via a voucher at a private school). You are moving away from dependency and towards self-sufficiency.

Second, because you oppose such programs as an immoral intervention of government against the rights of others.

Third, such a voucher may be considered a restitution of taxes taken from you that you could have used to pay for tuition without assistance.

Do not let statists wield an unearned guilt against you.

It has become nearly impossible and often illegal to function as a free and independent individual. When you advocate for freedom, the statists will sneer and ask why you are not living without the welfare state now. They will say that if freedom were practical, it would be working, ignoring the fact that we live in a mixed economy.

Warning: Check your beliefs for contradictions or these accusations will be correct. Is it hypocritical for a Tea-Party-like organization or individual to campaign for less spending and smaller government, while also defending the sanctity of its largest entitlement programs such as Social Security and Medicare? Yes, it is. But, these programs are so ubiquitous that they cannot be cut immediately, and require reform and a phasing-out period.

---

[7] Binswanger, Harry (ed). The Ayn Rand Lexicon. Online. aynrandlexicon.com/lexicon/government_grants_and_scholarships.html. Accessed 1 Aug 2011.

REVIEW

Q1: What would happen to the poor, the disabled, and the helpless in a free society?

_____

Q2: Is what context is it moral and immoral to accept government subsidies?

_____

Q3: Why would anyone want to freely help others?

_____

CHAPTER 20

HEALTH CARE

There is a difference, often overlooked in conversation, between health care and health insurance. This distinction is important because the access to, or ownership of affordable health insurance, does not guarantee the access to, or quality of actual health care.

Heath Care: the actual goods and services related to medical care.

Health Insurance: a way to transfer the risk of expensive health care costs.

Many political leaders today refer to health care as a "moral imperative" or an "ethical obligation" (note the "high ground" they are taking). Senator John McCain said, "It's a fundamental requirement to give people the chance to have affordable and available health insurance, or the option is to go into a big government program [notice the false dichotomy], such as we have in Canada, in England, and others. Americans right now are without health insurance. They need to get it."[1] Such claims, however, are morally wrong.

Recall that rights do not consist of any man-made good or service. Health care is not a right; it is a commodity, however needful. It is a con-

---

[1] McCain, John. youtube.com/watch?v=VXB3ELfLgdk. Fox News Sunday. 18 Oct. 2011. Online. Accessed 25 Aug 2011. Emphasis added.

tradiction to use force and violate the rights of anyone in order to supply the alleged "rights" of anyone else. The view that government must either mandate or guarantee the "right" to either health care or health insurance is both immoral and impractical. As Lin Zinser and Paul Hsieh write in their essay, "Moral Health Care vs. 'Universal Health Care,'" it violates "the rights of businessmen, doctors, and patients to act on their own judgment—which, in turn, throttles their ability to produce, administer, or purchase the goods and services in question."[2]

What is the proper role of government regarding health insurance and health care? The only proper role of government consists of protecting the individual rights (life, liberty, property) of people within a nation's borders. Rights are only violated through force. It is therefore an immoral violation of this role for government to initiate the use of force. Examples of such force are: mandates on employers to provide insurance; mandates on doctors to accept insurance or charge certain rates; mandates on insurance companies to cover certain conditions or individuals; making it illegal to purchase insurance in another state; restrictions on individuals and doctors prescribing what drugs and treatments are approved and "legal"; mandates on individuals or companies to purchase insurance, and so on.

WASTE AND CORRUPTION

My (Caleb's) wife, Chelsea, works in the Insurance and Financial Planning industry, and although she has her Life, Accident and Health Insurance license, she mostly does office assistant work for her boss. One December, her boss came in, handing her a bill for an elderly client who had a Long Term Care policy.

"What's this?" she asked, taking the folded pink paper.

"A bill for Mrs. Miller."

She looked it over, "For what?"

"Don't know," he answered, shrugging. "There's no description or itemized list of services or dates, just the amount they want Mrs. Miller to pay. So give them a call and figure out what Mrs. Miller is supposed to be paying $117/month for since October. Mrs. Miller thinks it's for her new walker, but that seems expensive for a walker."

---

[2] Zinser, Lin. and Paul Hsieh. "Moral Health Care vs. Universal Health Care." *The Objective Standard.* Winter 2007. Online. theobjectivestand-ard.com/issues/2007-winter/moral-vs-universal-health-care.asp. Accessed 17 May 2011.

Chelsea did some pricing research on the cost of walkers, as well as calling the client and getting their take on the walker and the bills. Chelsea also carefully looked the bill over before making a call— sometimes "bills" like this have a disclaimer at the bottom: "Don't pay this amount; this is just an invoice." But there was no such disclaimer. This was a legitimate bill. After the research was done, Chelsea calls the 800-number and is able to speak to a "customer service representative." (You'll see why that title is in quotes.) Chelsea discovers, after twenty minutes on the phone, that the company is in fact billing Mrs. Miller for the new walker, so Chelsea asks why Mrs. Miller had been billed for the walker twice in October.

"Mrs. Miller was billed for the setup and installation of the equipment in October," the representative replies.

"Set up. Does that mean that someone came to her home and put the walker together?"

"No, ma'am. It was constructed by the manufacturer and sent to her in one piece. No extra shipping costs incurred."

"Does 'installation' mean that—I can't even imagine. What does that mean?"

"It refers to the startup costs associated with beginning a line of service with us."

"So she is charged double in the first month, to have the privilege of being served by your company?"

"We have to set up her account information and billing."

Chelsea laughed a little, "And that costs $117? It must take a very long time to assign an account number and enter a billing address— unless you also enter her medical information?"

The rep seemed to miss the first part. "No, ma'am we don't deal with the medical side of things. We just provide the equipment."

"All right, then how do I get these other bills for November and December taken care of?"

The rep seemed genuinely confused, "Mrs. Miller has to pay them. Just send a check—"

Chelsea interrupted, "But she paid for the walker in October."

"Ma'am, Mrs. Miller will be billed monthly for the next thirteen months."

"What?"

"Mrs. Miller will be billed—and be expected to pay—for the next thirteen months until November of next year, if she intends to keep and use the equipment."

"Am I missing something? This is a walker, right?"

"Yes, ma'am."

"Is it made of platinum? Does it have a GPS? Walking WiFi?"

The sarcasm was not lost, and Chelsea heard the dry reply, "No, ma'am."

"Then please help me understand how a very basic piece of equipment—a walker with no special bells or whistles—the kind I could pick up down at Walgreens for one payment of $165 to $250 is going to cost my client $1,521!"

The rep was now pretty short with Chelsea, using a patronizing tone, and Chelsea noticed that the polite "Ma'am's" stopped altogether. "You're client won't actually pay that amount. Medicare will adjust the cost down to $53.22 per month, and that is all your client is responsible for."

"First off, that would still make the walker $691.90 to my client, on top of whatever Medicare is paying."

"No, Medicare will reimburse her for the cost of the walker. We bill that cost to them."

(Raise your hand if this makes sense to you.)

"You just said that my client was responsible for that amount."

"Medicare will reimburse her for the cost of the walker. That's what I meant: responsible through Medicare, but we bill them."

"Then why is my client receiving and paying these bills for $117, if the cost is supposed to be adjusted and paid by Medicare?"

"That's just how we do it."

"But Mrs. Miller has paid—personally—for the last three months. Will you send those checks back?"

"I'll have to look into it."

"Hold on, before you go, I still can't figure out why the walker should cost this much. I researched it online and, like I said, an identical or even fancier one shouldn't cost more than $300 at most. So, why, even with the adjustments, is this walker going to cost nearly $700?"

"You're client won't have to pay for it directly."

"That's not what I asked. Why does it cost more than twice what she could pay in a store?"

"Because that's what we charge. Medicare is contracted with us and with the company that makes the walkers. They can't buy them anywhere else or get them from anywhere else or they would get reprimanded and fined."

"What if my client just went to the store to get her own walker and asked for reimbursement?"

"She wouldn't get it. Medicare is contracted by the government to work with us and no one else for this equipment in her area." Emphasis was added by the representative, as though waving a "Get Out of Jail Free" card.

"Wow," Chelsea muttered into the phone, head in hands, very nearly speechless.

"Is there anything else I can help you with?"

Chelsea perked right back up, "Yes, you can refund the money Mrs. Miller paid directly to your company, since you have admitted that Medicare will pay the full amount and it is not her responsibility to do so. Then you can explain to me why this was NEVER explained to my client. Would it have even been noticed if she had kept paying this monthly?"

"No, ma'am. Not by us over here in billing."

"I can't believe you're saying that she could have kept shelling out $117 per month for another year to your company, and—even though your company is getting reimbursed by Medicare for the exact product and service—likely no one—no one—would have caught it or changed it. Please tell me you are saying something else."

"It's not our policy to do extra work with cross checks. As long as Medicare pays the reimbursement, we consider the account maintained."

"Then what has been done with this other money that Mrs. Miller paid directly? Those checks have been cashed. Did you guys think it was a gift?"

"No, it was credited to her account."

"So that means she should be paid up through, what, April?"

"No, her payment is due for January."

"But you just said that the $468 Mrs. Miller sent in was credited to her account, as well as Medicare having paid the adjusted amount. That comes out to eight months of adjusted service cost paid by both Medicare and Mrs. Miller, which should mean that she's paid up through April."

"Let me get you my manager."

"Oh, please do."[3]

Although the issue was "resolved" after another forty-five minutes with the manager, Mrs. Miller being reimbursed for two payments of $117, she apparently was required to have paid the first two payments—set up and installation—for a regular, run-of-the-mill wheeled walker. And why was it so expensive? Because the company that made the walker

---

[3] As told to the authors by Chelsea Nelson.

had a governmental contract (legal monopoly) with Medicare so the customer could not shop around for a better price, a better managed company, or better equipment. Competition was eliminated from the equation. So Chelsea's client may not have had to pay out of pocket, but her Medicare dollars were being overspent for an overpriced piece of very basic equipment that could have been purchased elsewhere for less than half the cost.

Now multiply such waste and incompetence by a billion and you see what is going on across the country. This violation of rights leads to unintended consequences, and such waste and price-inflation is ubiquitous across all areas of government spending from education subsidies to the military. Consumers disregard the need to "shop" around for better prices in health care because insurance or the government is footing the bill. They are also forbidden by law to shop for insurance outside of their state. Also, when government is responsible for your health, it necessarily leads to restrictions on your personal life such as "healthy eating" laws.[4]

Overcrowded emergency rooms result from a law requiring hospitals to diagnose and treat anyone within two hundred feet of a hospital, regardless of their ability to pay. Government violations of the rights of consumers, doctors, hospitals, and insurance companies to freely act on their own judgment and contract accordingly stifles productivity, hampers quality, and increases costs of both insurance and care.

For those who cannot afford to pay for their health care, they are free to rely on private charity, voluntarily given from family, friends, neighbors, strangers, and charitable organizations. Their need, however heartbreaking, does not constitute a valid claim against the lives of others.

Writer Paul Hsieh called this the "separation of charity and state" which means that the government doesn't tell us who to be charitable towards; it leaves us free to do so—or not—according to our own judgment. A proper government doesn't force anyone to support a particular religion. It also doesn't force anyone to "work in a soup kitchen or donate to the Red Cross. And just as a proper government does not compel a man to support his neighbor's church, so a proper government does not compel a man to pay his neighbor's medical bills."[5]

---

[4] Klein, Philip. "Blame Government-Run Health Care for Nanny Bloomberg's Soda Ban." *Washington Examiner.* Online. 6 Jun 2012. washingtonexaminer.com/article/699896. Accessed Sep 11, 2012.

[5] Hsieh, Paul. "Health Care and the Separation of Charity and State." *The Objective Standard.* Spring 2011. Online. theobjectivestandard.com/issues/2011-spring/health-care-charity-state.asp. Accessed 20 May 2011.

In Steve Forbes's book, How Capitalism Will Save Us, he offers a concise view of the issues and solutions he sees regarding the health care system of the United States. He identifies some false claims surrounding this issue that lead to violation of principle. The myth, he says, is that,

"Today's out-of-control health-care costs are the consequence of increasingly sophisticated medical technology and growing patient demand, compounded by greed throughout the system. Insurance and pharmaceutical companies, doctors, and hospitals all care more about profits than about patients. The only way to fix these complex problems is through a government-designed system with mandatory health insurance. Otherwise, health-care will become totally unaffordable and beyond the reach of the poor and middle class."[6]

The reality, Forbes writes, is that today's health care system shows how government dominance prevents a free-market from working. The individual consumers rarely directly pay for medical care or even insurance. The result of this is that the health care market then tries to meet the needs of big companies rather than individuals. "Policy reforms," he explains, "allowing customers to take charge of health-care buying decisions would correct this market distortion. Health-care and insurance providers seeking your business would lower prices, provide better service, and become more accountable."[7]

Further solutions include allowing people to buy health insurance policies across state lines, removing restrictions on health savings accounts, making it easier for small employers to pool together to buy health insurance for their employees, and allowing people and businesses to buy health insurance either with pre-tax dollars or a tax liability deduction for medical expenses.

We advocate transition to a free market in health care. We must leave insurance companies and hospitals free to innovate competitively for customers. We must leave customers free to contract with them. We must leave patients free to seek and use the treatments and drugs that they judge best for their condition. We must leave taxpayers free from the coercion of government intervention in health care, as well as Medicare and Medicaid. We must leave the doctors free to treat their patients to the best of their ability and judgment.

---

[6] Forbes, Steve. and Elizabeth Ames. *How Capitalism Will Save Us* (New York: Crown Business, 2009), 240.
[7] *ibid*, 270.

REVIEW

Q1: Why is health care not a right?

_____

Q2: What are some consequences of government involvement in health care beyond the violation of rights?

_____

Q3: What is the relationship of health care and health insurance to the proper role of government?

_____

CHAPTER 21

PRINCIPLES OF WAR

"If we desire to secure peace . . . it must be known that we are at all times ready for war."[1] - George Washington, 1793

THE PURPOSE OF WAR

A proper understanding of war and the foreign policy of a nation can be obtained by reference to the same principles that we've discussed and applied for individuals.

"Rational self-interest holds that every individual ought to live his own life for his own sake, by his own independent effort," Brook and Epstein write, "—without sacrificing himself to others or others to himself. It holds that the individual's self-interest is achieved, not by doing whatever he feels like doing, and not by placing his goals in opposition to his

---

1 Allison, A., Parry, J., and W. Cleon Skousen. *The Real George Washington* (Washington D.C.: National Center for Constitutional Studies, 1991), 670.

neighbors' freedom, but by living a life of reason, productivity, and trade."[2]

According to such a view, the greatest threat man faces in the achievement of his values and happiness—and thus the greatest threat to a harmonious and free society—is the initiation of physical force by others. Such violence, theft, or fraud is properly met with retaliatory force.

Man resorts to governments to keep himself free from the initiation of force so he can pursue his happiness. One of the primary proper roles of government is to protect those living within its borders from foreign aggression, as well as credible foreign threats of aggression.

An innocent nation does not seek to exist by force at the expense of other nations. When force is initiated against a nation or its citizens by another nation, it must righteously respond with force to neutralize the threat. Anything less is an injustice towards its citizens and a violation of that government's moral purpose—to protect rights.[3]

Going to war is moral only if it is in response to force, or the credible threat of force. A threat does not consist of perceiving a country's leadership or citizens as suspicious or shady. A threat would be just that—a state making a verbal threat of violence, and having the capability to act on that threat. Such threats include states giving financial aid to terrorist organizations and calling for the destruction of another country.

THE MORALITY OF WAR

"The principle that should guide our foreign policy is the same principle that should guide all governmental action: Our government should protect the individual rights of Americans."[4] - Yaron Brook

The only moral war is the war of defense, a war that eliminates threats initiated against the lives, liberty, and property of a nation's citizens.

---

[2] Brook, Yaron. Alex Epstein. "'Just War Theory; vs. American Self-Defense." *The Objective Standard.* Spring 2006. Online. theobjectivestandard.com/issues/2006-spring/just-war-theory.asp. Accessed 5 Aug 2011.

[3] *ibid.*

[4] Biddle, Craig. "America's Self-Crippled Foreign Policy: An Interview with Yaron Brook, Elan Journo, and Alex Epstein." *The Objective Standard.* Fall 2009. Online. theobjectivestandard.com/issues/2009-fall/america-self-crippled-foreign-policy.asp. Accessed 5 Aug 2011.

To fight and win a morally justified war requires two things:

1. Objectively identify the nature of the threat;
2. Do whatever is necessary to eliminate the threat with minimum risk to life, liberty, and property on the part of the citizenry. (Note: it is perfectly acceptable to use offensive tactics in a moral war of defense.)

There are also two types of immoral wars. These wars (and also some tactical actions within a war) are improper and unjust when viewed from the rational self-interest of a nation and its citizens. These are wars of self-sacrifice, or humanitarian wars, and wars of aggression. Both types violate the rights of citizens (especially the soldiers) because they sacrifice the lives and property of individuals for the sake of some "higher" cause, whether it is the suffering of the Bosnians or to satisfy the power-lust of a leader.

WARS OF AGGRESSION

"Statism leads to war because that is its nature. It is based on the principle of force, violence, and compulsion."[5] - Ayn Rand

Such wars are caused by a nation that pursues, through force, its irrational desires against other nations. They should be easy to identify: the German invasion of Poland and France in World War II, the taking of American hostages in Iran in 1979, the launching of rockets into the borders of Israel from its neighboring states and territories.

In some cases, aggressive nations may be dealt with through less violent means such as sanctions and ultimatums. However, when such means fail, military force is not just the last resort, it becomes the only resort.

The actions of aggressive nations are reprehensible, and such actions are only encouraged when they not dealt with swiftly. The proper response is with the destruction of the aggressors. History clearly demonstrates the folly in the appeasement of aggressors, which leads to more and greater violence.

---

[5] Harriman, David, ed. *Journals of Ayn Rand* (New York: Penguin, 1999), 315.

WARS OF SELF-SACRIFICE

"No government ought to interfere with the internal concerns of another,
except for the security of what is due to themselves."[6]
- George Washington, 1798

The popular modern theory of war is known as Just War Theory. It is based upon the self-sacrificial ethics of altruism, and has been taught explicitly to military recruits for many years.

According to Just War Theory an armed response is only appropriate under the following conditions:

- An openly declared war;
- A response to specific aggression against one's own people or a third party, or for a just cause;
- It must begin with the right intentions;
- It must be a last resort after other possibilities for redress have been explored.

In addition to this, according to Just War Theory, a nation may only wage war while observing that:

- The means are "proportional," meaning the level of force is commensurate with the nature of the threat; and
- "Discrimination" is practiced between combatants and non-combatants.[7]

"A soldier must take careful aim at his military target and away from nonmilitary targets," writes Michael Walzer in Just and Unjust Wars,

"He can only shoot if he has a reasonably clear shot; he can only attack if a direct attack is possible . . . he cannot kill civilians simply because he finds them between himself and his enemies.

"Simply not to intend the deaths of civilians is too easy . . . . What we look for . . . is some sign of a positive commitment to

---

[6] Allison, A., Parry, J., and W. Cleon Skousen. *The Real George Washington* (Washington D.C.: National Center for Constitutional Studies, 1991), 704.
[7] Elshtain, Jean Bethke. *Just War Against Terror* (New York: Basic Books, 2003), 65.

save civilian lives . . . if saving civilian lives means risking soldiers' lives the risk must be accepted."[8]

Such rules of engagement are the sort under which U.S. soldiers are
fighting and dying overseas. It is such rules that led the team of SEALs in
Operation Red Wings in 2005 to release the civilian goat herders who had
discovered them. Releasing them compromised their mission and position to militants in the area and resulted in the deaths of nineteen American troops.

Many of the altruistic notions of Just War Theory were first described by early Christians such as Augustine, for whom, "killing to defend oneself alone was not enjoined: It is better to suffer harm than to
inflict it. But the obligation of charity obliges one to move in another direction: To save the lives of others, it may be necessary to imperil and
even take the lives of their tormentors."[9] This means that it is immoral to
defend your own life, but in order to defend others it is sometimes required to risk your own life as well as those of the aggressors.

Such a theory denies the morality and necessity of a self-interested
approach to war, considering that a reference to self-interest makes
"most attempts at moral analysis irrelevant."[10] ("Moral," in this case,
means the collectivist ethic of altruism.) In *Just War Against Terror*,
scholar Jean Elshtain uses Augustine as a moral authority for such a self-
sacrificial theory. Augustine, she says, argues "that it is better for the
Christian as an individual to suffer harm rather than commit it." Augustine asks, "But is the morally responsible person also . . . permitted to
make for other innocent persons a commitment to non-self-defense? . . .
the answer is no."[11] Thus, if only you are attacked, it is immoral to defend
yourself. If your neighbor is attacked, you are obligated to defend him. It
is not a matter of defending innocence against evil, or peace against aggression, in Augustine's view. His standard used to judge the use of force
is that it must not be a self-interested act of defense, but a selfless service
to others.

Consider the Just War requirement that a nation may only go to
war for a "just cause." What constitutes a "just" cause? The only "just"
causes endorsed by Just War advocates have been humanitarian crises in
which a foreign people are suffering under oppression or genocide. Sacri-

---

[8] Quoted in Brook and Epstein, "Just War Theory," Online.
[9] Elshtain, *Just War*, 57.
[10] *ibid*, 189.
[11] *ibid*, 180.

ficing American soldiers to "peace-keeping" missions and humanitarian conflicts, in which no American rights are threatened, is considered morally mandatory in Just War.

What about the theory's claims that self-defense is an appropriate reason to enter into military conflict? The problem is that it means no such thing when rendered impotent by chaining a response to being a "last resort" and to means that are "proportional." Elshtain clarifies that, "For just warriors, both aims and means are limited, even if one has been grievously harmed."[12] Why? Because your sacrifice is good.

When should military action be considered when it is supposed to be viewed as a "last resort"? When a new Iranian regime held fifty-two Americans hostage for four hundred and forty-four days? "Did it rise to the level of a direct attack sufficient to place us at the point of 'last resort' with Iran and other nations that sponsor Islamic terrorism?" Brook and Epstein ask,

> "Not according to Jimmy Carter. What about after two hundred and forty-three marines were killed in Lebanon in 1983? Not according to Ronald Reagan. Or after Khomeini's fatwa offered terrorists a bounty to destroy writer Salman Rushdie and his American publisher for expressing an 'un-Islamic' viewpoint in 1989? Not according to George Bush, Sr. Or after the first World Trade Center bombing in 1993? Not according to Bill Clinton. The pattern is telling."[13]

What about the guideline that military action may only be used with "right intentions"? In this case, "right" means "altruistic." A nation which goes to war for the welfare of its own citizens is held suspect. A nation fighting for another nation's citizens is held as acceptable. Such a view can be seen in "Operation Iraqi Freedom," which was not called "Operation American Defense." Emphasis was placed on freeing the Iraqis from a dictator, bringing them "democracy," and loading them with food and collectively owned oil. The standard used for determining the success of such an operation was not whether Americans were safer, but, as Elshtain observed, the fact that "schools are opening [in Iraq], women are returning to work, movie theaters are filled to capacity, and people can once again listen to music and dance at weddings."[14]

---

[12] *ibid*, 58.
[13] Brook and Epstein, "Just War Theory," Online.
[14] Elshtain, *Just War*, 70.

Under Just War standards, there is no such thing as an enemy nation. As of this writing, the U.S. has not officially declared war against another nation since World War II—not against North Korea or Vietnam or Iraq or Afghanistan. Now we have a never-ending War on Terror where we wage war only against enemy combatants, not against the states that sponsor them, and in some unfortunate cases, it is the U.S. that is arming its own future enemies.

The altruism of Just War theory even extends to weighing the lives of one's own soldiers against the lives of the civilians in an enemy nation. According to Walzer, we should abstain from all judgments of the fighting and whether or not our cause is just. "We do this because the moral status of individual soldiers on both sides is very much the same: they face one another as moral equals."[15]

What do we expect our soldiers to accomplish when we tell them that their enemies are their moral equals? As to the civilians of enemy nations, Elshtain says, "According to just war thinking, it is better to risk the lives of one's own combatants than those of enemy noncombatants."[16]

This is what modern soldiers are being taught: that they are to fight and kill their moral equals with no regard for the justice of their cause, and that they are to hold enemy civilians in higher regard than their own lives.

This is what "discrimination" means in Just War Theory. Such a policy put forward by today's intellectuals, Yaron Brook says, undermines "Americans' moral confidence in our goodness and thwart[s] Americans' ability to unequivocally identify the evil of those who seek to destroy us. A country not sure of its own right to exist is sure to be weak in the face of those who challenge that right."[17]

Holding the lives of enemy civilians as more valuable than the lives of a nation's own civilians and soldiers is deadly and immoral. If it is possible to isolate innocents without military cost, then obviously they should not be killed. It is in no nation's or soldier's rational self-interest to kill innocents. But even if many of an enemy's citizenry may not support the aggressive actions of their government, we cannot hold their innocence above our own self-preservation. The important principle to be aware of here is that any innocent deaths in war are the sole moral responsibility of the aggressor nation. This is another reason why it is im-

---

[15] Quoted in Brook and Epstein, "Just War Theory," Online.
[16] Elshtain, *Just War*, 65.
[17] Biddle, Craig. "America's Self-Crippled Foreign Policy," Online.

portant to only go to war for proper moral causes. "The civilian population of an aggressor nation is not some separate entity unrelated to its government," Brook and Epstein point out,

> "An act of war is the act of a nation—an interconnected political, cultural, economic, and geographical unity. Whenever a nation initiates aggression against us, including by supporting anti-American terrorist groups and militant causes, it has forfeited its right to exist, and we have a right to do whatever is necessary to end the threat it poses."[18]

With the exception of objectors, the individual citizens in a country that goes to war bear some responsibility for that war. This is an important reason why people should be interested in the science of politics—they may ultimately reap consequences for the unjust and immoral actions of those they allow to rule them.

A nation's only moral concern should not be for the safety, comfort, or political freedoms of the enemy populace, but of ensuring the cheapest, fastest, most effective way to guarantee the safety of its own citizens and neutralize threats against their rights.

Both the Civil War and World War II were won this way, and "once massive defeats were handed to the enemy, the causes that drove the military threats were thoroughly defeated as political forces. There are no threatening Nazis or Japanese Imperialists today, nor was there any significant political force agitating for the reemergence of the Slave South after the Civil War."[19] (There is, unfortunately, a neo-Nazi resurgence happening among the youth in Europe, but this is a new threat, not the result of a failure to eradicate the old threat.)

In war, we must choose between the morality of victory and life, or the morality of death and defeat. It is the choice between self-interest and altruism. Let us choose to defend our life and happiness.

---

[18] Brook and Epstein, "Just War Theory," Online.
[19] *ibid.*

REVIEW

Q1: What are the requirements for going to war morally?

Q2: What are the moral principles the "just-war" theory violates?

Q3: If you could write your country's foreign policy, what would it be?

Q4: What, if anything, should your country do about terrorist threats abroad?

CHAPTER 22

ENVIRONMENTALISM

"Everything we have developed over the last 100 years should be destroyed."[1]
- Pentti Linkola, Finnish Ecological Activist

The science is in. Carbon dioxide is a greenhouse gas that traps heat. Mankind adds billions of metric tons of carbon dioxide to the atmosphere each year, and the temperature of the earth has gone up slightly in the last hundred years.

There is a vitriolic debate raging about whether mankind's contribution to global temperature is a serious threat. It is not within the scope of this book to evaluate or attempt to answer that question. Both sides of the debate have been guilty of fabricating evidence to support their side. It is very difficult to find unbiased and verifiable data on the issue. However, the purpose of this book is to apply objective principles to ethics and politics, and we can still do that.

We have focused on the necessity of having proper ethical principles. Mandatory ethics, which prohibits the initiation of force, is the minimum requirement for any ethical society. It is the foundation of all other

---

[1] Pentti Linkola Fan site. penttilinkola.com/pentti_linkola/ecofascism/. Accessed 6 Aug 2011.

ethical principles, but it is only the starting point. Individuals must seek their rational self-interest. This includes long-range planning. But truly long range planning should extend to the welfare of future generations. The majority of climate scientists warn that anthropogenic climate change is a serious problem. We should be responsible stewards that better our world and make sure it lasts for those who come after us.

Politically speaking, it does not matter that earth's climate is changing due to mankind's influence. It is not a problem that falls under the purview of government. Remember that the only job of government is to protect the rights of its citizens. It is not the job of government to address climate change any more than it is the President's job to make sure we eat our vegetables.

Man's relationship with his environment is a complex, multifaceted issue. Many particulars require experts in the philosophy of law and property rights, as well as ecology. We can, however, come to an understanding of some general principles to guide our decisions and actions in the particular issues surrounding man's relationship with the planet he lives on. We will address those here, recognizing that this is not a comprehensive list.

We will also examine the core philosophy and aims of the environmentalist (or green) movement and its incompatibility with capitalism and freedom. We will then examine the proper principles to guide a moral approach to the issue of man's interaction with the earth.

THE PERCEPTION

"The only hope for the world is to make sure there is not another United States. We can't let other countries have the same number of cars, the amount of industrialization, we have in the U.S. We have to stop these Third World countries right where they are."[2] - Michael Oppenheimer, Environmental Defense Fund

Many people may think of the environmentalist movement as a well-meaning movement (that is occasionally marred by crazy radicals) whose intent is to work towards awareness of man's relationship with his environment and solutions to maintain care over the planet to keep it beautiful, healthy, and productive for generations to come. Although this

---

[2] Quoted in Beck, Glenn. *An Inconvenient Book* (New York: Simon & Schuster, 2009), 21.

view is laudable, it is also exactly wrong to ascribe such beliefs and motives to the environmentalist, or green, movement. While many who support the green movement do believe such things, they are mistaken if they believe that such ideas are the essential principles guiding the movement.

Just as many self-proclaimed Marxists/Communists may naively have no understanding of core Communist philosophies, such as dialectical materialism and economic determinism, so also many well-meaning environmentalists have no idea what the movement they so passionately support actually, in its essence, advocates. (Perhaps, once they do, they can coin a new term to differentiate themselves from the "radical" environmentalists, such as "naturalists," or "stewards.")

Environmentalism is Anti-human

"If it were up to me, all the people associated with the Gulf oil spill, which is murdering the Gulf, would be executed. That would be part of the function of a state."[3] - Derrick Jensen, co-author of Deep Green Resistance

The core standard of value for the environmentalist movement is not that man's life has value and must be protected, but that nature has value intrinsically (in and of itself, with no consideration of any value that man may derive from it) and that it must be protected even at the sacrifice of man's life. If we hold man's life as our highest value, such a doctrine must be considered evil.

This doctrine is not easily found in press releases or on the front page of green websites, but it can be found explicitly nonetheless. Here is the anti-man doctrine in the environmentalists' own words:

> ➤ "I suspect that eradicating smallpox was wrong. It played an important part in balancing ecosystems." "Human beings, as a species, have no more value than slugs."[4] - John Davis, editor of Earth First! Journal

---

[3] Gabbay, Tiffany. "Militant Environmentalists Call For Executions and 'Decisive Ecological Warfare.'" The Blaze. 9 Aug 2011. Online. theblaze.com/stories/militant-environmentalists-call-for-executions-and-decisive-ecological-warfare/. Accessed 25 Aug 2011.

[4] Pushback.com. pushback.com/issues/environment/ecofreak-quotes/. Accessed 6 Aug 2011.

➢ "We advocate biodiversity for biodiversity's sake. It may take our extinction to set things straight." "Wilderness has a right to exist for its own sake."[5] - David Foreman, Earth First!

➢ "Human happiness, and certainly human fecundity, is not as important as a wild and healthy planet . . . Some of us can only hope for the right virus to come along."[6] - David Graber, biologist, National Park Service

➢ "The collective needs of non-human species must take precedence over the needs and desires of humans."[7] - Dr. Reed F. Noss, The Wildlands Project

➢ "We, in the green movement, aspire to a cultural model in which killing a forest will be considered more contemptible and more criminal than the sale of 6-year-old children to Asian brothels."[8] - Carl Amery, Green Party of Germany

The environmentalist movement today is not concerned with the health and well-being of mankind, either now or in the future. If it were, it would advocate for the one social system which ensures that the earth and its resources are used in the most productive, life-serving ways possible—that social system is capitalism.

ENVIRONMENTALISM IS ANTI-CAPITALISM

"We need a culture that is self-consciously oppositional to things like corporate power, capitalism, industrialization and ultimately civilization, because that is the arrangement of power on this planet right now."[9] - Lierre Kieth, co-author of Deep Green Resistance

---

[5] *ibid.*

[6] Rand, Ayn. and Peter Schwartz, ed. *Return of the Primitive: The Anti-Industrial Revolution* (New York: Penguin, 1999), 221.

[7] Pushback.com. pushback.com/issues/environment/ecofreak-quotes/. Accessed 6 Aug 2011.

[8] Rand, *Return of the Primitive*, 221.

[9] Gabbay, Tiffany. "Militant Environmentalists Call For Executions and 'Decisive Ecological Warfare.'" The Blaze. 9 Aug 2011. Online.

Environmentalism rejects capitalism because it rejects a basic epistemological premise of capitalism—that man must be left free to act on his own judgment. It also rejects a fundamental ethic of capitalism—that the requirements of man's life constitute the standard of moral value.

Instead of considering mankind as having intrinsic value, environmentalism holds that nature, or the environment, has value intrinsically. Nature is valuable in and of itself, regardless of what man requires to live; this value must be protected from nature's only enemy: mankind.

At a UN-backed conference in Venezuela of around one hundred and thirty green activist groups in 2014, the Margarita Declaration was issued: "The structural causes of climate change are linked to the current capitalist hegemonic system. To combat climate change, it is necessary to change the system."[10]

Though some environmentalists will often claim to be opposed to merely "indiscriminate" or "excessive" use of natural resources, their ideology actually compels them to oppose any interaction with nature for human purposes. "Preserving nature" is an idea that conflicts with mankind's requirements for life. To survive, mankind must interact with nature, alter it, and use it.

Today we see green activists even starting to criticize even the public's willingness to "go green." As Michael Ableman, an organic farmer and environmental author, said, "The assumption that by buying anything, whether green or not, we're solving the problem is a misperception. Consuming is a significant part of the problem to begin with." In other words, the problem isn't that the public is "buying green"; the problem is that the public buys anything at all.[11]

While there are many degrees of environmentalists (as in any movement) the core philosophy of this movement is not to value and preserve nature to benefit man, but to value nature untouched by man—which means man un-benefited by nature.

---

theblaze.com/stories/militant-environmentalists-call-for-executions-and-decisive-ecological-warfare/. Accessed 25 Aug 2011.

[10] Yeo, Sophie. "Venezuela Climate Summit Calls for End to 'Green Economy.'" *Responding to Climate Change.* 23 Jul 2014. rtcc.org/2014/07/22/venezuela-climate-summit-calls-for-end-to-green-economy/. Accessed 19 Aug 2014.

[11] Quoted in Lockitch, Keith. "It Isn't Easy Being Green." *Capitalism Magazine.* 15 Oct. 2007. Online. capitalismmagazine.com/science/environment/green-movement/5038-it-isn-t-easy-being-green.html. Accessed 6 Aug. 2011.

Environmentalism does not and cannot advocate capitalism, because if people are left free to act on their judgment, they will use the materials of the earth to prosper and produce the requirements of human life. Such use of the earth is necessary for any human to survive. We must have food, water, clothing, and many other things produced from the earth's elements in order to live.

DO PEOPLE REALLY NEED ALL THIS STUFF?

Some may argue that cars, computers, petroleum, and electricity are not requirements of human life. Actually, in much of today's society, they are. Take an average American worker as an example. First, his family lives by his income which he makes by driving to work at a local retail outlet in a car, bus, or train. His work only exists as it is because of automobiles and gasoline and computers, etc. If we didn't have those he wouldn't even have an income, nor would his employer even exist in the form it does today.

The worker also relies on all these things to bring him food from far away factories and farms. Most of the things he uses every day are either made with fossil fuels or are produced and distributed by them. If he didn't have them, and had to farm and hunt for subsistence, even with the help of neighbors, he and his family would probably die pretty soon. Without power or transportation, it's not hard to imagine that most of New York City would begin to starve in three or four days. So while these things were not necessary for life throughout most of history and don't exist in impoverished countries, they are necessary, literally, for the billions of people that can now only exist because of these things—billions that would have died in centuries past at much lower levels of production.

ENVIRONMENTALISM AS A POLITICAL WEAPON

"Even if the theory of global warming is wrong, to have approached global warming as if it is real means energy conservation, so we will be doing the right thing anyway in terms of economic policy and environmental policy."[12]
- Timothy Wirth, former U.S. Senator (D-Colorado)

Many politicians, parties, and bureaucrats do not care about the preservation or exploitation of the planet one way or the other. However, they still espouse the green movement for popularity and for political clout. This is admitted openly. Canada's former environmental minister, Christine Stewart, said, "Climate change [provides] the greatest chance to bring about justice and equality in the world." You should recognize the lingo by now. Those words mean "social justice" and "economic equality," i.e. wealth redistribution policies. Environmentalists have thus been humorously compared to watermelons—a thin skin of "green" on the outside, but mostly "red" (meaning Communist) in the middle.

Some scientists now claim that their studies, which show how global warming has been greatly exaggerated, have been suppressed from publication because it was "less than helpful" to the climate cause. Professor Bengtsson said, "The problem we now have in the climate community is that some scientists are mixing up their scientific role with that of a climate activist."[13]

Christine Stewart also said that "No matter if the science is all phony, there are still collateral environmental benefits [to global warming policies]."[14] So even if all the science is bunk, the government interventionist policies should still be enacted because they result in good things, we are told. The contrasting moral alternative to such a view is that even

---

[12] Quoted in Caruba, Alan. "What Greens Really Believe." Freedom Action Network. 20 Apr 2011. Online. freedomaction.net/profiles/blogs/what-greens-really-believe. Accessed 9 Aug 2011.

[13] Spencer, Ben. "Study suggesting global warming is exaggerated was rejected for publication in respected journal because it was 'less than helpful' to the climate cause, claims professor." 15 May 2014. dailymail.co.uk/news/article-2630023/Study-suggesting-global-warming-exaggerated-rejected-publication-respected-journal-helpful-climate-cause-claims-professor.html. Accessed 30 May 2014.

[14] Quoted in Beck, Glenn. *An Inconvenient Book* (New York: Simon & Schuster, 2009), 4.

if all the science is correct, it does not constitute a carte blanche for the violation of human rights by the government or by other citizens. Education and persuasion are the moral alternatives to government force.

OWNERSHIP AND STEWARDSHIP

The first true governing principles of the environmentalist controversy are the principles of ownership and stewardship. We discussed these in some depth in the early chapters of this book.

The morality of private property rights must be the foundation for any discussion on climate change or environmentalism. Yet, it is exactly such rights that the environmentalist movement denies. Such a principle includes the recognition that the initiation of force is evil, and that property should be privately owned, with the owners having the freedom to develop or preserve the property as they judge best. Capitalism is the only social system which enables this.

Under capitalism if a person or corporation pollutes someone's land or water, they are held accountable in a court of law. Property rights are protected, but otherwise people are left free to act on their best judgment.[15]

Rights can become very complex, especially when considering water rights, air quality, etc. Just because the issues become complex, however, doesn't make it okay to throw up our hands and give up trying to sort it out or merely resort to the force of government. It is precisely when issues appear complicated and tangled that the utmost care must be taken to sort out the principles involved, and base decisions accordingly. Many issues require the advice of specialists in law philosophy, land rights, ecology, etc. We will not presume here to have the answer to all environmental issues or conflicts that may arise between men. We do, however, have the key principles that will unlock the door to solutions and moral decision-making.

Capitalism recognizes and protects each individual's right to life, liberty, property, and the pursuit of happiness. Most people rationally recognize that in order to live well, they need a clean environment and resources to use carefully, while planning for the future.

---

[15] Biddle, Craig. "On April 22, Celebrate Exploit The Earth Day." The Objective Standard Blog. 18 Apr 2011. Online. theobjectivestand-ard.com/blog/index.php/2011/04/on-april-22-celebrate-exploit-the-earth-day-4/. Accessed 6 Aug 2011.

The next principle is stewardship. As the right of property is protected and understood, and as individuals are educated as to their effects on the environment, the principle of stewardship will increasingly result in effective and productive use of that property. Just as most people feel a sense of pride through ownership of their own home and land, and thus seek to maintain and improve it, so rational business owners and large landowners also seek to constantly improve their property. Nature must come to be seen as a responsibility, not to government, but to oneself, to improve and productively use.

It is contrary to the proper role of government to mandate, or attempt to mandate, responsible use of nature, except when improper use is objectively proven to violate the individual rights of others.

THE PROPER PRINCIPLES

The ideas necessary for a principled understanding of environmentalism and of the proper relationship between man and nature include the following:

- "Environmentalism," as an ideology or movement, is not meant to support and protect human life, but to support and protect nature, even at the expense of human life;
- Ownership (i.e. property rights and the social system which recognizes and protects them) and stewardship are the proper principles to govern man's interaction with nature;
- "Environmentalism" has been co-opted by Progressives to give motive power to their statist agenda;
- Persuasion and education are the moral tactics that should be used to further a healthy earth-man relationship, rather than coercion and government force.

REVIEW

Q1: Why doesn't it matter, morally and politically, if the earth is warming or not?

Q2: Contrast the perceived environmental movement with its actual declared principles.

Q3: How is environmentalism used as a political weapon?

Q4: Describe how ownership and stewardship solve ecological concerns.

CHAPTER 23

SOCIAL ISSUES

THE SEPARATION OF MARRIAGE AND STATE

This country is very divided on the issue of same-sex marriage. It need not be, and an identification of the principles involved will highlight this for the reader.

First of all, marriage is not a right. It is, however, an exercise of the right to liberty and freedom of conscience. As it is now, a marriage recognized by the state is a privilege for which licenses are given, similar to the idea behind the issuance of driver's licenses. The contention arises when the state includes the gender of the applying individuals as a basis for granting or denying a license.

To determine if this is right or wrong, and what actions should be taken to correct it, let us recall the definition, nature, and history of marriage.

Marriage is a social union or agreement between two people that creates a kinship; it usually involves some sort of ceremony.

In ancient Greece, no specific ceremony was needed, merely mutual agreement. There is also no "long-term" tradition of marriage between a man and a woman, nor has it always been the same type of relationship it is considered today. Polygamy was common in ancient times, and in many cultures women were not viewed as an equal partner but as a servant or a child-bearer or as a means to unite separate family lines.

The early Christian Church mandated that its members should only marry with the approval of the bishop. Thus marriage became primarily, in Europe, at least, a religious rite. Registration of this rite passed to the "State" during the Protestant Reformation, and by the 17th century most European nations had state involvement in marriages. State involvement is perpetuated today because of:

- Tradition;
- Expediency in many statist programs, entitlements and incentives;
- The State's desire to exert control over the lives of its citizens.

The foundational problem with this controversy is that marriage has become a state institution, rather than, or in addition to, its traditional religious, personal, or cultural foundation. In maintaining control of this institution, the government is violating the individual rights of its citizens by restricting legal recognition to some, while infringing on the consciences and personal judgments of everyone.

To further complicate matters, other privileges granted by government (1,138 total[1]) have been bundled up with marital status and are thus typically only accessible to those who are legally married. These include social security benefits, tax breaks, exemptions, and Medicare benefits. For some same-sex couples who want to get married, the debate is not so much about approval of their relationship by the state, but rather having access to those privileges now tangled up in it. Most, if not all, of the privileges now associated with marriage are functions of a statist government and their existence hinges on laws and institutions which violate rights. In a rights-respecting government, such laws and institutions would not exist and therefore neither would any sort of the statist privileges as we currently have. Government would have no role in ruling on hospital visitation. Social security survivor benefits would become a null issue with no welfare state, and so on.

Individuals have the right to act on their own judgment as long as they do not violate the right of others. Same-sex marriage does not vio-

---

[1] Shah, Dayna. U.S. Government Accountability Office Letter to Senate Majority Leader. gao.gov/new.items/d04353r.pdf. Online. 23 Jan 2004. Accessed 7 Jul 2012.

late anyone's rights—it initiates force against no one. (The exceptions to this are the politically militant pro-homosexuals who constantly attempt to use the power of government to force others to do what they wish, as in the case of the couple who sued the baker for refusing to bake them a cake for their wedding.) The proper role of government is to protect rights, not to authorize or deny to its citizens whatever definition of family and kinship they desire to pursue.

Marriage is (or should be returned to its source as) a cultural or religious ceremony, or ritual; in other words, a privatized ceremony. It is to celebrate and approve of the joining of individuals in a commitment of love.

THE SOLUTION

What must be advocated, therefore, is the separation of marriage and state, in the same way and for the same reasons as the separation of church and state. With this solution in place, we will see the following results:

• Same-gender couples can marry if they so desire, and if they can find a way to perform the ceremony, (if they even desire a ceremony at all).

• Political and contractual agreements would have to replace and function in political and economic arenas in the ways "marriage" was previously treated by government. This could be done via civil union, or "Family Contract," or "Contract of Kinship." These would be available to all individuals. Families previously married under license by the state could file one of these new contracts to continue under the same legal recognition that their "marriage" previously enjoyed.

In this way, all individuals can easily access all the legal rights available to them, while the government could not discriminate and imply approval or disapproval of the private lives of the citizens under its protection. It should appear to all as a win-win situation. The only people who would not be satisfied are those who would force their beliefs on others.

Some groups and churches have opposed such solutions on the understandable grounds that they are worried about lawsuits if gay marriage is legalized, as a result of which they might be forced to perform such ceremonies against their religious beliefs and rules. It should be common sense that consenting adults should be able to obtain all the same rights and privileges as any other person. At the same time, those who worry about protecting their religious traditions/rules, should not be forced, by fear of a lawsuit, to perform something their tradition considers a sin. Such fears must be assuaged by a strong guarantee of the protection of religious freedom and the objective separation of Church and State.

ABORTION

Abortion is a complex and emotional issue. Its complexity is exacerbated in the political and ethical realms by incomplete human understanding of the process and definition of human life. Reliance on certain principles, however, may still offer us some guidance as the human family comes to understand this issue more completely.

There are two main points of controversy: the genesis of human life, and individual rights.

HUMAN LIFE

A major hurdle to a common understanding is coming to an agreement on when, exactly, human life begins. This is both a metaphysical and ethical debate. Is it at conception? When the heart starts beating? When brain activity begins? When pain is felt? At full term? When the fetus becomes "viable"? After birth when breathing and digestion begin independently?

We don't know, and there is much debate on the matter.

Perhaps, to determine if a fetus is human life or not, we could remove the context of this planet. Imagine if we discovered some cells on a distant planet that were identical to the ones found in a developing fetus. Wouldn't scientists be excited that they found, not just life on another planet, but life like ours—human life?

HUMAN RIGHTS

The other point of contention is a political one. The mother owns her own body and has a right to do with it as she pleases. Does this agency extend only until conception or all the way until birth? What about in cases of incest or rape, when it was not the mother's choice to conceive? What about danger to the mother from prenatal complications? Depending on the answer to the former questions on when a fetus becomes a person, when do we begin to protect its right to life? Does the father have equal rights to decide the fate of his offspring? Should the abortion laws be different for minors than for adults?

THE PRINCIPLES

We don't pretend to have the answers to these difficult questions. We can identify some principles, however, to help guide our decisions in the best manner possible with our limited knowledge.

The first principles to apply are individual rights and personal agency.

(A note to religionists and conservatives: If you hold abortion as contrary to your religion, you should still do what you see your God doing: leaving people free to make their own choices and mistakes, all the while trying to educate and help them if it is a cause you feel passionate about.)

The next principle to guide us is that Perspective Determines Action. A change in perspective will change what people choose to do when faced with an unwanted pregnancy. We can support adoption and effective sex education programs, as well as education campaigns to lovingly inform people about the facts of abortion and what other options are available. We should do all this with the following code to guide us: err on the side of freedom rather than tyranny.

(A note to liberals and Progressives: Protect women's rights all you like, but leave public funding of abortions off the table. It is a contradiction to crusade for rights on one hand while violating the property rights of citizens (through taxation) as well as their liberty of conscience (through how those taxes are used) on the other. This is an initiation of force just as immoral as those who attempt to use force to stop these women. The principle to reference in this case is that Force Destroys Freedom and Prosperity.)

A REASONABLE SOLUTION

There are those, including us, who would argue that rights "are moral principles arising from the need for freedom to act on one's judgment in a social context," and they would be correct.[2] Some would further argue that rights apply only to individuals, that those individuals must exist in a social context. This is also correct. Then they say that because babies are encased in another individual, they do not yet exist in a social context. They do not base their argument on the ability of the child to survive outside the womb, or upon the child being distinct from the mother with its own DNA, merely upon being no longer encased inside another.[3] This conclusion is not necessarily correct.

The crux of this argument is that babies in utero do not exist in a "social context." Yet what does social mean? Social refers to interaction between human beings. Is not a doctor taking the life of a child, even in utero, still an interaction between two humans? Is not this an imposition of the most extreme force? Is a fully developed viable baby not an individual human simply because it of its spatial location? Partial-birth abortions require a child to be halfway delivered when a doctor kills them. Would it be half an individual with half rights if it was partially delivered? Is a baby not an individual since its head is still inches inside a birth canal? How would the distinction of "individual" be made if, like kangaroos, human babies could be replaced into a pouch? Would not that consist of being "encased" in another person? How does being encased in another cause individuality to cease to exist?

What is the difference between a baby killed in the womb vs. out of the womb? What about partially out of the womb? Out of the womb for less than ten minutes? Is killing a nine-month-old baby in the womb different from killing one delivered prematurely? An academic journal edited by Professor Julian Savulescu, then director of the Oxford Uehiro Centre for Practical Ethics, published a paper which argued that parents should be allowed to kill their children up to age two for reasons such as not being able to afford them, or simply not wanting them. Justification for this was based on the reasoning that a child is not yet a person with a moral right to life, possessing goals, dreams, etc. This revolting justification of murder is innocuously termed "after-birth abortion."[4]

---

[2] "Letters and Replies." *The Objective Standard.* Vol. 7, No. 1. Spring 2012. Online. theobjectivestandard.com/issues/2012-spring/letters-replies.asp. Accessed 31 Aug 2012.

[3] ibid.

[4] Adams, Stephen. "Killing babies No Different from Abortion, Experts Say." *The Telegraph.* 29 Feb 2012. Online. telegraph.co.uk/health/healthnews/9113394/Killing-babies-no-different-from-abortion-experts-say.htm.l Accessed 31 Aug 2012.

The distinction of in and ex utero is certainly a major event, but should it be the determiner between being an individual human and a lump of tissue? Is merely passing through the birth canal a significant enough event to make a meaningful distinction between avoiding an unwanted encumbrance and murder? Should the determining factor in such an important matter, not be the location of the pre-human, but the method that the human receives its air and nourishment—whether lungs and stomach or umbilical cord?

Perhaps, until mankind achieves further knowledge, the most reasonable answer to this issue would be to consider the beginning of life by the same criteria as the ending of life—with a detectable heartbeat. As has been said, this is a complex issue; however, making this distinction is perhaps the most rational middle ground for the purpose of having objective law which respects the rights of all involved. Abortion could be legal up to the point of the heartbeat, and for a time longer in cases of rape, incest, or where the life of the mother is in danger.

Another suggested parameter is whether or not a fetus would be viable if outside the womb. With improving technology, such a time-frame creeps ever earlier.

While a legal definition of life may be more narrow and restrictive for the purpose of determining moral actions of individuals, it is disingenuous and an outright evasion to argue that a growing human being is not "life." It does not matter how one seeks to evade the issue, whether it be by employing cold, distancing medical terms such as "fetal tissue," or otherwise to blank-out from the fact that the discussion of abortion deals with human life.

Does a woman have a right to choose what to do with her body? Certainly, but with rights come stewardship and responsibility for one's actions. When a woman risks pregnancy by her willful choices, her decision potentially makes her responsible for the life of another. A pregnant woman's actions have direct consequences over the life or death of a helpless human under her stewardship.

Contraceptives may fail, and one who has taken proper precautions to avoid pregnancy may still become pregnant. In such cases when a woman has acted responsibly and still becomes pregnant, surely she should have the right to do what she wants with her body, up until that action would infringe on the life of another. When a woman negligently becomes pregnant and passes to the point of being responsible for the life of another, should she be able to escape the responsibility from her poor choices by killing? Is this a morally justifiable way to evade the consequences of one's carelessness? The momentous choice to bear the responsibility for human life is not made at birth but before conception. Whatever your views on this issue, the destruction of human life should never be approached callously.[5]

REVIEW

Q1: How does the government violate everyone's rights by being in the marriage business?

_____

Q2: What principles should guide us concerning abortion?

_____

Q3: Using what you've learned in this book, what are principled solutions to other major issues such as the war on drugs, gambling, internet regulations, etc?

_____

---

[5] According to numberofabortions.com:
The number of abortions in the U.S. this year: over 1 million (50,000 after 16 weeks gestation).
The number of abortions in the U.S. since 1973: over 57 million.
The number of abortions worldwide since 1980: 1.357 billion.

CHAPTER 24

VOLUNTARY FUNDING

One of the first questions that is often asked of an advocate of a rights-respecting government and free economy is, "How is a proper government to be funded in a fully free society?" The implication here is that a free society sounds great in theory, but is impossible to practice. While this is often one of the first questions asked, it properly belongs as one of the last, and this is why we left this question until the end of this book. It belongs in this place for two reasons:

1. A proper understanding of the principles of freedom is necessary to understand the question and the answer;
2. The question is only practically relevant near the end of a long road to implement the principles of capitalism in society.

There are many milestones which must be reached before this in the journey toward a free society. People must be educated about the moral rightness of freedom. Government spending on illegitimate programs must be cut, and government must confine itself to only those spheres of activity which protect rights. The question of proper government funding is the last step in the transition to a fully rights-respecting society. Voluntary funding is only practicable in a fully free society that has been constitutionally reduced to its proper elements. It would not work today or for many years to come. But, it is important to be able to articulate the endgame and describe how government would be funded in a free society.

Let us remember why we do need government. We need it because not everyone respects rights in trying to get what they want, so we need to delegate our right to the retaliatory use of force to a government so we can go about living our lives. There are also foreign aggressors who desire to kill or coerce us, and we need a government to engage in our defense. Lastly, we need a rights-respecting government to arbitrate disputes among good people. Such a government would consist primarily of a police force, a military, and an objective court system.

The 2016 U.S. spending "budget" was as follows:

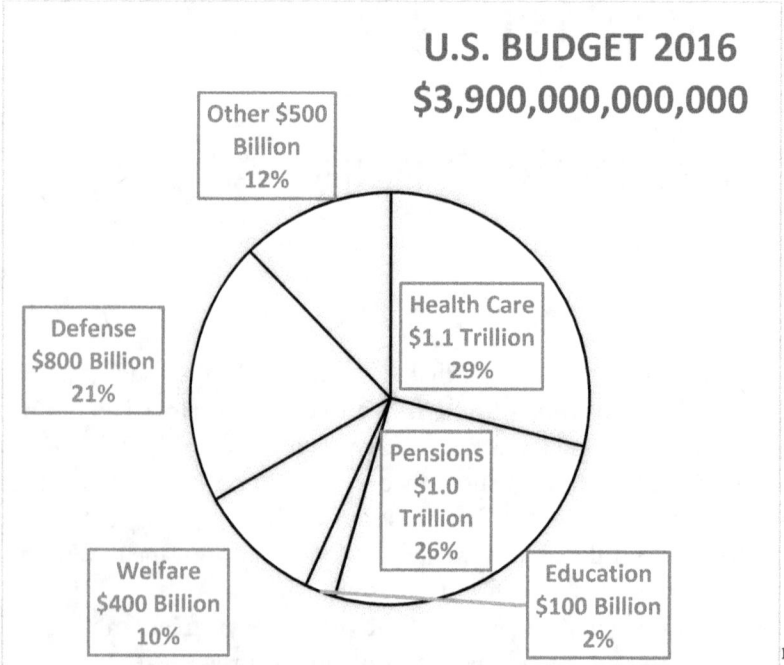

U.S. BUDGET 2016
$3,900,000,000,000

Other $500 Billion 12%

Defense $800 Billion 21%

Health Care $1.1 Trillion 29%

Pensions $1.0 Trillion 26%

Welfare $400 Billion 10%

Education $100 Billion 2%

The large majority of the U.S. budget is spent on welfare and entitlement programs. As we can see, if government can be confined to its proper roles, even with the bloated budgets of today's programs (which would also be drastically reduced in a rights-respecting government), it would only need about 20% of what it currently spends, less than 5% of the national GDP![2]

Of course, cutting out fraud, waste, duplication, and mismanagement would also make a huge dent. Senator Coburn says the government

---

[1] Data is from USgovernmentspending.com.
[2] USdebtclock.org.

throws away at least $200 billion a year on projects such as $5 million in crystal stemware for the State Department, $300 thousand to study angry wives, $1 million to promote romance novels with The Popular Romance Project, and $297 million for an overweight Army blimp that only flew once. $670 thousand to study the relationship between obesity and sexual orientation. And at long last, "the U.S. Embassy building in Islamabad, Pakistan won't have to get by without a 500-pound statue of a camel looking at a needle, because U.S. taxpayers are spending $400,000 to buy it one."[3] In an effort to wind down the wars in the Middle East, the military has decided to simply destroy $7 billion worth of equipment rather than sell it or ship it back home.

"CAMEL CONTEMPLATING A NEEDLE" BY JOHN BALDESSARI, $400,000

A proper government, one that only engages in activities that protect its citizens against the initiation of force against their lives, liberties, and properties, would, by nature, be much smaller in size and scope than the governments we see today. At a fraction of the bloated size of today's bureaucracies, the government would need a fraction of the funds. The current size of government is part of what makes the question of voluntary funding one for the distant future—a future after the widespread

---

[3] Longley, Robert. "US Spends $400k for Camel Statue in Pakistan." usgovinfo.about.com/b/2014/04/03/us-spends-400k-for-camel-statue-in-pakistan.htm. Accessed 19 Aug 2014. (Also see popularromanceproject.org to see that waste of money).

restriction of government to its proper functions. A program of voluntary government funding would adequately pay for the legitimate functions of government.

As a nation, we must come to recognize that government is the servant, not the ruler, of the citizens. This servant should not do its work gratis, as has come to be expected. It must be regarded by the people as a paid servant who does not dispense something for nothing. A servant does not coerce or extort payment from his employer. The employer voluntarily hires the servant to perform services.

The proper services of a government are clearly needed by every citizen and corporation, who would voluntarily pay for these services because they value their life, liberty, and pursuit of happiness, just as they recognize the value of and pay for other private services such as insurance. People buy health, auto, renters, and pet insurance. They purchase smoke detectors, security systems, and even bodyguards. They buy guns and take self-defense classes. Corporations buy liability insurance and key employee insurance, and hire law firms and advisors. All of this is evidence that people value their lives, their homes, their property, their businesses, their profits, their employees, and their happiness. Many proper government functions can be seen as a form of insurance. As writer Craig Biddle points out, the question of whether people would voluntarily fund a rights-protecting government is actually the question of whether people value the protection of their rights to life, liberty, property, and the pursuit of happiness.[4]

We will not use these pages to expound the elaborate details of free society funding. Such is not our aim, nor is it relevant any time in the near future. The question of implementing specific voluntary government financing is complex and belongs in the field of the philosophy of law. The philosophy of politics, on the other hand, is concerned with identifying the principles involved and proving their practicality and morality. Whether we can conceive of how a rights-protecting government would be funded or not, it is moral, and therefore practical once certain conditions are met such as education of the populace and the restriction of improper government programs.

There are many ways to fund a government that don't require taxation (not to mention the ways no one has thought of yet). The following

---

[4] Biddle, Craig. "How Would Government Be Funded in a Free Society?" *The Objective Standard.* Vol. 7, No. 2. Online. theobjectivestandard.com/issues/2012-summer/how-would-govt.asp. Accessed 23 Jul 2012.

are examples only and are not meant to imply that these policies should be advocated in today's political climate:

• Lottery—This is a viable way to raise large amounts of money without initiating force. These can range in size and purpose from a special War Lottery, to a local police force lottery, to a statewide interstate highway maintenance lottery. (This example of funding roads is an intermediary step before their eventual privatization.)

• Contract fees—One of the proper roles of government is the use of the court system to arbitrate and enforce contracts and property rights. Contracts range from personal rental agreements to credit card contracts to estate wills and trusts. For a legally fixed fee, your contract could be kept on file with the government. The fee could act as legal insurance in the event of a hearing or trial. Such a fee could be a fixed rate, or a percentage of the sums involved in the contract. It would not be compulsory, and those who do not wish to pay for the government insurance are free to make verbal agreements and uninsured contracts. They do so, however, with the knowledge that if they need to seek legal redress in the future, the cost will be higher, etc. Even a small percentage of all the credit transactions that occur every day would pay for many functions of government.[5] (It should be noted that in such examples, the amount of an individual's voluntary government financing would be in direct proportion to the amount of his economic activity and interests. The poor would pay little to none, while it would be in the best interest of the rich as well as corporations and businesses to pay the most to insure protection of their contracts and adequate protection from criminals.)

• Donations, fundraising, and volunteer work—Many functions of government may be filled with a combination of these. Americans are notoriously generous. How much more so would they be if they could retain their entire income tax-free and were able to decide where to send their donations—police, military, charities, etc.? It would be even easier if such donations could be set up as automatic withdrawals from paychecks as taxes are now, giving an amount to local police, judicial, legislative, or military funding. There are constantly new ideas on how to raise money. How about a Kickstarter or GoFundMe campaign for your city's new fire truck or street maintenance? There would most likely be patriotic businesses that would set, as a voluntary condition of working at their com-

---

[5] Rand, Ayn. *The Virtue of Selfishness* (New York: Signet, 1964), 116-18.

pany, the policy that a certain percentage of their employees' paychecks be devoted to "taxes." With a truly free-market there would be even more independently wealthy individuals than there are now, who would be willing, as were many Founders, to serve their country gratis.

(Isabel Paterson noted that, "Generally speaking, up to the Civil War any man seeking political honors expected to do so at some financial loss to himself, he lived by his private means. It is only when this condition prevails that men of intelligence, integrity, and good-taste—the productive character—will be inclined to enter public life.")[6]

The widespread lobbying and influencing of legislative and executive officials would also dry up and essentially disappear. Why pay to influence a legislator when he is chained down by a principled Constitution and has no real power to grant favors? (How would our world be different if the billions of dollars spent on lobbying—$3.5 billion in 2010[7]—were spent productively? What goods and services would we have that we do not now and how much cheaper would they be?)[7]

What about free riders? Are those who would refuse to pay taxes and "ride for free" really a problem? (Keep in mind that a full 46% or more of Americans do not currently pay any income tax.)[8]

In The Little Red Hen, the hen finds a grain of wheat, and asks for help from the other farmyard animals to plant it. However, no animal will volunteer to help her. At each further stage (harvest, threshing, milling the wheat into flour, and baking the flour into bread), the hen again asks for help from the other animals, but again she gets no assistance. Finally, the hen has completed her task, and asks who will help her eat the bread. This time, everyone eagerly volunteers. However, she declines their help, stating that no one aided her in the preparation work, and eats it with her chicks, leaving none for anyone else.

We can see from this story that the refusal to help does not constitute a violation of anyone else's rights. While they can assuredly be considered unwise, the other animals at no time attempted to stop the hen from her productive work—no force was initiated against her.

---

[6] Paterson, Isabel. *The God of the Machine* (Originally published in 1943. Qualiteri eBook, 2009), Chapter 15.

[7] Lobbying database. opensecrets.org/lobby/. 31 Oct 2011. Online. Accessed 2 Jan. 2012.

[8] Bingham, Amy. "Almost 1,500 millionaires Do Not Pay Income Tax." ABC News. 6 Aug 2011. Online. abcnews.go.com/Politics/1500-millionaires-pay-income-tax/story?id=14242254. Accessed 24 Jul 2012.

Those who would refuse to voluntarily support the government, for whatever reason, would not be a problem and may even have good reasons. Students, for example, may rightly refrain from doing so while earning money for school. Others may irrationally choose not to help because "the rest of the suckers will do it." Either way, neither group is violating anyone's rights because no one is forced to support them, and no one is stopping the self-interested from acting rationally to protect their own rights.

Craig Biddle offered an insightful idea that deserves to be considered at length. He called it Government Support Receipts (GSRs), and explained it this way:

"Under a system of voluntary financing, the government's budget department would periodically (perhaps annually) issue reports specifying how much money the government needs to fund its proper functions. Private individuals and watchdog agencies would scrutinize these numbers in great detail and offer their own related reports and analyses, as they do today when the government issues a budget.

"Upon reading the reports and analyses, individuals, businesses, and corporations would scrutinize the numbers, do the math, and determine, all things considered, how much money they reasonably think they should contribute. Socially acceptable standards would likely arise, but individuals and companies would be free to abide by or ignore them. Everyone would be free to act on their own judgment, with respect to their own values and their own context. For instance, an individual who barely uses the court system might decide that his contributions should reflect this fact. A large corporation that uses the court system heavily and regularly might tailor its contributions accordingly. Everyone would decide for themselves whether to contribute and, if so, how much.

"When an individual, business, or corporation contributed funds to the government, the government would issue a receipt—call it a Government Support Receipt.

"GSRs would have profound value in the marketplace. Those who held them would have evidence that they financially support a rights-protecting government and thus a civilized society. Those who did not hold GSRs would have no such evidence. Consider what this would mean.

"Suppose McDonald's wanted to establish a long-term contract with a beef supplier. Would McDonald's care whether the supplier was a rights-supporting, government-contributing corporation? Would McDonald's care whether the supplier contributed a contextually reasonable amount of money to ensure the continuation of rule of law, civilized society, and protection of contracts? The smart money says that McDonald's would care and that, given the existence of alternative suppliers, the company would choose to work with a vendor other than the free rider. (McDonald's might even put a clause in its contracts stipulating that its suppliers must contribute some percentage of their annual sales to support the rights-protecting government.) But even if McDonald's didn't care and opted to do business with the free-riding supplier, McDonald's would face the problem that a great many of its customers and potential customers would care—and that Burger King, Wendy's, Carl's, and the like might see a golden, patriotic advertising angle in the mix. Similar examples can be multiplied end over end.

"In a free society, large corporations would generally see great value not only in holding GSRs, but also in holding very large ones and making that fact known. Rational patriotism sells.

"GSRs would not likely come into play on small transactions, say, when someone purchases a cup of coffee at Starbucks. But they would certainly come into play on many major corporate transactions, and they might well come into play on lesser transactions, such as employment contracts, vacation rental agreements, and the like.

"Rational people and rational businessmen care about the protection of rights, and, by and large, they act in accordance with that concern—both in their personal lives and in the marketplace. In a fully free society, GSRs would be in high demand, and irrational free riders would discover that "riding for free" costs them much more than supporting the government would."[9]

We hope to have demonstrated that while not currently possible, the financing of a free society is desirable and would certainly be plausible as the final hurdle for free men to cross on their journey to a fully rights-respecting society.

---

[9] Biddle, Craig. "How Would Government Be Funded in a Free Society?" *The Objective Standard*. Vol. 7, No. 2. Online.

REVIEW

Q1: What are some important principles to understand about voluntary government funding?

_____

Q2: What are some ways it could be accomplished? Can you think of any that we didn't mention?

_____

Q3: Would you volunteer to fund a rights-respecting government?

_____

ΛFTERWORD

WHAT NOW?

"Be the change that you wish to see in the world."
- Anonymous, misattributed to Gandhi

The problems and upheavals in the world will persist so long as governments (and the individuals who support them) claim moral sanction to initiate force. Governments will continue to act immorally until citizens learn true principles of freedom and prosperity and work to move away from statism.

The world sometimes seems pretty bleak and hopeless. The minuscule minority of politicians who understand principles are mostly ignored and dismissed. Economic stability continues to worsen, governmental power continues to expand, the U.S. continues to take on unfunded obligations and debt that over the coming decades amount to many times more than the GDP of the entire planet, and the Constitution continues to be disregarded and misinterpreted. The abandonment of a sound monetary system will make the coming crash more devastating than we have ever seen. It will almost certainly get worse before it gets better. It is unlikely that we will live to see America, or any other country, decide to protect individual rights fully. The combined effects of all the global statist policies, if left unchecked, will one day come crashing down in utter ruin. The world will certainly change.

"The true source of our suffering has been our timidity. We have been afraid to think . . . . Let us dare to read, think, speak, and write . . ."[1]
– John Adams

Now that we have the tools necessary to understand and discover truth in the world around us, the question remains, "What now?"

The answer is going to be different for everyone, but some guidelines may be helpful. The best advice now is to strive for the best, prepare for the worst.

Striving for the best includes the following:

- Continue education for self, family, children, and friends.
- Work to change politics locally and nationally, by training current and future leaders and representatives to pursue the correct reason for the existence of government—the protection of individual rights.
- Work to support efforts such as those of ConventionofStates.org to constitutionally rectify problems that Congress refuses to fix.
- Love your life and follow your rational, life-centered values.
- Seek to spread the philosophy of freedom, the value of reason, the ethics of self-interest, and the politics of capitalism.
- Work to become an independent steward and producer. No one who is dependent on the government for subsistence will be effective in pursuing freedom.
- Seek to be a better person. For things to get better, you must get better; for things to change, you must change. Build and use the lost virtues of love, dignity, and respect—even as an answer to hate, bad manners, and no self-control.

Preparing for the worst includes emergency preparation for economic and natural disasters. This includes the following:
- Prepare food, toiletries, and water storage. Start with a 3-day emergency supply, then a 3-week supply, then 3-months, then a year.

---

[1] Quoted in McCullough, David. *John Adams* (New York: Simon & Schuster Paperbacks, 2001), 60.

Include garden seeds in your emergency supply. (There are many sources such as web sites and organizations available to assist in this preparation.)

• Have equipment and clothing for outdoor survival; go camping.

• Keep hard copies of important books, instructions, and documents.

• Learn old practices such as mending, canning, hunting, and farming; keep physical instructions of how to learn important survival skills.

• Live within your means and keeping a supply of cash on hand in case of bank or ATM failures (ATMs were down for days after Hurricane Katrina); if you have a large reserve of cash in savings, consider diversifying part of it into something like precious metals that can retain its value in case of a currency crash.

• Live near people you can trust to work together in an emergency rather than turn on each other; build relationships with them; learn their skills and needs.

> *"We're about to go through the crucible, but we'll come out the other side.*
> *We always arise from our own ashes."*[2]
> - film adaptation of *Children of Dune* (2003)

THE GOLDEN PATH

In Frank Herbert's masterful Dune universe, one of his key ideas is "The Golden Path." In his novels, this means the path that humanity must take in order to ensure its survival, not just across decades, but over tens of thousands of years—true long-range thinking.

This concept can be applied to each of us. There is a path to freedom, prosperity, and happiness. The path is the same for individuals, families, states, and nations. This path is strict adherence to the principles that govern human life, happiness, and prosperity. We've discussed many of these principles in detail in this book.[3] There is hope for humans to understand and embrace the philosophy of freedom because morality is a choice. The non-initiation of force against others is what paves this path into a bright future. Without a proper understanding and protection of

---

[2] *Children of Dune* (2003). IMDb. Online. imdb.com/title/tt0287839/quotes. Accessed 13 Sep 2012.

[3] A list of these principles can be found in Appendix A.

individual rights, our path winds instead into stagnation, destruction, and misery.

The Founders knew they had laid the foundation for the most spectacular experiment in freedom in the history of the world. They also knew that they were limited in what they could accomplish in their day—which is why the pyramid on the Great Seal of the United States is left unfinished at the top. It was for later generations to perfect what they had begun. In 1786, George Washington said, "The foundation of a great empire is laid, and I please myself with a persuasion that Providence will not leave its work imperfect."[4]

GEORGE WASHINGTON

They also knew that it was dangerous to leave it unfinished. What Washington warned of during the War of Independence also applies to the future country that survived it, "To trust altogether in the justice of our cause, without our own utmost exertions, would be tempting Providence."[5] To know what is right is useless without working to accomplish what is right.

We are reaping the benefits of thousands of years of intellectual and heroic struggle. Let us not be as the Israelites who, upon being freed from bondage, longed to return to the security of Egyptian enslavement. Let us, instead, work to understand and implement the philosophy of freedom and the principles of prosperity. It won't happen all at once. Freedom and the protection of rights must be won back by the same methods that they have been lost—via a cultural groundswell that pushes back progressively against the collectivism, rather than merely slowing it down through token resistance. American culture has been lost for decades to the Progressives. Freedom-lovers must win back movies, literature, music, television, and every other aspect that shapes our culture. We owe it to ourselves and our children to make a better world.

---

[4] Allison, A., Parry, J., and W. Cleon Skousen. *The Real George Washington* (Washington D.C.: National Center for Constitutional Studies, 1991), 701.
[5] *ibid*, 694.

REVIEW

Q1: What are some steps you can start to work on to increase your personal freedom?

_____

Q2: What can you do to help your country take steps towards greater freedom?

_____

Q3: Think of ways in which your family's emergency preparedness may be lacking. Write three things you can accomplish in the next month to improve on this.

_____

Q4: What further research do you want to start?

_____

APPENDIX A

LIST OF PRINCIPLES

MAJOR PRINCIPLES

- Existence exists.
- Principles govern.
- Happiness is the purpose of life.
- There is no truth without context.
- All that which is proper to the life of a rational being is good; all that which destroys it is evil.
- Collective action has no unique moral authority.
- Man's primary motivating force begins with self-interest.
- Force destroys freedom and prosperity.
- Personal freedom requires private property.
- Agency implies responsibility.
- The proper role of government is the protection of individual rights, which means the protection of individuals from the initiation of physical force.
- The government is only morally authorized to act in those spheres in which you, the individual also have the right to act.
- Taxes discourage production.
- Credit diverts production
- Production, not consumption, grows an economy.
- People are assets; (things are not).

- Exchange creates wealth.
- Happiness is a function of achieving rational, life-serving values; higher energy causes greater happiness.
- There is no exploitation without force or deception.
- Dollars follow value.
- Profit is a tool of validation.
- Human Life Value is the source of all property value.
- Productivity is the standard.
- Human behavior changes with incentives.
- Perspective Determines Action.

In addition to these major principles, you may want to take some time to articulate principles that are specific to your life and goals. Such principles should be based on true broad principles, but can be as specific as these examples:

- Morning exercise helps me feel more alert throughout the day.
- White lies aren't helpful in my relationship with my spouse.
- My "work" time needs to be away from the internet so I don't get distracted.
- My children feel and act better when they eat healthier.
- Thursday is laundry day (or an even broader: Every day of the week has a specific purpose, which helps me be more productive).
- I budget better and make fewer impulse purchases when I make a shopping list.
- Eating too late in the evening gives me heartburn.
- A weekly nature hike helps relieve stress.

APPENDIX B

RECOMMENDED READING

For further reading on the principles of freedom, we recommend the following (such a recommendation is not a blanket endorsement of everything these authors and organizations believe):

FOUNDING PRINCIPLES OF AMERICA

The Real Thomas Jefferson, by A. Allison, M. Maxfield, and W. Cleon Skousen

The Real George Washington, by A. Allison, J. Parry, and W. Cleon Skousen

The Federalist Papers, by Alexander Hamilton, James Madison, and John Jay

A Patriot's History of the United States: From Columbus' Great Discovery to the War on Terror, by Larry Schweikart and Michael Allen

The 5000 Year Leap: A Miracle That Changed the World, by W. Cleon Skousen

The Making of America: The Substance and Meaning of the Constitution, by W. Cleon Skousen

PRINCIPLES OF PROSPERITY AND ECONOMICS

The Law, by Frederic Bastiat
Loving Life: The Morality of Self-Interest and the Facts That Support It, by Craig Biddle
Kirk Duncan's collected audio recordings and trainings, published by 3 Key Elements
Killing Sacred Cows, by Garrett Gunderson and Stephen Palmer
Economics in One Lesson, by Henry Hazlitt
"Lecture Series on the Principles of Prosperity" by Rick Koerber, FreeCapitalist Radio, (May 19-June 26 2008), Podcast available from iTunes
The Selfish Path to Romance: How to Love with Passion and Reason, by Edwin A. Locke and Ellen Kenner
End the Fed, by Ron Paul
Atlas Shrugged, by Ayn Rand
How An Economy Grows and Why It Crashes, by Peter Schiff and Andrew Schiff
The Wealth of Nations, by Adam Smith
TheObjectiveStandard.com

CAPITALISM AND COLLECTIVISM

The Collected Works of Ayn Rand, especially *Capitalism: The Unknown Ideal, Atlas Shrugged, Anthem, The Virtue of Selfishness, and Philosophy: Who Needs It?*
The Decline of American Liberalism, by Arthur Ekirch, Jr.
Objectivism: The Philosophy of Ayn Rand, by Leonard Peikoff
The Ominous Parallels, by Leonard Peikoff
The Naked Communist, by W. Cleon Skousen

PHOTO CREDITS

Cover ---Caspar David Friedrich, Wanderer above the Sea of Fog (1818), Wiki-media.

7 ------ By Doug Smith, National Park Service [Public domain], via Wikimedia Commons

20 -------Immanuel Kant (painted portrait) by unspecified -/History/Carnegie/kant/portrait.html. Licensed under Public domain via Wiki-media Commons.

24 -------The Leaning Tower of Pisa, [Public Domain], Wikimedia.

(wolf) By Doug Smith, National Park Service [Public domain], via Wikimedia Commons

29 -------By Etching created by Cadell and Davies (1811), John Horsburgh (1828) or R.C. Bell (1872). The original depiction of Adam Smith was created in 1787 by James Tassie in the form of an enamel paste medallion. Smith did not usually sit for his portrait, so a considerable number of engravings and busts of Smith were made not from observation but from the same enamel medallion produced by Tassie, an artist who could convince Smith to sit. [Public domain], via Wikimedia.

35 -------Official Presidential portrait of John Adams, by John Trumbull, circa 1792 - whitehouseresearch.org/assetbank-whha/action/viewHome. Licensed under Public domain via Wikimedia Commons.

62 -------Bust of Frederic Bastiat. "Buste-bastiat" by Thbz - Own work. Licensed under Creative Commons Attribution-Share Alike 3.0 via Wikimedia Commons.

80 -------Hengist and Horsa, mentalfloss.com/article/30912/rejected-designs-great-seal-united-states.

82 -------John Trumbull's painting, Declaration of Independence, depicting the five-man drafting committee of the Declaration of Independence presenting their work to the Congress. The painting can be found on the back of the U.S. $2

bill. The original hangs in the US Capitol rotunda. [Public Domain], via Wikimedia Commons.

83 -------Portrait of Thomas Jefferson which hangs in the Thomas Jefferson State Reception Room on the 8th floor of the main U.S. Department of State building in Washington, D.C. It was painted by Charles Willson Peale while Jefferson was Secretary of State. It is probably a replica of Peale's 1791 portrait of Jefferson which hangs in the Independence National Historical Park, [Public domain], via Wikimedia Commons.

85 -------Howard Chandler Christy, Scene at the Signing of the Constitution of the United States, (1940). [Public Domain], via Wikimedia Commons.

112------Portrait of Journalist and Economist Henry Hazlitt. By work-for-hire (Mises Institute; Henry Hazlitt estate) [CC-BY-3.0 (creativecommons.org/licenses/by/3.0)], [Public Domain], via Wikimedia Commons.

129------According to clause 50 of the Copyright Act of Zimbabwe, Chapter 26:1, this work is in the public domain because it is either an image of a bank note which has been demonetized in terms of the Reserve Bank of Zimbabwe Act Chapter 22:10, or an image of a coin or the artistic work defining the design of a coin.

142------Bust of Auguste Comte in Place de la Sorbonne, Paris. By MLWatts (Own work) [CC-BY-SA-3.0 (http://creativecommons.org/licenses/by-sa/3.0)], via Wikimedia Commons.

148------ John Dewey by Eva Watson-Schütze (1867-1935) [Public domain], via Wikimedia Commons.

156------Official Presidential Portrait of Woodrow Wilson. By Frank Graham Cootes [Public domain], via Wikimedia Commons.

181------Marx, [Public Domain], Wikimedia.

186------Engels, [Public Domain], Wikimedia.

190------Statues of Karl Marx and Friedrich Engels - Near Alexanderplatz - Eastern Berlin. By Adam Jones, Ph.D. (Own work) [CC-BY-SA-3.0 (http://creativecommons.org/licenses/by-sa/3.0)], via Wikimedia Commons.

188------Candy bar. By Evan-Amos, [Public Domain], Wikimedia.

192------"Roosevelt" by Frank O. Salisbury - whitehouseresearch.org/assetbank-whha/action/viewHome. Licensed under Public domain via Wikimedia Commons.

198------Mussolini and Hitler, [Public Domain], Wikimedia

246------"Cornelius Vanderbilt three-quarter view" by unattributed - Heritage Auction Galleries. Licensed under Public domain via Wikimedia Commons. commons.wikimedia.org/wiki/File:Cornelius_Vanderbilt_three-quarter_view.jpg#mediaviewer/File:Cornelius_Vanderbilt_three-quarter_view.jpg.

367------Camel Contemplating a Needle. www.HallWines.com

378------Washington, [Public Domain], Wikimedia.

CONTACT US

FACEBOOK.COM/THEPHILOSOPHYOFFREEDOM

ABOUT THE AUTHORS

Caleb Nelson holds a BA in English (a minor in Latin American Studies) and lives in Utah with his fabulous wife, Chelsea, and three great children. When he isn't writing political treatises, he's probably playing with his kids, exploring Utah's wilderness, inciting hilarity with witty ripostes, or pwning noobs on his Xbox. He enjoys singing and acting on stage, as well as oil painting. He is an avid reader, consuming the likes of Robert Jordan, Ayn Rand, Brandon Sanderson, and Frank Herbert.

Kenneth Jeppesen holds a BS in Child and Family Studies, a master's degree in Marriage and Family Therapy, and is mentoring many awesome people. He calls Utah home with his lovely wife, Heidi. His interests include writing author bios, meta jokes, and *hygge* with kith and kin. Kenneth is an INTP who enjoys finding the perfect words to express thoughts, making things more efficient, fleshing out his theory of everything, and working to be a fully-stocked dispenser of helpful knowledge.

www.ingramcontent.com/pod-product-compliance
Lightning Source LLC
Chambersburg PA
CBHW072133290526
45794CB00004B/1304